Caring for Kait

A True Story of Young Love & Cancer

Travis Ruhland

ISBN-10: 1540397742
ISBN-13: 978-1540397744

Marcia Thompson

DEDICATION

Dedicated to Kaitlyn, of course.

CONTENTS

	PREFACE	1
1	A LOST MEMENTO	2
2	CUPID STRIKES	4
3	CANCER'S RETURN	18
4	SURGERY	27
5	INTRODUCING OUR NEW ONCOLOGY TEAM	33
6	A FRESH START	38
7	A SOMEWHAT DECENT PROPOSAL	42
8	ANOTHER RETURN	49
9	SHOCKING DISCOVERIES	61
10	ROUND ONE WITH IL-2	70
11	RETURN TO NORMALCY	77
12	DING DING: ROUND TWO	81
13	IPILIMUMAB & THE CALM BEFORE THE STORM	88
14	THE BEGINNING OF THE END	103
15	LOYOLA	119
16	FAMILIAR SURROUNDINGS	130
17	CRANIOTOMY	144
18	HOME SWEET HOME	156
19	WORLD OF PHARMA	169
20	NOT ANOTHER SEIZURE	174
21	TOMOTHERAPY: A FALLING OUT	178
22	DESTABILIZATION	184
23	GRANDMA'S FUNERAL	186
24	COMFORT IN THE LORD	190
25	ZELBORAF	192
26	TALES OF TWO LIVES	196
27	DIVINE INTERVENTION?	200
28	UPON FURTHER REFLECTION	203
29	SEIZURE SCARE…AGAIN	205
30	WEDDING PLANNING RECOMMENCED	209
31	CONFIRMED SUCCESS	211
32	TRANSITIONING PERIOD	214

33	DARKNESS LOOMS	218
34	ARIZONA BOUND	228
35	A COLD RETURN	237
36	A CRUSHING BLOW	243
37	PLEASE DON'T GO!	250
38	THE RING	275
39	FAREWELL MY LOVE	285
40	FINAL GOODBYES	292
41	A DESOLATE APARTMENT	299
42	FAITH RENEWED	309
43	EVOLUTION OF MIND	326
44	REDISCOVERING PURPOSE	335
45	UNTIL WE MEET AGAIN	348

PREFACE

First of all, nothing in this book should be construed as medical advice. It's only the irrelevant opinion of an uneducated man.

Secondly. I didn't write this book because I am seeking sympathy, attention, a pat on the back, or to be seen as a hero of any kind. Not at all. I don't want any of that. I wrote this book because I wanted to share Kaitlyn with the world. I wrote this book because I wanted to give an accurate account of what goes on in the lives of a family struggling with cancer. I wanted to give people an honest look inside the mind of a man faced with the idea that the love of his life may be taken away much too soon.

Lastly, I've changed the names of Kaitlyn's family, friends, and doctors for a number of reasons.

Oh, and one more thing. You might come across things in this book that you disagree with, which is great. But, before jumping to conclusions, I would simply encourage you to ask questions. A lot of thought and consideration goes into just about everything I ever say.

And, as I write this portion of the Preface, it has been a few years since I completed this book. I considered giving it a complete overhaul in terms of structure and content, but ultimately decided to keep most as is. For me this provides a snapshot of who and where I was at the time, and I find some value in that. Also, maybe there is a reason I felt compelled to write everything I wrote when I was writing this. Even though some parts may sound silly, or even though you might be able to tell I was trying too hard to sound like a real "writer" in certain areas, I decided to leave everything unchanged for the most part.

With that, thank you for reading our story!

1 A LOST MEMENTO

December 22, 2012. A Saturday.

My Kaitlyn lay in front of me on her bed, hardly able to move. For a week she had been confined to that bed as the tumors growing in the right portion of her brain caused complete paralysis of the left side of her body. Her ability to comprehend anything was worsening by the day, and moments of conversation happened less and less. My beloved, sweet Kait. The love of my life. Was dying. Right before our eyes. And I wasn't ready to let her go.

Time stood still. Everything seemed to happen in slow motion. At certain points I would wish for it to all be over, for her suffering to end. At other points, I would grow angry at the thought that we were giving up hope and consequently giving up on treatments. It was torture for her. It was torture for everyone having to witness this slow – and rapid – disease progression in someone they loved so dearly.

Just two weeks earlier, Kait was up and walking about. She had spells of extreme pain here and there, but her mobility was almost 100%. We even went ring shopping for our wedding. She already had her ring, but we needed to quickly get one for me since we moved the wedding up to January 5th instead of May 25th like we originally planned.

We found the perfect ring.

Wanting to make a special request with the jeweler, Kait had me step outside of the store so I wouldn't hear her secret. Moments later, she exited, smiling from ear to ear. "So, where is it," I asked excitedly.

"It'll be here in a couple weeks," Kait vibrantly replied.

Well, that couple weeks brought us to December 22nd. My ring had arrived. But how drastically things had changed. The ring was picked up and brought back to the house. To me. I grabbed it, brought it upstairs, and placed it on the dresser next to Kait's bed where she laid, keeping it in its small box. Kait was asleep at the time so I didn't want to wake her.

It saddened me, because in her state of mind, it was likely she would never be able to comprehend that this symbol of our love was resting in its box right next to her. Though, no material item could ever define our love, it was still important to me because it was a gift from her that represented the next step in our relationship - marriage. And there the ring lay on her dresser, possibly never to be opened.

Numb and deflated, I sat next to her bed rubbing her arms, watching her sleep, kissing her forehead. Millions of thoughts ran through my head. I looked at her engagement ring, remembering the day I proposed to her, how unbelievably happy she was, how happy we both were. And that was merely a year ago. How the hell did we ever get to this point?

I started reminiscing about the first day we ever met. I remembered it as if it were yesterday.....

2 CUPID STRIKES

It was early-September, 2008. The hallways of the Wells East Dorms were packed with mostly confused, oblivious, and impressionable freshman anxious to throw their belongings into their rooms so they could focus on more important matters, like who would buy them alcohol or where the location of their first kegger would be. Unfortunately, I could be of no assistance in that regard. I mean, I was the RA on the 9th floor, after all. I considered myself to be wise beyond my years, and risking my free room and board on the first day seemed quite unwise, indeed.

My door remained open all day. Even though I wanted to hide away in my room and play Mario Golf, I couldn't reveal my true antisocial self just yet. It was my sworn duty to help facilitate a friendly, community environment, answering questions that arose from students and parents. The only problem was, I invested almost none of my attention toward learning during RA training, zoning out through a large portion of the drawn-out lectures. Every day was long and boring. I'm a hands on learner, like many others, and theoretical "what-if" discussions do little to stimulate my mind. Needless to say, I was ill equipped to answer any questions on move-in day, resorting to my default response every time. "Let me look it up and I'll get back to you." It never failed, and I never got back to them.

They all survived.

As I sat on my jagged futon watching the Milwaukee Brewers, constantly having to reposition myself to avoid the metal bars pressing up against the crack of my buttocks, I found myself suddenly blinded by a

4

bright light. Squinting heavily to regain my vision, I discovered the source. It was the huge, sparkling, friendly, nervous smile of a blonde-haired girl hovering at my doorway. Standing at about 5'2", weighing maybe 110 pounds, she was as cute as a button. Who was this ethereal being emanating with warmth and happiness?

"Hi, I'm Kaitlyn," she said. Her voice was sweet. Full of energy and life.

She was certainly an attractive girl, but as the RA, courtship of my residents was strictly prohibited. At least I thought that was a rule. Maybe it wasn't. Like I said, I didn't pay attention during training. But, I wasn't about to jeopardize my job. Not yet.

"Hey Kaitlyn. I'm Travis, the RA."

Of course she knew that already. RA's are somewhat of celebrities during the first few days, until they start busting underage drinking parties. I tried to be the cool RA, turning a blind eye as long as the kids weren't too rowdy.

Wearing her smile the whole time, her eyes shimmering with a crystal blue as the sun reflected off of them, she sheepishly requested, "My roommate is gone and I'm trying to put our bunk beds together. Do you think you'd be able to help us out?"

Smiling back, "I think I could do that."

Of course I agreed to help. No man turns down an opportunity to flex his muscles and prove chivalry is not extinct. Walking down the hall, in need of a male assistant, I pointed to the first guy I saw and asked him, no, no, ORDERED him to help me.

With my mosquito bite arms exposed through my cutoff shirt, we walked into her room. The first thing I noticed? They had a freaking air conditioner! The only residents on the floor to have one. Divas? Yah.

In all honesty, Kaitlyn's roommate, Carla, had an acute allergy problem, so she needed the cleaner air. Lucky. It was great during the upper 80- to 90- degree days of September. Although, in Wisconsin, those temperatures quickly begin to drop as the month moves forward. Still, great way to lure people into your social circle for those sultry first two weeks.

Anyway, the guy and I (I don't remember the dude's name sadly) simply lifted Kaitlyn's bed and placed it on top of Carla's. The beds were efficiently designed so that the legs fastened together like a puzzle piece.

Done. Piece of cake. After Kaitlyn thanked us, we exited her room. I walked away a hero for the day. And, I got to meet a nice lady.

Days later, classes began. Ugh. With my head hanging and my feet dragging, I trudged out of my dorm room. I didn't want school to start.

As I approached the elevator, my lifeless eyes were suddenly called to attention. Kaitlyn was waiting there. I couldn't give off the impression that I was boring and had a bad attitude toward life, so I instantly perked up.

Surprising myself that I remembered her name, we greeted each other. Out of the 40 students who moved in within a couple days, somehow I remembered hers and forgot most everyone else's.

After making small talk for 20 seconds, we both stood in awkward silence. Curious what she looked like from the side, I took a short, silent step back and glanced over at her out of the corner of my eye. She was smiling. She had a craterous dimple on the right side of her face. It was adorable.

While analyzing her every movement, I found myself becoming curious. Thinking back to our first meeting just days prior, I recalled she had a smile the whole time. And now she was smiling the whole time we stood by the elevator. How interesting. But why? Why was she always smiling? Was she nervous? Was she always happy about something? Did she have a disorder? I didn't get it. She was literally always smiling. It was a beautiful smile, though, so obviously there was nothing wrong with her always wearing it, but I was just curious. It hurt my face to smile for 10 seconds let alone three straight days. Nevertheless, it was endearing and I found myself feeling that same comfortable warmth in her presence. Without even knowing her, I felt like I could trust her with anything.

The elevator finally came and we entered. When we exited, I made sure to walk extra slow so that she could get a safe distance ahead of me. Walking and talking with someone in a situation of forced conversation was always awkward for me. Maybe it was because my brain didn't do well with multi-tasking, and having to talk and focus on putting one foot in front of the other at the same time was mentally draining. So, I typically avoided it.

Kait and I both went on our merry ways. And I suddenly felt injected with energy. My day felt brighter.

A week, maybe two weeks went by, and I was sitting on my cheap futon playing Super Mario Bros. 2 for the regular Nintendo. That's right. The old school system with the blinking problem where you have to blow in the games to make it work. The theory of blowing in the games to make them work may have been just a myth, but I swear it helps. However, I had a "top loading" Nintendo. It was released in 1993 as a solution to the blinking malfunction, but was only on the market for a year. The Nintendo games work every time, meaning you don't have to worry about a game shutting off on you just as you're about to send Bowser tumbling into the molten hot lava.

I digress. Clearly.

Anyway, I was playing Super Mario 2. One of my favorites. Suddenly, Kaitlyn floated by and took immediate notice. Stopping on a dime, she marveled at the classic 8-bit game being projected on my TV screen. "Oh my God, you have an old Nintendo? We used to play Super Mario 2 all the time when we were kids."

"Shut up.....no way," I responded with a smile.

"No seriously, we used to watch my dad play. We used to yell and scream in his ear every time he would get in trouble." She laughed at her fond memory. "I know a whole bunch of secrets."

I was intrigued, but didn't believe her. Everyone blows his or her gaming knowledge and skills out of proportion.

Talking at a speed of about a million words per minute, Kaitlyn proceeded to tell me about all of the secrets in Super Mario 2 that she knew about. I couldn't believe my ears. She wasn't lying after all. The secrets she was listing off actually existed in the game. I was shocked. A girl who was interested in videos games, old Nintendo games for that matter, was a rare occurrence and not to be taken lightly or for granted. I felt my interest begin to pique a bit. Was it just a fluke? Even with her knowledge, I assumed she was terrible at the game anyway.

In her reminiscence, she began rattling off all of the other games she used to play, Tetris and Mario Kart 64 being her favorites. I suddenly found myself captivated by her every word.

Talk of classic video games ignited a whole slew of conversation pieces. My head was racing. This girl was super friendly. Super cute. She enjoyed playing Nintendo. Her smile was intoxicating. She wasn't vain like seemingly many college girls. She was a sophomore, and quite mature for her age, though she still maintained the exuberance of a 5 year-old. I felt extremely comfortable in her presence. I didn't feel judged. I felt like I could be vulnerable and reveal my flaws, though I wouldn't. She seemed to be the whole package.

After she left, I quickly turned my head and rested my chin on my shoulder, placing the back of my hand against my face. *Travis you mustn't. She is one of your residents. You cannot fall for her.*

As much as my mind resisted, it seemed as though my heart had already been pierced with thine sweet, searing arrow. A spell had been cast upon me and soon I would have no control.

To my surprise a week later I found out she could actually back up her talk when it came to video games. She proved to be AMAZING at Tetris. Better than I, which was a rare feat when it came to the classics.

Over the next couple months, Kaitlyn and I got to know each other more and more. From walking down the hallway making Pac-man sound effects as she helped me decorate my Pac-man themed RA board, to helping me organize floor events, she was around quite often. And I found myself thoroughly enjoying her presence. She always seemed ready and willing to help me or anyone out whenever we needed assistance, and I appreciated it. She was making it increasingly difficult to keep my attraction for her locked away.

And I found it fascinating because whenever Kaitlyn came around, other residents on the floor seemed to come out of the woodwork and join in on the conversation. It would start out being only Kait and I in my room. But, after ten minutes we would find ourselves surrounded by a hoard of others.

I quickly realized that Kaitlyn had this special gift of bringing sunshine into an otherwise gloomy environment. With her friendly and positive personality, people seemed to gravitate toward her. She made everyone feel comfortable, like they belonged. You were always certain to leave her presence feeling happier, as though you were worth something. And there was never a doubt that she genuinely, truly, sincerely, absolutely cared about you. She wasn't just "fake" nice to you because she felt like she had to be or because she wanted the attention. If you were speaking, she would give you her utmost attention, and you felt like whatever you were saying mattered. She treated everyone like this, like they were the most important people in the world. Naturally, people wanted to be around her. Every human wants to feel like they matter in this world, and Kaitlyn made you feel that way.

In my observations I was taking notice of all these wonderful subtleties. All of the traits she exhibited were everything I looked for in a woman. She took generosity and friendliness to a whole new level, a level I had never seen in anyone before. She was extremely witty and funny. She was fun and easy to pick on. She understood and played along with my unrelenting sarcasm. She didn't take things too seriously. She valued her family over everything else. She loved her friends. She played the violin. She was energetic. Bubbly. Caring. Compassionate. Sincere. Honest. Trustworthy. Down-to-earth. Selfless. Secure. And the list of superlatives goes on to infinity. The only flaw that stood out among her enormous inventory of positive attributes was her terrifying road rage. I quickly learned that whenever she would get into the driver's seat of a car, she would transform from sweet, little, smiley Kaitlyn into this red-faced, sharp-toothed, snarling monster as she frequently spewed expletives and flipped the bird at drivers she deemed crazy. Because it deviated so far from her typical personality, though, I found it hilarious…while I would sit in the passenger seat making the sign of the cross with my fingers, holding it up at her to protect me from her demons. But because she was completely different than anyone I'd ever met, it was something I was happy to overlook and confident I could work with. Otherwise, everything else about her was perfect to me. Hell, even the road rage!

Was this one of those situations where I should ignore the rules and pursue her? I mean, she seemed to be one in six billion! The perfect catch men spend years in pursuit of. I almost had to.

Needless to say, after weeks passed and she continued proving what a special person she was, I gave into my overwhelming attraction for her. We began by going on a few dates. I still had to dig deeper to see if she was the real deal or an imposter.

Not wanting my fellow RAs to find out, we sort of snuck around campus when we were together. Kaitlyn thought the sneaking part was ridiculous, but I really didn't want to have to answer questions. I felt like my boss or other RAs would think I was "taking advantage" of my own resident since I was in a position of "power" and normally younger girls are highly impressionable. Obviously this wasn't the case. I actually liked this girl.

After weeks of spending quality one-on-one time with Kait and getting to know her, it became obvious that she was the real deal. Definitely for me.

Once I finally broke through the invisible barriers I created in my head about not being able to date residents, our relationship took off and quickly blossomed into something wonderful. We moved fast. I even popped the "L" word almost right away. But, it felt right, so I found no sense in holding back. The only thing that mattered to me was that when I was with her I laughed, I smiled, and I just felt great all around.

On a side note, one thing I did notice early on was that Kait had this small brown mark on her forehead. It looked like it could have been some sort of birthmark or maybe a mole. When I asked her about it, she just said it was simply a "sun spot." *What's a sun spot?* I wondered. *Must mean that it's just a birthmark or something?* I accepted her answer as is and didn't ask too much more about it. She said she had it checked out before and the doctors basically told her it was nothing. Fair enough.

Over the remainder of the school year, Kaitlyn and I spent almost every day together, quickly falling deeper in love (giggle, giggle). I felt electric when I was with her. Everything felt great right from the start. Even after only three months of dating, my buddy Dan asked me if I could see myself marrying her in the future, and I responded, "Yes."

We did everything together. From going to museums, and going to baseball games and weddings, and playing video games, and watching movies, and going to dinners, to simple things like grocery shopping, or just sitting and talking, or playing board games. Bottom line, I really liked spending time with this girl, and I never seemed to get sick of hanging out with her. I felt like I could talk to her about anything. For the first time ever I felt like I could truly be vulnerable and let my guard down. I didn't feel like I was being judged no matter what crazy thing I was saying, and I said many crazy things. My mind was always filled with outlandish thoughts and ideas, differing greatly from the norm, and with her I could actually share those thoughts rather than keep them to myself. It felt relieving. It felt good.

Also, for the first time ever, I became dependent on someone else. Before Kaitlyn came around, I was about the most independent person you could find. I could spend all day entertaining myself either through working on my hobbies like writing or moviemaking or doing leisurely things like playing video games or basketball. I didn't realize I was missing something in my life. I never knew how much my life could be enhanced by including a special girl in it, until Kaitlyn came along. She would help me on my projects and praise me often when I did something well. I quickly got used to the support and positive reinforcement that I didn't have before I met her. I became drunk off it. I needed it. It felt good and made the pursuit of my goals seem more worthwhile.

As another measure of assurance, my whole family absolutely loved her. They couldn't get over her personality, how friendly she was, how cute she was, and how funny she was. My dad often said that I was lucky. It wasn't easy to find a woman so accepting of the typical male annoyances. At one point I remember him telling me not to lose her.

She fit in so well. She played board games with us, video games, bowling, etc. And her initial bowling technique was so pitiful that we couldn't help but be entertained by watching her feebly throw the ball down the lane. Her technique? She would slowly approach the foul line, and using her dainty momentum to propel the ball forward instead of swinging her arm like a normal human being, she would simply twist her wrist and drop the ball. It was adorable. Eventually, she learned the more proper technique of actually swinging her arm to throw the ball, which improved her game by leaps and bounds. She even bowled over 100 once or twice.

One of the first cute things she did around my family that got them hooked was when we played Pictionary together. The opposing team was taking their turn trying to draw and guess the picture. When one of our opponents (my brother, Tyler) correctly guessed the drawing, she cheered for them, clapped, and said, "Nice job!"

Slowly, I turned my head in gleeful disgust. "What did you just say?"

"What? They did a good job," she responded with her head slightly sunken into her shoulders, bashfully looking at me with a smile.

We all laughed. She didn't realize how competitive we all were when it came to games. This made her even more endearing and heartwarming in my eyes.

Kaitlyn also demonstrated her uncanny knowledge when it came to animated Disney movies. The first and only time she played the Disney Scene-It game (one based on trivia of the films) with my family and me, she absolutely destroyed us. After she (I was on her team, but everyone forgot) made it to the final question whilst leaving the competition in the dust, a challenge came up where a silhouette of a character appeared on the screen and we had to guess who it was. I'm not exaggerating when I say this, but the image was literally displayed for less the ONE second before Kaitlyn yelled out as she bounced in her seat and hesitantly pointed her finger at the screen, "BOO!!!" Boo is the little girl from the *Monsters, Inc.* movie.

"Oh my Godddd," my mom responded. We couldn't believe how fast her mind could generate an answer. And she was right!

"Sorrryyyy," Kait sheepishly responded. As competitive as she was at times, she felt bad crushing her competition like she did that evening.

Once again we all laughed, dumbfounded by her unmatched skill-level. After we packed up the game and called it a night, the rest of my family was sent off to bed licking their wounds.

I also found out really quickly that Kait had this profound love for children and babies. Apparently, she knew she wanted to teach young kids all the way back to when she was only in grade school. Kaitlyn was like a kid-magnet. Children would naturally drift to her whenever she was around. That same warm resonance that attracted adults seemed to be amplified around kids. It was something that always made me smile.

I remember one instance, we were hiking at a place called Devil's Lake near my hometown in Wisconsin. As we were preparing to head up a trail, Kaitlyn saw a mother and her baby. Kaitlyn, staring at the cute baby, said, "Uhh, I just love babies! Sometimes, don't you just want to go up and steal one?"

Bursting out into laughter I replied, "Haha, nooooo! Do you?"

"I just want to grab that baby and take off with it." She started laughing with me as we imagined her sneaking up, grabbing the infant, and running away with it. Obviously, she was joking.....I think.

After the laughter had calmed, she got serious and said, "If I ever found out I couldn't have kids, I would be devastated. I don't know what I would do."

"Yeah, that would be sad. Hopefully that's something you never have to worry about."

Holding hands, we began our hike.

Her love for kids melted my heart. I was indifferent toward them. I had never changed a diaper in my life, and I rarely held them because I was afraid one would slip out of my hands. But, I did think they were cute. Not as cute as puppies, though.

Around April of our first school year together, in 2009, with the encouragement of her family, Kaitlyn decided to get that spot on her forehead checked again. It seemed as though it had gotten a bit bigger since we first met in September, so she figured it'd be wise to get it looked at.

A biopsy was done on the enlarged mole, and days later it came back as being positive for melanoma. *Melanoma? What is that?* I'd heard the word before but was never familiar with it. I never really knew that melanoma was skin cancer until she told me.

After Kait called me with the results as I exited class, I walked as fast as I could to return to the dorm. The moment I entered her room, she began sobbing. "I'm sorry, sweetheart," I said. I felt terrible for her. All I could really do was hug her, rub her back, and just be there.

"It's okay...," she responded through her tears, "It's really not a big deal. It's just kind of shocking when someone tells you cancer is growing on your body."

"Yeah. I agree."

Cancer. Such an ugly and frightening word. Even though it was only Stage 1, it was still scary hearing her name and cancer in the same sentence. Naturally, the thoughts in our minds escalate to terrifying places. To places of toxic, damaging chemo and radiation. To places of a hairless head and a haggard body. To a place...of death. However, Kaitlyn quickly brushed those thoughts and worries from her mind, realizing she was only wasting energy and causing unnecessary stress on herself. She knew that once the doctors removed that spot on her forehead, cancer would be out of her life forever. Stage 1 melanoma has a cure rate in the upper 90 percentile, so the chances of it coming back were minimal.

As we sat on her futon, Kaitlyn quickly subdued her tears and took a deep breath. "Okay...I'm better now. Sorry, I just needed to get that out."

"That's okay, honey. You shouldn't apologize," I said with a half-smile. "Did you call your parents, yet?"

"Yeah. My dad is really worried about me. He made me promise I would never use a tanning bed again."

At one point in her life, Kait did use tanning beds to darken her complexion and "improve" her outward appearance. Though she was always stunningly beautiful just the way she was, society, advertising, and media have a way of making you feel like you're never quite beautiful enough. And most girls (and guys, of course) have no idea how dangerous using tanning beds can be and how much damage they can cause one's skin cells. Going forward, Kaitlyn upheld her promise she made to her father.

Shortly after discovering cancer was growing on and in her forehead, Kaitlyn had that overgrown mole removed. The doctor had to dig deep, to the lower layers of skin to extract every last bit of disease. Kaitlyn returned to school with a big letter "I" stitched to her forehead, and the bruising drained down from the incision, temporarily giving her black and blue eyes.

Though her physical appearance had been altered for the time being, she never let it bother her. She was so comfortable in her own skin, so secure with herself she didn't care if she was aesthetically abnormal. We went to a wedding just two weeks after her surgery, and though she had a large bandage on her forehead and leftover bruising under her eyes, she smiled and mingled with everyone with zero inhibitions. Kait was just relieved to no longer be tethered to cancer, freeing her from any future worries.

One side effect that did bother her after surgery, however, which she found out a few months later, was that she had lost feeling in her forehead. When I kissed her near the spot of the incision, no longer could she feel my lips. That made her sad. She loved the sensation of a kiss on her forehead, and she feared she would never feel it again. Out of everything, that was the one aspect of the whole situation that caused her to be upset. Not the surgery, the stitches, or the bruising, but because she wanted to feel my kiss. Such a minor thing it would seem, but it's the little things that really matter in life, right?

Fortunately, after a few more months of healing, the feeling in her forehead was completely restored. She could now officially strike the thoughts of cancer from her mind.

Over the next few years, Kaitlyn and I quickly built a strong relationship together. One full of love and happiness. For the first time in my life I felt complete. Even after just a few months of being with her, it felt like I had known and loved her for many, many years. Every day we verbally expressed a hundred times over how much we loved and cared and adored each other. Sure, it sounds like overkill, but, oddly, it never felt forced. I mentioned to Kait at one point that maybe we said "I love you" too much, but then I ended up being the one who said it even more. It just felt right.

What we had together was certainly more than simple puppy love. We had something special and unique. We seemed to complement one another perfectly. I was always calm. Composed. Safe. Boring. She was there to breathe life into me and give me a jolt of energy. She was there to teach me that spontaneity can be interesting and fun every now and then. On the other hand Kait was a worrier. Nervous and high strung at times. I was there as a gentle voice. A gentle touch. I was there to calm her and ease her fears. Kait complemented all of my flaws, and I complemented all of hers, though there were very few. I always told her she was perfectly flawed or flawed to perfection.

We did everything together. We told each other EVERYTHING. Even if I did something as small as eat a delicious candy bar, I told her about it, and I knew that she genuinely cared and that she was interested. Our relationship was never about control, about who wore the pants or anything childish like that. We both treated each other like royalty. From my perspective, I would see myself as a peasant and her my royal highness. Conversely, from her perspective, she would see herself as the peasant and I the king. In essence, we were always trying to make the other happy, even if it meant sacrificing our own happiness. But making her happy made me happy, so I guess there really was no sacrifice. And I know she felt the same way.

We almost never fought, either. Arguments were very few and very far between, and when they did happen, we would communicate well with each other, resolving issues without worrying about "winning" the fight. If ever one of us was wrong, we would swallow our pride and apologize. Our common goal was to always be on the same page, and we could only achieve that through strong communication. When relationships do falter, it seems like the lack of effective communication is the prime suspect, as pride, misunderstanding, and failure to compromise act as accomplices.

15

Then, feeling as though talking through issues and concerns has become pointless, leading nowhere, couples give up and their relationship spirals downward.

I give Kait so much credit, though, as she taught me not to bottle up my concerns. During the early portion of our relationship, getting me to express my feelings was like getting a child to eat his greens. I suppose I was a typical guy. Kait could always sense when something was brewing in my mind. She could sense the tension from whatever thoughts I had stored up, whether it was about our relationship or something completely irrelevant. When I sat with a blank stare as the wheels in my mind were spinning, she would notice and then urge me to release whatever was causing me stress. Typically I would resist for as long as I could before eventually giving in and expressing my innermost concerns. But, when I did give in, I always found myself feeling much better afterward. It helped me to feel relaxed and less burdened by my thoughts. She was so patient. That's why I give Kait so much credit for why we got along so well.

Well, I guess I'll take some credit. I was able to teach her how to control her little Irish temper.

We both helped each other grow I suppose.

Her support for me never wavered throughout our time together no matter what endeavors I chose. One of my hobbies was to write and make movies. At one point I began making a feature film on no budget. The project was extremely time consuming and quite stressful. But, Kaitlyn supported me throughout the whole process, especially during the times when I was burning out and becoming easily agitated. She even came on set and helped out with setting up food, organizing equipment, and taking pictures.

I had a wonderful companion. She was my little buddy.

I graduated before Kait, moving back to Madison to be near my place of employment. Because Kait began student teaching in her hometown, she moved back home to Kenosha. For a year and a half, being two hours apart, we made the whole long distance relationship work. Every day we spoke on the phone, usually multiple times, texting almost every 15 minutes. On every weekend, we spent time together. Either she would drive to Madison or I would drive to Kenosha. It was certainly an adjustment, and sometimes exhausting, but Kait was certainly worth it.

Aside from the long distance, our relationship seemed to be going perfect, and I wouldn't have changed anything about it. We started talking about getting a place and moving in together, which led to talks of getting a dog. She wanted one that would remain a puppy forever, but because that wasn't possible, and because of my obsession with pugs, Kait agreed to let me be the one who got to pick out our first breed - a pug, obviously. And Kait even suggested we name him GusGus. I loved it. That chubby mouse from Cinderella was so cute, making the name a perfect fit for a roly-poly, snorting pug.

I was even beginning to think about popping the big question. She had expressed to me very early on that she saw marriage in our future, and she was adorably anxious for that future to come sooner rather than later. For the first couple of years in our relationship, even though I saw Kait in my future, the thought of marriage terrified me. So, I put it off. Another typical male trait, right?

Well, after about three years together, conjuring up a proposal didn't seem as outlandish or spooky of an idea anymore. It started to feel right. I never imagined I'd find a love as strong as the love we shared, and it continued to grow every single day. I truly found my soul mate in Kaitlyn. Prolonging an inevitable marriage seemed pointless and silly. It was time to get serious. If only..........

3 CANCER'S RETURN

Everything in our lives seemed to be falling perfectly into place. I had a good job. Kait had just graduated college. We were preparing to move in together. And, she was ready to start her career in teaching youngsters - her passion. Like most people our age, she was 22 and I was 26 at the time, we had no reason to believe our ultimate goal of living a happy life together would be thwarted. Unfortunately, sometimes we have no control over our destiny. Sometimes life forces our plans to shift. But we had no way of predicting how significant that shift in our reality would be.

It all really seemed to begin in June of 2011. Kaitlyn and I were enjoying each other's company one weekend when she alerted me to an abnormality as we were getting ready for bed. "Trav, come here. Feel this," she said nicely.

With her left index finger, she was feeling something in front of her left ear, at the upper part of her jawbone. As I walked over, she removed her fingers and guided mine to the exact spot in question. Right away, I could feel it. It was a small bump. Very small. About the size of a pea. The spot was hard like a rock. "Hmmm, that's interesting."

"What do you think it could be," she asked.

"I don't know. Does it hurt?"

"No."

"Hmm, maybe it'll go away in a week or so. If not, I would definitely make an appointment."

And that was it.

We went to bed thinking nothing of it, really. At least I tried thinking of it as nothing, but I couldn't stop my mind from assuming the worst. I just had to hope and pray it would disappear, like a pimple.

Well, a week had passed, and that pea-sized bump on the side of her face did not go away. In fact, it had grown slightly. There was no cause for alarm just yet, but it seemed wise to have the spot checked out by a medical professional.

Kait's local doctor, after briefly analyzing the area of concern, initially assumed the bump was merely an infection of some sort, so she prescribed a weeklong regimen of antibiotics.

Good! I thought to myself. *It's just an infection.* We both felt relieved. We had no reason not to trust her doctor's expertise, so we felt confident that the prescribed medication would do the trick.

Unfortunately, we were wrong.

Kaitlyn took her antibiotics for a week as suggested, and the medication proved to be futile in combating the small protrusion by her ear. And, what was even more disconcerting was the fact that the bump continued to grow. My initial confidence was quickly fading as fear began to slowly propagate. I was still just hoping and praying the bump was nothing.

By mid-July, after the antibiotics failed to destroy the hard spot by her ear, Kait scheduled another appointment with her local doctor. Worried about my baby's health, I suggested she should have a biopsy done just to make sure it wasn't cancer. Of course, in trusting the years of knowledge her doctor must have acquired, I assumed a biopsy would be automatic, especially after looking into Kaitlyn's records and noticing a history of melanoma. I know doctors don't like to make rash judgments, but it seemed careless not to consider cancer as a possibility right off the bat. It had all of the superficial signs. It was hard. It was uniform. It didn't hurt. And, it was growing!

Well, during her second appointment with her local doctor, Kait was advised to simply wait it out for a couple more weeks to see if the bump dissipated on its own.

When Kaitlyn told me that, my jaw dropped. I couldn't believe it. That bump had been growing for over a month, and her doctor wanted her to sit on it even longer even though melanoma was in her history. I found the doctor's medical advice to be completely unacceptable, but I couldn't do much about it since I lived so far away. All I could do was sit and stew in my accounting cubicle at work, admonishing to Kait how much we needed a biopsy done just as a precautionary measure. She shared my concern, but we didn't know what we could do.

Following her doctor's suggestion, Kait waited another two weeks, which led us into August. As we both expected, the bump next to her ear continued to grow, and so did my fear and concern for what it might be. That lump was becoming increasingly prominent, as it had become visible now from every angle, whereas in the weeks prior it was unnoticeable. I didn't want to panic, but it seemed obvious we needed to take this very seriously.

Kaitlyn made another appointment with her local doctor.

Finally, after more than two months of the bump increasing in size, her doctor ordered a simple test.

On August 15th, a Monday, Kaitlyn received an ultrasound on the growing hard spot. When asked when she would find out about the results, her doctor told her she should expect a call in three days. We just had to wait.

Well, three days had passed. It was Thursday now, and Kaitlyn kept a close watch on her phone all day, anxious to hear the results. But as the hours ticked by, the call never came.

Just out of curiosity, I asked my mother, who happened to be a nurse, how long it should take to read the results of an ultrasound. Her answer. "Almost immediately."

I could only shake my head in further disgust over the seeming incompetence her clinic had been exhibiting.

Friday arrived, and Kait continued to wait anxiously for the results. Because the clinic wasn't open on the weekends and time was running out on the day, Kait decided to call them. The operator politely told Kait she would leave a message with the doctor and that the doctor would give her a call back later.

Well, the hours kept passing by. Soon, the evening was upon us as the sun began to tuck itself into the horizon. It became increasingly apparent that that phone call was not coming.

Frustration was growing within me at the level of irresponsibility her doctor was displaying. It was a pattern of carelessness that had been repeating itself for two months. I understand clinics are busy, but when you are told "three days" for the results, you expect three days. It had been a week. As much as Kait tried to push her assumptions aside, she couldn't help but begin to worry about all of the possibilities. And now she had the weekend to sit and ponder over it as the results hovered over her head.

But, Kait was not the type to sit and dwell on things like me, so she was able to repress all those troublesome thoughts and enjoy her weekend. To her, two days was not substantial, and she was confident the results would arrive on Monday.

Well, Monday came and Kait waited anxiously for the expected phone call. By about 1 PM and still no results, Kaitlyn decided to call them again. And again, she was told that a message would be left with her doctor and that someone would call her back later.

As daylight waned, her phone remained silent. The results didn't come.

With my frustration boiling over, Kait's patience began to diminish, too. The potentially negative conclusion from her ultrasound had been lingering over her head too long, and she just wanted to know if something was wrong with her.

Tuesday came. Still, no phone call. Kait called again at noon and was told the same exact thing she was told during her previous calls.

That was it. She had had enough. It was time to be proactive and obtain the results herself. Exhausted from a full day of dealing with unruly children in the sultry heat at the day camp where she worked, Kait calmly walked into the clinic.

Being polite as she always was, even through her fatigue and frustration, Kaitlyn nicely explained to the medical staff how she had been waiting and waiting and waiting for the results that should have been received a week ago, and that she had to call three times and was told she would get a call back but got nothing. Her frustration while explaining the situation had reached a tipping point. Kait broke down and began sobbing. And she had every right to be upset.

Finally, a doctor came out and delivered the results to Kait. The images from the ultrasound were inconclusive. She needed to schedule an appointment with a specialist for a biopsy. Finally! That's all we needed, and the message was so simple. Fighting back her emotions and exhaustion, she thanked the doctor and immediately set up her next appointment.

I was furious at how Kait was being tossed aside at her clinic! I wanted so badly to unleash a verbal assault on her doctor, but I couldn't because I was two hours away, and, let's face it, I'm too passive. Kaitlyn should not have had to walk into the doctor's office herself to find out important results that should have been delivered to her a week ago. What kind of practice were these people running?

It was now almost September, and Kaitlyn was finally scheduled for a biopsy, something that should have been recommended back in July. That bump had three months, and probably more, to grow and potentially spread to other areas of her body. I wanted to explode at the way Kait's situation was handled.

Finally, on September 2nd, a biopsy was done on the protrusion by Kait's ear, and six days later, on a Friday evening after Kait picked me up from work, we received a phone call from the clinic on our drive home. The results were in.

Melanoma.....

With a partial smile, attempting to conceal her emotions while she spoke on the phone, she thanked the person on the other line and hung up.

"So what's up," I anxiously asked.

Trying to remain calm as she became increasingly distraught, she replied, "They said it came back positive for melanoma."

I went completely silent for a brief moment. I was not too surprised, but still shocked. Cancer was back. As I looked concernedly at Kait, I could see her bottom lip beginning to quiver.

"Sweetie.....why don't you pull over quick," I suggested as I pointed to an opening by the curb.

She complied.

As soon as her car came to rest at the side of the road, Kait began weeping. I felt terrible for her. All I could do was put my arms around her and give her my love and encouragement.

"I'm sorry, sweetheart..."

"It's okay....I just need a moment."

I rested my forehead against the side of her head and rubbed her back. It pained me to see her sad.

"You know......we'll just do whatever we need to do, get that stupid bump taken out, and hopefully never have to worry about it again," I said.

But deep down, I didn't know what to think. My knowledge of melanoma was almost nonexistent, and I just assumed surgery would solve the problem permanently. I really had no idea, though.

After wiping the tears from her face and taking a few deep breaths, Kait called her family to deliver the negative news. Like myself, they were also ignorant on the seriousness of melanoma. We all thought it would just be removed and we'd never have to worry about it again. We couldn't have been more wrong.

During the remainder of our drive home, I did my best to comfort Kait and calm her worries. But behind that façade of positivity, my mind was racing with concern for her future. Naturally, when one thinks of cancer, the thought of death seems to creep in unabated. My heart palpitated as I attempted to fully grasp our situation. I was dumbfounded.

Here was a bright, smart, wonderful girl, only 22 years old, having to face cancer. No young person should have to face that. I mean, no one no matter what age should have to endure cancer, but it seems so tragic when it is a person in his or her youth. They have yet to experience so many of the joys in life that come with age. Kait had so many goals and aspirations, so many things she wanted to experience.

I sat in the car reflecting on our lives and our relationship together. While trying to hold a conversation with Kait, I was playing out hundreds of different scenarios in my head, ranging from the cancer being taken out and never coming back to cancer spreading and taking her life. My head felt like a balloon.

What would happen now? How will this affect our lives? How will this change our plans going forward? Everything is falling into place, and this has the potential to completely turn our lives upside-down.

It seemed so unfair. But, being the strong one in our relationship Kait reminded me that others around the world were dealing with hardships much worse than she, young and old, and she wasn't going to feel sorry for herself. That meant I couldn't either.

Wanting to move quickly, surgery to remove that melanoma tumor was scheduled for Monday, September 19th.

In the interim before the procedure, I briefly researched the disease we were facing. In my research, I was surprised to find out melanoma is actually the deadliest form of skin cancer. Once it spreads past its original sight, into what the medical world denotes as Stage 4, it's almost impossible to cure and becomes extremely aggressive. A very small percentage of people with Stage 4 melanoma live past five years.

Of course, at the time, I had no idea what stage Kait's melanoma was at. It seemed like a quick and simple fix with surgery. Also, even if it was serious, I mean, it was 2011 after all. In my mind medicine had become so advanced that I was confident a great treatment would be available to completely destroy her cancer. Boy was I in for a rude awakening.

On Wednesday of the following week, I went into my boss's office in the morning to inform her of the recent events in my life. I told her about Kait's tumor, and that I would need a few days off for her surgery. Of course she was receptive to my request. It was odd, because for the first time, talking about it out loud to someone else, I could feel a surge of emotions coming on. I felt like I wanted to break down and start crying. I don't know why, because I was truly confident that Kait was going to be just fine. Luckily, I held my tears back.

Later on that day, after Kait had an appointment with a doctor to talk about her situation, she called me on the phone at lunch to give me an update.

"Hey sweetheart," I exclaimed as usual.

"Hi honey, are you on break?"

"Yupyup….so how did the appointment go?"

"Good, good. The doctor just kind of talked about the surgery and what was going to happen."

"Yeah, so do you feel good about everything, I mean, I'm sure you're nervous and stuff, but…"

"Yeah, I feel pretty good. I just want to get this surgery over with and move on to the next step."

"Did he talk about what stage it was," I asked.

"Well, he said because it's in the lymph node, that means it's stage 3."

"Stage 3?!?!"

I was shocked. At the time, all I knew was that there were 4 stages with cancer. The 4th stage was obviously the worst and meant you basically didn't have much of a chance, and the fact that Kait was one stage away was quite jarring for me. As I stared at the wall in front of me, I could feel that surge of emotions once again coming to the forefront of my head and my eyes. But, no way was I going to cry with Kait on the phone. Not with what she was facing. I wanted to be the tough one for her. To get some fresh air while on the phone, I stepped outside in hopes that it would calm my nerves.

However, the cool breeze and crisp air was not enough. As Kait continued talking, I could no longer hold back the rush of built up emotions just waiting to burst through my face. I finally broke down and started crying. But I tried keeping my whimpers silent, pulling the phone away from my mouth when I needed to take a breath so Kait wouldn't hear me. But that didn't work. She could sense my sobs.

Doing her best to try and comfort me, even though she was the one with cancer, she said, "Sweetie, don't be sad for me. It's okay. I'm going to be okay."

"I know, I'm just worried about you because I love you and don't want you to have to go through this..."

"Aww, I love you, too, but seriously we'll just get the surgery, get this thing removed and we won't have to worry about it anymore."

I couldn't believe it. She was the one directly dealing with cancer, yet I was the one having to be consoled. A part of me felt ashamed that I couldn't maintain my composure for her, but it spoke volumes to me on how strong she was. From that point on, I knew that even though she was the one dealing with the life threatening disease, she would still put everyone else ahead of herself, just like she did when she wasn't dealing with cancer.

After talking a bit more, we said our goodbyes.

"Alright, honey, well, I'll let you go," she said gently.

"That sounds good."

"Well, I love you, and please try not to worry about it too much. Just think, after the surgery, I'll be fine."

"Yeah you're right. I love you sweetheart, and I'll talk to you later."

"I love you, too, Trav."

As soon as we hung up, I walked behind a large pillar outside of the office building and released the rest of my tears. I didn't want people to see me. I then made my way back inside, checking myself in the bathroom mirror and wiping away all of my tears before heading up to my desk. I was hoping the redness around my eyes wasn't too noticeable.

As I sat in my cubicle, all I could think about was Kaitlyn and what her, our, future would now possibly entail. Shock perpetuated throughout my body as the phrase "Stage 3" kept on flashing in my head, and I felt a constant rush of emotions wanting to burst through like before. Just wanting to be by myself and with my mind on everything but work, I decided to leave the office so I could sit and process everything without people around me.

I was never one to cry, especially not in front of other people. I had too much insecurity with it. Before this situation with Kaitlyn and cancer, I could probably count on one hand the amount of times I cried (I exaggerate). Kaitlyn meant so much to me, and the mere thought of such a sweet and loving person having to struggle through such hardship was crushing. It was unfair.

4 SURGERY

September 19th had arrived. The big day. The day of surgery.

With our posse of Kait's family members – Mark (dad) and Vicky (stepmom), Kathy (mom) and Tom (stepdad), Jessica (sister), Brian (brother), Vicky's mom and sister, and I – we accompanied her to the hospital as we crammed into the waiting room, taking up much of the limited free space. The only immediate family member missing in the bunch was Kait's kid brother, Benjamin. We were all anxious, but none more than Kait. As nervous as she was as she awaited her name to be called, she just wanted the procedure completed and the tumor out of her body forever.

Some time during mid-morning, Kaitlyn was called back to begin surgery prep. As she walked away, I hugged her and wished her good luck. We all did.

Along with removing the mass by her ear, a lymphectomy was scheduled, which required the surgeon to remove roughly 40-50 lymph nodes surrounding the tumor just in case it had traveled outside of the primary spot.

With Kait in surgery, we all stood by patiently, but on pins and needles.

The waiting room had a monitor that displayed the status of every patient in surgery so that family members could follow the progress of their beloved. Of course, it didn't show the names of the patients, but each patient was assigned a special number. I couldn't stop looking at the monitor. Every 30 seconds my eyes would wander to the screen to see if

Kait's status had changed. And every time I looked up, the monitor would display "466137 – In Surgery." For hours, my neck received a good workout as I performed probably over 1000 head lifts.

Finally, at about the three-hour mark, Kait's status changed. Just to make sure my eyes weren't playing tricks on me, I approached the screen for a closer look. Sure enough, it said "466137 – Recovery." We were all relieved. Kait was out of surgery and in recovery.

Another hour went by before the surgeon, a young lady named Dr. Darsey, came out and briefed us on the procedure. After informing us of the success of the surgery, she went on to explain that the tumor was about the size of a walnut! *A walnut!?! Holy shit!* To make the surgery even more delicate and complex, she said a nerve was wrapped around the large growth, which was why the surgery went a bit longer than expected. We couldn't express our profound gratitude enough as we thanked the doctor multiple times for doing a wonderful job.

Now, we just wanted to see Kaitlyn. But she was in recovery, so we had to wait a couple hours to allow her to rest.

At around 5 or 6 in the evening, after Kait had an appropriate amount of time of convalescence, we were allowed to visit. I couldn't wait to give her a hug.

We walked into her room. When I first saw her, I couldn't get over how adorable and sweet she looked. The anesthetics and the pain medications caused her to remain groggy and very tired even hours after surgery, and we could see she was experiencing some pain and discomfort.

Her voice was very soft and cute, and she could barely keep her eyes open. For some reason, I don't know if it was because she was cold, or anxious, or if it was a side effect from surgery, but her lower jaw was shaking uncontrollably. Her teeth were chattering and she looked uncomfortable. I felt terrible for her. It became apparent she needed rest, and she wasn't prepared to be talkative and social.

As we were visiting with Kait, some aunts and uncles arrived, wanting to say hello and express their love and support for her. It was sweet, and I know Kait appreciated feeling the love from all of her family. But, as I was observing Kait's body language, I could tell she just wanted to rest. She didn't feel like entertaining us.

After about an hour, we all decided it was time to let Kaitlyn be. Kathy volunteered to sleep in the hospital room with her daughter, making sure she wasn't alone for the night. With that, we all hugged and kissed Kait goodbye and left the medical center.

We headed back to the hospital right away the following morning.

When we arrived, we began packing up Kait's belongings to move her out of Urgent Care and into a different wing of the hospital. Kait was explicitly informed not to perform any physical activity such as lifting objects so as to not over exert herself. We told her to just sit in her wheelchair and relax.

She agreed, but I should have known better.

As we were gathering her things, suddenly, out of the corner of my eye, I saw someone in a bright green hospital gown walk by. It was Kait. And she was not empty-handed. Slowly making her way to her wheelchair, a couple bags hung from her hands, her legs kicking them with each step.

I could only shake my head and smile as she set the bags on her lap.

"Kait! Darn you," I said, scolding her for her insubordination. I tried taking the bags off of her legs as she sat in the wheelchair. "Let me grab those."

"Nope. I got it," she replied.

For being so cute and stubborn and for disobeying orders, I smiled more and kissed her on the forehead.

Kait was the type of person who always wanted to feel like she was contributing and doing her part. Even if she was completely weakened, she was still determined to find a way to help out in any capacity. It was a loveable and endearing trait of hers.

We settled into our new room. It was actually quite big.

That evening, we all gathered around Kait to join her in watching one of her favorite television shows at the time – "Glee". Lacking a sufficient amount of chairs, Kait asked if I wanted to lie in bed with her. I didn't know what to do. Was it safe? Would her dad be giving me the evil eye the whole time?

I looked around at the faces in the room, trying to gauge if anyone was giving me a look of condemnation. No one seemed to disapprove, so I climbed in bed with my girl as she scooched over to make room.

But as soon as I settled in, the bed started going haywire. "Uh ohhh......I think I broke it," I said nervously.

The bed wouldn't shut up as the mattress moved up and down to compensate for the sudden change in weight. Every single movement I made, the bed adjusted. It was annoying as hell. Finally, I just decided to remain completely still once I found a comfortable position. The bed stopped complaining.

With Kait leading us in conversation and laughter, we spent the next couple hours joking around and enjoying each other's company. That was one of her specialties – bringing people together and putting smiles on their faces. I enjoyed watching the interaction.

That evening, I was the chosen one. The one bestowed with the ultimate honor of staying with Kaitlyn for the night. I had been looking forward to a hospital slumber party with her all day. Lucky for me, no one had any quarrels with the idea of a simple "boyfriend" accompanying her.

Little did they know, however, that in addition to our plans of moving in together on November 1st, a proposal was also on the horizon. But with Kait's new health scare I decided it would be wise to postpone asking her to marry me in order to give her adequate time to recover.

As I set up a cot and pushed it tight up against Kaitlyn's bed, the family kissed Kait and said their goodbyes. It was *finally* just the two of us. I could *finally* let my guard down and unleash an onslaught of affection toward her, something I would never do in front of others. With everyone out of the room, I could *finally* tell her how much I loved her, and how proud I was for how she handled surgery and her situation with cancer. And I was so proud of her!

Surprisingly, sleeping in the hospital was not as dreadful as I thought it would be. It was actually quite peaceful. And it certainly helped being next to Kait since she always soothed my worries and put me at ease.

We could have never imagined that sleeping in a hospital room next to each other was something we would soon have to get used to.

The next day, Kaitlyn was discharged and we were off to Kenosha. With surgery out of the way and the cancerous lump removed from her body, she felt a huge weight lifted off of her shoulders. We all did. She was ready to move on with her life and continue chasing her goals and dreams. We just had to hope and pray that the cancer hadn't spread. From the time we actually discovered the bump to when it was removed, it had been over three months. And it's impossible to say how long it had been growing before Kait discovered it. We just had to wait for the results of the pathology report before we could feel completely safe.

In the meantime, we set up an appointment with Kait's future oncologist – Dr. Thomas Robertson. Fortunately, he was located in Madison, just minutes away from where I was. That meant Kait and I could follow through with our plans of moving in together in a month. We were both excited!

To add to our good news, Kait received a phone call from her surgeon about the pathology report. The 40 to 50 lymph nodes removed around her tumor came back negative for melanoma, and the PET scan done prior to surgery showed no signs of disease anywhere else in her body. Kait was free of cancer!

We were all overcome with elation and joy. While Kait was delivering the news over the phone to me, I could hear everyone in the background hooting and hollering! It was the news we had been waiting to hear. Now it seemed we could officially move on with our lives and put cancer behind us.

Though I was happy as hell to hear Kait was cancer free, there was still a part of me that wasn't completely satisfied with the results. A part of me worried that cancerous cells could still be growing in her body, but the scans just couldn't detect them.

That night, for some reason I felt compelled to dig deeper in finding out more information about melanoma. As I was researching the Internet, I came across a chart that showed survival rates. For those with Stage 3 melanoma, the 5-year survival rate was only 50%. The 10-year survival rate was even smaller. A mere 25%! My heart skipped a beat.

How could that be? Only one person out of four survives 10 years after being diagnosed with Stage 3 melanoma? But, all of the cancer was removed, so Kait should be in the clear, right? Maybe those other people had it in multiple lymph nodes. Maybe the pathology report for those other people came back showing it had spread to other areas of their body? Kait's situation is different from others in Stage 3. She only had it in one lymph node, and it was removed, and it didn't show up anywhere else. So she should be just fine. I think? God, I hope so.

Discovering that grim information was unsettling to say the least. Not wanting to search any deeper I closed my computer. At that time, I didn't want to know any more. Kait was a unique person, and I didn't want any

31

general statistics hovering over my head. For all we knew, the cancer was gone, and it was a waste of energy to stress over it.

Nevertheless, I shrugged off my negative thoughts and told the worrywart in me to 'zip it'. Cancer was behind us and it was time to start looking forward to a bright future.

It was time to start looking at rings!

5 INTRODUCING OUR NEW ONCOLOGY TEAM

With a free muffin and a cup of hot chocolate, complements of the Carbone Cancer Center at the University of Wisconsin in Madison, we waited in the waiting room as Kait checked in at the registration desk. We were set to meet Dr. Robertson for the first time.

Slowly sipping on my cup of chocolaty deliciousness, I could hear a brood of women behind me squawking away. Of course, Kaitlyn was at the source of all the chatter. With her beaming smile, with those soft and jolly cheeks, and with her shiny blonde hair, the nice ladies working behind the registration desk lit up as soon as Kait entered the clinic. Her personality and positive energy was contagious, so I wasn't surprised that the tranquility of the waiting room was temporarily disrupted upon her arrival. It was almost as though smiling and laughing became an uncontrollable reflex when Kait was around. A wonderful power she unknowingly possessed.

I filled up my Styrofoam cup one more time before Kait came and sat down with us. It was just too good to pass up!

Shortly after she took her seat, a nurse called out a name. "Kaitlyn!"

"Oh, that's us." Kaitlyn stood up and waved at the nurse, "Hii! Um, is it okay if my family comes back or do you just want me for now?"

In total there were six of us, so we needed a slightly bigger room to fit into.

"Oh no, your family is certainly welcome to come back." The nurse took a look at our group. "Ohhhh. Let me see if we can open up the conference room."

"Okay, that sounds good, thank you," Kait gleefully exclaimed.

Moments later, the nurse came back out and led us into the family room where we all found a seat.

As we waited anxiously to meet our new medical team and learn about our next steps with melanoma, a woman walked in. Her name was Nurse Sue, at least that's what we called her. We never really knew her last name, or if she even had one. She was Dr. Robertson's right hand woman.

Nurse Sue was a very nice lady, and she took to Kaitlyn instantly.

With Kait's happy and sparkling face, all of the nurses fell in love with her immediately. I can't help but fawn over my girl, but it was as though a piece of the sun broke off and fell to earth and transmuted itself into this little ball of shine named Kaitlyn. Months down the road, every staff member in the cancer center quickly got to know and love Kait. It was impossible not to.

Anyway, after Nurse Sue spent some time acquainting herself with us, mainly Kaitlyn, she began educating us on melanoma and our treatment options. For those in Stage 3, a treatment called Interferon was about the only option. Nurse Sue explained that Dr. Robertson would be recommending Interferon. As she explained it, basically Kait would have the treatment administered for one year, and though it would make her feel sick for the most part, it wouldn't completely inhibit her ability to live a normal life.

We listened intently to every word Nurse Sue spoke. When it came to cancer, we were very ignorant and fearful. With our limited knowledge base, we were willing to do every possible treatment we could in order to make sure cancer never came back. As far as we knew, the best plan of attack was radiation and chemotherapy, because that's all we knew about. In our minds, radiation and chemotherapy were the one and only answers. In our minds, radiation and chemotherapy were great options.

As Nurse Sue continued giving us our much-needed lecture, Dr. Robertson walked into the room. Wearing his white gown and glasses, with very short hair and a stubble beard, he immediately approached Kaitlyn and shook her hand before going around the room and meeting the rest of us. Likely in his 50s, we instantly got the feeling that this guy was well educated just based on his look. Of course he was, he had been specializing in melanoma for, I don't know, 25 or 30 years.

Bashfully confident is how I would describe the doctor, a trait Kait found quite endearing. When he spoke he didn't always make much eye contact, but he spoke clearly and concisely and was confident in what he said. A typical genius, I suppose. Kaitlyn and the rest of us admired him from the beginning.

After spending time getting to know Kait, he shifted his focus to her health. He started off by speaking in detail about Interferon and what Kait should expect while receiving the treatment. We were curious as to the purpose of doing any treatment in the first place. Wasn't the cancer gone from Kait's system?

"Interferon has shown to keep melanoma from coming back for two years," he explained.

We were all somewhat confused. Keep melanoma away for two years? But, Kait no longer had melanoma. Is he saying that it inevitably comes back? We needed clarification.

"Wait, what? Two years," Kait asked, unsure if maybe she misheard what he said.

"Yes, Interferon has been shown to keep the cancer away for an average of two years."

We understood we likely needed Kaitlyn to receive some sort of treatment just in case tiny remnants of cancer remained undetected in her body. But, we assumed that whatever treatment we chose would completely eradicate the disease.

"So, wait, this Interferon won't kill the cancer completely," we asked.

Dr. Robertson wanted to choose his words carefully. Certainly, with some people the cancer never returns. I suppose looking back on my research, it stays dormant in roughly 50% of people, at least for 5 years. But Dr. Robertson didn't want to use the word "cure," because in the world of oncology that term can be considered irresponsible. Even if cancer doesn't show up on scans, it doesn't necessarily mean one is cured.

Nevertheless, we were somewhat disappointed because our hopes were high coming into the clinic that whatever treatment Kait received would destroy the cancer forever. Once again, our ignorance shone brightly.

"Well, is there anything else we can do to increase the chances of this cancer not coming back," we asked.

"Yes. You could do radiation first."

Basically, as he explained it, they would simply radiate the area surrounding the location of her tumor to kill any remaining cells. Like I said, we wanted the whole package, leaving no stone unturned. We wanted to make sure we did everything possible to increase our chances, so we elected to go with radiation first before commencing Interferon.

Now, many months down the road, after I became more educated on melanoma and the available treatments, I regret the fact that we elected to put Kait through radiation. In my studies, I found out that melanoma is typically "radioinsensitive." It is resistant to normal levels of radiation. Consequently, in hindsight and in my irrelevant opinion, radiotherapy seemed more like a waste of time than anything, and actually would cause more harm than good since it damages healthy cells, too. Had I not been so ignorant at the time, I think our course of action would have certainly differed.

Nevertheless, we happily agreed to do radiation first, and we were eager to start. It was scheduled to begin in early-November. Kait would receive the radiation every day for five consecutive weeks, getting Saturday and Sunday off.

That was it. We shook the hands of Dr. Robertson and Nurse Sue, thanked them, and we prepared to leave the hospital. We had a treatment plan laid out, and we were happy!

That night, Mark and Vicky came to my hometown and met my parents for the first time. It was chaotic because our beloved Milwaukee Brewers were playing a deciding Game 5 in the playoffs, and it was a close game in the late innings. Right as Mark was telling a compelling, but unfortunately-timed story, the Brewers had a walk-off hit that won the game for them and sent them to the next round of the playoffs. We all rudely interrupted his story with cheers and high fives. I felt bad, but we couldn't help ourselves. It was the first playoff series the Brewers had won in my lifetime.

Even Kaitlyn was in on the cheering. She jumped ship on the Chicago Cubs and became a Brewer fan once we began dating. She still liked the Cubbies, but the Brewers were a likeable team, and I was a fan of them, so it was easy to make the switch. Plus, I mean, let's face it, the Cubs kind of, well…..sucked. However, Kaitlyn ensured her dad not to worry, because she would NEVER ever become a Green Bay Packer fan. She would always be true to the Chicago Bears. A compromise that Mark could accept. The Packer/Bear rivalry extended almost 100 years, and it would be sticking a dagger in her father's heart had she jumped on the Packer bandwagon.

After settling down from the exciting victory, we ate dinner and had a great night of laughing and socializing.

The next day, Kait, her dad, stepmom, and I went to a place called Devil's Lake for hiking and sightseeing. It was a beautiful location that included a lake and tall bluffs (small mountains) that surrounded the sparkling water. Because it was Fall, all of the leaves were changing color, so we were in for a visual treat.

When we got there, we decided to hike the first path that we saw. Unbeknownst to us, this was one of the steepest trails at Devil's Lake. The ascent was basically a 90-degree vertical hike. There were stepping stones, though, so it's not like it was that dangerous, but some of the stones were slippery. As we traversed the mini-mountain, we had to stop for Mark and Vicky a few times. I mean, they were elderly (40s/50s) and didn't workout as often as Kait and I, so it was expected they'd be winded. What I didn't expect, however, was how well Kait would do on the trail. I mean, she was about two weeks removed from surgery, and there she was on those bluffs, climbing up without much of a struggle at all. I was so proud of her.

When we eventually arrived at the summit, we were awarded with a view of the beautiful scenery from high above. The midday sun pierced the crisp air and shimmered off of the water below. And a sea of trees painted in a wide array of bold autumn colors blanketed the infinite landscape beneath us. It was a wonderful sight to see.

I put my arm around Kait while we soaked in the gorgeous view. We felt good about everything. We felt confident. She was going to be just fine.

And if there was one positive we could take from facing adversity through that pestilent cancer, it was that it brought us closer together. Through hardship, our love grew even stronger!

6 A FRESH START

With October upon us, Kaitlyn was finally able to move in with me in Madison for the final few weeks of my lease before we moved into our new place. We were excited to get a chance to act like a real adult couple, and I couldn't wait to be able to come home from work every single day to embrace and cherish my very best gal.

And to further our return to a normal life, Kaitlyn would finally have an opportunity to begin teaching children in order to bring in some fat dough. She couldn't wait to get started.

Then there was this idea of marriage occupying my brain.

Proposing had been on my mind for months, but with the cancer diagnosis and subsequent surgery, I forced myself to sideline those plans temporarily. Now that the dust had finally settled, I felt like I could get back on the saddle and begin planning again to make the big move. The time felt right.

First I needed to pick out a ring, which terrified the heck out of me because my eye for fashion was pathetic. Nevertheless, I forced myself to dive into the world of jewelry and become familiar with the various styles.

After a grueling week of research and two sweaty, nerve-wracking hours at a local jewelry store, I finally made my great purchase. I felt confident that the ring I picked out was going to complement Kait's personality perfectly. It wasn't too plain, yet it wasn't over-the-top gaudy. It was dainty, just like she was, with diamonds aligned around the twisted band. I was happy with my selection. I surprised myself!

With step one of my proposal out of the way, my next step was to figure out how exactly I was actually going to propose. The thought of getting down on one knee mortified me more than the thought of buying a ring. I didn't know what to do. I wanted it to be unique, and I wanted it to be personal. It had to be clever, and it had to fit who Kait and I were. But how?

Ideas flooded my mind, like a carriage ride with a fancy dinner, and a few others, but they all seemed too cliché and overdone. I wanted something completely different and hopefully memorable. For days I tried thinking of all the different things Kaitlyn was interested in. Puppies, flowers, polar bears, candy, the color pink, penguins, cookies, popcorn, etc. My mind was firing blanks. Then, one day, an idea just popped into my head. It was like a bolt of lightning penetrated my ass and made its way up to my brain. It was an idea that I felt particularly excited about.

Every year we had been going to this special Christmas Market located in Chicago called the Christkindlmarket. It was basically a small Christmas village adorned with cute little shops, Christmas decorations, music, and good food. At the center of it all was a huge Christmas tree. And one thing Kaitlyn loved just about more than anything else in the whole wide world was Christmas. She loved everything about it, the family, the love, the lights, the snow, the trees, the giving, the music, everything. So, I wanted to incorporate Christmas into my proposal.

My idea went a little something like this. I would place her ring in a large box and wrap it in wrapping paper to make it look like a big present. Then, on the day of the Christkindlmarket, I would have whoever we were with stealthily place the present under the huge Christmas tree. Kaitlyn and I would eventually stroll on over to the colorful fir and admire its splendor. Then, after a moment or two, my eyes would catch notice of something. "Hey, what's that," I would say, pointing to the present. Confused, she would then grab the gift, see her name on the tag, open it, and that's when I would get down on one knee and beg her to spend the rest of her life with me.

Perfect! At least the way it played out in my head it was. It was unique and very personal to her interests. Now, figuring out how to execute my idea was another issue all together. Nevertheless, I had my ideal plan in place, and that was the most difficult part, I think.

Kait's birthday came on October 29th, right around Halloween. She turned 23 that day. To celebrate, a bunch of friends and us got all dressed up in our costumes and went out in downtown Madison, famous for its huge party on State Street where tens of thousands of freaks join to drink beer and act stupid. Being a little older, we avoided State Street. It's more chaotic and crowded than it is fun. We elected to celebrate at a couple neighboring bars instead, which included a karaoke bar where I got to live out one of my longtime dreams – singing "I'm Gonne Be (500 Miles)" by the Proclaimers. Using the thickest Irish accent I could muster, my friend, Jeff, and I shouted the lyrics like champs. We were stars. I wasn't going to let the fame get to me, though. Kait taught me to be humble.

Overall, it was a great night to spend with my baby along with our friends. After everything that had been going on, we needed a day to let loose and have fun. Never in a million years could we have imagined that it would be the last Halloween we would get to celebrate together in that same fashion.

The week following Halloween, we finally moved into our new apartment, and Kait began her radiation therapy. She also started substitute teaching in the Madison School District, so she was a busy girl.

Every day, Kaitlyn would get up and go teach loud, misbehaved, snot-nosed children (I only use harsh words for effect, and Kait didn't think of them that way). That in itself was exhausting, but immediately after work she would drive straight to the UW hospital in the busy downtown, stop-n-go, Madison traffic for her radiation. Normally she would come home just pooped, and I felt bad for her. But, at least when she came home I could greet her with a hug and help her relax. Stresses for the day seemed to quickly vanish when we were in each other's company.

Kait's grueling schedule aside, we couldn't have been happier at the time. Everything was falling perfectly into place once again. We were all settled into our new apartment, and I got to come home every single day to hang out with my best friend. Her presence gave me a new spark. My energy level was the highest it had been in a long time.

Many experts opine that moving in with your partner before marriage can be detrimental to the relationship, but with Kait and I it seemed to be the complete opposite as our relationship was finally allowed to flourish. Instead of having to travel two hours to see each other every weekend, cramming our love into just two days, we could see each other seven days a week. And instead of fitting a day's worth of events into an hour of conversation on the phone every night, we could spread out all of our trivial stories throughout the day. We could seemingly do anything now without feeling rushed. We could cook with or for each other. We could watch our shows together. We could play video games or board games. We could catch a talkie or go to dinner. Or, we could just lie at home in comfortable silence, doing nothing and saying nothing. I could kiss her or she could kiss me any time we felt like it. We could hug or snuggle or cuddle. It was great!

And outside of the home, Kait's teaching career was taking off as she had found a long-term subbing position at a Madison elementary school. That school had a position opening up and they were prepared to hire her on permanently.

Cancer really was not much of a worry in our heads at that point. To us, it was gone.

7 A SOMEWHAT DECENT PROPOSAL

December was upon us which meant violent shopping sprees for disposable goods, Christmas songs on repeat, and the forgotten birth of a divine baby whose name escapes me. It's the best time of the year!

All kidding aside, Christmas was right around the corner, which meant the pressure was on me. It was time to get my right knee dirty. It was time to ask Kait to take my hand in marriage.

A week before the proposal, I called each of her parents, not to get permission, but to let them know I was planning on asking their daughter to marry me. The whole "asking for permission" thing was kind of cheesy to me, because even if I didn't have their permission I still would have asked Kait to be my wife. It was important to me, however, that they at least be in on the secret, as long as no one spilled the beans.

Saturday, December 3rd, 2011 was marked on the calendar in my head as the big day. For a whole week leading up to it, I was filled with constant anxiety. I just wanted everything to go as perfectly as planned, the way I envisioned it in my head with dancing penguins, Christmas carolers, and raining graffiti. Very few things make me nervous in life, but proposing was certainly near the top of that short list.

And then to add to my anxiety, with Saturday just around the bend our plans to go to the Christkindlmarket fell through at the last minute, sending my nerves into a panic. Scrambling to figure out a new time and date to make my proposal, I didn't know what to do. As I was freaking out on the inside, I started to question whether or not I should just scrap my idea entirely and think of something completely different.

However, all was saved when I found out my mother and brother, Nathan, just so happened to be heading to the Christkindlmarket the next day, Sunday, December 4th. So, we decided to go with them. My plan was back on track.

Without Kait knowing, I gave the ring to my mom a few days prior and had her wrap it in a large box. Hoping to capture the wonderful moment on video, I also made a request to Nathan to have him bring his camera.

I was ready!

On the Sunday car ride to Chicago, my nerves could not be calmed as I could feel my armpits perspiring the whole day. My thoughts were driving me crazy. *How the hell am I going to do this? How will it play out? Will it be stupid? Did I choose an adequate method of proposal? Shit! I didn't. What was I thinking? This idea is terrible. It's not romantic at all. There's no way it's going to work. I should just cancel. No, no, no, it'll work out just fine. Just shut up and enjoy the ride, Travis. Ok, yeah you're right.*

If Kait could have only gotten a glimpse inside my head to see how insane I was, I think she would have had second thoughts about me. Nevertheless, I was prepared to postpone my proposal if the circumstances weren't right.

Just after noon, we made our arrival into the Windy City. Surprisingly, the city was not that windy at all. It was calm, crisp, and cool. Comfortable for those accustomed to the wintry feel of December.

Wanting to save my proposal for last, we planned a number of activities before making our way to the Christkindlmarket. To be inconspicuous Nathan used his camera throughout the day, pretending like he was interested in all that Chicago had to offer.

After spending the afternoon ice skating, sightseeing, and eating pizza, my time to shine was fast approaching. With the sun tucked away for the evening, we made our way to the Christmas village.

The closer we got to the market, the more apprehensive I became as I began to doubt myself and my idea. In my head I started coming up with every excuse I could in order to convince myself to cancel. Needless to say, I was scared!

When we arrived to the little town, my mother took Kait inside a small hut to shop for Christmas ornaments, temporarily distracting her so Nathan and I could scope out the area surrounding the humongous tree. We investigated every angle, trying to figure out the perfect spot to place her gift. After a couple minutes and a plan sort of figured out, we made our way back to the women.

As my head was racing trying to plan every detail to the second, the four of us walked around the village and admired all of the wonderful lights and decorations. With time quickly elapsing, I tried finding the perfect opportunity to execute my plan, and as the night waned it seemed less and less likely that perfect opportunity would present itself. Then the second-guessing began. *Travis, what are you thinking? This is such a dumb idea. It scores about a 1 out of 10 on the romance meter. And there are people everywhere. It's cold. And, we'll never be able to pull it off without Kait noticing. There's no way this can work.*

That's it. I'm canceling. I'll just propose to her on another day, with a simpler idea, at our apartment, just to get it out of the way. I can't do this now.

"Mom," I said quietly so Kait couldn't hear, "I think we're going to have to cancel."

"Ok. Whatever you want to do," she replied.

I pursed my lips and discretely shook my head in disappointment that I couldn't find the courage to execute my plan. I had failed. *Well, that's okay, I suppose. At least we tried, sort of. I'll think of something else, something better.*

To conclude our evening in Chicago, we walked around a bit longer, checking out other areas of the Christkindlmarket. As we navigated through the village, Kait's attention turned to a kiosk serving hot chocolate. "Mmmm, I'm gonna get some hot chocolate," she declared.

Kait took off toward the hot chocolate stand, slinking her way through the crowd. Suddenly, with her distracted, I felt a jolt of positive energy. A resurgence. It was time. *I can do this!* Putting my "game face" on, I glanced over at my family members and nodded my head slightly. "Mom. Nate. Go! Now!"

They both nodded and took off for the large Christmas tree.

After watching them disappear into the crowd, I walked up to Kait as she stood in line. "Did you still want to get a picture by the Christmas tree," I asked.

"Ahhh, yeah."

"Grab your hot chocolate and let's make our way there."

The vendor handed Kait her drink, and we slowly made our way to the tree. *Oh my God this is it!* Adrenaline secretions tunneled through my body as my legs began to feel wobbly, like Jell-O. I looked all over to see if I could see my mom. "I just love Christmas," Kait obliviously exclaimed as we got closer and closer.

As we approached the tree, I could see my mother standing there. She made eye contact with me and immediately fled the scene. It was just a good thing Kait was so short so she couldn't see over the crowd and notice my mom waiting at the tree.

Though the Christmas village was packed with people, it truly felt like we were the only humans in existence at that moment. My nerves began to vibrate throughout my body, and I could feel a tingling deep within the pits of my stomach.

Arriving at the tree, I quickly spotted the gift and led Kait to the area where it was laying. Facing the bright conifer, we leaned against the fence and started talking. What were we talking about? I have no clue. Words were completely muffled at that point.

After a moment, I pretended as though something peculiar had caught my attention. "Hmmm? Kait, what is that," I asked, staring at the gift below.

Following my line of vision, she spotted the object my eyes had been rested upon. "Oh it's a present. That's nice."

I was hoping she would grab it, but she didn't because she didn't think it was for her.

"I wonder who it's for," I said, hoping to ignite her curiosity enough so that she would want to pick it up and check.

"Hmmm, yeah I don't know."

She still wasn't picking it up. *Dang it!*

Finally, I reached down and grabbed the present. "What does the tag say?"

"Trav, I don't know if you should be taking that," she said, nervously.

"No, no, it's fine."

We both looked at the tag. It read '**For: Kaitlyn**'. Employing my best acting skills, I pretended to be baffled as we both exchanged puzzled looks. How odd that the present just so happened to have her name on it.

"That's weird. It's got your name on it," I said.

"Hm. Yeah that is weird."

"Maybe you should just open it?"

"Well I don't know. I really don't think I should."

"It has your name on it! Just open it," I said.

Looking around, unsure if she'd get arrested for stealing, she finally decided to open the gift. As she gradually unwrapped the paper, she scanned the area to make sure she wasn't breaking any rules. No one seemed alarmed, so she continued. Slowly and slowly she revealed more and more of the box. Finally, after tearing away all of the paper, she removed the lid off of the decoy container, and the small red jewelry box was exposed. At that moment, under the colorful, twinkling lights of the Christmas tree, I lowered myself to the ground, resting on my right knee.

Seeing me on one knee looking up at her with a smile, I could feel her heart speeding up. "Oh my God...," she said. With that, she opened the box, revealing the dazzling ring. Tears immediately began streaming down her face. "Oh my GOD...," she said once again.

At that point, with the ring exposed and water gushing from her eyes, I began making my plea for her to spend the rest of her life with me. To be honest, with the rush of blood drowning out my thoughts and the tension plugging my ears, I have no idea what I said. Because I rehearsed certain phrases, I know that the gist of my speech went something like this, "Kaitlyn Julia, I love you more than anything in the world and I want to spend the rest of my life with you. Will you marry me?" I promise I did say more than that, but I really have no clue what else was said.

Sobbing uncontrollably, Kait bent over, kissed me on the cheek, and said, "Yes, of course," smiling all the way.

With her acceptance, I stood up and joyously put my arm around her as tears of happiness continued to race down her cheeks. She was shocked, which was a good thing.

After giving us our moment, my mom and brother joined in on the celebration. "Congratulations," my mom said with tears as she hugged Kait.

"Thank you! I'm sorry.....I'm a big mess right now....," she said. We all chuckled.

"Did you have any idea, Kait," Nathan asked.

"No! No!" She chuckled. "I didn't even think the present was for me." We all laughed with her.

"Oh my God...," she kept repeating. "You poor thing. This must have been so stressful with all of the plans changing."

"Yeah, you could say that," I said with a smile. I was so relieved it was finally over.

"Oh my God!" Kait buried her head into my shoulder. I squeezed her tightly and kissed her head.

After fully taking in the moment, Kait wanted to call her parents and tell them the big news, so we found a secluded area where she could call them. Once she composed herself, she called her dad first.

Her dad answered, "Hello."

"Hey dad!"

"Hey, Kait, what's up?" He had an inkling.

"Guess what?" Tears started flowing again as she prepared to deliver the news. "I'm engaged!!!"

Mark and Vicky were ecstatic. Through her tears of joy they could hear the happiness and excitement in her voice. They were jubilant, wanting to know all of the details as Kait did her best to recreate our special moment.

After ending the conversation with her father, Kait immediately called her mother to spread the word.

Kathy answered. "Hellooooo!?!"

"Hi mom! Guess what?"

"Hang on Kait, hang on."

"Okay." Kathy wanted to put Kait on speaker so that everyone could hear.

"Okay, now you can say it," Kathy said.

"I'M ENGAGED!!!"

Everyone at the house instantly started cheering for Kait, congratulating her. It was such a nice moment. Everybody was so happy for her and for us.

Between the proposal and calling our family and friends, it was complete elation and I wished I had the power to freeze time and experience it forever. For hours we were overcome with joy, and we couldn't stop smiling. Strong waves of positive energy flowed freely throughout our bodies the entire night. We were on Cloud 9.

Obviously, in the end, I was quite satisfied I decided to execute my plan. Was the proposal idea itself very good? I don't know. I liked it. It was personal and hopefully memorable. Was the execution perfect? It could have been better. Was it romantic? It depends on one's idea of romance. Reflecting back on it, I don't think it was very romantic at all, but it was unique I suppose. Overall, I was extremely happy with the way it went down. And, it was SO relieving to finally get it out of the way since it had been dangling over my head for weeks.

Now newly engaged, we were extremely excited and couldn't wait to begin a new chapter in our lives. We were flying pretty high at that point. With the way everything had been going, it felt like we were on top of the world!

8 ANOTHER RETURN

To add to our string of good fortune, the cherry on our ice cream sundae, Kaitlyn completed her radiation treatments just days after we became engaged. That meant no more late evenings. No more uncomfortably tight facemasks fastening her head to the radiation table. No more burns and skin irritation on her neck. No more fighting through bumper-to-bumper downtown traffic after school only to recommence that battle immediately following her appointment. And no more added, unnecessary fatigue to her everyday life. She was so relieved to finally be done!

And I was extremely proud of my little blonde girl. Her schedule for that five-week span was grueling, but the way she handled herself amazed me. She never complained. She never took a day off from work. And she never once resigned to self-pity. She was much tougher than I, because there was no way I could have carried myself the way she did. Kait would have been drowning in my incessant bitching and petulance for those five weeks. Heck, I already whined and complained about my job enough, and that was without having to endure radiation therapy. But to Kait it was just something that had to be done, a necessary annoyance, and she was going to buckle down and do it. Her focus was on the finish line, on 100% health. If she had to go through hardships along the way, that was acceptable to her, as long as it was helping her achieve her ultimate goal of destroying cancer.

With radiation therapy officially in the can, Kait had roughly a month off before embarking in the next phase of treatment - Interferon-alpha2b or just plain Interferon.

As a simple explanation, Interferons are proteins naturally produced by our body's immune system. However, Interferon-alpha2b is a drug synthetically engineered and mass produced in the lab. The plan for Kait was to receive Interferon for a full year. During the first month it was to be administered 5 days a week, and for the remaining 11 months, she would receive it only 3 days a week.

Many doctors, not all, typically recommend Interferon treatment if the melanoma has spread to only the lymph nodes, which, as noted earlier, is considered Stage 3. Even after surgical excision of the affected nodes, melanoma has a high probability of recurrence. In theory, Interferon is supposed to lessen the chance that it will return. Studies have shown that those receiving interferon didn't relapse "as quickly" and the patients lived a year or two longer without recurrence, but that data itself isn't consistent among many clinical trials. Some studies have come back reporting no statistical significance in overall survival, and some have reported a slight benefit. So, one can take that information and interpret it how he wishes, but in my own conclusions Interferon did not sound overly effective. Basically, the patient is miserable for the year they are on the drug with side effects ranging from fever, nausea, vomiting, headaches, fatigue, heart problems, hallucinations to depression, memory loss, cognitive dysfunction, breathing difficulties, paranoia, mania, disorientation, and so much more, and if melanoma is still present in one's body even after surgical excision, it will likely come back whether or not Interferon is introduced. In my cynicism toward the pharmaceutical industry I merely perceived it as a revenue maker for the manufacturer.

In hindsight, I concluded that both the radiation and Interferon treatments were a waste of time and did more harm than good for one's body in the long run.

Anyway, with the excessive nausea and other side effects expected to be felt due to the Interferon treatment during her first month, it was likely Kait was going to be unable to teach. After the regimen eased to three days a week following the initial month, she would be able to work, but likely only part-time. Taking that into consideration, unsure of her future reliability, Kait disappointedly had to turn down the full-time position that opened up in the school she had taught at for the previous months. But like everything, she took it in stride and kept her chin up. She was just eager to begin proactively fighting her disease again.

Though Kait was scheduled to soon begin her new treatment, overall our life finally seemed to be leaning in our favor. We had a comfy, cozy beginners' apartment adorned with bright, colorful Christmas decorations and a humble little tree. Kait was able to care for young children and bring some revenue into our modest household. Radiation was an afterthought. And, we were getting married!

We were riding blissfully high atop our wave of happiness. But I suppose it was foolish to think our good fortune would last forever. It was foolish to think our peaks wouldn't be met with the occasional troughs along the way. However, I couldn't have predicted how soon our wave would come crashing down.

Taking advantage of the peaceful ambiance, finally devoid of outside distractions for the day, we laid in bed holding our almost ritualistic pre-bedtime conversation. Every night before falling asleep, in the dark calm of our apartment and with the world seemingly on temporary reprieve from chaos, we talked. About everything. We talked about our day. About puppies. About our philosophies on life. About family. About friends. Everything. And nothing. It was really the only time we could truly be alone. No people. No TV. No cell phones. Just us. That's when we held our most intellectual and most elementary conversations.

But that night, whilst subjecting Kait to one of my typical garbled diatribes, she politely interrupted.

"Hey Trav?"

I stopped talking and turned my attention to her. "Yeah, sweetie?"

"Feel this."

The muscles in my forehead contracted with curiosity.

"What's up?"

"Here." Kait took my hand and placed my fingers on her belly, just above the navel.

Immediately, I felt it. It was another hard, bead-sized bump, similar to the one by her ear.

"Hmmm….." With silent concern, I clenched my eyebrows even tighter as a cold chill traveled through my body. For Kait's sake I didn't want to panic, but I know we were both thinking the same thing. "I wonder what it is?"

"Yeah, I don't know. I'll have to call Dr. Robertson and see what he thinks I should do."

"Hmm. I suppose he'll probably want a biopsy done, just in case."

"Who knows, maybe it's just a side effect from the radiation or something," she said, merely trying to calm her fears.

"It could be."

Both in denial, we were grabbing at straws trying to find possible explanations for the new protrusion. Maybe it was an infection. Maybe it was a polyp. Maybe it was an ingrown hair. We just had to pray cancer hadn't returned already. But, we knew.

And the biopsy just days later confirmed it.

Melanoma had returned. The worst possible conclusion, at least that I could think of. And pouring salt on the wound, Christmas was just under a week away.

However, to be completely honest, as much as we absolutely did not want the biopsy to express cancer, I didn't feel overly worried by the positive test result. In my mind I just assumed the small tumor would be easily removed through surgery, like the one by her ear, and that she would still begin Interferon treatments in January as planned.

So naive, I was.

Receiving the update, Kait immediately received a PET scan following her oncologist's orders. We needed to know if it had spread elsewhere in her body.

And with Kait's favorite day less than 48 hours away, we entered Dr. Robertson's lair hoping for good news to send us into the holiday. It would have been the most satisfying Christmas present of all.

As Kait and I sat in one of the many small clinical rooms, Dr. Robertson walked in, greeting us with a handshake. Kait first since she was the main attraction. Then again, even if I was the one with cancer, he'd probably shake her hand first anyway just because she was that likeable.

Rapidly tapping my feet under my chair while holding Kait's hand, we anxiously awaited the results as Dr. Robertson took his seat. Understanding we were on pins and needles, he wasted no time in explaining the report from the PET scan.

It wasn't good.

Multiple tiny spots had lit up in the images, mainly in the fatty tissue around her legs and abdominal region. Though no spots appeared in any of her organs, yet, the cancer was spreading. Dr. Robertson explained that the melanoma had "metastasized" – a foreign word to me at the time – meaning it had spread from its original location and was now travelling throughout the body, most likely through her blood stream. Though we couldn't fully grasp the gravity of his words, we knew it was bad.

Kait began gently sobbing as we tried to comprehend the situation we were facing.

"So is Interferon still the plan going forward, or…," I inquired while the air in me was quickly deflating.

"No. With the disease now in the blood stream, Interferon is no longer an effective solution."

Dr. Robertson continued explaining, tactfully divulging as many details as he could without completely crushing our spirits. But, it was his job to be 100% honest and forthright with us, not to fill us with false hope, and we wanted it that way. Basically, with the cancer metastasized, he informed us we were now dealing with a different beast entirely. A beast that would be difficult to control.

We couldn't help but feel discouraged.

"But, there's more reason to hope now than ever before," Dr. Robertson said, trying to restore a sense of optimism in us. "In the last year, two new treatments have been approved to fight melanoma, the first, really, in the last 25 years. Before this, our only options were Dacarbazine and Interluekin-2. Now we have more options."

"That's good," Kait said with a smile, maintaining her friendly demeanor as she tried holding in her sobs. Though a few tears escaped Kait's eyes, she remained relatively composed for the most part while Dr. Robertson delivered the disheartening news. Because it was almost Christmas, he felt awful sending us into the holiday with thoughts of cancer looming over our heads, but it was important we knew. We were given the option of waiting until after Christmas, but we chose to find out as soon as possible. We would have been worried about the potential results, anyway, so we just wanted to get it out of the way.

Our next step was to return in a week to develop a new treatment strategy.

Holding hands, we quietly walked out of that office and through the hospital, unsure of what to think. Everyone seemed to zip past us at warp speed as we proceeded in slow motion, trying to fully grasp our situation.

What were we up against now? What does it all mean? We didn't really know. Neither of us talked much as we attempted to absorb and interpret all of the information, but it was overwhelming. As much as we tried remaining positive and upbeat, our heads were heavy. We both felt a certain emptiness inside. Even though our understanding was lacking, we knew the situation had become very serious.

After entering our vehicle, finally secluded from the masses, we tightly, silently embraced. Words need not be spoken in that sad, yet wonderful moment, to express how deeply we loved and cared for each other. With our hearts pounding as one, we knew we could count on the other to always be there for love, comfort, and support. As long as we had each other, we would never have to face anything alone.

Our next seemingly daunting hurdle was only 45 minutes away – we were set to celebrate Christmas at my family's house. But how the heck were we supposed to do that? We couldn't. Not with cancer on our mind, on everyone's mind. It was Kait's first time celebrating Christmas with my family, but the activity-filled night seemed ruined.

"Should I call my parents and tell them we won't be able to come over tonight?"

"No, no. Let's go......... It'll be fun. It'll help take our minds off of everything," she said. She was so sweet. Of course, I was going to do whatever she wished. She deserved it.

On the car ride home, my mind was racing. *It has spread to her fatty tissue. What does that mean? Does that mean it will be easier to fight? What were we going to be up against now? What does this mean for Kait's future? At least it's not in her organs. That gives her a better chance of beating the cancer, right? I would think so.*

While my mind was on overdrive, Kaitlyn had the task of calling her family to update them on the results. She contacted her mother first. As soon as Kathy answered the phone, Kait's tears began pouring out as she struggled to deliver the news. I felt terrible for her. It was Christmas, her favorite time of year, and instead of being able to freely enjoy the holiday and family and everything else that comes with it, she would have to worry about what her life was going to be like from here on out.

About a half mile away from my parents' house, I pulled over on the side of the road. "I just figured I'd stop here so we can gather ourselves without them seeing us. How you feeling?"

Kait took a deep breath to try and calm herself. "Phew.......I think

I'm good," she said as she perked herself up, "It'll be fun!"

"Well, you just let me know when you're ready and we can go."

Kait gave me a smile, "I'm ready.......Let's go!" She leaned over and gave me a kiss. "Thank you."

"I didn't do anything," I said with a smile.

"Yes you did. You always make everything better."

I wrapped my arms around her and squeezed her tight. "I love you, sweetheart.......more than anything in the world."

With that, we both released a long exhale before taking off. Kait was going to make the most of her Christmas, cherishing every moment. No way was cancer going to ruin it for her.

Entering my parents' house, everyone was there waiting for us – my mom, dad, two brothers, and Lane (Tyler's wife – girlfriend at the time). To prepare them, I had called my mom on the ride home to inform her that the cancer had returned, but I didn't go into much detail. As we stood at the doorway removing our coats, we went through our typical greetings as usual, but there was this uncomfortable ambience in the air, a giant pink elephant in the room. Cancer was obviously on everyone's mind, but no one was really sure what to ask or what to say. Finally, my mom chimed in.

"So...what did your doctor all say," she cautiously asked.

There was an uncomfortable silence as everyone awaited details. I looked over at Kait, and I could see her fighting to swallow a lump in her throat. The last thing she wanted to do at her future in-law's was break out in tears, so she tried regaining her composure before speaking. But after a second or two, with all eyes fixated on her, it was apparent to me that she wasn't going to be able to. "It came back," I quickly interrupted, trying to deflect attention away from her. "It spread to her fatty tissue, but it hasn't gotten to her organs, yet. So, next week we have to go back in and figure out our next steps."

You could literally feel the pressure in the air release at that moment.

"Oh. So can they just go back in and do surgery, I wonder," my dad asked.

"No. Surgery is not an option, and Interferon is now off the table, too," I replied.

Kaitlyn, released from her temporary stranglehold, felt comfortable enough to speak. "Dr. Robertson said it's in the blood stream, so even if they did surgery, it would still be in my body."

"Huh, so next week you find out what to do next," my dad continued asking.

"Yup. He said we have a few options, and some new treatments have been approved, so we have to figure out which one to go with," Kait said.

"Oh good. Well at least it's not in any organs, so that's good at least." My dad always tried staying optimistic. That or he just said what he wanted to hear in order to convince himself of what he wanted to believe.

"Yeah, exactly. It's not like it's out of control or anything, so hopefully whatever treatment we go with will kill it."

"And you have such a great, positive attitude. That's really important," Tyler added.

"Yeah, that is definitely important," I said.

After discussing Kait's situation for a couple more minutes, we settled in and got comfortable. Cancer wasn't brought up for the rest of the night.

The evening schedule included dinner and then board games, which was customary for every Christmas Eve at the Ruhland household. Of course, it wasn't Christmas Eve, but we decided to move it up a day so that Kait and I could visit both families.

Monopoly was first on the list, a game in which we were all fiercely competitive with. Kaitlyn was used to our rabid behavior when it came to competition, so she was prepared as always.

Unfortunately for Kaitlyn, she was the first one out since her ability to effectively land on open properties was lacking. Weeks prior, I told her to practice up on her dice rolling, but she didn't listen. Though the early exit briefly pissed her off, Kait was a good sport and decided to help me with banking duties. What a noble loser. I should talk, however, I was out second.

Once Monopoly was finished (Nathan was the winner), we played a couple of other games, like Clue and Scattergories. Overall, we ended up having a wonderful night considering the circumstances. We shared some laughs, opened some gifts, and just had a gay old time. At least for a few hours we were able to take our minds off of disease.

That night, before climbing into bed, I softly said, "Come here," with my arms held out.

Kait walked into me, melting into my body as I wrapped her in my arms. I hugged her for a good minute before letting go. This was the first time we were truly alone since receiving the bad news, and we both needed each other's comfort.

"We're gonna be ok," I said, kissing her forehead as she closed her eyes.

"You think?"

"I have absolutely no doubt in my mind."

"Good," Kait said as she came in for one more hug. "I love you, Travis Dean. So, so much."

"I love you, too, Kaitlyn Julia."

With that, we went to bed.

The next day, the actual Christmas Eve, we traveled two hours to Kenosha for Christmas on her mom's side. None of the family had seen Kait, yet, since her new diagnosis, so we were both a bit apprehensive about how we would be received. Would there be tension? Would there be tears? Would people be hesitant to laugh or smile? We couldn't know.

When we walked in the door, people greeted and smothered Kait with hugs. Of course I got hugs, too, but not the same kinds.

As expected, Kathy was quite concerned about her loveable middle child. We went through a similar explanation as with my parents, trying to divulge as much detail as we could. It's not like we had much information to begin with. We only knew that it had metastasized, that it was only in the fatty tissue, and that Interferon was now off the table. After delivering as many details as we could, we moved on to other topics. For the most part, we tried not to bring up cancer for the rest of the evening. I mean, it was Christmas after all, and it was supposed to be festive and happy. At least that's how Kait saw it, and nothing was going to take that from her.

Throughout the night I found myself subtly observing other family members, seeing how they were reacting and interacting toward Kait. Everyone seemed to do a great job of pushing the thoughts and questions of cancer aside, a task made easier by Kait herself since she was smiling, joking, and laughing the whole time. Was her happiness sincere? I think so. For the most part. Sure images of cancer were lurking in the dark alleys of her mind, but the loving distraction of family and friends always has a unique way of steering thoughts to a pleasantly bright sanctuary.

Later that night, we all sat down to open gifts. There had to be at least 20 of us. With all of the commotion taking place, I found myself preoccupied by conversation with some of the aunts and uncles, not really paying attention to Kait opening gifts with her siblings and cousins. All of a sudden, when I looked across the room and found Kait, I noticed she was wiping tears from her eyes. *Uh oh! What happened? Did someone say something?* However, the tension and worry on my face quickly transitioned to a calm smile when I finally realized they were tears of joy. Kait's cousin Alexa (Lex) had gifted her a wedding preparation kit along with a shirt that said "Future Ms. Kaitlyn Ruhland". Seeing her name with my last name gave her happy thoughts of a future she had been envisioning for a long time – the day we would finally become husband and wife.

To lighten the mood even more, Kait and Lex put on their recently purchased Christmas outfits – red adult-sized "onesies" with cartoon Santa Clauses and Rudolphs printed all over. I wasn't sure what to expect, but when I saw Kait with it on, I wanted to tackle her because she looked so incredibly adorable. She looked like a kid even without the onesie on, but with it on, it exemplified her childlike exuberance even more. It was great!

As the night concluded, round 2 of spending Christmas at each other's families was done. Once again we experienced another wonderful night of happiness and laughter with good company, allowing us to set aside our health problems for yet another moment.

Christmas day, Kaitlyn's favorite day in the whole wide world, had arrived. I was worried she wouldn't be able to enjoy it the same, but after seeing how successful the last two nights were, I knew it was going to be a great day, extremely busy, but great.

Right away in the morning we headed over to Kait's dad's house. Upon entering, Mark and Vicky both gave Kait long hugs. Like any father would be about his little daughter, Mark was always extra concerned about Kait's medical situation. But, on this day he figured it'd be best just to save the cancer conversation for later. Of course they wanted to know all of the details, but he and Vicky were okay with a simple, brief explanation for the time being. Again, it was Christmas. I think they both wanted to do their best at keeping Kait's mind off of the negative stuff so she could enjoy the day as much as possible.

After eating lunch and opening gifts, we had to quickly head over to her grandparent's house for some good dessert, good conversation, and a few more gifts.

~~Grandpa~~ Papa Don, a goofy jokester of an old man, always had a special place in his heart for his sweet little Kaitlyn, just like he did for all of his children and grandchildren. He loved everybody. But I could always see Don's face light up when Kait walked in, and it was heartwarming for me to observe their loving social dynamic.

See, when Kait was a young child, Papa Don and Grandma Phyllis would host cookouts with the whole family. Don would grill steaks or ribs outside while everyone enjoyed their beers, lawn games, or whatever else they did for entertainment before food was served. But, you wouldn't find Kait with that larger group. Nope. At least not when Don was grilling. When Don was standing over the flames, Kait would be right next to her Papa, helping him spread the barbecue over the meat like the good little helper she was. She would have made a great Christmas elf, always wanting to be of assistance, even if it wasn't needed all the time.

And then there was Grandma Phyllis, a sweet lady who doubled as a lawn gnome to help support the family. Okay, I'm kidding, I'm just trying to poke fun at her for being really short. The first time I ever met her was when Kait and I joined the family out for brunch at one of the local diners. Phyllis thought she'd be funny and threw a glob of whipped cream on my pancakes after I expressed my repulsion to the white fluff. I was SO pissed off by her middle schooler antics that I picked her up and shot-putted her through a window. She thought twice about sullying my pancakes the next time we went out. Okay, I'm joking about that, too. She really did put whipped cream on my pancakes, but I just laughed about it. To me it was an indirect way of letting me know I was accepted.

Also, Phyllis was the only person allowed to call Kaitlyn by the nickname "Katie." Since she was a child, Kaitlyn adorably thought that "Katies" were mean-spirited people, and she did NOT want to associate with those types. But, Phyllis had special permission.

Whenever we were with Kait's grandparents, it was funny because usually the women did all the talking. Typical. And, then, over in the corner of the living room, Papa Don would sit in his chair, talking about some obscure topic, hoping someone would listen to him. Once I realized he was basically talking to himself, I would turn my attention away from the squawking hens and focus on Don as he talked about the Aztecs, or his childhood, or whatever was currently on his mind. Maybe that's why he liked me. Then again, he liked everybody.

With so many events packed into our schedule that Christmas day, we couldn't stay too long. We still had to travel two hours back to my part of Wisconsin to attend the huge family Christmas on my side. So, we said our goodbyes and gave our hugs. Everyone's hug to Kaitlyn was a little bit tighter and lasted a little bit longer.

With that, we were off.

Back in my neck of the woods, our family Christmas was being held in a cabin where the congregation of my father's 11 brothers and sisters, along with the mass of offspring they produced, created a madhouse of disorderly conduct and enjoyable chaos. That's how every family gathering was.

By the time we arrived at the party, it was late and everyone had already eaten dinner. All of the talking throughout the day left Kait's vocal chords severely weakened and her voice just about gone.

We made our rounds, trying to talk to everybody, and Kait did her best to be sociable even though she could barely speak. After a couple hours, we had had just about enough of Christmas for the year. The craziness from our busy three-day schedule left us both exhausted and we were ready to close up shop for the holiday.

Our first Christmas celebrating with each other's families was officially over, and it turned out to be great. We couldn't wait to do it every year in the future.

9 SHOCKING DISCOVERIES

Through the early stages of Kait's diagnosis with cancer, I stayed away from the Internet for the most part. The possibility of discovering soul-crushing truths frightened me, and I preferred to keep my head in the sand because I trusted that her future treatments would extinguish the invading cancer cells. Therefore, it seemed unnecessary to become enlightened about melanoma. Plus, it was my understanding that statistics on the web were generally unreliable, at least that's what I told myself.

A few evenings after Christmas, Kaitlyn and I were relaxing in the calm of our apartment. I was sitting on the couch watching television, and Kaitlyn was lying on the floor with the laptop in front of her surfing the web. As I was flipping through the channels, all of a sudden I saw Kaitlyn bury her head into her hands. She began sobbing. *Oh no! What did she find out?* For the last week, our ignorance kept us happy. Kept us positive and encouraged. What did she find out that would change those feelings? "Sweetheart, what's the matter?"

I rushed over to her and started rubbing her back. "I don't know why I looked.......I shouldn't have looked."

"What, sweetie?!?"

She pushed the computer toward me and pointed to the screen. The website she was exploring displayed information about melanoma. As I was reading it, I discovered the cause of her tears – Life Expectancy - 7 to 9 months after it has spread. Suddenly, my face began to tingle as blood rushed to my head. *Holy shit!* I was shocked. *This can't be true. Please tell me this isn't true. Please tell me this website has outdated information.*

I felt a wave of emotions barreling through, but I couldn't lose my composure, not when Kait needed comfort and strength from me. I swiftly forced myself to suppress my enormous worries, putting up a blockade to keep my emotions under control.

"Sweetie, don't worry about that. Who knows how accurate that is? And who knows how old this data is? Treatments have gotten so much better. I mean, back in the day, people probably had almost no options at all. Now, we have all of these new medicines coming out. Plus, you're young, you're active, you're healthy, and you have a great attitude. You're going to beat this thing, there's no doubt in my mind."

Kait's face remained buried in her arm. For the first time since being diagnosed with melanoma, the possibility of death became real. And if the information displayed on the website was accurate, her time was potentially coming much sooner than we ever could have anticipated.

For moments, Kait remained silent, inhaling deeply to conquer her emotions as I continued rubbing her back. "Do me a favor.....don't let me look up any more stuff on melanoma."

"Yeah....that's probably a good idea."

Minutes passed before I felt Kait finally begin to relax. As she slowly regained her composure and perspective, I allowed myself to gradually release the mental barriers I had constructed to ward off those stress-inducing thoughts. Consequently, with my guard down, my worries started seeping through the cracks. I quietly began thinking more and more about what we had read. 7 to 9 months. That statistic was sinking in, throwing my heartbeat into a panic. I could feel my nerves stabbing my skin. 7 to 9 months! It was inconceivable. It was terrifying. It was crushing. And it was all I could think about for the rest of the night. *Could it really be true? Could it be that THIS perfect girl that I'm sitting next to RIGHT NOW, laughing, crying, will be GONE in just a few short months? Will she soon be a memory? It can't be. This is KAITLYN JULIA we are talking about here, beloved daughter, sister, granddaughter, aunt, friend. Please, God, this can't be. Please take this illness away from her. She deserves to live. Bad people roam the earth repeatedly doing evil things, and they seem to get a pass. Kait has done nothing wrong. Please help her!*

Kait stood up to get some water, and I gave her a big hug. As we separated, I put my hands on her arms and stared straight into her eyes. "I KNOW you are going to be okay," I sternly exclaimed.

Sniffling, she replied, "Yeah.....you're right." She merged into me one more time, melting into my arms. I just wanted to absorb all of her worries. All of her stress. All of her sadness. All of her cancer. I wanted to take it all.

"Thank you...I love you so much, Trav."

"I love you, too, sweetheart..........more than anything in the world."

About an hour later, both feeling despondent, we laid on our bed together, on top of the covers with the lights on. It wasn't bedtime, yet, but we had zero desire to do anything but hold each other. We both needed the quietness, away from all other distractions to shut our brains off and focus only on us.

It was hard to breathe. 7 to 9 months. That thought was suffocating both of us. It was disturbing.

Eventually, as we talked about our now unstable future, tears finally began to break through my walls. I absolutely did not want her to see me visibly sad. But as much as I wanted to remain strong for her, I couldn't hold back all of my tears anymore as a few drops forced their way to the surface.

I couldn't help it. Thoughts of a world without my Kaitlyn were overpowering my mind, and I couldn't control it. The thought terrified both of us. It was unfathomable. Beyond our comprehension. Every morsel of my being was completely invested in her. She was my future. And if she were to...... die .... essentially a big chunk of me would die, too. I'd become a zombie. My soul would be on life support, barely living, but I'd still be required to walk the earth and perform menial tasks.

"If you ever did....pass...," I muttered weakly, as my voice began to crackle through my gentle sobs, "I think I'd rather just live the rest of my life alone."

"Nooo, I wouldn't want that," she was sobbing with me, "I would want you to find a way to be happy again, someone that would make you happy."

"I don't know how I could. You're the only thing that makes me truly happy. You're really the only person that can put a real smile on my face."

It was true. Putting a sincere smile on my face was almost impossible, but she did it with ease.

We both fell silent for a moment as I squeezed her tightly. She couldn't hear the shrill cries from within me, but they were deafening.

For the next couple of hours, we simply laid in bed, holding each other, exchanging sobs, talking. We talked about everything. Our stomachs were all knotted up from the enormous worry and stress. One minute, Kait would start crying, and I would have to reassure her that she was going to be okay, that she was going to beat cancer. Then, after her tears would subside, my thoughts would drag me to a dark, scary place, drawing me to tears, and then she would be the one having to reassure me. It was a sad cycle that continued as the night progressed. Luckily, we both had each other to lean on during those depressing intervals.

Impatiently fidgeting inside the family room with her four parents, waiting for Dr. Robertson to discuss our next step in our cancer-fighting process, it seemed Kait and I were becoming way too familiar with the Carbone Cancer Center in Madison, and I didn't like it. Unfortunately, with Kait's disease progressing to Stage 4, our familiarity with the clinic was likely to grow.

Equipped with pens and notebooks to scribble as much information as we could, Dr. Robertson stepped in the room, accompanied by his trusty sidekick, Nurse Sue. After the usual polite salutations, they both sat down, preparing to deliver the disheartening information we were all eager and not so eager to hear. Unfortunately, with his profession, Dr. Robertson was all too familiar with these difficult discussions. It made me wonder if doctors become desensitized to it. I would assume not. Then again I'm sure some do. I feel like it would be extremely difficult and stressful to watch the heartbreak on someone's face, even if it was the 100th time I had to do it.

To begin the informational session, Dr. Robertson started by re-explaining the progression of the disease in Kait's body - how it had metastasized, that it was only in the fatty tissue, and how it hadn't appeared in any organs, yet. As we were listening to him speak, he received a message on his pager from another doctor explaining the results of Kait's head MRI, which we were waiting to hear. He showed us the message. Kait's brain was clear of any cancer. Of course this was great news, but we had no idea of the significance of it. To help us understand how important that was, Dr. Robertson explained that once it gets into the brain, it becomes almost impossible to treat effectively. *Phew! Then thank God it hadn't spread to her head, yet.*

We then shifted our focus onto the next important topic – figuring out a treatment plan for Kait since Interferon was no longer an option. Dr.

Robertson listed three different options for us – Interleukin-2 (IL-2), Iplilimumab (Ipi), and Vemurafenib (Zelboraf). Ipi and Zelboraf were the drugs that had just been approved by the FDA, so they hadn't been out on the market for very long. With that in mind, Dr. Robertson recommended that Kait start off with IL-2. Like Interferon, IL-2 is a natural part of our immune system. It's responsible for activating and stimulating the growth of immune cells. Considered as another type of immunotherapy, the genetically engineered form of IL-2 was approved in 1998. In short, it basically revs up the immune system so that the body's T-Cells can grow and mature more rapidly. T-cells are white blood cells whose responsibility is to attack foreign intruders, like cancer. Unfortunately, IL-2 lacks effectiveness. The success rate of IL-2, defined as a partial or complete response, falls in the 5-10% range, a pitiful measure in my opinion.

Was it even worth it? Couldn't we go with something else to begin with, something more effective, like the recently approved Ipilimumab? Do we even want to mess around with IL-2, considering if it doesn't work we will have wasted precious time while the cancer continued to grow? Though my mind was casting doubt on the overall efficacy of the treatment, I didn't feel like I was in a position to question or make suggestions with my lack of education. All of my concerns aside, Dr. Robertson was recommending IL-2, so IL-2 is what we settled on. On the plus side, if it did happen to work, the potential was there for long-term results.

It was decided. Kait would start her IL-2 treatment on January 18th. She would be required to stay in the hospital for 5 or 6 days. Due to the level of toxicity in the treatment, she would experience some nasty side effects, causing a high level of discomfort. Lastly, she would gain about 15 to 20 pounds in water weight, which would be immediately lost in a day or two at the completion of treatment. We were actually humored by that last part.

Then, there was one more bit of detail Dr. Robertson provided to us about melanoma. A detail none of us wanted to hear, but one we were all curious about. Without intending to scare us, he explained that typically someone with metastasized melanoma lives about a year on average. But before we could even think about that statement too hard, he quickly interjected once more by reassuring us that there were plenty of people who've made it well beyond that simple average.

We all silently nodded our heads, acting encouraged by his final statement. As a chronic pessimist, I fought hard to convince myself that Kait would be one of the few who skewed the data in the positive direction.

With our meeting concluded and a treatment plan fleshed out, we thanked Dr. Robertson and Nurse Sue as they exited the room. Next, we just had to wait for scheduling to be completed before we could leave.

"I'll be right back," Kaitlyn said as she stood up and left the room.

The family and I waited patiently, discussing Kait's situation in her absence. We all shook our heads, confounded by the incomprehensible circumstances we found ourselves in. Kait's life was in jeopardy! It was unbelievable. A nightmare. But with all of the treatment options available, we felt good reason to be optimistic (though I later found out the repertoire of tools in the melanoma treatment kit was quite pathetic).

A couple minutes passed and Kaitlyn hadn't returned, yet. *Where did she go? She must have gone out to schedule appointments or something.*

Another five minutes passed by, and Kait still had not returned. When I poked my head outside of the room, I didn't see her anywhere. So, with everyone wondering where she had gone, I decided to step out and investigate.

Exiting the room, I initially walked past the front desk. She was nowhere to be found, so I continued forward, taking a left down a hallway past the schedulers. Looking around, I still didn't see her anywhere. *Hmmm.* Perplexed about her potential whereabouts, I decided to return to the room and simply wait for her.

On my way back, just as I was passing a bathroom with its door closed, I heard a faint sniffle from within. I immediately stopped, perking my ears on alert. With my full attention aimed at the bathroom door, listening intently, I heard a couple more sniffles and what sounded like the whimpers of someone crying. My heart sank. *Could that be Kait?*

Assuming she wanted to be alone, if it was indeed her, I hurried back to the room. Obviously, if she was crying in the bathroom, she didn't want anyone to see her in that "weakened" state. If anything, I planned on addressing it later, in the seclusion of our apartment.

Upon my return to the family room, I simply told Kait's family I couldn't find her.

If Kait was, in fact, in the bathroom sobbing, I felt terrible that she felt like she had to conceal her sadness from her family, but could understand why she would want to. Kait knew us all well. Like any family member, if we became aware she was struggling emotionally with her situation, we would all worry even more. And the last thing she wanted was for us to worry about her. She wanted to bear the entire burden. Something I truly admired her for.

As a few more minutes ticked by, Kait finally returned, and we took off. I tried analyzing her facial expressions and body language to assess whether or not she had been crying. It didn't look like it, but it was difficult to tell. Maybe it wasn't her in the bathroom. I couldn't be sure.

Leaving the hospital, I felt sick to my stomach. I wanted to jump in a hole with Kaitlyn and stay there for an eternity. I wanted to forget about everything else in the world and just hold her tight. Dr. Robertson's words kept on playing back in my head over and over again – "About a year on average." Reading life expectancy data online, you never know if the statistics are accurate or skewed. But, coming from the mouth of a medical professional, it becomes all too real. I wanted to burst into tears. Tears for her, of course. Never me. I couldn't care less about myself, but I cared immensely for her and what she had to deal with. Knowing what she had to face, knowing how much she was looking forward to our future and possibly having that taken away from her, it was painful. I was THE person she looked to for comfort and safety, and her safety was no longer in my control. Coming from a guy who needed to feel like he had some sort of say in any situation, it was tough to surrender that control during the most important situation I had ever been involved with. It was the most helpless feeling I had ever experienced. The only thing left I could provide her with was......me. My presence. My voice. My love. Unfortunately, that wasn't enough, not by my standards. That wouldn't cut it. My love and everything else wouldn't keep her alive. There had to be something more I could do. I couldn't just stand idly by as the love of my life slowly withered away.

In an attempt to reclaim some semblance of control, I began by researching cancer-fighting foods. What I found to be common on most websites was the fact that blueberries were great as an antioxidant. Garlic, green tea, tomatoes, onions, wine, turmeric, mushrooms, blackberries, spinach, and more all appeared on a number of websites, too. My head was spinning trying to keep all of the information straight. But, I narrowed my list down and we went out and purchased the goods.

Now, the next step was somehow getting Kait to eat those foods consistently, because she was a picky eater. Not nearly as picky as I was, but there were many foods Kaitlyn would not eat. She didn't like blueberries. She didn't like green tea. She wasn't a fan of spinach or many of the foods we purchased at the store.

Aware of what was at stake, however, Kaitlyn told her pickiness to take a hike. She found ways to incorporate all of the cancer-fighting foods that we bought into her diet. At first, it was difficult to choke down the blueberries and drink the green tea. The flavors were not too appealing to her taste buds. But, after a couple weeks of toughing it out, she actually began to like most of the foods she once found repulsive. I was so proud of her for stepping outside of her food boundaries. If only I had the courage to start eating healthy like that. Her mental strength was much greater than mine, though.

Over the course of the next few days, I found it incredibly difficult to focus at my job as an accountant. My mind was on one thing and one thing only – Kaitlyn, of course. Each minute of thoughts was completely different from the next. One minute all I could think about was a grim future where Kait was no longer in my life. The next minute I was upbeat and positive about her conquering the disease. One minute I'd be ready to shed tears. The next minute I'd be smiling. The roller coaster of emotions made it nearly impossible to be an efficient employee.

Normally when I'm at work, I put together a playlist of songs to listen to throughout the day. If I'm looking for inspiration for my writing, sometimes I'll listen to movie soundtracks. As I was sifting through scores of Hans Zimmer, I came across a Lion King video clip. Intrigued because I hadn't seen that movie in ages, I clicked on the link.

The video began playing. It was the scene where a grown-up Simba is speaking to his deceased father, Mufasa, as his spirit appears in the clouds, imparting profound wisdom onto his son. Then, when Mufasa slowly starts to disappear, Simba begins running after him, pleading with him not to go. The whole time, I had Kaitlyn superimposed over Mufasa's spirit, and I was Simba. In my imagination, Kaitlyn had passed on and was speaking to me beyond the grave. And, that was me chasing after her, pleading with her not to leave me. That very thought made it difficult to repress my tears. Luckily, I didn't cry at work. It's strange to think that a child's movie could evoke any kind of strong emotions out of me, but it did. From that point on, I began noticing that the slightest things could trigger a thought that would snowball and develop into something much worse.

10 ROUND ONE WITH IL-2

Monday, January 16th, 2012. Kait was scheduled to begin her IL-2 treatment in Milwaukee, about two hours away from Madison. The plan was, I would work during the first few days of the week and then return on Thursday to stay with Kait for the remainder. We figured I should save my accrued vacation just in case we needed to travel at some point in the future.

Accompanied by her family, we arrived to St. Luke's hospital and settled into Kait's room. The previous two weeks to her felt like wasted time just sitting around as the cancer grew, so Kaitlyn was excited to finally begin her treatment, to begin actively attacking her cancer, or at least attempting to. But based on the statistics Dr. Robertson provided us, I wasn't overly confident that the IL-2 drug was going to help much. Pessimistically, I was already looking forward to the next form of treatment – Ipilimumab.

On that Monday, I was only able to hang out with my Kait for a few hours before heading back to our apartment. Luckily, she had a great support system in her family during my absence. There would always be someone around to keep her company, so I knew she was in good hands.

I hugged and kissed my baby goodbye, and with that I was off, back to Madison for work. I knew it was going to be a struggle without Kait around, but I assumed I could manage for three whole days.

- - - - - - - - - - - - - - - - - -

70

It was a typical morning. After slowly log-rolling out of bed, I trudged through the sticky cobwebs of our gloomy apartment, arriving to the porch door where I opened the shades, exposing myself to the fiery morning sun. The powerful beams of blinding light hit me like a freight train, sending me flying back into the couch as I lifted my left arm to shield my face from the burning rays. Smoke began emanating from my pale, flaky skin. After regaining my eyesight, I pulled myself up from the couch and stumbled through the sea of pungent garbage bags that was our living quarters and entered the bathroom. Looking into the mirror, the ghoulish figure sneering back at me was nearly unrecognizable. His beard hung low, almost to his belly button. His nails, mangled and yellow, were nearly a foot long. Tiny eight-legged arachnids roamed free through the thick brush of his dirty, oily hair. He was hideous. He was me!

Deliriously wandering into the kitchen, I found myself foraging through the empty cupboards, confused, before my meager hands clutched a box of unopened cereal. I gazed listlessly at the colorful cardboard, confounded. What was I supposed to do with it? How does it open? Grabbing a fork from the dusty countertop, I stabbed the box. As food particles and sugar trickled through the tiny holes, I held the box above my head and stuck out my tongue hoping to satisfy my great hunger. It wasn't enough. Rage and frustration quickly grew. I tightly grasped the box with both hands and violently pulled. The cardboard container burst open. The explosion sent flakes of whole grains soaring through the air, and the cereal rained down on me and on the tile below. Success! Wide-eyed and drooling at the mouth, I lunged to the ground, desperately gluttonizing like a famished pig.

Simply put, I was lost. It had been three whole days without my Kaitlyn, and I. Was. Lost! The time elapsed felt like months. I could never have anticipated just how much I would miss Kait and how much I needed her in my life, but I did. Fortunately for me, it was the day of my reunion with her, and I couldn't contain myself.

After cleaning myself up, I jumped into my Ford Focus and headed to the hospital, bouncing up and down in the car for the whole two-hour trip. I was excited!

Upon arrival, I called Kaitlyn to let her know I was in the parking garage. "Hey, sweetie! I'm here!"

"Yay! Do you remember how to get up here?"

"I think so." I really didn't remember, but I'm a guy and we always have to act like we know our way around. "I'll be up in a few minutes."

As I entered the hospital, I searched for familiar markers to guide me back to where Kait was stationed. Navigating this building was analogous to navigating a life-sized maze. Slowly, I made my way through, but not without hitting a couple dead ends, forcing me to back track until I discovered the correct path. Eventually, I made my way up to the 9th floor. The "few minutes" I had told Kait turned into 15 to 20 minutes.

When I exited the elevator I took a left and then an immediate right. Down the hall and through the door that separated the waiting room from the oncology wing, I could see Kaitlyn waiting at the opening of her room. My face immediately lit up. My smile stretched from ear to ear. Bursting through the door, I approached Kait, stretching my arms outward as far as I could.

Oh my God! I couldn't believe my eyes. As expected, the IL-2 caused her to gain about 15 pounds in water weight. What I didn't expect, however, was how unbelievably, absolutely, positively adorable she would look. She was soooooo puffy and soooooo soooooooooo cute. Her cheeks were even jollier than usual, and I just wanted to pinch them. When she smiled, her dimple was more craterous than it had ever been before. I loved it!

"Sweetie! Oh my God, look at you! You look so cuuuuute!"

Smiling back at me she stamped the ground with her foot and said in an excited tone, "Baby, where were you?!? I was waiting by the elevator."

With my smile nearly ripping my face apart, I hugged Kait and kissed her on the cheeks. "I'm sorry….I got lost trying to find this place. Oh my gosh, look at how cute your face is!"

"I know. Isn't it crazy? I look like a beached whale."

Amidst my chuckling, I wanted to tackle her. I could barely contain myself. If her family wasn't there I seriously would have smothered her with obnoxious affection. We were both elated to be reunited once again. IT HAD ONLY BEEN THREE DAYS! What was wrong with us?

When I entered, her family was gathered around her hospital bed inside the room. It was spacious, but still felt like a hospital, e.g. a dungeon.

Taking a seat next to her bed, we went through the usual catching up. I mean, Kait and I had been speaking on the phone every day so I was mostly updated with her status. Thus far, she was handling the treatment wonderfully with minimal side effects for the first three days. However, I arrived on day number four, and the first signs of nausea were setting in.

As we were all talking, I just could not get over how cute she looked with the extra 15 pounds of water pushing her skin out. I began rubbing her legs as she was sitting on the bed, and they were extremely tight. The tautness inhibited her mobility some and she couldn't bend her arms and legs completely. It was a bit uncomfortable for her to say the least.

Being encased for multiple days in her small white cage, tethered to monitors and other medical equipment, Kait was becoming stir crazy. Her normally active muscles were being forced to shut down for a week, and they didn't like it. Every 30 or 60 minutes, Kait would get up and take a walk to try and calm the nerves from her muscle anxiety. On our first walk upon my arrival, we passed by the room of an elderly man who had been housed in the cancer wing for weeks. Rumor had it, he was a mean, grumpy old man, always in a bad mood, and even the nurses were skittish in his presence. He was a man to avoid at all costs! So I was hesitant as we approached his room. But Kait seemed to have no fear.

"Hey!!! How's it going?"

My eyes widened upon hearing her address this supposedly sinister being. *Kait what are you doing?* I thought to myself. But, suddenly, to my surprise, but not really, the man lit up with life. His face and demeanor completely changed as he was seemingly injected with positive energy.

"Hey, there she is!"

I stood behind Kait as she hovered just outside of his room for a few moments, mesmerized by her ability to lift the spirits of a man who allegedly refused to speak to anyone else (apparently Kait had started talking to the man as soon as she arrived on that Monday). It just further reinforced what I already knew, and that was that everyone's attitude improved in Kait's presence. Everyone found themselves smiling and invigorated. I was truly a lucky man! After exchanging a few more words we continued on our walk.

St. Lukes had a beautiful greenhouse type of room just down the hall for patients to go and relax, so we decided to give it a visit. Dragging the monitors with her, Kait and I entered this "Zen" room. It was filled with plants, both large and small. Soft, gentle music played over the speakers. And a small pond of water, fountain included, rested in the center of it all. The room was actually a nice little sanctuary for patients to try and escape the confines of their cells.

As we were walking around, I quickly noticed the bricks that were placed throughout the room labeled with the names of those brave souls who had lost their battle to cancer. Though it was a lovely tribute, and a great way to honor those wonderful people, all of the wrong thoughts began entering my head and my heart rate and breathing started to increase. *That could be Kaitlyn's name on one of these bricks someday.....* Butterflies began flying around in my stomach as Kaitlyn took a lap around the big room, smiling with her chubby cheeks, oblivious to the images my brain was producing. I was not good at hiding when something was on my mind, but I was hoping I didn't make my worries too apparent. Then again, she might have been thinking the exact same thing. I certainly hoped not.

And when Kait needed exercise to stretch her legs and muscles, but didn't feel like walking all the way to the Zen garden, we would take a couple laps around the oncology wing. Passing by the rooms of other patients, an eerie feeling crept through my body. A number of these patients, mostly quite old, were on heavy sedatives to help ease them into the afterlife. The sedatives put these elderly people into a deep sleep. As we would walk by, they would be sleeping on their beds with their mouths, and sometimes even their eyes, wide open as they laid there, completely motionless. They seemed to be as close to death as one could possibly be without actually being dead. I don't know why, but the sight of these poor souls was unsettling to me.

At other times during our walks, we would witness a group of nurses wheeling a gurney through the hall. Resting on top of the gurney would be a black body bag. They would enter a room and then put a curtain up so onlookers couldn't see what was happening. Of course we knew that someone had passed away, and that they were preparing to wheel that person to the mortuary area.

Like in the Zen garden, a part of me was wondering, worried that seeing this would cause Kaitlyn to think deeply about her own situation, about her own mortality. I was hoping that didn't cross her mind, but I would assume it would be impossible to inhibit those thoughts.

That night, I slept on a cot next to Kaitlyn's bed just like during her first surgery a few months back. Whether or not the cot itself was comfortable was of little importance. What was important to me was that I was finally with Kait, by her side again, like I was supposed to be, like I yearned to be. For all I cared that cot could have been covered with thumbtacks, and it still would have been more comfortable than sleeping *without* Kait at the apartment.

As we settled in for our long winter's nap, I quickly realized the key word there was "nap," because short naps are all one seems to be afforded while staying at these hospitals. Every hour or so a nurse would walk in to check on Kait, administer medication, or take vitals, waking her/us up every time in the process. Getting a good night's sleep at a hospital seems all but impossible, which is actually really counterproductive for patients whose bodies are fighting and need the rest in order to heal. I know the nurses are just doing their jobs, but it seems there should be a more efficient way so that patients can get their much-needed sleep. Kait's body was undergoing a serious event with the cancer and treatment combined, and adding any sort of undue stress through sleep deprivation seemed unnecessary and possibly detrimental to her overall health and ability to fight. Needless to say, Kait did not get much rest that night or any of the nights.

The next day, Kait really began feeling the side effects from the drug. Nothing tasted quite right, and she was only able to eat foods that were easy to digest. Her heart rate was constantly hovering around a whopping 150 beats per minute, which was expected to some degree, but anything over 150 was cause for alarm. Because of her increased heart rate approaching the recommended limit, it was advised that Kaitlyn forego her last dose of the synthetic IL-2.

At first, skipping her last round of treatment caused Kait to worry. Her thinking was that by not receiving her final dose, the treatment wouldn't work properly. But Dr. Stockton, her doctor for the week, explained that the overall objective was to get her immune system to a certain level, and that certain level had been reached. At that point, additional doses would have been unnecessarily excessive and could have done more harm than good. That put Kait at ease.

Following the doctor's orders, the nurses began prepping Kait to be discharged. But, for monitoring purposes and because she still had 15 to 20 pounds of water-weight to shed, we had to remain at the hospital for one more night. To help quickly drain the fluids from her body, Kait was given a medication that caused her to constantly have to pee. Sadly, that meant her extra jolly cheeks were going to be deflated back to their normal jolliness. She was so unbelievably cute as my little puffball for those two days that I didn't think I was ready for her to return back to her usually tone, fit self. But, our love was unconditional, so I had to accept her no matter what.

Friday quickly became Saturday, and we were allowed to leave. After a week of confinement, unpalatable food, and overall discomfort, Kait was excited to be out of that hospital. Round One of her bout with IL-2 was officially over, and she made it through with few hiccups or side effects. I couldn't have been more proud of her. She battled like a champ, as I knew she would. With her first interval concluded, Kait had three weeks to recover before squaring off with IL-2 a second time.

We returned to Kenosha, victorious, well, Kait was victorious. The rest of us were merely in her corner, cheering her on and lending a hand when we could (not to diminish anyone's role). The weeklong battle and minimal sleep had left Kait exhausted and ready to crash. I suppose I was pretty tired, too. So, upon our arrival to her mother's, we headed straight to her room and melted into her bed. It was glorious! For three days I had to sleep without Kait. For two days I could only sleep in the room she was in. Now, I was finally able to lay shoulder-to-shoulder with my best gal, and it was wonderful. I felt euphoric. Holding my baby's hand, we exchanged "I love you's" before dozing off. Once again, things were good!

11 RETURN TO NORMALCY

By the time we arrived to Madison on that Sunday to begin our three-week layoff, Kait's weight had already dropped to her usual 110 pounds, and she was quickly regaining the strength she had lost due to the treatment. Determined to maintain some semblance of normalcy in her life, Kait began substitute teaching just two days after her return, even with side effects still lingering. Though I questioned to myself whether or not teaching was healthy for her due to all of the mental stress that comes along with keeping children in line, I didn't say anything because I knew it was what Kait wanted.

As for me, I had a burning desire to exit the world of accounting and take on new challenges, but I needed a backup plan first. For years I had a strong interest in computer programming and web development, so I decided to build and improve upon the base of knowledge I had already acquired. And after spending 30 days of learning various computer languages (HTML, PHP, JavaScript, CSS), I began building my first website from scratch, using an idea Kait helped me develop, one based around the classic Nintendo.

Though we tried our best to live a normal life, we naturally found it impossible to ignore the not-so-subtle footsteps constantly clomping behind us. Cancer was always on our minds, even when we weren't consciously aware of it.

One cold night in early February, after just finishing my weekly shave and splashing away the remaining few clumps of white cream scattered across my face, Kaitlyn walked into the bathroom, her face fraught with concern. I noticed it immediately. "Hey sweetheart! What's the matter?"

Kait didn't respond right away, pondering the validity of her thoughts. She looked down at the floor before returning her disconcerted glance at me.

"Trav, do you think this will take my life," she asked gently, "Will I die?"

Completely unprepared for a question of such magnitude, I quickly tried to align my web of frantic thoughts whilst remaining aesthetically unfazed. Too long of a pause would indicate to her my deep level of concern and overall negative outlook. Unfortunately, the left hemisphere of my brain often dominated the right, molding me into a very logical person. As hard as I tried to shut down the logical part of my brain, the statistics from the Internet made it difficult to be optimistic. The reality was, under 10% of Stage 4 melanoma survivors made it past five years. And as for the 10-year survival rate, it was between 3 and 5 percent. It was nearly impossible to ignore those numbers and was cause for constant worry and stress. However, I was determined to keep that worry and stress solely within me, never to be conveyed on the outside. If Kait were to sense my worry, her worry would increase tenfold. Even though she was the one in the fight for her life, she was still selflessly more concerned about her family and me than she was for herself. And, with worry comes stress. Stress causes one's body and immune system to shutdown in various ways and function inefficiently. Kait needed every single part of her body to be working properly in order to successfully fight cancer.

With almost no delay, wearing the most positive face I could while staring intensely back at her, I said, "There is no doubt in my mind you are going to beat this! There are plenty of treatment options out there, plus, your attitude is unbelievable. You got tons of people praying for you, and you have strong faith in God. You will beat this. I'm sure of it."

As I looked into her eyes, I could sense her analyzing me, debating within herself whether or not my answer was sincere.

"Yeah, I hope so," she replied.

"I know so!"

Her disheartened tone had my heart aching for her, because I knew those thoughts were crossing her mind, torturing her throughout the day, every day. And I could do nothing to alleviate it.

I approached Kait for a hug, clasping her tightly against my body.

Early on in our journey against cancer, I realized I had become a pretty good actor, for Kait's sake, quickly discovering the ability to suppress my innermost concerns so as to minimize Kait's stress. Conversely, I didn't know it at the time, but so did Kait. When it came to our deepest worries about cancer, we both acted for each other in an attempt to keep the other person from worrying. But we were both secretly terrified.

Another part of me sometimes wondered if my inner doubt could have played a part in inhibiting her body's ability to fight the disease. I know it probably sounds absurd, but maybe her body could sense my negative energy, which in turn kept it from reaching its maximum positivity level, which would then keep it from functioning at its maximum healing potential. As strange and "pseudo-sciencey" as that seems, you never know, I guess. I never tried showing my negative attitude on the outside, but on the inside I was mainly sad and discouraged.

With that sadness and discouragement, sometimes I had to slap myself in the face. To change my attitude, I often recited to myself, "Travis, shut up. She is going to beat this. There are so many reasons to remain positive. She's young. She's healthy. She exercises. She has a great attitude. They caught it before it traveled to any major organs. New treatments are available. Her faith is strong. She is GOING to beat this, so quit being so negative and start BELIEVING!" Did that motivational speech to myself ever work? Yes. Sometimes. My emotions were a roller coaster of optimism and pessimism, changing by the hour, if not more frequently. It was rough.

I remember another instance in February, I was just heading out the door to go to the gym before Kait briefly stopped me. She wanted some ideas of what we should have for dinner. We began discussing our options. And at that moment, I remember my brain started producing a dichotomy of thoughts. Down one path, we were conversing about dinner. Down the other path, all I could think about was this beautiful woman standing in front of me and her potentially grim fate. While talking about food on the outside, on the inside I kept thinking how she was so kind-hearted, so caring, so friendly, so funny, so innocent, so adorable, so blonde, so selfless, so special. How she loved life so much. Yet there she was, standing in front of me, facing the prospect of death. There she was, trying her best to live a normal life, cook food, teach, love, laugh, all while knowing her time may be cut tragically short. I remember feeling so sad for her in that moment. She didn't deserve the hand she had been dealt.

All of that and more were flashing through my mind while we discussed dinner plans. After I said goodbye and left for the gym, all I wanted to do was cry for her. But I held my tears back.

12 DING, DING: ROUND TWO

Kaitlyn's vacation from treatment seemed to be over before it even began. We had three weeks of normalcy, and then it was back to St. Lukes for Round Two where she would have to endure five more days of IL-2.

Sadly, that meant I'd be alone at my apartment for another four days, longing to be reunited with my sweetheart every minute we were apart.

It seems so strange, yet amazing to me at the same time how a person can become so accustomed to someone else's presence, to the point when that someone else is absent, everything feels off. The void in your life is unmistakable, and you just don't feel quite like yourself. As independent as I once was, it had become apparent that I was completely dependent on Kaitlyn being in my life in order to function normally in my daily activities. But I knew I was surrendering my independence to someone I could trust, someone who could handle my vulnerability with love and care, someone who always had my best interests at heart, so I was okay with becoming dependent on her. At times, I felt like Kaitlyn knew me better than I knew myself, which was great for those moments when I'd lose sight of my true identity.

Upon returning to the hospital on Thursday, I quickly learned things hadn't gone as smoothly for Kait the second time around, unfortunately. Her body was definitely feeling the effects of the IL-2. She felt nauseous, she felt restless from being cooped up in that claustrophobic room for consecutive days, and she couldn't sleep. The nausea turned eating into a painful chore, and her stomach was prepared to deflect anything she put inside it. She was only able to ingest foods that were easier to digest, like applesauce, rice, potatoes, etc.

On top of that, I was starting to get a cold, bringing into question whether or not I should even stay with Kaitlyn, fearing my sickness could leach on to her. Needing her body to be in tip-top shape to endure her second round of treatment, she couldn't afford another ailment. Nevertheless, I decided to stay with her. I couldn't bear another night without her by my side. Was it a poor decision on my part, putting her health in jeopardy? Probably. I justified my decision by telling myself she had already been exposed the moment I walked in, so if she was going to catch a cold, she was going to catch it whether I stayed with her or not.

That first night proved to be a rough one. Kaitlyn couldn't sleep. She had gone stir crazy again, unable to find a comfortable position in bed, and with the ill effects from the treatment and medical personnel constantly intruding, it all culminated to one long restless night. For me, as the hours ticked by, my cold worsened. I had to get up several times throughout just to blow my nose, constantly waking Kait up in the process, something I wasn't too proud of myself for. The night was a mess.

The next day, Friday, was much the same. Kait's restlessness had doubled from the previous day, and with the lack of sleep, her fatigue levels had hit their peak. However, as was a part of Kait's many wonderfully endearing personality traits, she never liked sleeping when guests were present, and we were her guests. She always felt like she was being rude by falling asleep on people, even when we would urge her just to close her eyes and rest. "Kaitlyn, sweetie, don't worry about us. Your body is desperate for sleep right now," I would say.

Her dad would add, "Yeah, just close your eyes, pumpkin. We don't need to be entertained."

For a moment she would listen to us. "Ok. Are you guys sure? Maybe I should just close my eyes for a little while."

"Yes, please!!!"

When Kait finally closed her eyes, we did our best to keep our mouths shut for the duration. But after a half-hour, assuming Kait was asleep, we figured it was at least safe to whisper. "Have you guys gotten through Season 1 of Modern Family, yet," her dad asked.

"Almost. We got, like, three episodes to go."

"It's a good show isn't it?"

"Yeah, I was surprised at how good it is. Normally shows don't make me laugh much, but this one does. Did you see that episode where Cameron dresses up as the clown for the first time?"

I received a response to my question, but it didn't come from the mouth of Mark.

"I love that episode," a girly voice interjected. It was Kait! When I slowly tilted my head to look over at her, her eyes were still closed but she had a bashful smirk on her face.

"Kait, you're supposed to be asleep!"

"Sorryyy," she replied softly.

Mark and I both laughed and shook our heads. Kait was always on alert, never sacrificing a moment.

With Kait refusing to nap consistently during the day, I worried another night of no sleep would put her body into panic mode as it already seemed as though it was operating on fumes. Luckily, we received good news. Kaitlyn was going to be released from the hospital a day early since her immune system had reached its threshold and further IL-2 doses were no longer needed. Dreary-eyed and running out of energy, Kaitlyn perked up enough to help gather our belongings together before being discharged.

From the drugs, lack of sleep, and lack of nutrition, Kait experienced a string of hallucinations as we were preparing to leave. While I was packing her clothes in a duffle bag, all of a sudden I heard, "Did you guys just see that spider walk across the floor?"

I looked over at Kait sitting on her bed. "You saw a spider?"

"Yeah. I know it wasn't real. But it was big and red and I saw it walking across the floor. Then it disappeared. I think I was hallucinating."

I didn't know whether it was okay for me to laugh or if I should be concerned. "Oh that's weird. Your brain must be exhausted."

Finally, at about 7:30 that night we were discharged from the hospital. It had gotten to the point where Kait was actually feeling pain due to being so sleep deprived. The eyelids around her drawn in eyes felt like 50-pound weights, and her head, it felt like a thousand buffalo were stampeding through. She was miserable! As much as she tried, she was unable to fall asleep during the bumpy car ride home. The only remedy was her warm Kenosha bed. "Hang in there, sweetie. We're close."

Eventually, we made it to Kathy's house as I pulled our car into the driveway. "Alright, sweetie, now you go straight upstairs. Don't worry about this stuff, we'll get it," I said, referring to the suitcases and other junk in the car.

"Are you sure," she replied with her head bobbing and her eyes barely open.

"Yes. Absolutely!"

"Okay. Thank you."

Kaitlyn immediately headed inside and went straight up to her room. And by the time I had unloaded everything from the vehicle, Kaitlyn was already in her bed. The soft, fluffy pillows and her cloudlike mattress were shouting her name. When she finally dozed off, and it didn't take long, she ended up sleeping for 12 hours straight that night. Her body desperately needed it.

With round two of treatment officially completed, our next step was a full body scan to assess whether or not the IL-2 was working.

Sadly, wedding planning had almost become an afterthought in lieu of cancer.

Toward the final portion of her stay at St. Luke's while receiving IL-2, Kait was restricted primarily to the B.R.A.T. diet – Bananas, Rice, Applesauce, and Toast – foods easily digested by a battered stomach. However, three days after receiving her final does of treatment, and with her feeling much improved, we figured it was safe for her to begin eating normal food once again.

Big mistake!

Almost as a celebratory meal for Kait victoriously completing another cycle of treatment, we made chicken parmesan. It was deeelicious on the way down! Unfortunately, the unpleasantness afterward for Kait turned it into a regrettable meal.

With the heaviness of the chicken parmesan, and the pasta and cheese that accompanied it, Kait's stomach began churning, trying hard to digest the large clumps of food. It was very painful for her as she laid curled up on the couch next to me. We didn't know what to do. This wasn't your typical "take Tums or Pepto" situation. The food in her stomach was just sitting there and her body wasn't quite to the point where it could handle such a heavy order. We just hoped that it would eventually pass.

Well, a couple hours later as we tucked into bed, the stomach pains persisted.

"I don't know what to do," she groaned, "I just wish this medicine would work."

When I placed my hand on her tummy, I could feel how bloated she was. Her protruding belly felt solid.

"Geez, Kait, you have so much gas or air built up in there! That's what's causing the pain."

Something had to be done! Cerebrating as hard as I could with my skittle-brain, I arrived at a 'genius' conclusion. "Somehow we need to get that gas out of your body. If you could just fart a few times you would feel so much better."

Genius! Just like I said.

"Gross," Kait replied.

"It's not gross."

"I know. Trust me, if I could fart right now I would and I wouldn't even care."

Kait was whimpering in pain, but those soft whimpers sounded like screeching fingernails on a chalkboard to my ears, so we had to do something quick. Then, a light bulb flickered in my head.

"Kait, I'm gonna try something. Tell me if this hurts and I'll stop. We just need to get that built up pressure out of your body."

Putting my plan into practice, I placed my hand gently on her stomach, about four inches above her bellybutton. The accumulation of air caused her tummy to feel like an inflated balloon. "Does that hurt?"

"No."

With that I then pressed down slightly on her belly, adding just a bit of pressure. "Just tell me if it hurts."

"I will."

Slowly, so as to not cause her more pain, while maintaining the same amount of pressure, I began sliding my hand downward. Logically, it made sense in my mind that the technique I was using would eventually force the air from her belly and out her backside. A technique likely not found in medical literature.

As stupid as the idea seemed, I continued my attempts at forcing the built up pressure out of Kait's stomach. Oddly enough, after just a few strokes, it began working.

"Oh my God, I think I'm actually gonna fart," she exclaimed, unsure of whether to be elated or disgusted with herself.

"Good! Don't worry, I'll plug my nose," I said excitedly. I never thought I'd be so happy for someone to break wind.

Silently, Kait began passing gas. (Sorry, Kait, I know this is so embarrassing for you.) With the effectiveness of my technique, I continued my strokes and she continued farting. The pressure in her belly was slowly releasing. Like an almost-empty tube of toothpaste, I pressed until every last bit of gas seemed to exit her body. My wrist had become fatigued and sore, but I couldn't stop. Kait's stomach pains were being alleviated, and that was worth the sacrifice!

After about 15 minutes of constant belly depressions and a haze of green gas in the air, Kait's stomach discomfort seemed to completely dissipate. "My stomach feels so much better!"

"Really?"

"Yes! Thank you." She was quite relieved.

"I can't believe that worked. I'm so happy!"

We rejoiced! Normally a cause for asphyxiation, we welcomed the liberating flatulence that night. The enemy of our enemy had become our friend. We were finally able to sleep soundly.

During our two-week wait before Kait's body scans, I began researching clinical trials for the treatment of melanoma. Like I mentioned earlier, I wasn't all that confident that IL-2 was going to do its job, so I decided to see what other options were in existence aside from the newly approved Ipilimumab and Vemurafenib (Zelboraf). As I was navigating through the main Clinical Trials website, I discovered hundreds of available trials. Overwhelmed at first, I wasn't sure how to even sift through all of the data. But, one by one I narrowed down my search and dug up a few that sounded promising.

With the help of my grandma, we began calling the various medical institutions, trying to set all of our ducks in a row just in case we were forced to change course with our treatment plan.

As another precautionary measure, unable to predict the long-term effects her treatments and cancer might have on her body, we began looking into Embryo Cryopreservation, in case Kaitlyn was no longer able to have children. I mean, to put it bluntly, it really really sucked knowing Kait's fertility was being threatened and possibly in jeopardy, and because one of her biggest dreams in life was to raise children, we wanted to take measures to ensure our future was secure. At least when it came to children.

The procedure was quite costly, but with the help of my grandparents, we decided to give it serious consideration. So, Kait set up some appointments to see a specialist.

Unfortunately, as the days passed, we decided to forego the embryo preservation because there was legitimate concern that the procedure could stimulate her cancer, and we couldn't risk that. We just had to hope the cancer would disappear before excessive damage was done to her body.

13 IPILIMUMAB & THE CALM BEFORE THE STORM

Two weeks after treatment, the results from Kait's PET scan came in, and it was as I cynically expected. The IL-2 was not working. With the cancer's continued growth, we were forced to figure out a Plan B. Unfortunately, the one clinical trial I had focused my attention on had struggled to acquire funding, so they couldn't accept new patients for the time being, forcing me to scratch that option off of my list. They had the labor, equipment, and resources prepared, but lacked money. I was disappointed because the procedure sounded innovative and promising.

With that, we began discussion with Dr. Robertson about deploying the newly approved, Ipilimumab (Ipi), another form of immunotherapy, like IL-2 and Interferon. The way it works is it blocks the protein in a person's body that regulates the production of T-cells. With that specific protein blocked, one's immune system is essentially always 'turned on,' and T-cells are able to constantly grow, uninhibited.

To my ignorant ears, the process seemed very similar to IL-2. However, Ipi's success rate fell between the 20-30% range, a big improvement compared to the 5% of IL-2, and that's all I needed to hear to increase my confidence in the synthetically produced protein. So that we wouldn't too hastily jump to negative conclusions after not seeing immediate benefit from the treatment, our oncologist explained that it could take a few months before we saw any results, meaning the cancer would continue to grow while Kait's immune system fortified its defenses.

Hoping to add another weapon to our treatment plan, we introduced to Dr. Robertson an idea we had come across on a news story just a week earlier. The story focused on one particular woman who just happened to be suffering from melanoma, and who just happened to be receiving Ipilimumab. While she was waiting for her body to respond to the therapy, she had a growing tumor that had begun pressing up against her spine. Needing to make a quick decision before the growth caused excess damage and to alleviate the pain, her oncologist elected to use high-dose radiation on the mass. A week or two later, after introducing radiation therapy, they noticed that not only did the main tumor by her spine nearly disappear, but multiple surrounding tumors also shrunk rapidly, even though the beams were focused only on the one mass. The hypothesis behind this "Abscopal Effect" was that the radiation weakened and exposed the hidden melanoma cells to the billions, or trillions, of T-cells that the woman's body had produced from receiving Ipilimumab. The melanoma cells were essentially bleeding and the shark-like T-cells could finally sniff them out, whereas the cancer went undetected before.

That method of using radiation along with Ipilimumab made so much logical sense to me. And we figured it would do little harm to Kait's body if we simply irradiated a single tumor. In my opinion, any attempt to potentially increase the likelihood of destroying cancer cells without causing excess harm to her body, seemed worth it. However, Dr. Robertson was not too keen on the idea since it had not been fully tested and proven, yet. I understood his concern. And, it was against protocol. That meant the method we had in mind in hopes of achieving that abscopal effect through the combinational use of radiation and Ipi was off the table.

So, Ipilimumab it was, as a single agent, and Kait was scheduled to begin in two weeks. We went home with a new plan and a newfound confidence that success would accompany our new treatment. I know I felt genuine encouragement.

As the schemer that I was, I began devising a strategy in my head, thinking that maybe Kait could lie and say a tumor was causing her a lot of pain and then request radiation on that single spot. But after pondering that idea for days, I decided against lying about her condition. Looking back, I wish we would have.

In the meantime, before commencing Ipilimumab, small tumors began appearing in various areas across Kait's body. All of them were subcutaneous, under the skin, but they were visible and we could feel them. Though they were aesthetically unpleasant for Kait, they weren't all too noticeable, didn't cause discomfort or impede her ability to perform her daily activities, so she didn't allow their physical appearance to effect her – at least not often. I mean, Kait already knew she had cancer, but those bumps served as a constant reminder of her affliction. And for me, the ability to now monitor their growth triggered my obsessive compulsive tendencies, causing me to slowly become an annoying pest as the days passed.

See, whenever I have something in my life I care deeply for or am passionate about, it becomes an obsession. When I used to gamble in the stock market, I would check the ticker every 30 seconds. Whenever I was awaiting an important email from someone, I would refresh my inbox every few minutes. If I ever had money riding on a football game, my eyes would remain glued to the TV or computer screen, keeping track of every single play until the clock hit zero. I know it's not healthy, but I can't help myself. I know that looking at the prices of stocks or at the scores of football games won't change the outcomes, but I still NEED to know what's happening. Maybe it helps me feel like I'm in control to a certain extent. I just don't know.

Anyway, I obviously cared deeply for Kait and the situation we were in, and, consequently, with her tumors now visible, giving me a rough marker to monitor the progression of Kait's disease, I became obsessed. I just HAD to know how fast those tumors were growing in her body. Or, I just HAD to know if they had begun shrinking, miraculously.

I didn't do it too often, but in the beginning I would simply try and sneak a peek at her visible tumors when she wasn't looking. I didn't want her to see me staring, because I figured it would cause her to think about her cancer and possibly become discouraged by the fact that we weren't seeing results, yet, and I didn't want that. So, I felt an obligation to remain secretive about my observational habits. And sometimes, not all the time, when I hugged her, I would brush my hand across one of the tumors on her back to check its size. She was no dummy, though. She knew what I was doing. But she accepted my mental deficiencies because she loved me.

On March 16, 2012, Kaitlyn received her first Ipilimumab treatment. Unlike that insufferable IL-2 where she was sequestered in a claustrophobic white chamber for a full week, Kait was in and out of the hospital in a matter of hours. The simplicity was so relieving to her. Me, too! And, as an added bonus, side effects were expected to be minimal, meaning Kait would be able to work and perform all of her daily activities with little interference, which was great. Our next steps were to simply go home, live as normally as possible, and wait for the results to occur over the next couple of months.

In total, Kait was to be given four rounds of Ipilimumab, and each one was to be administered every three weeks. It was possible for shrinkage to happen relatively fast, but unlikely. Ipi stimulates T-cell growth within the immune system, which is a gradual process and needs time in order to proliferate enough of an army to successfully seek out and attack those pernicious melanoma cells. In some cases, patients don't see results until a month or even two months after their final dose of treatment. So, we just had to be patient.

Following the first round of our new treatment regimen, we felt supremely confident that Ipilimumab would be the therapy to obliterate the cancer in her body. We were going to beat this disease! We were going to overcome cancer! We believed!

And after the first week, Kait felt great! She experienced zero side effects and was able to do everything she did on a normal basis. At times, it made it easier to forget she even had cancer in the first place. Not that we ever truly forgot.

To resume her life of normalcy, Kait taught at various schools in the Madison area as many days a week as she could. And the one school, Kennedy Elementary, which she had to turn down for a full-time position, frequently asked her back. All of the children were just ecstatic whenever she came around. They adored her!

Back in the Fall, when she initially began at Kennedy, there was one boy in particular who had certain behavioral issues, and no one could successfully "reach" him. That is, until Kait came along. Soon after being introduced to each other, the boy's attitude began to drastically change, and he opened up to Kait unlike anyone before. To him, she was finally someone he felt like he could trust and look up to. Someone who wouldn't let him down.

So, on Kait's first day back to the school following her stage 4 diagnoses, the teachers wanted to surprise the young boy. As Kaitlyn began making her rounds, greeting faculty and all of the children she had become familiar with, the young boy was in a room receiving one-on-one attention from another staff member. And when he was finally allowed recess, the teachers brought him to see Kait. As soon as he saw her, his face immediately lit up, and he ran straight into her arms for a big hug.

In another instance, during another one of her days teaching at Kennedy, a magician was invited to entertain the children. The magician instructed the kids to choose one teacher to come up so he could perform a special magic trick. Without hesitation, the crowd of children overwhelmingly began shouting Kait's name. Of course, with a smile and rosy cheeks, she accepted their request before walking to the front of the audience as the magician's unlucky victim.

It was apparent to everyone who knew Kait that she truly had a special gift when it came to interacting with children. Her warm presence made it so that every child wanted to be around her. It was that very presence and ability to speak to children that earned her the name "Child Whisperer" by the principal at the school.

Whenever Kait humbly told me these stories, I would secretly melt inside. Everybody absolutely loved her. Both children and adults. And, it made me happy!

Yes, I was confident in our new treatment, but that confidence wasn't always consistent.

While Kait was teaching and doing her best to live a normal life, I was doing the same. And it wasn't easy. Every day at work I experienced a roller coaster of upward and downward emotional swings. Sitting at my computer chair, staring at my spreadsheets and financial reports, my mind would often, and quickly, wander. Sometimes I would conjure up positive thoughts, visualizing the day when I could joyfully kiss my beautiful bride as we walked hand-in-hand down the aisle of red and white rose pedals. I would imagine what we would look like together when we were 60-, 70-, or even 80-years old, all chubby and wrinkly and fragile, playing card games or Rummikub on the porch as the sun set in front of us. Those thoughts would help put a nice smile on my face.

Other times, however, my thoughts would spiral out of control. The worst possible scenarios would be at the forefront of my mind and I couldn't shut them out. *What if Kaitlyn passes away?* The hairs on my body stood tall as a cold chill pulsated through. My imagination produced pictures of me standing at a podium with a suit and tie, giving a speech to a watery-eyed crowd. Just thinking about it accelerated my heartbeat. *What would I even say? ...... ".....Kaitlyn was the sweetest person I have ever known. It didn't matter who you were, what your social status was, or anything trivial like that, she was going to give you all of the love and respect she had........."* My eyes would begin watering up at work just picturing myself speaking at her funeral. It was unbearable. But before anyone could see me, I had to quickly snap out of my sadness. *No, no, no. Stop! Stop thinking about that, Travis! Quit thinking those depressing and negative thoughts. She's not going anywhere. She deserves a miracle, and a miracle will happen.*

I often found myself dumbfounded, unable to grasp how our life could have changed so drastically, almost in an instant and with hardly a warning. I longed for the days of worrying over trivialities. I wanted so badly to go back in time to when we could happily daydream about our future without having to second-guess if that future would ever be realized. Those were the good ole' days. But it almost felt like that world never existed.

We're gonna beat this disease, Travis! I had to remind myself to stay positive.

Some moments seemed to challenge our upbeat attitude.

Violently stamping the slush and snow off of my shoes as I walked into our door after a typical day of work, Kait greeted me with her usual warm hug and her usual candy kisses. And, as usual, she helped me take off my puffy winter coat while we discussed the events of our day. What was unusual on this particular day, however, was the obvious look of concern on her face. I sensed she was being mentally bogged down by something unpleasant.

"Are you okay, sweetheart," I asked, navigating through her feelings to locate the source of her worry.

"Yeah, I'm fine," she replied with her sweet voice, but with only a half-smile. One of those smiles that really says 'I'm not fine, something is on my mind, but I'm trying my best to hide it.'

"Are you sure," I asked, trying to summon the concern she was obviously masking.

Pausing for a moment, pondering whether or not she wanted to revisit what had bothered her earlier in the day, she caved slightly. "Well, when I called you at work today, it was because I was having kind of a rough moment."

She did call me that day while I was at work, but with my phone completely silenced, I didn't get to it until hours later. "Oh nooo! I'm sorry, sweetie, and no one was here with you….," I said with an upward inflection in my voice. It saddened me to know she had to manage her emotions all by herself.

"It's okay, I called Alexa, and she was able to help me."

"Ohh, well that's good at least. I'm sorry you were feeling that way………I wish I was here. Do you want to talk about it anymore?"

"No, that's okay, honey. I'm good. It was just one of those weak moments, I guess."

To my knowledge, Kait had told me everything. However, I would later find out there was more to her "rough" day than what she was leading me to believe, but she just didn't want to burden me with worry at that moment.

On April 6th, Kaitlyn received her second round of Ipilimumab. Though it was still way too early in the treatment-process to expect results, it didn't keep us from optimistically hoping. Unfortunately, every time I spot-checked her bumps, it was apparent they continued to grow. Nothing to be discouraged about, however.

"We will triumph against this cancer! We will one day be married!"

Feeling relatively stable in our life, Kait and I finally felt like we were in a place where we could dive back into wedding planning. Over the previous months, our engagement was certainly not forgotten about, but it naturally took a backseat to Kait's health, which was infinitely more important than anything else, at least to me.

To recommence the planning process, we first visited the reception hall we planned on booking for our wedding, conveniently located just miles away from her home in Kenosha.

After the manager of the hall walked us through planning and budgeting, explaining about the food, the booze, DJs, etc., she took us into the dining area to partake in the portion of our visit we were most looking forward to. Taste-testing!!!

One by one, the chef brought out all sorts of delectable items - chicken marsala, chicken parmesan, chicken-this, chicken-that, steak, beef, pasta, mashed potatoes. Like the mindless dog that I was, my mouth was salivating the whole time. "Kait, make sure I only eat small portions of everything! I'm already fat enough as it is."

"Ditto, babe," she replied with a smile. Discipline was not my strong suit. The temptation to just shovel everything into my mouth was too great. Every single variation of chicken that was brought out was delicious. On top of that, the garlic mashed potatoes were amazing! And mashed potatoes are my favorite food, so it was agony staring at the fluffy white mound of scrumptiousness and telling myself to stay away.

For the most part, we both did a good job of practicing moderation. But, as we were sitting there, waiting for the manager to return to send us on our way, I couldn't resist. My hand, brandishing a fork, had a life of its own. I tried stopping it, but it was too strong as it kept on reaching in for just "one more bite." Well, after ten "one more bites" later, the manager finally returned and escorted us from the building.

We left the reception hall feeling electric! It was such a wonderful day for the two of us to share together. It made us feel like marriage was becoming more and more of a reality, and that was a happy thought for both of us. Once again we felt on top of the world, like nothing would get in our way.

After the taste-testing event, we continued making wedding plans.

Now, I'm not going to sit here and lie by saying the planning duties were shared equally, because they weren't. Kaitlyn definitely took on the lion's share. But it wasn't because I was lazy. Not at all. I TRULY wanted to help with every aspect of the process. I did! But every time I took initiative to try and do something on my own, I would wind up crossed-eyed, sucking my thumb while curled up in a fetal position on the living room floor, overwhelmed and confused by it all. I desperately needed Kait's guidance. I needed her instruction on what to do.

Kaitlyn devoted much of her free time and took great pride in planning for our day of "official" unity. With the help of my aunt Wendy, she and Kait spent hours decorating red candles with silver glitter to be placed on the dinner tables of our reception. By the time they were finished, it looked like a strobe light had exploded in Wendy's garage.

Ever the crafty one, Kait implemented an idea she stumbled across on the Internet for designing ornaments to be hung from the church pews during our wedding. After purchasing red and cream colored fabrics along with a glue gun and Styrofoam balls, we spent hours together cutting and gluing the material onto the foam spheres. I was actually quite surprised and impressed by how great they turned out.

We started coming up with various ways for how we wanted to present our picture slideshow during the reception, tossing around a whole bunch of creative ideas in order to make it as entertaining as possible for the spectators. The idea that resonated most humorously with us was the one involving the two of us actually recording our own voices singing the songs in a really cheesy way as the pictures were being projected on the big screen. Kait and I laughed just thinking about it.

Then, I started coming up with an idea about how we would walk into the reception hall together. My idea was that I would make a video that would be shown to everyone as they awaited our arrival. The video would include me as a video game character traveling through the Mushroom Kingdom in the Super Mario Bros. game. All of the enemies would have the faces of our wedding party superimposed onto them as I ran through defeating them along the way. Then after I would defeat Bowser (the final boss), Kait, doubling as Princess Peach, would be awaiting my rescue. She looked just like the character, after all. In the game, I would then pick her up and carry her off screen, and that's when the doors to the reception hall would open where I would walk in with Kaitlyn in my arms.

I loved it! I couldn't wait to get started!

I had a dream! That one day, I would finally have the privilege of telling Kaitlyn, "Sweetie, guess what? They're shrinking!!!"

With that announcement we'd both jump up and down, dancing and rejoicing and skipping about the apartment. We would call our families and tell them the news they had been waiting to hear for months, and they would hoot and holler and sing songs in the background. We would laugh. We would cry. It would be pure elation! If only that moment would hurry up and become a reality. But for the time being, it was simply a dream that I constantly replayed in my head.

Almost every other day I would feel her tumors, hoping to be surprised by a decrease in size, hoping my dream would finally come true.

But through April, no shrinkage had taken place. It had only been six weeks, though, so we needed to continue our exercise in patience. And if I was becoming too overzealous in my physical assessments, Kait would politely let me know, and I would abide.

"WE WILL BEAT THIS DISEASE!" We remained confident!

Around April 27th, Kait completed round three of her treatment with flying colors. Her fourth and final dose of Ipilimumab was just three weeks away, scheduled for May 18th, and we were looking forward to it along with the subsequent results. The finish line was around the bend!

Thankfully, Kait still had not experienced any adverse side effects, allowing her to continue teaching, exercising, dancing, playing Super Mario 64 with me (a game she claimed was her "all-time favorite"), spending time with her beautiful niece, or anything she liked without worrying about feeling ill or weak. It was great! We tried fitting in as many normal activities as we could without overwhelming ourselves.

On one particular weekend, with her father and stepmother, we traveled up to a church near Green Bay where sightings of the Virgin Mary had been confirmed. It is one of only a handful of churches around the world to have allegedly experienced this supernatural phenomenon. When we arrived at the holy ground, we did our best to soak in and feel its significance. Inside the church, we each took turns lighting candles and praying, hoping Jesus would hear our calls. Ashamedly, my belief, or lack thereof, prohibited me from fully investing my energy into praying. I didn't really think anyone would actually be listening. Lack of faith aside, it was a great experience overall, and we hoped healing would accompany the visit.

On another weekend, with Vicky escaping the clutches of her evil husband, and with Mark all alone, we decided to pay him a visit, because, well, let's be honest, he's a Chicago Bears fan, so he's obviously not right in the head, and we needed to make sure the house wasn't burning down. It was Jessica's birthday, so we tried convincing him to come out and throw a few back with us. Kait and her father hadn't had many opportunities to share drinks together since she turned 21, and it seemed like a perfect chance. The next month or so was extremely busy with the Relay for Life and Milwaukee Zoo walk soon approaching, and with Mother's Day and Memorial Day just around the corner.

Reluctant at first because he wasn't sure how his damaged pancreas would hold up, Mark decided to join us. It was a decision he wouldn't regret. We (with Jessica's boyfriend, Carlos, and best friend, Christie) all had a blast knocking down Long Islands, laughing, spinning quarters on the table and stopping them upright with our finger, telling jokes, and shooting the shit for hours. For the time being our future was completely unpredictable, and we were all fully aware of how important it was to take advantage of as many prime opportunities as we could. For all we knew, it could have been the last time Jessica would get to spend her birthday with her sister. And it could have been the last time Mark would be able to spend a special night with his two little girls, creating a memory to cherish forever. Though it was such a simple night, it sticks out in my head and always makes me smile.

Aside from wedding planning and all other activities, I continued honing my web developing skills. And after a few months of building, I finally finished my first website, instilling confidence within me that I could start developing for third parties. Clapping her hands together, Kait was excited for me. Her unwavering support and constant encouragement always motivated me no matter what I was doing, and I became dependent on it. Whenever I would accomplish anything, whether it was something minor like beating a video game or something major like solving the world's hunger issue, she would shower me with compliments and positive reinforcement, and it felt nice I must admit. I quickly acquired a lust for the attention and praise that came along with "being a good boy."

While she was overcome with joy that I had finished my project, I just sat there and listlessly smiled at my achievement because I'm boring and I internalize my emotions. Typically I try not to let my accomplishments go to my head, but because I try so hard to be modest, I completely brush off my successes and act like they don't happen. So, Kait normally celebrated for the both of us. Then again, she was the same way. If she found success in any of her endeavors, she wouldn't even tell people about them. The main difference was she was NATURALLY humble, whereas I had to actually TRY being humble. While I would accomplish something and secretly want people to find out about it, Kait would accomplish something and not care if it stayed hidden for eternity. In fact, she preferred her good deeds remain anonymous.

"Will we conquer disease? Or are we just in denial?"

One night, lying in bed with the pale moonlight twinkling through the bedroom window as Kait rubbed my back to lull me to sleep like she did almost every night, and with her final treatment only two weeks away, Kaitlyn came clean about something she had been withholding from me.

"Trav, do you remember a few weeks ago when I was having that rough day by myself, and I called you and couldn't get ahold of you, so then I called Lex?"

"Yeah, why?"

"Well, the reason I was having a rough moment was because I got this really bad pain in my head, above my right eye. It scared me because I thought it was a tumor."

"Oh sweetie, I'm sorry you had to deal with that by yourself. I'm sure it was just a headache. Maybe it was a side effect or something. Maybe it was just stress from everything."

"Yeah," she paused for a moment, "I called Nurse Sue and she said that if it persisted I should let them know right away."

"Has it happened since?"

"No. So, hopefully it's nothing."

"Exactly. Hopefully it's nothing to worry about."

"Are you mad I didn't tell you?"

I began laughing at her question. "Sweetie! Absolutely not. I know your intentions. You knew it would cause me to worry and you didn't want that. But, I really want you to understand that I'm here to share as much of the burden as I can with you."

"I know, I just don't want you or my family stressing over me. I know my dad is always super worried. I feel bad."

"That just shows how amazing you are, sweetheart. You still think about everyone else even though you're the one dealing with this. That's why I love you so much! I mean, you have to know, I'm going to worry no matter what, so…..I mean….you might as well tell me those bothersome things." I put my arm around her and kissed her.

"I love you, Trav. You're an amazing man, too, you know that?"

"Oh no…….nope, nope, nope. I do nothing."

"Yes, we will overcome our affliction!" We truly believed!

With the persisting belief that her treatment would kick in soon, Kaitlyn was not content with merely sitting idly by, feeling sorry about the hand she had been dealt. She realized that even though her situation was highly unfavorable, it was also a unique opportunity that gave her a voice and an ability to hopefully promote further awareness of such a devastating disease. Young girls are being diagnosed with the highly aggressive and deadly melanoma at an alarming rate. They have no idea how dangerous those tanning beds are to their skin cells, all in the name of having a darker complexion so they can look more "beautiful."

Like Kaitlyn and all of us before her diagnosis, people around the world are mostly oblivious to how dangerous melanoma is. We all just think, "Oh skin cancer, that's nothing. Just get it removed." Kaitlyn had a desire to help change that perception.

Trying to find a way to be proactive and kick-off her journey into health advocacy within the cancer community, she began by enrolling in a couple events. One was a Relay For Life walk on May 11th, and the other was a melanoma walk being hosted at the Milwaukee Zoo just a week later. Kait invested more of her time in the Milwaukee Zoo walk, raising money to stimulate further research and continued awareness. She was looking quite forward to that particular event. I couldn't have been more proud watching her take pride in something she felt was highly important, expending a good deal of time and effort in building support for the cause, for those walking in similar shoes as she. And it would be just the beginning for her, a way to network and become acclimated within the charitable community.

On May 11th we drove down to a Chicago suburb to participate in the Relay For Life walk. Kaitlyn was particularly excited because that meant she would be able to spend time with her cousin (best friend) Alexa who lived in the town hosting the event.

When we arrived at the Relay For Life walk that night, we were invited to take a seat on the main stage. We were in awe of the vast amount of people that had volunteered to come out and lend their support.

Before the walk commenced, two attendees were brought on to speak about their journeys with cancer. The first speaker was a sweet teenage girl whose mom had recently passed away after a long, strenuous battle with the disease. Her story of her mother's trials and tribulations as she walked that terrifying path with her family was moving to say the least. One could only shake his head in sadness upon realizing how much that whole family had gone through.

The second speaker was a high school boy who was battling some form of cancer himself. From the stories the brave young man was telling us, it was clear he had been through hell. He had undergone multiple surgeries, had bits and pieces of his organs removed, had been told on a number of occasions that his time was about to expire, and had many instances where his life almost had been taken from him. Yet, there he was, still alive, still fighting, upbeat and positive, sharing all of those details that you would think would cause a person to want to give up, but he hadn't.

Kaitlyn was especially moved by this boy's inspiring story. When she turned to look at me, she had tears running down her face. All I could do was give her tissues and put my arm around her. "Trav, if you ever hear me complaining about my situation, I want you to remind me of this boy. I have no excuse to be down."

I simply pursed my lips and nodded my head at her, signaling that I would adhere to her wishes. However, if I ever really did hear her complain about her situation, I really had no intentions of reminding her why she shouldn't be complaining. Anyone in situations as unfortunate as theirs should be allowed to complain at least some of the time. If, however, her sadness and grief was causing her to give up and stop living, then I would certainly help her put things into perspective, which would probably include a reminder of this boy's story. But, we were talking about Kaitlyn Julia here, a girl as strong-willed as anyone I knew. I could never imagine her throwing in the towel.

After the two speakers were finished telling their stories, the walk commenced. On the first lap, each cancer survivor was given the option to take the microphone and state their name, what type of cancer they had, and how long they had been a survivor. I wasn't sure whether or not Kait would take the mic. I never really pictured her as being much of a public speaker, then again talking was one of her strong suits, so I wasn't about to underestimate her abilities to address a crowd.

As we approached the microphone, I started feeling nervous for Kait. Would she stutter? Would she start crying? Would her mind go blank? With a group of us standing alongside her, Kait grabbed the microphone. To my surprise, instead of simply answering the three questions, she went a bit further. "Hey, everyone! My name is Kaitlyn Zolper and I was recently diagnosed with Stage 4 melanoma in January. And, I just wanted everyone to be aware of how dangerous tanning beds are, and they're not worth it. I will beat this!"

I was amazed. Sure it was just a couple simple sentences, but I was still amazed at how calm and composed she was, saying exactly what she wanted to say in a concise manner without becoming too overindulgent. I was not expecting that at all. She was wonderful.

As she passed off the microphone and began her first lap, we all sped up to congratulate her. "Oh my gosh, honey! You were great! I was not expecting that," I said excitedly as I put my arm around her and squeezed. She just smiled as we continued walking. It was nothing to her. For me, it was reason number 1,294 as to why I was so proud of her.

After we left the walk, a small group of us decided to go out and share a couple drinks. Attending the cancer event was a great experience, and Kaitlyn was especially pleased with the turnout and support. Now she couldn't wait for next week's event at the zoo.

Everything was normal and wonderful that night. However, what I noticed, and what I later found out Alexa noticed, too, was that Kaitlyn was just a little bit off. I mean, she was herself for the most part, but something was just slightly amiss as she was just a bit different than usual. But, I wasn't about to let it worry me. I assumed it was probably just because of all the excitement and the couple alcoholic beverages she consumed.

We went to bed that night happy and carefree, looking forward to driving back to Kenosha to spend Mother's Day with her mother and stepmom, but not at the same time of course.

14 THE BEGINNING OF THE END

It was May 12th. A Saturday. Before departing for Kenosha to spend Mother's Day with Kait's mothers, we accepted an invitation to join Lex and her father, Dale, for breakfast at a local diner. We were in no hurry, and being the penultimate lightweight that I am, I needed time to quell my hangover from consuming a whopping three drinks the night before.

Conversation and laughter were flowing as usual at the restaurant - nothing felt amiss. After indulging in a sugary, caffeine-laced specialty coffee, Kaitlyn was put up to the task (by Lex) of convincing her Uncle Dale to fire the piano man he had hired for Lex's upcoming college graduation party, the very same piano man he employed some five years earlier for her high school grad party where her friends arrived expecting trendy hip-hop music, only to be surprised by a goateed man pouring his heart out onto piano keys, belting out the words of hits from a variety of genres. He was great, but not high school age material. So, when Dale surprised Lex with the news that he had hired him again for her post-college celebration, she wanted to find a way to put the kibosh on those plans.

Her ace-in-the-hole? The sweet, persuasive voice of the lovely Kaitlyn. It was a lofty challenge, but with her charm and entrancing smile, she could convince anyone to do anything she asked.

Endearingly batting her eyes and smiling bright, she nicely said, "So, Dale, I hear you hired a piano man again for Alexa's graduation party."

Suddenly perking up, Dale gleefully responded with a glint in his eyes, "Oh yeahhh. I've been friends with him for years. He's great!"

The man sounded proud of his accomplishment. He came through for his daughter, at least in his mind. Sensing the proudness and excitement in his voice, and knowing the disappointment he would feel to be told that his party planning endeavors had fallen miserably short, Kait decided to raise the white flag before the manipulation ever began. She couldn't break his heart. So, instead of crushing the man's dreams, she decided to positively reinforce his decision, sparing his fragile ego.

"Oh yeah! That sounds gooood! I'm sure it'll be a great time," she replied, strategically matching the glint in his eye.

Lex's plan had been aborted. When I looked over at her, she was staring blankly at her cousin, as if to sarcastically say, "Nice effort, Kait......"

For the remainder of the morning we continued talking, laughing, and shoveling flapjacks and greasy bacon into our mouths before eventually leaving the diner. Breakfast was great! Nothing seemed out of the ordinary.

Just as we exited, the sun had decided to take refuge behind the smoky rain clouds, and sprinkles began descending upon us, quickly increasing in number. Trying to avoid the wetness, we jogged to Lex's car, giggling along the way.

"Shotgun," I yelled. I really didn't want to be in the front, I just said it to be childish. But when I saw Kaitlyn already jumping into the back behind Lex, I didn't say anything and hopped into the passenger seat.

On our way back to Lex's, we talked and joked as usual. Like the immature kids that we were, the topic of farts came up, and I made a backhanded comment about Lex's flatulent tendencies. Expecting Kait to laugh or add a witty remark as she typically did, I glanced back at her to see what she had to say. To my surprise, she was silent. In fact, she had no reaction at all as she calmly stared out the window, completely removed from the conversation. *Hmmm. Did my comment offend her? Is she mad for some reason? Maybe she's just enjoying the peace and isn't really paying attention to what we are saying?* Returning my gaze to the front of the vehicle, I tried not to put too much thought into it. She was likely just relaxing, at least in my mind.

Throughout the remainder of the drive, Kaitlyn didn't speak a word. And when we finally pulled into the garage, I looked back at her and asked, "Are you okay, sweetie?"

"Yeah, I'm just not feeling so good."

"Okay," I replied, accepting her answer as it made sense since we just had a heavy brunch.

We exited the car. "I think I need to lie down or something," Kait said in a quiet voice.

"Oh you're not feeling well? Yeah, just rest before you guys leave," Lex replied.

We entered the house. I walked into the kitchen to set my things on the counter. Out of the corner of my eye I saw Kaitlyn head toward the bathroom. Lex followed.

After sending a quick text message, I closed my phone and approached the living room. No one was present. So I made my way toward the bathroom to see how Kait was doing. I passed Alexa in the hallway as she exited.

Upon entering the bathroom, I immediately noticed Kaitlyn standing about three feet from the toilet, calmly gazing at the floor beneath her. Concerned, I asked, "What's up, sweetie?"

Her voice was soft, monotone. "I don't know…..," she said as she continued staring at the ground. Just blankly staring.

I began rubbing her back. "Do you not feel well?"

"Nooo…..."

At that moment, she lifted her head and stared forward. She then slowly turned her head and eerily looked right at me. The look on her face was frightening. It was as though a stranger was staring at me. The confusion. The disorientation in her gaze. She wasn't there. Her eyes, they had an unusual glaze to them, and her pupils were dilated. I started to grow nervous.

"Something's not right…..," she emotionlessly continued.

The palpitations in my chest grew louder by the second. "What's not right sweetheart?"

Staring blankly forward, she did not immediately respond, and I became increasingly concerned. I didn't know what to think.

"I can't stop thinking of him…..."

What?!? I was taken aback by her response. "Who, Kait? Who can't you stop thinking of?"

"The old man…..."

Every single hair on my body immediately stood up. A shockwave of chills was sent pulsating down my spine. Suddenly, I felt scared. For

Kaitlyn. "Lex! You wanna come in here?!"

Lex's degree was in the medical field, so I figured she might have a better idea of what was happening.

Alexa quickly entered the bathroom. "What's the matter?"

"I don't know, something's not right here. She's not making much sense."

"Kait, what's up," Lex asked.

As time quickly passed, the glazed look in Kait's eyes increased. The words she was saying were making less and less sense, and her nausea was becoming more intense. Feeling like she was going to vomit, she sat down in front of the toilet. Uncle Dale entered the scene.

"Kait, what's wrong, honey," he asked.

"I don't feel well….," she replied, staring blankly in front of her.

"Hmm, maybe that coffee was a bit strong. It did have a lot of sugar and caffeine."

"I think she's about to have a seizure, dad," Alexa worriedly exclaimed.

"Should we call an ambulance," I asked, not knowing what to do.

Alexa returned her attention to Kait, trying to evaluate her to make a decision on how we should proceed. Dale turned his focus to me. "I don't know, I'm sure it's just that damn coffee that's making her feel this way."

It was a valid thought, indeed, but in the back of my mind I had suspected what was happening, and it had nothing to do with coffee. Scrunching my eyes and pursing my lips, I gave him a concerned look and said, "Dale, I don't think it's the drink……" As my breathing accelerated, I then lifted my left arm and tapped the top of my head with my index finger. "I think it's in her brain……..the cancer." My worst fear…….

"Dad, we need to call an ambulance! She's GOING to have a seizure!"

"I'll grab my phone," I said.

"Maybe we should get her up and just drive her to the hospital," Dale suggested.

Hastily skimming our options, we decided to get Kait into the car and transport her to the nearest medical facility.

"Okay, Kait, we're gonna get you up and take you to the hospital, okayyy," Lex told her.

"I don't want to go. I don't feel good."

Lex and I slowly helped Kait up from the floor where she was seated. "I'm sorry, sweetie, but we gotta get you to the hospital."

Kaitlyn was on her feet as Lex and I slowly walked her out. "I'll grab our stuff," I said, letting Dale replace me in keeping Kait steady.

I walked into the kitchen and grabbed my wallet and Kait's purse, just in case she needed it. When I came back out, Lex and Dale were already to the entrance of the garage. Trailing about ten feet behind, I watched them approach the passenger side of the car with Kait.

All of a sudden..... "DAD! She's SEIZING!!!"

Immediately, I felt a crack ripple through my heart. Time froze. In slow motion, I watched Kait's body sink to the floor as Dale held her in his arms, easing her to the ground. Likely preventing severe injury.

Kait began convulsing. Surrounded by metal objects and cement, Dale kept her body controlled. A constant, unsettling groan projected from her mouth. It was terrifying!

Shock consumed my body for about two seconds, which felt like two hours, but once I unfroze I immediately pulled out my cell and dialed 911. The phone began ringing. Rapidly pacing back and forth in the garage, I desperately awaited an answer.

"Oh my God, she's turning BLUE!"

My heart was already pounding violently, but after Lex uttered those words, I could feel it hammering through the walls of my chest.

A dispatcher finally answered. So as to deliver the information clearly and concisely, I forced myself to quickly regain my composure.

"Hello! My fiancé has cancer, she just had a seizure, and we need an ambulance right away!"

After giving the dispatcher our address, an ambulance was sent out, and we ended the call. I returned to Kait and was relieved to see her face had regained some color.

I then quickly called Kathy to notify her. When she answered the phone, they were literally just walking in the door after returning from vacation. As fast and as clearly as I could, I explained the situation.

"Ok, I'll call Mark and Vicky, and we'll come down immediately," she replied before we hung up.

I walked back to tend to Kait. Dale was still holding her upright as she was seated on the garage floor. Alexa was knelt down in front of her, assessing her as best she could. Her seizing had stopped, but her eyes were still positioned toward the back of her head. She was not conscious. My baby....

I was frantically looking around, back and forth, trying to figure out what I could do. But, there was nothing I could do. We were all so helpless.

Off in the distance I could hear sirens! I knew the ambulance might have difficulty finding Lex's place, so I ran a block or two to the end of the street to flag them down.

In the middle of the empty road, I paced back and forth. Waiting impatiently. Finally, after about 8 seconds, flashing lights entered my view and I began waving my arms. When it was clear they saw me, I ran back to Lex's, stood at the driveway, and continued waving my arms.

Hurry, hurry, hurry. Come on!

After the ambulance pulled into the driveway, the medics ran out and began assessing Kait.

"Okay, can you explain to me what happened," one of them asked as he turned to me.

I did my best to explain everything – what happened, her cancer situation, all of the relevant information I could think of.

"Thank you. Okay, can you tell me when her birthday is?"

Oh shit! "Uh, 10/28/88." In my panic I couldn't even remember her birthday. "Wait no! 10/29/88." *What the fuck is wrong with me?*

The EMTs swiftly secured Kait onto a stretcher and fastened her safely in the ambulance. As I jumped into the front seat of the medical vehicle, we took off.

Rushing to the hospital, millions of thoughts were speeding through my head. The girl I cared about more than anything in the world had just suffered a major, possibly life-altering, life-threatening event, and it killed me inside. I wanted to burst into tears. But as the EMT was talking to me, I used every ounce of mental strength I had to hold back my cries.

Ten minutes passed before we arrived at the Silver Cross hospital where Kait was wheeled inside and into a room to wait for a doctor. Her eyes were closed and she wasn't saying anything, but she wasn't completely unconscious.

Dale and Lex walked in shortly after. We were all very concerned and on edge, and we didn't know what to say. All we wanted were answers! "Maybe that coffee was just a little too strong. I don't know."

"DAD! IT WASN'T THE COFFEE!"

To break the tension, a doctor finally entered the room with his clipboard in hand, and we told him everything we could think of as he rapidly jotted down all of the pertinent information. Wanting to know what was happening in Kait's head, he ordered a CT scan right away, and Kaitlyn was wheeled out.

Tapping my feet, my fingers, my hands, everything while I sat despondently in a chair, the three of us waited anxiously. I couldn't calm my heartbeat. My adrenaline was still at a maximum and sitting still was impossible. Eventually, I got up and left the room. My innards were in a frenzy!

In the hallway, I slowly paced back and forth, trying to get my blood pressure under control. As I scanned the area, hoping to see Kait skipping through the doors, Lex and Dale joined me. We stood in a circle and talked. I could barely keep my emotions subdued, but somehow I managed.

A half hour later, Kaitlyn was wheeled back into the room, and the doctor followed behind. He began explaining the cause of Kait's seizure - a hemorrhage within the left side of her skull. "It looks like she has some lesions in her brain…..I'm sorry," he said.

I was confused. I didn't know what "lesions" were at the time. I needed clarification.

"Cancer???"

"I'm afraid so….," he delicately replied. My face transitioned from concern to dejection.

Shortly after, the doctor left the room. For a moment, I could only stare forward as blood rushed to my head. My worst fears had been realized, causing partial shock and dizziness. The cancer had moved to her brain……

With that revelation, all hope seemed lost. Recovery, almost insurmountable. Once a cancer metastasizes to one's brain, it becomes extremely difficult to treat because our Blood-Brain Barrier blocks most treatments from entering. Our situation suddenly went from bad to dire, and I was crushed. I was angry. I was sad. *Why couldn't we catch a break? Why must we hit one barrier after another?*

I walked over and stood quietly by Kaitlyn's side as she laid motionless in her hospital bed. I couldn't take my eyes off her. She was so beautiful. I wanted so badly to have the power to absorb her sickness. Unshackle her from the suffocating constraints of her cancer.

When Kathy finally arrived with Tom, she walked directly to Kait. Staring at her daughter, she began petting Kait's head as she tried to talk to her. The thought of delivering the terrible news to the unsuspecting mother was strangling me. The pressure in my head from my built up emotions was ready to explode. I had to step out.

Kathy followed. She needed to know what was going on. With my back to her as I walked through the hallways, I could feel her presence as she approached me. At that moment, I could no longer hold back my tears. They began pouring out from my eyes. As I covered my face with my hand to hide from the world, Kathy came and hugged me.

"It's bad....... It's really bad....," I whimpered.

Kathy continued to hug me as the water from my eyes flowed unabated.

"It's moved to her brain."

She took a deep breath as I revealed the new finding, knowing we were now facing another major roadblock. But she wasn't fully aware of the severity of it all, not yet at least.

Worried about sullying her shoulder with tears, I briefly pulled away to wipe the moisture from my face. Kathy was doing her best to console me, and eventually I was able to get my emotions under control, temporarily. I took one long inhale before having to take the next dreaded step - notifying my folks.

"I better go let my parents know what's going on."

"That would be a good idea," Kathy replied.

I stepped outside of the hospital and pulled out my cell phone to dial home. At that moment in time, they were preparing to leave for a wedding reception.

The phone rang. I took one last gulp of air, trying to bury my emotions deep within my diaphragm. I was ready.

My mom answered.

"Hello?"

"Mom....??" I burst into tears, immediately. But I didn't want her to hear me crying, so I pulled the phone away from my mouth.

"Trav!?!"

As hard as I tried, I couldn't restrain my emotions. I could barely even speak. Finally, I swallowed hard and muttered, "It's Kait......"

"Trav what's wrong?!? What happened?"

I could hear the panic in her voice. I tried desperately to get my composure back so I could speak clearly, knowing that every second I made her wait for an answer was torture.

"Kait had a seizure. She was taken by ambulance to the hospital. And, her cancer has moved to her brain."

My mom began sobbing. "Ohh Trav....oh nooo...."

As a nurse, she was well aware of the seriousness of the situation. "What hospital are you at? I'm going to come down."

"She's going to be transferred to Loyola in Chicago. I don't know when but it'll be sometime soon."

We didn't talk long. After ending the call, I cried for another few minutes before rejoining Kait's family.

Back inside the hospital, Mark and Vicky had finally arrived. Everyone was gathered in a small conference room after just having been briefed on the results of Kait's CT scan. They were all quiet. "Take a seat, Trav," Tom said as Mark and Vicky left the room to go check on Kait.

"Huh?" Sound entering my ears was muffled.

"Why don't you take a seat?"

Nodding my head, I slowly sat down at the table, across from Tom and Kathy. "The doctor told us that there are five tumors inside Kait's head," he informed me.

With reddened eyes, I stared blankly at the table in front of me, slowly shaking my head. I wanted to cry, but my tears were all dried up for the moment. The only response that came to mind was, "This fucking thing...."

They agreed.

We three sat in silence for a few minutes as I tried to breathe and calm myself. Numbness was already setting in.

Back in Kait's room, she was mostly out of it, mainly responding to pain. Because her head was throbbing, a nurse came in and administered morphine intravenously. As the nurse pressed down on the syringe to deliver the liquid into Kait's system, a burning sensation could be felt at the entry point of her tiny veins, and she began wailing in pain. It was excruciating for her, and all her dad and I could do was stand there and watch. We were powerless.

Toward mid-afternoon, an ambulance was ordered to transport Kait to the Loyola Medical Center in Chicago, but we had to wait for a vacancy first. Trying to plan ahead, with all of our belongings back at Uncle Dale's house, we decided it would be wise to leave then to collect it all, agreeing to meet everyone in Chicago. So, Lex and I took off.

On the car ride back to the house, my emotions were constantly spilling over. Every word I spoke about Kait caused me to burst into tears. I just couldn't believe what we were facing. Everything I had known, everything I had come to love was likely changed FOREVER. The "simpler" life we had just hours earlier had vanished, never to return. It was a difficult notion for me to grasp, and I didn't want to accept it.

As Lex and I crawled through the bumper-to-bumper Chicago traffic on our way to Loyola, I feared for Kait as she was being transported by ambulance. I worried that the constant braking and accelerating would rattle her brain and cause further bleeding. Luckily, I was wrong.

We arrived to Loyola while Kait was still in transit, so we were placed in a small room to await her arrival. Finally able to sit back and collect my bearings, my reflections on the day left me stunned as I tried piecing everything together. My mind was manufacturing an assembly line of thoughts, producing the same cycle of tormenting images over and over and over again.

After about a half hour of recycled thoughts, Kait had finally arrived. Providing a bit of levity to an otherwise despairing situation, Kathy informed us that Kait vomited in the ambulance, which is normally not funny at all, but the fact that Kait was actually awake and calmly warned the EMTs beforehand made me smile for some reason. Maybe I was just relieved that she was actually conscious. Maybe it was the comical way Kathy described the scene. I don't know.

Once the medical personnel secured Kait into her room, we were finally allowed to visit with her. I knew she was awake, but I didn't know what to expect from the aftermath of her seizure. Nevertheless, she was alive! And I was ecstatic to see her.

When we first walked into her room, she was sitting upright in her bed, which was a wonderful sight for my sore eyes. We all immediately greeted her with hugs and kisses. However, when we tried speaking with her, we quickly learned how extensive the damage in her head was, and whether it was temporary or permanent was yet to be known. The hemorrhaging in the left temporal lobe of her brain caused her to experience a form of aphasia, where the words she was thinking in her head were not the words being projected from her mouth. For the time being, she was unable to effectively communicate with us. Her sentences were jumbled together, and she used the same few words to describe multiple things. Her voice was soft, and it was missing its usual vibrancy, understandably, but it was the sweetest voice I had ever heard. She was far from "herself," but she was still Kait, nevertheless.

When she looked at us, I recognized that same glazed-over, out-of-focus look in her eyes that I saw when she was standing in Lex's bathroom right before her seizure, like her consciousness was not completely present. And, in a way, she had sort of reverted to a more childlike mindset for the time being, simple and mostly oblivious. Oddly, though, she had moments of almost complete clarity, as though her mind would temporarily snap back to normal and she would talk to us in a completely coherent manner, clearly describing what she had experienced right before her seizure. At those moments everyone thought she was turning a corner, but shortly after she would fall back into her somewhat bewildered state of mind. That let me know that the 100% Kaitlyn was still in there, but mainly dormant for the time being.

As difficult as it was to see my beautiful gal incapacitated, I felt grateful that she WAS still with us and there WAS still hope for recovery, no matter what any medical professional told us. And, I must say, she was as adorable as ever with her innocence and her soft, sweet voice. I just wanted to squeeze her. I just wanted to hold her and rest my head on top of hers and never let go. I just wanted to let her know that she was going to be okay.

A couple hours later my mom arrived, accompanied by my brother, Nathan, and my grandparents. As much as I didn't want them to see me in such a vulnerable state, it was nice having some familiar faces around. Older brothers have a harder time letting their guard down, but I had to accept the fact that I didn't have a choice in our particular situation.

After explaining all of the details to my family, a priest stopped in to offer prayer for Kaitlyn. I was not much of a "believer" myself, but I thought it couldn't hurt. And, it's not that I didn't believe in God, but my logical brain had a hard time making sense of an imaginary, all-powerful entity. Sometimes I believed. Sometimes I wasn't sure, and I would doubt the plausibility of it all. So, when the priest came in, I didn't think his presence would accomplish much, but I knew for Kait and our families, they would appreciate and be comforted by him.

We all gathered around Kait's bed as she laid there, half awake. When she saw the priest walk in, a soft smile appeared on her face. She recognized that this man preached the word of the Lord, and that made her happy. With her gentle, sweet, sweet voice, Kait greeted him with a, "Hiiii!"

"Hello, Kaitlyn," he compassionately greeted her back. "Is it okay if we say a little prayer?"

Kait slowly nodded her head, "Mmhmm."

"Okay, let's all join hands. We're going to say the 'Our Father'."

Just as we were about to begin the prayer, with her eyes closed, Kaitlyn gently, weakly lifted her forearms up and folded her hands together near her chest. My heart and everyone else's heart collectively melted from Kait's adorable, yet simple action. She was so cute!

We all began praying together as Kaitlyn, with her eyes closed, did her best to listen.

After finishing the 'Our Father' prayer, we all said "amen" and performed the sign of the cross. With cords and IVs hanging from her right arm, Kait slowly lifted it up and touched her forehead, then her heart, and then both shoulders. Her simple gesture put a smile on all of our faces. I couldn't stop staring at her, mesmerized by how perfect she was!

That night, we were informed that family and visitors were not allowed to sleep in the same room as the patients, which I thought was rather silly. A part of me worried that Kaitlyn would wake up and, upon realizing she was alone in a dark room, have a panic attack that would stimulate her brain too much and cause more hemorrhaging. In order to be able to frequently check up on her and also get some sort of sleep, Lex decided to stay with me so we could tradeoff between sleeping in the waiting room and sitting with Kait.

The small private room we were allowed to stay in had no beds or cots, only chairs, but they were padded chairs, so they were at least somewhat comfortable. Being creative, we each put two chairs together and laid across them, and I was able to doze off here and there, probably totaling a half hour of sleep for the night. Of course, we were much better off than Kait, so I wasn't about to complain.

Morning seemed to arrive before night even ended, and at about 5 AM, I headed into Kait's room and stayed there until she woke up.

At around 7 AM, a group of doctors and fellows and residents and other "doctors-in-training" entered the room. Every morning it was their duty to evaluate each patient and run certain tests. With Kait, they asked her to perform simple motions, like lifting her arms up, pressing her feet against their hands, raising her legs, etc. Unfortunately, she had difficulty understanding what the doctors were asking of her, so I would repeat their orders. And for some reason, when the instructions came from my mouth, she was better able to comprehend them. With the massive blood clot in her head, much of the movement on her right side was inhibited since the obstruction was in the left portion of her brain, and she had difficulty performing many of the actions being asked of her.

After the physical evaluation, the doctor began asking her simple questions, like "what day is it?", and "where are we?", but Kaitlyn was unable to answer his questions correctly. Then again, technically her answer of, "Here," was correct when asked where we were, which gave me a healthy chuckle. Overall, Kait showed some signs of cognitive improvement from her previous day, but not much.

Before finishing the testing session, the doctor pointed at me and asked Kait, "Do you know that guy's name right there?"

Kaitlyn looked at me, paused for a short moment, and said, "Brian."

The doctor looked to me for confirmation, "Is that right?"

I shook my head. Of course I was not disappointed one bit. I didn't expect her to be able to say my name.

Eventually, the head doctor entered the room. And, well, to put it bluntly, I thought he was a real jackass. I immediately got the feeling that he perceived the Loyola patients as numbers rather than as humans. As he spoke (shouted, really) toward Kait as if she was an alien, his voice severely lacked compassion. Then, he asked similar questions to Kait as the previous doctor, and when he completed his evaluation, he turned to me and disingenuously offered his condolences about the tumors in her brain. I sensed very little sincerity. Curious about his interpretations of her scans, I asked, "Do you know how many there are?"

With almost a smirk on his face, he looked at me and said, "5 or more." I don't know, maybe that was his way of becoming numb to all of the tragedies he witnessed on a daily basis, but to me his attitude was unacceptable. Or, maybe I was just extra sensitive given everything that had taken place in the previous 24 hours. I don't know. I think he was just an asshole, plain and simple. Even when he left the room, I could overhear him arrogantly chastising his students simply in an attempt to remind them that he was in charge, that he was the one in power.

I did not like that man.

For the rest of the morning, I held Kait's hand, rubbed her arms, stroked her hair, kissed her cheeks, her forehead, her lips, until her family arrived. Though she was far from complete health, I felt great satisfaction in knowing that I was still able to sit right next to her, still able to hear her voice, and still able to feel her breathing. And she may have had difficulty responding to me, but I felt like I could sense just about every word she wanted to say, and in my head we were communicating clearly. Maybe I was going crazy.

Once everyone returned to the hospital, I decided to head to the hotel my mom booked in order to rest since I was running on no sleep. To keep from dozing off, I drove with the windows down and my rock music blaring, but traces of adrenaline were still flowing in my body so I had no trouble staying awake.

When I arrived at the hotel, my brother and mother were there to let me in the room. It didn't take long before Nathan said, "Trav, I think I might have found something that can help Kait."

"Oh yeah?" My eyes felt heavy.

"Yeah, it was weird. I had this dream last night that I was researching the Internet and found a website that could help. So, then, when I woke up this morning I started researching and found a website that looked just like the one in my dream."

I was intrigued. "Hmm....go on. What's it about?"

"It's this stuff called Hemp Oil. I've been doing my research and it looks like a lot of people have been helped by it. There's this guy, Rick Simpson, he's kind of the main person in all of it."

"Hemp oil? You mean, like, Marijuana?" No one in our family ever used the "drug," so I wasn't so receptive at first. "I don't know. I can't buy into it until I've done my own research. There are tons of scams out there."

My mom surprisingly intervened. "I think it's legit, Trav."

"Hmmm. Well, I'll have to look into it then." Was it possible that

Nathan received some sort of sign or premonition? Was it even possible for such supernatural things to occur? I didn't know, but it seemed unwise to ignore any potentially viable option, so I put it on the backburner until I had time to research myself.

A few minutes later, my family left for the hospital so I could rest, and I immediately threw myself onto the warm bed. As I stared up into the ceiling, I finally felt like I could let my guard down. With everyone present at the hospital, I was never able to shut my mind off and fall into an awakened coma like I wanted to. But, finally alone, I could do just that.

As I sat in the hotel room, every thought that ran through my mind caused emotional pain and heartache. My body was instinctively trying to find a way to cope with the elevated stress levels, and as a defense mechanism, I could feel my brain slowly being silenced by my subconscious. It wanted to go into eternal hibernation.

But, consciously, I knew I couldn't shut down. Not yet. Kaitlyn was still with us, and that meant I still had a job to do. My sole responsibility was to her, and I wasn't about to cower away as she faced the fight of her life. The stakes were higher than ever before, and the odds against her were increasing by the minute. She needed me, and I needed her. It was my fight, too. It was everyone's fight. Everyone was in it together, and no one was going to run. If only I could barter with her disease, I wished. Offer my body in exchange for hers. If only I could acquire every last one of those horrible cancer cells. I would be gratified. I would be so happy.

As much as I tried temporarily blanking my mind while I was in the sanctuary of the hotel room, the mass of thoughts and questions continued to bombard my brain. *What will our life be like now? Just 24 hours ago we were laughing and playing and talking about our future. Then, in the blink of an eye, our future might be gone. Will she ever recover her speech? Will she ever recover, period? Is this it? Is this the end now? How much time do we have remaining together?*

No, no, no. Stop it! She will beat this. A girl as pure as her, she deserves a second chance. Something good will happen. She has hundreds or thousands of people thinking and praying for her. A miracle will happen.

But, what if it doesn't? Should we move up the wedding? Yes, we probably should.

No, no, wait, we shouldn't. If I throw out the idea of moving up the wedding to Kait, she might think, 'why?' If we move up the wedding, it will indicate to her that I don't think she will survive. So, no, we can't move up the wedding. I don't want Kait

thinking that we're throwing in the towel. Plus, we need something to shoot for,
something to look forward to.

Coping with such a rapid and drastic change in our life was difficult
for me to accept. Tears came and went with my thoughts as I sank into the
hotel bed, and I had no control over them. I just felt so horrible for Kait.
She was so innocent. So sweet. So kind. All she wanted was to get
married, have children, and teach youngsters. That's it! Nothing
extravagant. And she worked so hard to set herself up to accomplish those
goals, doing everything the right way and never cutting corners. In my
opinion, she earned an opportunity to fulfill those goals. But with her very
way of life threatened, that opportunity was likely lost, and it was so sad. It
was so unfair. I felt like for all the people she picked up in her life when
they were down, she deserved a chance to be the one who was picked up
for once. It was only right.

Eventually, as the mattress and pillows engulfed my body, I was able
to doze off amid my bipolar thoughts. My mind needed the reprieve,
because I suspected the next few weeks or even months would be taxing, to
say the least.

15 LOYOLA

Over the course of the next two days, we watched Kait slowly regain some of her intellectual abilities. She had recovered to the point where she could spell out our names, but she had a hard time saying them. For instance, a nurse asked her, "What's that guy's name right there," and pointed to me.

Her response was, "I know his name is," and she began spelling it, "T-R-A-V-I-S, but I just can't say it." I smiled big. Even though I knew it was such a minor improvement in her overall recovery, I wanted to start jumping for joy on her bed.

And then when it came to her memory, it seemed some things she was able to remember, and some things escaped her. For instance, she mentioned multiple times during her stay at Loyola about the gifts she had purchased for her mother and stepmother to celebrate Mother's Day, inquiring whether or not they had opened them, yet. She also remembered that the melanoma walk at the Milwaukee Zoo was only a week away, and she was worried about missing it. A large group of our family and friends had signed up, and Kait planned on bringing sandwiches and drinks for everybody, something she had been looking forward to for weeks. Sadly, in light of the circumstances, it was unlikely she would be able to attend.

And, throughout all of the fuzziness, she still maintained her knack for making us laugh, whether she was trying to or not. Comedy was one of her natural gifts. Kait always made people laugh, and she never cared if it was with her or at her. When she tried to be funny, she was hilarious. When she wasn't trying to be funny, she was hilarious.

One afternoon at the Loyola hospital, Uncle Dale walked in with a surprise for Kait – a bag of homemade chocolate chip cookies. Her favorite. Throughout our relationship, Kait had expressed to me multiple times her affinity for the tasty treat, even saying, "I don't know if I could go a day without eating a chocolate chip cookie." Chocolate in general, like most women I know, was something she always had a craving for.

When Dale entered the room with the bag of cookies, he intended to reach across Kait's bed and hand them to Kathy. Right as he lifted his hand above the mattress, Kait's eyes locked onto the bag. As the cookies were travelling across her line of vision, her eyes followed them every inch of the way and she passionately hummed, "Mmmmmmmmmmmmmmmm!!!" Everyone in the room started laughing. That was Kait in her truest form, and it was wonderful to see that her sweet tooth was still intact.

During her stay in Loyola, it became apparent her craving for junk food was in full force. The next day, her little brother, Benjamin, brought in a Hershey's chocolate bar and set it on the tray next to her bed. It was lunchtime, and the nurses were just bringing in some grilled cheese. But based on Kait's expression, she wasn't all too excited to eat the "normal" meal, as she sat back and said, "I don't want this….."

Reaching with her right arm over the lunch tray, she began weakly gesturing toward the candy bar that was only a couple feet from her grasp and gently asked, "What about that over there?"

She wanted the chocolate! As much as I knew her body required regular food, too, I couldn't help but smile and give in to her adorable demands. But, being the person of reason, Mark offered her a deal, "Kait, how about you eat some of this first," as he pointed to the grilled cheese, "…and then you can have some chocolate."

Looking up at us with those beautiful blue puppy dog eyes, Kait took a deep, cute breath and sighed, accepting her father's offer. As became the norm, my heart melted once again. I just couldn't get enough of her.

After two nights of being kept in Urgent Care, Kait was transferred to the neurological wing just down the hall on that Monday night. It was just her and me.

As we entered our new room, we quickly learned we would not be alone. On the other side of our room, behind a tall curtain, an older Mexican lady was staying with us, drawing Kait's ire. And I don't know how to explain it because I am not knowledgeable about the mechanics of the brain in its labyrinth of complexities, but in her irritation Kait instantly snapped into a heightened state of awareness, becoming more coherent than she'd been throughout the previous couple of days. I attributed that temporary shift to the adrenaline possibly causing the neurons in her brain to fire more rapidly. And, maybe her anger caused an increase in blood flow and oxygen to her brain. Who knows.

Anyway, upon seeing that we had a roommate, Kait went from barely speaking to vehemently arguing on my behalf with the medical staff. At first, she was quite concerned for MY well-being because with the room being so small, she was worried I would have nowhere to sleep. "No, no! This is unacceptable! We cannot stay here," she demanded. "Where is Travis supposed to sleep? There is no room!"

"Kait, it's okay, sweetie. I'll be okay."

"No. Honey, there is nowhere for you to sleep. You'll be miserable."

The nurses glanced at each other, not really sure what to do. I looked at them and assured them I would be all right, and there was nothing to worry about. But for those nurses, it was a potentially contentious moment where one of their residents starts becoming hostile. While they tensed up, I was secretly elated on the inside. At that moment, Kait was speaking more clearly than she had since suffering her seizure. Even if her episode of clarity was only temporary, I was relieved to see it.

Trying to hold back my smile, I walked up to Kait, put my hands gently on the sides of her head and began petting her hair. "Sweetie, I promise you, I'll be okay."

Looking back at me, I could see the genuine concern in her face. She cared about her man and she wanted him to be comfortable.

Like I mentioned earlier, through her hemorrhage, most of the wonderful traits that made Kait who she was remained intact. However, one particular tool was absent for the time being, and it was that very particular tool, that filter stored in one's brain that keeps us from saying everything we are thinking. We, the family, quickly learned that if Kait had something on her mind, it would be said, and she was generally unaware if others around her would be offended or not. She didn't know. However, I must assure you, never once were her unfiltered words offensive or harmful in the least. I mean, it was Kaitlyn we were talking about - our sweet, innocent, harmless little girl. Plus, we understood the circumstances, so she certainly deserved a pass. If anything, her frankness was refreshing.

I can remember only one time when someone took offense to a comment that Kaitlyn uninhibitedly made during her recovery, and that was when Jessica's butt crack was showing above her pants, and Kaitlyn said, "Jess, your butt crack's showing." Jessica was embarrassed because some of her family were present at the time, and she didn't appreciate it. I laughed hysterically over the incident.

Anyway, during Kait's frustration, our elderly Hispanic roommate slowly shuffled her body to our side of the room. She intended to comfort Kait. Let her know she was not to be feared.

That poor woman. She had a large, stitched-up gash just above her forehead, and it was quite clear she had suffered some sort of traumatic event and had recently been through brain surgery. Maybe it was a lobotomy. Maybe it was a craniotomy. I didn't know. But I felt sympathetic toward her.

Intending to calm Kait down, the short, pudgy old woman stopped right in front of Kait and stood face-to-face with her. Looking on attentively, I prepared myself in case I had to spring into action to protect my girl. It wasn't that I thought the woman would do anything intentionally malicious, but she was obviously not all there mentally, and it was possible in my mind that she could fall over on Kait or do something accidental that would set back her recovery.

Facing Kaitlyn, the woman slowly raised her right hand and moved it toward Kait's head, heightening my alertness even more. What if she was one of those crazy Christians or spiritual people who recite a prayer and then slap the forehead of the recipient? In her fragile state, Kaitlyn couldn't afford any more trauma to the head, even if it was minor. With that, I tensed up and put one foot forward.

However, to my relief, the woman gently placed her hand on Kait, and with the few remaining teeth in her mouth, said a nice prayer. No harm. No foul. Kaitlyn thanked the woman for her kind gesture, and she returned to her quarters. I could exhale and relax.

With Kaitlyn finally at ease, I pulled up a chair into the 2.5-foot space between the wall and her bed. A cot wouldn't fit in the room, so I had to make do. Unfortunately, the chair was one of those small, old wooden ones that didn't have any padding on the backrest and sat at almost a 90-degree upright angle. Somehow, I had to find a comfortable angle to sleep

— an unlikely proposition. But I didn't care. It was small fries compared to our much, much bigger problem.

Preparing to shut down for the night, Kait was all tucked in and cozy in her bed. Not wanting to rest until I knew Kait was asleep, I sat quietly in my chair and waited. "I love you so much, sweetheart!"

"I love you, too, Travie." Kait's eyes were closed.

Suddenly, through the drawn curtain, the woman next to us began talking. I couldn't make out a single word she was saying, but she was definitely speaking to us. Not wanting to be rude, I responded to her attempt at conversation with simple "Oh yeahs" and "Uh huhs" and "Oh that's interestings". But, Kaitlyn was very tired and just wanted to sleep. After the woman finished talking, Kaitlyn interjected and said, "Okay, thank you, I think we're gonna go to bed now."

With that, the woman halted her words and the room fell comfortably silent. However, after only 30 seconds of tranquility, our silence was interrupted by the woman's second attempt at mumbled conversation. Slightly perturbed from having her rest disrupted the first time, Kait grew more annoyed. Once again, trying to be friendly, I continued to respond to the old woman even though I hadn't a clue what she was muttering.

"Travis just ignore her," Kait whispered to me before responding to the Mexican lady, "Okay, it's getting late....I think we're gonna go to bed now....good niiiight..."

I could sense the growing agitation in Kait's voice. I mean, it was 12:30 AM after all.

The lady adhered to Kait's request once more. But after only another 30 seconds of peace and quiet, the chatter started up again. At that point, in her adorable feistiness, Kait had had just about enough and just wanted to sleep. Because I'm a hopeless people-pleaser, I couldn't help but respond to the Hispanic woman even though I knew that she probably had no idea what was going on or what she was saying.

"Travis, just go to bed. Ignore her."

But I didn't listen to my wife-to-be, something most veteran husbands would agree is a regrettable mistake. Finally, fed up as the senseless banter continued, Kait decided to put her foot down, and with an elevated, loveable voice, demanded, "TRAVIS, I'm gonna tell you one more FUCKING time, GO TO BED!"

Immediately, the room fell into a permanent silence as I sat in my chair, wide-eyed and holding my hand over my mouth to keep from bursting into laughter. Never in my life had I witnessed a response from Kait like that, and I loved it. It was hilarious because it was completely out of character, and completely unexpected. Of course, the attitude was only brought on as a side effect from her seizure, so I took zero offense to it.

The Mexican woman conceded and didn't speak for the rest of the night. I guess she got the message. With a contained grin, I reached over and whispered, "Good night," and kissed my stubborn doll on the forehead.

"Good night, honey, I love you." Her tone had completely shifted back to normal.

"I love you, too, sweetheart."

After only a few minutes of peace, Kait fell comfortably asleep.

Me on the other hand, I couldn't get comfortable for the life of me. Even with a pillow to lean against, the thin wooden backrest dug into my neck with every single position I tried, eventually causing a shooting pain that traveled from my spine up into my head. After a couple hours of restlessness and discomfort, I started feeling nauseous. I desperately needed to lie down. So, though I felt terrible for doing it, I left Kait's room to go into our small private room just down the hall. Only intending to be gone for a brief period, I set my alarm for an hour later, hoping she would remain asleep the whole time.

In our private room, I laid out a couple thin blankets on the hard tile floor, and because no other position felt comfortable, I laid face down on a fluffless pillow. Even though gravity was pressing my ribcage into the solid surface, it was the most comfortable position I could find. But I was so tired I hardly cared. And eventually I fell asleep, awakening a half hour later to the shrill cries of the alarm on my phone. The short catnap felt great, though, as it put my neck back into alignment and nearly alleviated my headache.

After slipping on my shoes, I walked back to Kait's room to find she was still asleep. Phew. For the rest of the morning, I sat silently next to her, admiring how peacefully she was resting. How beautiful she was. All I could think about was how much I loved her and how much I loved being around her. We desperately needed a miracle. *Please, God, help us!*

With Tuesday upon us, it had been three full days since Kait suffered her seizure. Though her communication skills were still coming and going, she was making progress. Sometimes she would be more "out of it" and other times she would be more "with it." It came in unpredictable cycles.

When our families returned to the hospital that morning, I couldn't wait to report the events of the night. I began by telling them all about our Mexican roommate (she had been taken to therapy and wasn't present at the time) and how Kait was none too pleased. Because her comprehension had improved, Kait had an adorable, off-centered, bashful smirk the whole time I was telling the story. It was off-centered due to the hemorrhage in her brain temporarily paralyzing certain parts of her face. Anyway, when I got to the climax of the story where Kait delivered her sharp expletive, everyone in the room burst into laughter. It was so unlike Kait, but we loved it. We thought it was so cute and endearing.

That morning, my mom and brother decided it was time to head back home toward Madison. Trying to think with sound logic, we all figured it would be wise if I went home to try and work a couple days to save my sick leave. Since Kait was scheduled for transfer to our UW-Madison hospital the next day, I'd only be away from her for one night.

So, with that, I packed up my bags and prepared to leave, saying my farewells to the family. Then, ready to take off, I looked at Kait lying upright in her bed. I had to say goodbye for now. "Alright, honey......"

But as soon as I began to speak, her face tensed up and she began sobbing. It almost broke my heart. Everybody scurried out of the room to allow Kait and I to be alone for as many minutes as we needed.

Just the two of us, I wrapped my arms around her and rubbed the back of my index and middle fingers against her whimpering cheek. "Sweetheart, it's gonna be okay. I'm only going home for one night. Then tomorrow when you come back to Madison, I'll be there waiting for you. It'll only be one day."

Sniffling, with tears falling on her lap, she nodded her head. "Yeah... Okay."

"Plus, now someone else will get to hang out with you tonight, and you can watch your TV show." *Glee* was coming on that night. I rested my cheek on hers and gave her a big hug. "I love you so much, sweetheart!"

"I love you, too...."

"It'll be okay, I promise. Just one night, that's all."

A few minutes later, the family walked back in. I said my goodbyes once more and we took off. It was only going to be one day, but I was going to miss my sweet Kaitlyn every second we were apart.

Upon my return to Madison that afternoon, I decided to make up some of my lost hours and went into work. From 5:30 PM to 1:00 AM I focused on completing the menial tasks of my job, knowing my mind wouldn't be present through the duration of the evening. And if I was making mistakes, I wasn't about to catch them. All I could think about was Kaitlyn.

On Wednesday morning, while I packed my bag in preparation for Kait to arrive in Madison that afternoon, I received a call from Kathy as they were set to depart Loyola. Plans had shifted, unfortunately. Wanting to take all of the necessary precautions to ensure Kait's safety, an ambulance was scheduled to transport her to the UW hospital. She was still considered high risk and any of her brain tumors could begin hemorrhaging at any moment, so having trained professionals on board during the drive was the safest way to deliver her.

But, of course, when dealing with hospitals it seems like things can never go smoothly (I know, they're busy).

With everyone's bags packed, Kaitlyn was in her wheelchair, ready to go as the ambulance was waiting outside to chauffeur our beautiful, yet fragile little sweetheart. She was then escorted outside, exposed to the golden rays of sunlight for the first time in four days. But, just as they were about to enter the ambulance, a hospital official came out and abruptly halted them. They weren't going anywhere. Due to an apparent insurance snafu, it was decided that Kaitlyn's transfer to Madison would not be covered financially. To add insult to injury, Kaitlyn had to be wheeled back into the dingy, dirty Loyola facility to be kept indefinitely. The family disappointedly unpacked their bags.

I was furious upon receiving the information about the insurance flap. I thought it was complete BS and that it seemed cruel to tease a girl who had been through so much only to let her hopes down. Medical staff should have had their shit figured out way before the ambulance had even arrived.

At that point we were faced with a choice. We would either remain at the dysfunctional Loyola facility where the incompetent-seeming doctors decided just to let Kait's blood clot sit and dissolve naturally, or return to

Madison, a nice, organized, clean facility where you actually felt like you could trust the doctors. The answer seemed obvious. We had to get Kait to Madison.

After some deliberation, the family decided it would be best to stay in Chicago and allow one more night of recovery for Kait. Kathy and Tom would then transport her in the morning. Caution and safety could not be stressed enough, but I was ever anxious to see my girl.

Alone in my bed after just tucking myself in that Wednesday night, my heart began palpitating wildly, and I could feel the temperature in my body rise as beads of sweat formed just above my upper lip. With a strong, persistent pain in my right calf, my imagination was leading me to believe a blood clot was brewing. *I'm dying!* At least that's what I thought.

You see, earlier that evening, while eating a processed meal in my apartment with Kait gone and no one else around to encourage me to eat properly, I felt a small bump on my right calf. Because the protrusion above my muscle was soft and spongy, I ruled out cancer immediately. I knew that it was likely nothing to worry about, but nevertheless, a seed was planted in my mind.

With the gray twinkle of the pale moonlight blanketing my bed where I laid, that small seed of thought had mutated into a ghastly beast. It caused me to grow nervous, wondering if a blood clot was actually about to ensue, a blood clot that would ultimately exhume my spirit from my body. It seemed silly, but I had given that small seed all of the fuel it needed to blossom into the frightening thought it had become.

Over the previous many days, during our nightmarish ordeal, I tried desperately to speak with God. And as I said before, my religious and spiritual beliefs were always coming into question by the logical portion of my mind. I believed, yet I wasn't sure if I believed. The notion of God was easy to dismiss, because for most of my life it seemed I hadn't needed him. Ashamedly, I was one of those pseudo-Christians, only calling on our great Creator during times of need. Now, with Kait's life in the balance, I was turning to him for help.

Every day I prayed. *Please, God, help Kait. She loves you. She loves people. She's kind and caring to everyone that crosses her path. She deserves a second chance. Please, God! Help her!*

Was anybody listening? I hadn't a clue. I wasn't sure. Doubt had been cast in my mind. For days I was pleading with every deceased relative I knew of – my Grandpa, my Great-Grandma, my cousin Nicholas, Kait's Grandpa and Grandma. Everybody. I was hoping someone would hear my pleas. I was hoping someone would lend a divine hand.

Well, that Wednesday evening, after I devoured my processed meal, I felt more desperate and determined to reach God than I had been out of any of the days prior. In my apartment, I got on my knees, folded my hands together, and began to pray. *Please, God! Save my Kaitlyn. Please, God! Save her. Please, take me instead. Take my life and spare hers. Please, I will spend a thousand years in hell if I have to, as long as it means Kaitlyn can be allowed a full, fruitful life.*

With my enclosed fists pressed against my head, I continued to pray. *Please, God! Take me instead! Save Kaitlyn. Please, God! Let us trade places. Please! I beg you!*

So, that night as I laid nervous in my bed with thoughts of a fatal blood clot blocking my arteries, and considering my emphatic cries to the Lord just hours earlier, I wondered over and over again if He had listened. I actually wondered if I was going to die. As dumb as it seemed, the power of the mind can really take hold of one's sense of reason sometimes. It did at that moment as my thoughts snowballed into an avalanche of irrational stupidity. But those gestating thoughts caused my heart to flutter out of control as I became more nervous. I was scared of death, and I feared the potential pain that would come with it. I was apprehensive of the unknown.

However, after about 20 minutes, the pain in my leg completely vanished. My desired sacrifice had not become a reality, and I did not die. Eventually, I fell asleep, only to wake up the next day, partially disappointed.

But then I got to thinking. Which scenario would be worse? To die and leave Kaitlyn with the rest of her life to suffer my loss? Or, to have Kait pass away, leaving me to carry on without her? The more I pondered that question, I realized that if it came down to it and one of us HAD to go, it would seem wrong for me to choose to leave Kait behind, forcing her to live her life in emotional anguish. IF one of us HAD to go, I would rather be the one to stay on Earth and bear the pain.

Plus, Kait would never ever ever accept me sacrificing myself for her. As selfless as she was, she would take a bullet for me 1000 times out of

1000.

So, with that, I called off my offer to God. Instead, the miracle I began pleading for was merely one-way, only involving Kait. *Please, God! Save my girl!*

16 FAMILIAR SURROUNDINGS

That next morning, Thursday, I anxiously sat in a wheelchair just outside the UW entrance, waiting by the patient drop-off area as Tom pulled up in their blue minivan. Through the tinted windows, I could see Kait resting soundly, fastened securely in the backseat with pillows stacked all around her to buffer any bumps from the road. As the automatic van door slowly slid open, I greeted Kait with a smile, trying to contain my excitement so as to not whip anyone with my tail. "Hi, sweetheart! How are you?"

"Hi," she replied softly. The two-hour ride coupled with having to wake up early had left her tired and weary.

Dressed in her cute purple pajamas and a pink sweatshirt, we grabbed her arms and guided her gently into the wheelchair. Overjoyed to finally see her, I felt honored just being able to escort her through the hospital, sneaking in kisses on top of her head when I could.

We couldn't have been more relieved to finally be back in Madison with Kait where she belonged. We headed straight up to our room that had been waiting for us. Comparing everything side by side, UW blew Loyola out of the water. They were more organized, cleaner, more accommodating, and much more efficient.

Though Kait had made improvements with her speech and comprehension since I last saw her a couple days earlier, the large obstruction inside her head was still impairing her neurological abilities. She was still unable to recognize certain objects, or at least come up with the words for them, and she was only able to partially follow along when others were speaking. In terms of her overall cognizance, it seemed as though her awareness fluctuated throughout the day. Like in Loyola, sometimes she was almost fully aware and "present," and at other times her "presence" would be, more or less, absent.

Even though it was difficult seeing her plagued with her hopefully-temporary cognitive defects, we did our best to soak in every moment of her sweetness as we could. After all, it was unclear how many more moments we would have with her.

With everyone settled into the new room, Kait was able to relax and take a nap. She needed it!

A MESSAGE?. Later that afternoon, after Kaitlyn gradually woke up from her nap, I slowly helped her out of bed and guided her to the nearest chair; she was sick of lying down. And for the time being, it was just the two of us as the others left to grab food.

Still feeling groggy from her short snooze, Kaitlyn rubbed her eyes in silence as she tried to regain her senses, a task that took much more time and effort than normal due to her seizure. As I stood next to her, we did not speak. I didn't want to bog her mind with conversation, and besides, the peace of the room's natural ambience sufficed. I was there to serve, not pester.

But, as Kait sat silently in her chair, she suddenly hunched over and placed her hands on her forehead. Taking a deep breath, almost sighing, she began shaking her head as though she was disappointed, or even disgusted with herself for some reason. I was confused. Flexing my eyebrows, I tried figuring out what was going through Kait's mind, but I couldn't. Then she spoke.

"Ughhh. This isn't good….."

Even more confused, I stared at her with a bewildered look and asked, "What's not good, Kait?"

She did not immediately answer. Her breathing began to accelerate and she continued to shake her head. She sighed once more.

"This is NOT good………..I was SUPPOSED to die for you….!"

For a split-second, I stood motionless, in complete silence as chills instantly ran down my spine. I immediately attempted to interpret her words, and my first thought was - Near-Death Experience.

"What do you mean, Kait? Who told you that?"

"This is not good….," she repeated without answering my question.

"Kait, honey, what do you mean? Why do you feel that way?"

She didn't respond.

Feeling slightly light-headed, I took a step back, trying to decipher the meaning of her one statement. Thoughts were zooming through my mind of the endless possibilities.

Did Kait have an Out-of-Body experience or a Near-Death Experience? Did she meet someone on the other side? Jesus? A relative? If so, was she told she was supposed to die for me? Why? Why would she have to die for me? What about me is so significant? Was it to teach me a lesson? Was it because I lacked faith? Am I being punished? Did I do something wrong? If so, why does it have to be Kait? Why can't the message be delivered to me in an alternate way? Or, is there an even greater purpose for her having to die for me? What possibly could that purpose be? Or, maybe there is nothing supernatural about her statement at all. Maybe she just feels bad for "putting me through this" and doesn't want me to have to suffer anymore at her expense. I just don't know.

I was beside myself. Without a clue of how to interpret her words. I should have asked her one more time to clarify her statement, but I didn't, leaving me to ponder the meaning of those seven words likely for the rest of my life.

And I didn't know it at the time, but that one statement would turn out to be the catalyst toward changing my perspective both spiritually and how I would view the world.

Shortly after retrieving my head as it floated toward the clouds, Kait's family returned, followed by our prospective neurosurgeon, Dr. Kuo. For the moment, I kept hidden what Kait said because I needed more time to digest her heavy words. Anyway, after introducing himself, Dr. Kuo laid out a few options for us to mull over. Basically, we could either wait and allow the blood clot in Kait's brain to dissipate naturally or we could elect brain surgery – a craniotomy to remove the hemorrhage.

We already knew that brain surgery always carries with it considerable risk, and Dr. Kuo cautioned us that a previous girl in a similar situation to Kait's (she had melanoma and was receiving Ipilimumab, too) actually passed away following her procedure. While I became light-headed once again with my knees almost buckling from under me (Mark experienced the same thing), Kait remained generally unfazed. "Will it fix it," she asked.

"Well, we would go in and evacuate the blood clot and maybe some of the tumor and then go from there."

"Oh…..but will it fix it," she repeated.

Dr. Kuo seemed to grow irritated at the fact that Kait asked the same question twice, somehow unaware that Kait's current mental condition left her unable to process thoughts fully. "Wellllll, that's what we're trying to figure out," he replied in a somewhat agitated manner.

"Hmm…..I just want it to be fixed," she said one last time.

With that, Dr. Kuo left the room, leaving us with much to discuss. Because Kait was not of sound mind with the large blockage in her head, we were tasked with having to make the weighty decision on her behalf. And unfortunately, it seemed as though we were in a "damned if we do, damned if we don't" situation.

That week, it felt like the bomb shells just kept on dropping, one after another. Emotionally, we couldn't catch a break. On Friday morning, Tom, Kathy, and I sat in the lounge area while Mark and Vicky kept Kait entertained; rather, she entertained them. As I sat emotionless in a rocking chair in the lounge in an attempt to rest my brain, I noticed Dr. Kuo approaching down the hall. I expected him to veer off into some patient's room, but he didn't. He headed straight for us.

"Can I speak with you all for a moment?"

"Certainly," I said.

"Tom, can you go grab Mark and Vicky quick," Kathy ordered.

Dr. Kuo led us to the empty coffee area within the lounge, signaling for us to take a seat at one of the small tables scattered about. Kathy and I complied as Tom hustled to the room to get Mark and Vicky.

As the remaining three joined us (leaving Kait alone briefly), Dr. Kuo took a seat in front of us. We assumed he was preparing to speak to us once again about surgery.

"Now, I just wanted to speak to you about the surgery and what to expect."

The small corner we were sitting in was isolated from other families in the lounge.

"As you know, melanoma is very difficult to treat once it has entered the blood stream."

I rested on my chair with the knuckle of my index finger placed below my nose, leaning my mouth against my hand as I stared at Dr. Kuo. I knew the severity of Kait's situation with the tumors spreading to her brain, but we hadn't seriously talked about it with a doctor, yet.

"Now that it has entered her brain.......it changes everything," he continued, "Even if we go in and do surgery.....and even if we do brain radiation.....we're talking months."

MONTHS?!?

Loud thuds could be heard as everyone's heart hit the floor. The crack in mine widened.

"Oh noOoOo...," Tom muttered with a shaky voice.

I could only stare forward. Paralyzed. I felt lifeless. I could feel my soul desperately trying to escape my body. My head felt like a balloon floating toward the ceiling. Mentally, I was flat-lining as my glossy eyes connected with Kuo's. Others began to cry. And the doctor continued.

"I mean, this is....cancer," he said, hoping his statement would help us accept Kait's tragic fate, "...and this is the final stage."

Looking back at me, Dr. Kuo could see the agony beneath my blank stare. After pausing for a few moments, he stood up. "...I'm sorry."

With that, he walked away.

All I could think about was my poor baby alone in her room, completely unaware of what laid ahead for her. Thoughts in my head were firing at will. I was crushed. Kaitlyn was my life. *This can't be happening. He can't be right. There's got to be something we can do. There's got to be some treatment out there that can help her.*

What happens if Kait finds out she only has a couple months to live? She would be devastated. She would no longer be able to live her last months happily. Death would constantly be looming over her head. She would essentially be living with a countdown in her head. She can't know.

My poor baby.......

As my breathing rapidly accelerated, tears began gushing from my eyes. I began bawling uncontrollably. Trying hard to suppress my cries, I felt like I was hyperventilating. My world was caving in on me.

Knowing Kait was all by herself in her room, I felt I needed to be with her. So, I attempted to squeeze every last bit of tears out of my eyes, preparing myself to enter her room with a smile on my face. I didn't want her to know we were crying. I didn't want her to suspect anything. So, standing outside of her room, I took a deep breath, gently wiped my eyes one last time, and entered.

"Hi, sweetheart," I exclaimed as she greeted me with a smile. Doing my best to pretend like nothing was wrong or out of the ordinary, I walked up to her and gave her a kiss.

Just minutes later, Kait's grandparents, Don and Phyllis arrived along with her aunt and uncle. It was the first time her grandpa and grandma were seeing her since her seizure, and I anticipated they'd be devastated by her debilitated state.

As they walked in, Kait smiled and said, "Hiiiii!"

At the sight of Kait, Don playfully stopped in his tracks, as though her beauty left him paralyzed and speechless, something he did often for levity. Kait smile! "Ohhhh, there's my beautiful, Kait!"

"Hey, Kaity," her grandma said as she entered the room.

Don walked up to me, shook my hand, and put his hand on my shoulder. "I hear you've been taking such good care of her."

Flattered and humbled, I replied, "Welllll, we've all been doing our best."

"Thank you!"

They both stood at the side of Kait's bed. Don held her hand while Phyllis rubbed her legs as she continued to smile. Watching their interaction made me feel so warm inside. I felt the stronghold on my emotions quickly weakening. The weight of our big secret about Kait's prognosis was pressing down on me; they had no idea they had a mere couple months left to spend with their beloved granddaughter. It was a thought that became more and more difficult for me to swallow.

"Ohh I just love seeing that smile," Don said, kissing Kait on the forehead. He was always the charmer.

I sat in my chair observing, smiling, and crying on the inside at how sweet, yet devastating that moment was. All that love being shared felt so temporary, like it would soon be coming to an end. My tears quickly built up inside.

"Oh Kaity, you look so good," Phyllis added.

Kait kept smiling. She always enjoyed their company.

Watching the endearing exchanges between the three, my emotions could no longer be contained as I felt them spilling over. I had to get out before they flooded the room.

"Hey, sweetie, I'm gonna step out for a bit, ok," I said hastily. The tears were right under my eyelids.

"Okay," she said.

I briskly walked out of the room, and as soon as I turned the corner into the hallway, I burst into tears yet again. My sadness for Kait and everyone who loved her was just too overpowering.

Covering my face with my arm as I walked slowly toward the lounge, I suddenly felt the arm of a stranger gently nestle around my shoulders. I glanced briefly out of the corner of my eye. It was Don. He followed me out of the room and accompanied me to the lounge, patting my back along the way, doing his best to comfort me. Of course he knew my sadness for Kait was profound, but he didn't realize at that moment the great source of my tears derived from her terrible prognosis - months. I wanted to tell him, but I couldn't. I feared the devastating news would potentially collapse his fragile heart.

Almost a year's worth of emotions had been storing up within me, and the result was this sobbing, watery baby I had become as I sat despondently in the lounge chair. I was sick of crying. But no matter how desperately I tried to wring all of the tears from my eyes, I just couldn't stop the constant outflow. The levees inside me had failed. I had never felt more sorry for someone in my life, and it was painful.

And to make matters worse, even in her mentally weakened state, Kaitlyn still had the sensibility to know she was "different" from her seizure.

Just a day earlier, sitting calmly in her bed, she said to me in her soft voice, "I'm broken..."

I was crushed. "Sweetie.....nooo.....you're not broken! Once you recover fully you'll be completely back to normal."

I didn't want her to feel so hopeless, but in her state of mind, the normally fiery Kaitlyn was dormant as she sat quietly; thinking.

"You should move on...."

My heart skipped a beat. I knew her intentions were well-meaning, selflessly trying to put my health and feelings above her own, but hearing the defeat in her voice as she realized she may be burdensome to me, it broke my heart. She felt like she was dragging me down.

"Nooo sweetheart....I'm not going anywhere. You're my girl and I love YOU!"

So, as I sat in the lounge with Don, I began crying again as I recalled her words. The thought of moving on to someone else, leaving her to fight her battle alone made my insides churn. Running was absolutely out of the question.

What Kait didn't realize, and what I told her family, was that she and I might as well have been married already. The one and only reason we decided to push the wedding further into the future was so she had time to fight her awful disease. But in my head, we were as husband and wife as we could be, minus the constant bickering and bitterness toward one another. The only thing we were missing to make it "official" was the phony piece of paper with scribbled ink.

And I didn't care if she never recovered 100%; even if I had to feed her for the rest of her days, I was committed. Forever. I wanted to be! Kaitlyn was the love of my life, and the most important person in my world. As much as she felt bad for "bringing me down," she didn't realize she was actually lifting me up, helping me strive to become a better person. Also, I knew with unwavering confidence that if roles were reversed, she would feel the exact same way.

I wasn't going anywhere.

As the day wore on, feelings of hope slowly replaced despair as the initial shock of Dr. Kuo's words faded away. Options were still on the table, and that meant a chance for long-term survival existed. Though the road to recovery seemed arduous, and the odds ever so slim, the white flag was staying in our pocket. Actually, that white flag was being sullied and burned; it was no longer an option.

That afternoon, while dragging her monitors with her, Kaitlyn slowly made her way out to the lounge to entertain us all. Even if she was merely 50 feet away from her room, she certainly enjoyed the change of scenery.

From the day of her seizure to where we were at that moment, Kait had made drastic improvements. Though her speech was still slow and her ability to listen and fully comprehend remained inhibited, she was able to participate in conversation much more than she could just six days earlier. It was so nice actually being able to talk with her.

"Um…did you open the gifts I got you," she asked, looking to Vicky and Kathy in reference to the Mother's Day gifts she had purchased.

"No, we haven't opened them, yet. We're going to wait until you're back home with us," Kathy replied. Mother's Day was almost a week in the past, but Kait would never forget.

As she calmly sat in her chair looking adorable in her glasses, enjoying everyone's company, I began gently rubbing her back. Over the previous week, I had completely forgotten to monitor her tumors like I had been doing before her seizure. I guess it no longer seemed important. But, since my hand was already combing the region on her back, I decided I would feel the larger tumor near her spine, just out of curiosity.

Using my index and middle fingers, I slowly grazed the middle of her back, trying to locate the tumor that was so prominent and easily detectable before; but I couldn't find it. Because it had been so long since I evaluated her bumps, I thought that maybe I had forgotten their exact locations, so I continued searching, intensifying my focus as I explored down her spine.

And then, I found it. To my absolute amazement, the tumor had significantly decreased in size! I couldn't believe it. Intrigued and with my excitement level increased, I began feeling around for her other tumors. First, I scanned the one on her neck. It was barely present! Then, the one under her armpit. It was roughly half its size from a week earlier! I was astounded! We were finally seeing results from her treatment. Kait's immune system, her T-cells, were finally starting to recognize those evil cancer cells.

Then I started thinking, because T-cells are able to cross the blood-brain barrier, it seemed logical that they could begin attacking the tumors in her head, too. Or, maybe they already were attacking them. Maybe that was what caused the hemorrhage in the first place, because the tumors were being attacked.

A rush of positivity began to percolate throughout my body as we were presented with a possible silver lining, a reason to hope. Or, maybe it was too little, too late. I couldn't know for sure, but I certainly felt compelled to tell Dr. Robertson. He had mentioned Kait's final dose of Ipilimumab was no longer needed since her brain tumors had developed, but I thought maybe he'd reconsider given the fact that it was actually starting to work. It was worth a shot!

In the meantime, after much deliberation, we elected to go with surgery to evacuate the blood clot from Kait's brain. The surgery was subsequently scheduled for the morning of Sunday, May 20th. Our hope was that by relieving the pressure in her head, she would recover faster, and it would increase the likelihood of regaining most of her normal functions. Of course, with the delicacy and complexity of the brain, we knew nothing was a sure thing.

With a plan in place, we weren't necessarily able to relax, but we were relieved of one less decision to stress over.

Over the prior couple months, Kaitlyn had a special book she would read often to herself. The book had a page for every single day of the year. If it were October 29th, one would read the particular excerpt for October 29th. Each page contained a summarized passage from the Bible. For the most part, the passages were positive and uplifting, and Kait found the book helpful and comforting while she managed her life-threatening disease.

At various points throughout our stay at UW, in between Kaitlyn stacking her chocolate chip cookies together and eating them like a sandwich, we would read passages from her book. We all took turns reading a page. When it was my turn, I tried reading slowly, putting extra emphasis and inflection on certain words to help her understand. Unfortunately, Kait admitted she had a difficult time understanding what we were reading, but just listening to the words helped put her at ease and made her feel warm. Kaitlyn's faith and trust in the Lord was much stronger than mine.

Aside from being transported from hospital to hospital, Kaitlyn hadn't been able to enjoy a moment in the sun for a whole week. So, on Saturday afternoon, exactly a week after her seizure, we assisted Kait into her wheelchair, dragging her monitors and IV bags along with, and led her outside atop a large rooftop balcony above the 5th floor.

It was beautiful outside with temperatures hovering around the mid- to upper-70s. Finally able to breathe in the fresh, crisp air, Kaitlyn was calm, serene, absorbing every bit of warm sunshine she could. She loved it.

"This is nice," she said, reiterating her sentiments more than once.

With everyone circled around her, helping her embrace this simple, yet wonderful moment, Kaitlyn seemed completely at peace as the gentle breeze calmly whistled past her skin, massaging her scalp as it ran through her hair. She closed her eyes, just listening to all of the life, all of the energy that was absent within the walls of the medical facility. She didn't want to leave.

Eventually, as we basked in the tranquil simplicity of the moment, Dr. Robertson joined us on the balcony, wanting to meet with his young patient before she went into surgery. He approached Kait and knelt down at the side of her wheelchair. As he prepared to address her, you could see the conviction in his eyes – he truly cared for her.

"Hi, Kaitlyn."

"Hi doctor, how are you?"

"I'm good, thank you. Now, I understand you all made the decision to go with surgery."

We all nodded.

"I think this is a good decision and puts us in a better position to treat this disease going forward." He paused. In a soft voice, trying not to sound overly assertive, he continued, "Now, now, from the beginning I always wanted to be as honest and open as possible with you, and with everyone. I don't feel like I'm doing anyone any good by not being honest."

As I observed Kaitlyn, she was staring forward, expressionless. I wondered to myself whether or not she was understanding anything Dr. Robertson was saying, keeping in mind her brain was still functioning at about half its normal capacity, maybe less. I assumed not.

Dr. Robertson looked to Kait as he spoke to her. "This is pretty serious. Now that this disease has traveled to the brain, it becomes much more difficult to treat. Even if we go through surgery and radiation, there is a chance that this...could end up taking your life."

I was hoping he wouldn't say that. I didn't want Kaitlyn to have to consciously hear those words, ever. I never wanted the notion of death to become a reality in her head, and by hearing it come from the mouth of a doctor, it made it all too real.

Looking at Kait, she still seemed unaffected by Dr. Robertson's words. I hoped it swooped right along the top of her head, never entering her ears.

"With that, I think it would be a good idea to do the surgery and radiation, and then we will devise a treatment plan from there, and there is a possibility we can achieve long-term results."

Suddenly, I could see tension developing in Kait's forehead. Her lips began to quiver. And at that point it was clear. She understood. Seemingly everything. Her future was bleak, and she knew it.

She began to sob.

"Why don't you just let me die.......?"

Immediately, the 10 or so of us closed in on her, trying to comfort her as tears streamed down her face. "Honey, no! With surgery and then radiation, we can still fix it," I implored.

"I know, but what's the difference if it's now or in a couple of months," she whimpered.

For the first time, it seemed, Kaitlyn was comprehending the severity of her situation and the likelihood of a future where she was no longer present.

Everyone gathered around her, nary a dry eye among us. Just sensing the utter dejection and hopelessness in her voice and in her facial expressions was probably the most heartbreaking, most soul-wrenching moment throughout our whole journey up to that point. My tears must have dried up from the previous few days, because somehow I didn't cry, but I was crushed. Seeing her endure such emotional struggle as she tried to grasp her situation, the pain was intense.

We all desperately assured her there was good reason to continue fighting. There were still options available. There was still reason to hope.

Dr. Robertson did his best to comfort Kait with us. At seemingly the proper moment, he left us be. As he was walking away, I followed behind.

"Hey, doctor, can I talk to you quick?"

"Sure."

"Well, when I was feeling her tumors the other day, I noticed that most of them had decreased significantly in size. It seems as though the Ipi just started working and her T-cells have been attacking her tumors. Do you think we can still get Kait in for her final dose?"

"That's good news, but at this point I'm much more worried about what's going on up here," he pointed to his head, "as opposed to her body."

"But, isn't there a chance that her T-cells could travel to her brain and attack those lesions up there?"

"Well, at this point, because she's been taking the steroids to reduce brain inflammation, the Ipilimumab would no longer be effective."

Shit!

Kait had been receiving Dexamethasone, an anti-inflammatory drug, since her seizure, which basically had been knocking down her immune system. So, all of the work the Ipi did to help build it up was likely being negated. *Dammit!*

I felt defeated.

We spoke for another minute or two before I left him on his way, and I returned to Kait.

Back on the balcony, the mood had completely changed to a more somber tone. Kait was no longer in positive spirits like when we first entered the sunny rooftop. Everyone continued to do what he or she could to lift her back up.

"Like I said Kait, it's going to be a long road, but you can do it. We just gotta take it one step at a time like we've been talking about," Mark explained, "Step 1 is surgery. Step 2 is radiation. After that, we decide what Step 3 is."

"That's right. There's still hope Kait. If anyone can do it, it's you."

"Yeah….," she replied softly, still despondent. For many moments, she stared off into the distance. "…….I think I want to go back inside…..."

Following Kait's request, we wheeled her back to her room.

I felt so helpless. I wanted so badly to be able to do something, but there was nothing I could do. I wanted so badly just to be able to magically place my hands on her body and expel the disease. Seeing her in such a sad state of mind and health, it was awful.

As a side thought, I became curious about how Kait knew she only had "months" left? I was curious why she mentioned "months" on the balcony? Dr. Robertson never gave any time frame. No one ever told her how much time she had left. Was she just making a wise, logical guess? Did someone tell her what Dr. Kuo told us? It made me wonder.

That night, with our emotions finally settled down, we all gathered around Kaitlyn as she sat up in her hospital bed, each one of us taking a turn reading a passage out of Kait's book in hopes that it would help ease her worries before going into surgery the next morning. In reality, however, we were the ones who needed our nerves calmed. The thought of that other poor girl who had passed away from the same procedure was lingering over our heads, making the possibility ever so real that our last night of seeing Kaitlyn awake may be upon us, and it was unsettling.

After everyone took a turn reading to Kait, they all said their goodbyes and took off to their sleeping quarters for the night, leaving her and I alone. Before drifting off to sleep, I sat awake with Kait and lightly talked with her for an hour. She seemed completely unshaken and comfortable with the idea of being put under the knife, and that made me feel confident.

17 CRANIOTOMY

Sunday, May 20th, 2012. Marching alongside Kait, Mark, Tom, Vicky, Kathy, and I accompanied her as a nurse wheeled her down to the surgery wing and into the prep room where we were to wait. Still groggy from just waking up, she was completely calm and unfazed with surgery on deck.

As we sat and talked with Kait, trying to squeeze out every last second we could with her, a nurse eventually came in and nicely told us it was time to go. So we all took turns hugging and kissing her and telling her how much we loved her before exiting the room. As we were walking out, I turned one last time and gazed at my precious girl. With a smile, I raised my hand and waved goodbye. Then, we left. In my mind, however, I wasn't nervous. I had a strong feeling she was going to be just fine.

Sitting in the lounge, we all waited impatiently.

Thoughts were zipping by my head at breakneck speeds. They were all over the place.

God please guide Kait through her surgery. Please guide her!

Wait, wait. Actually, you know what, God, maybe it would be best if you took her during this surgery. Maybe it would be best if it all ended now. If she passed away during the procedure, it would be peaceful. Being on the anesthetics, she wouldn't feel a thing. That way, she won't have to suffer through the heartbreak of knowing she may only have months to live. She won't have to suffer through brain radiation and losing her hair. She won't have to suffer through chemo and throwing up and feeling nauseous every day. She won't have to deal with the mental anguish of the possibility that all of her hopes and dreams may never be realized. She won't have to suffer through the potential physical pain if her cancer were to progress and the tumors in her body began to press up against her muscles and organs. By going now, she would never have to struggle through any of this. Yeah, God, if it is inevitable that this disease will eventually claim her, maybe today would be the best day for her to go.

Once again, a sequence of images began playing in my head of me standing at a podium, having to deliver a speech to a somber audience. What would I say as they all stared at me? *'Kaitlyn was the sweetest, most loveable girl I have ever met. In a world filled with selfish, "me first" behavior, her selflessness allowed her to stand out from the crowd. Never did she put herself before others. Kaitlyn was truly one of a kind. I believe she was an angel sent to earth, disguised as a human.'*

Wait, wait. No, no, no! Quit with this stupid negative attitude, Travis! She will make it through surgery! She will end up beating her cancer! And we will have a long life together, cherishing every single moment we have with each other because we would both know how close we came to being separated! I will get to brag about how my wife was months away from death, but through her strength and courage, she overcame the incredible odds and came all the way back and the cancer has now been gone for years! On our wedding day, before dinner I will get to hold up my glass and give a toast to the "strongest person I know", saying how proud I am of her, how happy she makes me, and how deeply in love with her I am! We will all proceed to give her a long standing ovation that will bring tears to everyone's eyes. When we're old and wrinkled, we will still be playing Tetris and Mario Kart together, telling our kids and grandkids about our connection to those ancient games. We have a lot to look forward to! We can't give up now! She has to survive this surgery! Please, God, guide Kaitlyn through this surgery!

My mind was a mess.

To interrupt my thoughts, we received a number of pictures and messages from a group of family and friends who attended the melanoma walk at the Milwaukee Zoo to honor Kait, our fallen angel. Since she was looking so forward to attending, we couldn't have been more thankful for their support as they represented her and our family.

Throughout the whole week, the support we received from everyone was absolutely wonderful. When the chips are down, you really begin to realize how great people can be.

While waiting in a rocking chair, suddenly I saw Mark walk nervously into the lounge. *Uh oh! Something happened.* I thought. "What's up Mark?"

"I just got off the phone with the nurse. She told us to come down!"

"But, did they say that she's out of surgery?"

"No, the nurse just said for us to come down."

Visions of a failed procedure danced in Mark's head, and it caused him great anxiety. His unease transferred over to the rest of us. But, for some reason, I felt little concern. My intuition kept telling me Kait's surgery was successful, which helped me remain calm and confident.

For the next 15 minutes we scrambled through the halls in search of Kait. We arrived at the site where we originally dropped her off only to find out the procedure had been performed in a completely different location. But we didn't know where. So we backtracked, asking whoever crossed our path for any information they could provide, but nobody seemed to know much. Mark's nervousness was morphing into a panic. Finally, as we were trekking through the halls, we just so happened to see Dr. Kuo walking by. Waving our hands, we got his attention and anxiously asked him how surgery went.

"The surgery went well. We were able to successfully remove the blood clot, and now she's in patient care in the neurology wing."

A huge weight was instantly lifted off of our shoulders as we all released a sigh of relief, and Mark's nerves were partially silenced.

"Thank you so much, doctor!" We were truly appreciative of his delicate work.

Even though Kaitlyn was successfully out of surgery, we still weren't out of the woods just yet. Excessive swelling in the brain during the recovery period is what caused the death of the previous girl, so the next 24 to 48 hours were crucial. We packed up Kait's belongings in her old room and made our way down to the neurology department.

Because the recovery wing housed high-risk patients, and because too much stimuli could potentially result in setbacks during the healing process, the area was dark and quiet, and only a couple visitors were allowed back at one time – a rule we broke once or twice.

Quietly, a few of us walked into Kait's room as she was just awakening, exhausted and in a ton of pain from just having her skin ripped open and her skull busted through. Thick white bandages wrapped tightly around her head, resembling a turban, and it caused her excessive irritation and a persistent, unreachable itch that nearly brought her to tears. She continuously tried scratching the hard, shell-like bandages, hoping to alleviate the awful discomfort, but scratching and clawing didn't work, so she would resort to tapping her head with the palm of her hand. Alarmed, we urged her to stop. Hitting her head was exactly something that could cause detrimental inflammation.

But much worse than the extreme irritation, was the pain, as indicated by her frequent, yet quiet whimpering and her tortured facial expressions. It was excruciating for her, at a constant "10 out of 10" during the early portion of the afternoon. Not even pain medication could reduce the immense throbbing as it persisted throughout the day.

My heart ached for my girl. I couldn't stop feeling sorry for her. All she had been through. All she had endured. It was unfathomable to me. And to think, her treacherous journey was only beginning. However, she was a tough little shit, much tougher than I, so I felt confident in her ability to persevere.

My parents showed up for a visit. Though she was tired and in unbearable discomfort, Kait still greeted them with a smile, doing her best to be hospitable as she always did. But rest was imperative for her, so my folks only visited for a short while before retreating to the waiting room (I followed), allowing her to convalesce in peace.

With my wheels spinning, I was convinced that practical solutions existed to remedy our cancer plague. As we sat with the rest of Kait's family just outside of the recovery wing, I bombarded my mom with medical questions, trying to educate myself as much as possible. I sat in my chair and began logically thinking through our situation.

Dr. Robertson concluded that the Ipilimumab didn't work. His explanation was that the brain tumors wouldn't have developed if it had. But I wasn't buying that argument. It had been stated to us over and over again that tumors would still grow in the early stages of treatment, and that it would likely take a couple months before we began to see results. I even read a story about a man who began receiving Ipi. While he was waiting for the treatment to begin attacking his cancer, tumors began growing in his brain, just like Kait. After his fourth and final treatment, he received brain scans, and the images revealed he had 19 brain tumors. Nineteen! They thought all hope was lost. But, about a month and a half after receiving his final dose, he went in for further scans in order to devise a next step. Miraculously, the images came back showing all 19 of his brain tumors had been obliterated. The treatment just needed more time. So, just because tumors began growing in Kait's brain, it didn't necessarily mean the Ipi was unsuccessful, especially considering the fact it was working within her body.

For all we knew, her T-cells could have already been working on her brain tumors. It was impossible to know because we never saw them at their maximum size. In my opinion, the treatment just needed more time. Unfortunately, time was limited, and no matter how hard I tried, we likely wouldn't be allowed to administer Kait's final dose. I had to move on, it seemed. Look ahead to other options. Plus, doctor said that the steroid she was receiving would negate the effects of Ipi anyway.

That night, as Kaitlyn slept, I wanted desperately to regain a semblance of control in our battle against cancer. So I made a decision. I decided I was going to do whatever it took to obtain as much knowledge about melanoma and cancer as I could. I wanted to become an expert on the subject. As much as I admired all of our doctors, especially Dr. Robertson, I did not fully believe or trust in their ability to alleviate Kait from her ailments. Doctors see many, many patients throughout the days and weeks, spending a small portion of time with each one. They don't have the luxury of becoming an expert on an individual's case, so the way I saw it (whether right or wrong) was they generally employ a one-size-fits-all approach to treating the cancer, which is inefficient and usually ineffective. Everyone's cancer is different, and everyone's body reacts differently to each method. I, however, had the luxury of devoting all of my time to one patient – Kaitlyn - and I could become an expert on her case. In my mind, there had to be a better solution out there for her. Simply following protocol and receiving a single treatment at a time, one after another, was not the answer. It rarely is. If it were the answer, then the mortality rate among melanoma sufferers wouldn't be so high. There had to be a better approach.

For Kaitlyn's case, I knew what Dr. Robertson's recommendation would be after she completed brain radiation – the newly approved drug called Zelboraf, which works for six months on average. But I wasn't satisfied with that single approach. Simply extending someone's life for six, seven, or eight months is not a victory in my eyes. It's a failure. There just had to be more effective strategies out there.

With that, I was bound and determined to find out everything I could about melanoma and all the treatment options in existence, both mainstream and alternative. I wanted to become completely dedicated. I wanted to expend as much energy as possible in reading medical literature to become as knowledgeable as I could on exactly how tumor cells interact, how different proteins send signals to other proteins, which ones are the messenger proteins, etc. I figured that would allow me to use common sense and logic to formulate effective treatment strategies. Unfortunately, I was aware of the one major aspect that was going to hold me back, and that was my lack of formal education. I knew that no matter how knowledgeable I'd become, no matter how good my strategies would sound, getting the right people to listen would likely prove futile. But for the love of my life, it was certainly worth the effort. I had to try.

As the bell tolled the midnight hour during our first night of recovery, Kaitlyn awoke, restless and in pain. Her medication had worn off, but thankfully her pain didn't rise above a level 7, which was still high, but tolerable compared to what she was initially experiencing. Because she could no longer sleep, I remained awake to keep her company until she felt tired again.

In the quiet of our room, I began talking to her, asking her questions. And when she responded to my initial inquiries, I immediately found out how much the surgery helped as her ability to speak and process thoughts had improved immensely. Evacuating the massive blockage in her head seemed to have an instant impact. When she spoke to me, her answers were no longer simple sentences consisting of few words. She was actually able to hold a full conversation, expressing thoughts and concerns that she hadn't been able to express since before her seizure. It was wonderful! I was beaming so brightly on the inside I just wanted to jump for joy atop her bed.

Being able to partake in coherent conversation with my girl for the first time in over a week, I took full advantage. Her voice was so soft. So sweet. And I could literally <u>feel</u> her following along and comprehending my every word - finally. I loved it! As I sat with her, stroking her arms, massaging her legs and feet, and staring into her heavenly blue eyes, I felt a week's worth of stress and worry instantly evaporate. And it was because of Kait. It was because she was awake, aware, and smiling. It was like she had been in prison for years and had finally returned to me. I felt so happy. I felt at peace. All of our problems seemed to vanish. Everything felt perfect, and it was because I had the privilege of being in her conscious presence. If only I could freeze time…

By Tuesday morning, the 48-hour window of risk had just about passed, and Kait's recovery was proceeding as expected. I was relieved and thankful! But we still had to be cautious, of course.

At around 6 AM, a dose of doctors entered our room to run their daily neurological tests on Kait to assess her progress. Weary-eyed and with the bandages still wound tightly around her head, Kait followed along as the doctor instructed her to perform a multitude of relatively simple tasks. He had her follow his finger with her eyes as he moved it up and down, and side to side. She passed. He put his hands on her feet and told her to push down, then pull up, making note of the increase in mobility and strength on her right side. He had her stick out her tongue. He had her smile. She passed. He held up various objects for her to name. He asked her what day it was and where we were. She passed! Everything! I was elated!

Moments later, Dr. Kuo came to evaluate his patient's progress. After doing much of the same tests as the previous doctor, he had one final hurdle for Kait to jump over. He pulled out his pen and held it in front of Kait. "Kaitlyn, can you tell me what this is?"

Every day during her stay at UW, Dr. Kuo would come in, perform his tests, and at the end he would always pull out his pen and ask Kait to name the object. On her first day at the Madison hospital, she couldn't find the word for it. On every subsequent day, her answer would simply be "a pencil," which was close, but not quite. The brain surgeon would then correct her and tell her it was a pen. But, with the blood clot removed from her brain, the ultimate test to assess her progress was being waved right in front of her face. After Dr. Kuo asked Kait to describe the object in his hand, she didn't hesitate.

"Well, you keep calling it a pen, but I call it a pencil."

Perfect! The surgeon and I both laughed. He considered her answer as a passing one. With that, Dr. Kuo decided Kaitlyn was well enough to be released from the hospital, possibly as early as 9 AM, which was great news! Woohoo! I quickly called her family to notify them, and they rushed to the hospital to prepare to head home! We were so excited!

As the doctors filed out of Kait's room, a nurse walked in carrying scissors. The bandages were coming off. My curiosity and imagination woke up my nerves as I prepared myself for what laid beneath the white gauze. I questioned my ability to stomach it at first sight.

The nurse started slowly unraveling the bandages around her head, revealing little by little the aftermath from surgery. With her head completely exposed, seeing the incision for the first time, I felt slightly uneasy, only for a second, though. I mainly felt bad for her. All of the hair on the left side of her head was shaved off. The incision started at the back of her neck and ran around her ear, toward the top of her head, before circling off and ending near her temple. It covered a large area, and it looked painful. Luckily, she still had enough hair atop her head to cover up the hairless region if she wanted to.

Shortly after having her bandages removed, Kait's family returned to the hospital. At first glance, seeing Kait's wounded head exposed for the first time was also a bit jarring for them. Like me, however, they quickly adjusted. Ultimately, we just felt so sorry for her. The large scar would serve as a constant reminder of why her life would likely never be the same. But she wasn't going to sit back and feel sorry for herself, so she wouldn't allow us to, either. All we could do was live in the moment and take advantage of the time we had left. And what was important at that moment was that Kait was still with us, and we were finally going home! It was something to be excited about as we packed our bags and waited for the discharge papers.

With our suitcases zipped, we sat and waited for our release. We were looking forward to leaving! But 9 AM quickly came and went, and we hadn't received any word on our discharge. Of course, we never really expected to leave at 9 AM, but we hoped. We had grown accustomed to lowering our expectations when it came to scheduled times at hospitals. Usually if someone says five minutes, that actually means five hours. We had to be patient.

The small hand on the clock slowly moved from 9 to 10, and then from 10 to 11. Still, no one had come by. Becoming anxious, Kait then made the assertion that we had been forgotten about.

"No, Kait. They didn't forget about us. They're probably just really busy. We just have to be patient," we said.

We certainly couldn't blame her impatience. If I were enclosed in a small living space for 11 straight days, my patience level would have been surpassed much sooner.

While we talked and kept each other company, time seemingly leaped from 11:30 to 12:30, missing all other minutes in between. And still, no word on our release. Kait's agitation slowly escalated. She just wanted to go home so badly.

"Someone needs to go ask the nurse when we can leave. I know they forgot about us."

"Well, next time she comes in we'll ask."

We ordered food for Kait, hoping to keep her distracted from the clock, and of course because she is a human and required sustenance. Just as Kait's meal had arrived, and just as I took the first bite of her cheeseburger to test for poison, a medical staff member walked into the room. Our hopes were uplifted. We were about to be released! Not... Unfortunately, the lady's job was only to give us a detailed explanation of all the medications being sent with Kait and how often they should be administered.

Upon entering, the nice woman took a seat right at the end of the bed, facing Kait with a clipboard in hand. Staring down at her papers, she started at the top of her list and began explaining to Kait all of the names of her medications and how to take them properly. Now, Kait's ability to comprehend things had improved immensely, but not to the point where she could understand complicated medical jargon, especially when the explainer was speaking at 1000 words per minute. Also thrown into the mix was the fact that Kait was famished and had a delicious cheeseburger sitting right in front of her. Needless to say, Kait didn't want to waste time listening to this lady, and she made it hilariously apparent.

With all of us in the room, the lady continued to explain to Kait all of the information attached to her clipboard. Not really listening because she was mentally unable to follow along, Kait looked at the woman and said, "I just want to eat."

Smiling, the woman replied, "Okay, I'll be done soon."

Kait's confusion and agitation grew with every sentence the woman spoke. The added commotion in the room due to other visitors checking on Kait made it simply too much for her mind to sort through. With her eyebrows cocked, she started shaking her head, indicating none of the information coming in was being retained or understood.

The lady continued. "Now, these pills here are the Dexamethasone, this is the Keppra. You want to take the Dexa when you wake up and at night, the Keppra...."

With multiple conversations going on at once, Kait was done trying to listen. Her mind was overwhelmed. Still shaking her head, Kait turned to me as I stood next to her, and with an adorably concerned, confused look, she said, "I don't know what she's saying and I don't know why she doesn't get that I just want to eat."

Those who heard Kait – mainly my brother (Tyler) and I - got a healthy chuckle from her comment. She meant no harm or offense by it, and I could sense the lady understood. Heeding Kait's blunt, yet innocent message, the woman smiled and conceded. "Okay, I will let you eat."

So, as the nice woman turned to Kathy to divulge the remaining information, Kait finally was allowed to dig into her cheeseburger. All became right. I put my arms around Kait's head, staying clear of her wound, and kissed her for being so cute.

After devouring the half of the burger she left for me, I glanced at the clock and couldn't believe it was almost 2 PM. Five hours had passed from our original estimated departure time. Finally, a nurse walked in. With the task of unhooking all of the cords, tubes, strings, etc. from Kait's body, we figured she was prepping us to leave. Phew!

As the nurse pulled the IV tube from the back of Kait's hand, blood began seeping aggressively from her veins. The sight of blood would normally cause Kait to feel faint, but in her indifferent state of mind she wasn't bothered in the slightest. Though, her dad had to turn his back away so he wouldn't keel over.

While trying to stop Kait's bleeding, the nurse politely informed us of our foolishness for believing we'd be able to leave after she was finished. We still had to wait for one more person to evaluate Kait and give us the discharge papers, apparently. Fortunately, she said that person should be by shortly.

With the bleeding stopped and the nurse gone, Kait's restlessness reached its peak. She had been anxiously waiting to leave the hospital for far too long and it was becoming too much. "I know they forgot about us. Someone needs to go ask."

"Don't worry Kait, that nurse said someone will be coming by shortly."

Continuing our exercise in patience, we waited, and waited, and then waited some more. It was almost 4 PM and nobody had stopped by. Kait once again asserted that we had been forgotten about, insisting we go ask somebody. Then, she gave us a warning that grabbed all of our attentions. "That's it! If no one shows up by 5, I'm gonna grab my stuff, walk out of here, and go wait in the van….and there's nothing you guys can do about it."

Everyone in the room tried desperately to hold in their laughter. Kathy had to turn her back. Her cuteness was too much to bear. Quenching my lips, fighting the urge to laugh, I replied, "Alright, sweetie, you're absolutely right. We will go ask someone."

Finally taking Kait seriously, Tom and I ventured off to find someone of knowledge. After asking around, our small quest led us to a man in a pink button-up shirt who agreed to help us.

"Oh I'm so sorry," the man said, "Somehow we must have forgotten all about you."

Sheepishly turning our heads to look at each other, Tom and I were thinking the same thing – Kait was right the whole damn time. They had actually forgotten about us. How could we be so blind, deaf, and dumb? All we had to do in the first place was ask.

At around 4:45 PM, the discharge papers were finally signed and we were FREE!!! Relief filled the air, and Kait couldn't wait to be back in the comfort of her own home.

As we exited the hospital, Kait closed her eyes and took one long inhale, breathing in the clean, fresh air. She was finally liberated! We knew the road ahead of us was still a long and treacherous one, but just being able to walk out of that hospital after having a brush with death was a victory in and of itself. A victory that could only be surpassed by a complete recovery from her cancer.

After throwing our bags into the van, we drove off, headed back to Kenosha.

That week and a half had been the longest of our lives. The 11 days felt like one continuous day crumpled together, leaving me unable at that moment to ascertain where one day ended and another began. And after everything, it was likely that Kait would never be the same. None of us would be.

Over the course of the almost two weeks, our emotions were pushed to their limits and well beyond, as though they were bound to a medieval torture rack. With every passing day, the executioner turned the wheel a little bit more, stretching our emotions further and further. It was agony, and it was painful, but we all made it through. And, to think, our suffering paled in comparison to what Kait was experiencing.

One thing was certain as we moved forward; no day would be taken for granted. No day would go to waste. The amount of time we had left together was completely unknown, and we were going to cherish every single minute we were given.

18 HOME SWEET HOME

Kaitlyn walked into her house for the first time in weeks. The moment was a touch euphoric. All the familiar smells. That familiar warm atmosphere. She was so happy to finally be....HOME! No more seclusion in a 10x10 foot room. No more hospital food. No more chaos. No more alarms and whistles going off in the middle of the night (scaring the crap out of me) due to her getting out of bed to go to the bathroom. Kaitlyn was free once again!

However elated she felt to be in the comfort of her wonderful home, her exhaustion pushed her to bed sooner than she would have liked. After a quick shower to wash all of the guck from surgery out of her hair, she nestled into her warm, cozy mattress. I followed.

Finally able to lie next to my girl, I put my arm around her, smothered her with love, and showered her with affection as she slowly faded off into the night. I was so happy! Having my life partner back, even if things were far from okay, my soul twinkled with bliss. My dulled aura emanated with colorful brilliance once again. Like in the hospital, I wanted so badly just to be able to freeze time. Sometimes, in my daydreaming and wishful thinking, I would imagine Kait and I lying in a large vat together. I would be holding her, and she would be holding me. Liquid gold would then begin pouring down on us, filling the tank until we were completely submerged. Eventually, it would harden, and we would be forever entwined. In a sense, we would be frozen in time.

Shortly after sinking into bed, Kaitlyn fell asleep, and I pulled out my computer to begin learning some more. I'd been digging deep over the previous couple of days, storing vast amounts of information within the library of my mind. And in just two days, I had already stumbled upon numerous alternatives, numerous clinical trials, and numerous articles to educate me about the workings of melanoma. There was so much to learn in so little time, and my research could only cease once Kait was cured. I knew the likelihood of me falling flat on my face was high, but I didn't care about the odds. I had to at least try. If I didn't, I would never forgive myself, always wondering "what if?" But I was confident that if I kept amassing knowledge, a logical, viable strategy would emerge.

For the first time in what seemed like an eternity, we both slept-in the next morning. After finally feeling adequately rested, it was time to start working our way up to the point where we could actually live life once again. To do that, we had to help ease Kait back to health while making sure she remained safe.

During my stay at her mother and stepfather's residence, my main responsibility was to shadow Kait's every move. With her mind still not functioning at full capacity, the chances of momentary disorientation and a subsequent fall remained relatively high. So, I was her watchdog. When she went up the stairs, I followed. When she napped, I napped. When she ate, I ate. When she burped, I burped. It was an effective excuse to constantly be by her side.

Every single day, Kait made drastic improvements with both her cognitive abilities and physical strength. With the help of a therapist, simple tasks like standing on one foot or walking backwards became easier during each session. And to keep her moving, get her blood flowing, and strengthen her muscles, we went on about three short walks on a daily basis, as recommended by her therapist.

One observation I made about Kait, and when I mentioned it to her, she noticed it, too, was that when she was outside walking, her mental abilities seemed to improve instantly. When we were inside the house, her ability to listen and speak was better than at the hospital, but nowhere near her normal abilities as certain things still confused her, and she was much quieter than she used to be. But on our walks, we were suddenly able to have full, snappy conversations. She would ramble away, she would tell jokes, she would laugh. It was as though she was returning to her old self. Then, as soon as we returned inside, her mind reverted back to its cloudy state where things weren't quite so clear. It boggled my mind. The simple answer, to me, was that the fresh oxygen and exercise increased blood flow, thereby increasing the activity in her brain allowing neurons and such to fire more efficiently. Or, maybe going for walks triggered a memory or a certain mindset, since walking is normally accompanied with conversation. I didn't know for sure, but I nevertheless found it fascinating how much she improved by simply being active. It made walks much more enjoyable.

During our first few walks, we kept the pace at a nice, leisurely speed, easing Kait back into physical activity. But as the week progressed, we picked up the pace with each walk, and by the end of the week, Kait was doing full power walks. She was focused and determined on exercising her way back to health and strength. And whenever Kait had her mind set on something, she would do it. Even when I would tell her to slow down a bit, she insisted we keep up the pace.

Her determination and newly acquired feistiness all culminated into one comical moment after I had left Kenosha to go back to work for a few days. With me gone, the torch was passed on to Kathy to accompany Kait on her walks. Needless to say, I'm in just a tiny bit better shape than she. But, that miniscule difference made all the difference.

One morning, as Kathy was working from home, preparing for a conference call, Kait insisted they go for a quick walk. With 25 minutes until the meeting commenced, Kathy thought "what the hell, I'll do it quick." So she told her colleagues she might be a bit tardy, and they took off. However, at that time, Kathy had yet to experience how fast and far Kait liked to walk. She was expecting a comfortable, leisurely pace just around the block. I guess I should have warned her.

The walk started out nice and slow, just as Kathy had hoped on that calm, beautiful morning. But then, as soon as they turned the corner, Kait was off. Her speed accelerated to that of "grueling mode," and Kathy struggled mightily to keep up. "Kait, slow down...!"

"Nope, mom. You gotta keep up," she replied, stubbornly.

Oh what the hell, they were just going around the block, Kathy could endure. At least, that's what she thought. The distance between the mother and daughter duo was quickly increasing, and soon Kait was 20 yards ahead. But instead of taking a right turn in order to make a circle around their block, Kait kept on walking straight – straight out of their subdivision. "KAIT!" Kathy yelled as she violently waddled to keep pace.

"We gotta go back!"

"Come on, mom! You gotta keep up!!"

At that point, Kathy couldn't keep up any longer as Kait continued on her walk. Winded and sore, Kathy was forced to throw in the towel. Instead of maintaining pace, she stopped and monitored Kait as she reached the end of her destination and back. Kathy admitted to being a bit frustrated, but not that much. She couldn't be upset with a daughter who was moments away from death just a week and a half earlier and now just wanted to walk. It was an endearing moment! And it was beautiful watching her energy return!

As another form of exercise, I began doing light mental activities with her in order to stimulate her mind and help her regain some of her cognitive abilities. By playing simple games like Wheel of Fortune, Words with Friends, and various card games, I figured it could help improve her mental strength. When we played Words with Friends, I was surprised at her ability to place words in locations that earned her high scores. Sometimes she would attempt to place words that were clearly not words, like "CVEM" or "WHLA," but as she continued to try she would eventually find words that she recognized.

The one area that seemed to lag behind all other aspects of her recovery was her short-term, associative memory when it came to associating words with objects. Everything she learned pre-seizure, she remembered. But after her seizure, if she was just learning the name of something for the first time, she would quickly and easily forget it. The information would enter one ear, and it would remain in her brain, but the whereabouts of that name remained hidden in the recesses of her mind. She simply needed more time to heal.

Kait was back in the comfort of her own home. That meant she could finally give Kathy and Vicky the Mother's Day gifts she had often reminded them about since that day passed two weeks ago. And she couldn't wait! As the two mothers each took a seat, Kaitlyn excitedly handed them their wonderful mementos to unveil. I stood back, outside the circle, becoming a quiet observer with my eyes glued to Kait the whole time. Watching her adorable facial expressions, seeing her happy, it melted my heart.

Giving to others was an activity Kait enjoyed almost more than anything in the world, providing her with much more satisfaction than being on the receiving end. It was that sudden burst of positive energy, that look of pure joy on their faces upon discovering their hidden treasure - that's what Kait loved most about it!

So with Kait standing calmly beside them with a beaming smile, Kathy and Vicky slowly unwrapped their presents. She couldn't wait to see and feel their happiness. And I couldn't wait to watch Kait's reaction.

After clawing their way through the colorful wrapping paper, both mothers finally revealed their gifts. Their faces lit up with joy! So did Kait's! And it mattered very little what the items actually were, but the fact that it was Kait who was able to physically hand deliver the Mother's Day gifts meant everything to them. Kathy and Vicky each gave Kait a big hug, expressing their extreme love and gratitude toward her. Over in the living room, my eyes glistened as I felt all warm and fuzzy on the inside. My girl was such a beautiful person, and it was such a lovely moment to see.

During Kait's first week back in Kenosha, everyone wanted to stop by and visit. We received visits from both our friends and family. Because most people hadn't seen Kait since her seizure, I was afraid they would be startled by how different she was. And it's not that she was a completely different person, she was still Kait with all of her wonderful core qualities - her generosity, hospitality, and sweetness - but the physical and mental effects from the seizure and surgery were noticeable, and seeing her so weakened was emotionally challenging for those that hadn't seen her in weeks or months.

And, when supporters would come to visit, it was sad for me watching her struggle to converse normally with them. Usually she was a sharp, quick talking, witty, social butterfly. Now, as much as she tried, she couldn't be that. Thoughts took longer to process and sometimes she repeated herself. Sure it made me happy watching her talk to others in such a sweet manner, but it was difficult knowing she was being so inhibited by her ailments. Seeing her functioning at a fraction of her normal capacity was a tough pill to swallow, because I know she so desperately wanted what she had just weeks prior. I just had to keep in mind, though, she was improving every day, and it would only get better with time.

For a few days, I reluctantly returned to work in Madison. As much as I didn't want to leave my Kait, I knew I had to go back for at least a portion of the week to complete some hours. I trusted she would be well looked after in my absence, and I was right.

Sitting at my cubicle for the first time in what felt like months, focusing on my mundane tasks was no simple feat as people continually approached me, expressing their deep sorrow and concern. My colleagues wanted to know if everything was "okay," and I couldn't lie to them. Even if I tried lying, my pathetic poker face revealed the truth.

When asked whether everything was all right, I could only shake my head and say "no." Things were far from all right and I couldn't hide it. The only time I would lie was when people would inappropriately ask about her prognosis. I knew they were well-meaning, so I didn't let it bother me, but I responded with, "We will see. There are still treatments out there so hopefully one of them works." They didn't need to hear that she was only given months.

When it came to actually performing my job, I simply went through the motions, completing everything like a zombie. Luckily, I had become so used to my daily routines that I could afford to lose focus for extended periods of time, as became the norm. Kait was always on my mind. Always. It's just that sometimes I was able to find a way to share my mental space with other thoughts.

Once my work chores were completed, I spent the rest of my time researching the web. With so much information and so little time to ingest it all, I expended as much energy as I could into memorizing and understanding everything I read. It became tiring at times, but with my adrenaline always on high, ignoring the fatigue was easy.

My first priority in my research was to find a clinical trial for Kait. Like I mentioned earlier, even though it hadn't been discussed yet, I knew that after completing brain radiation, her oncologist would want her to go on the chemotherapy called Zelboraf. With the knowledge I was acquiring, I knew that I didn't want Kaitlyn to take that route. Not yet. Zelboraf was the lazy and uninspired choice, in my opinion. Sure, it had a success rate of 60% or more, but it only lasted 6 or 7 months on average, making that percentage seem like an inflated one in order to win investors and the FDA's approval. How can something be considered successful if it only works for a few months? And to add to it, once the drug stopped working, the floodgates were essentially released and the tumors grew at a much, much faster rate, pretty much rendering all subsequent treatments useless.

It was basically an "end game" treatment to merely extend one's life just a little bit longer, but wasn't going to cure. Again, unacceptable to me, and I was convinced we could do much better.

Monotherapy in general was unacceptable to me. It seemed the best chance at curing was to combine various methods. Many clinical trials existed where they combined Zelboraf with other methods or drugs. If anything, I would rather we chose one of those options.

So, I began scouring the clinical trials website, trying to find a study that best suited Kait. I created a spreadsheet listing all of the potential trials, researching each drug to see how effective it had been so far through the testing phases. I poured over various message boards, finding out what others in Kait's position were doing, how effective it had been, and so on. It got to the point where I had devised strategies which I thought were more than formidable, giving Kait a better chance than simply receiving Zelboraf.

My next hurdle was, how would I convince everyone else? How would I convince Kait? For the most part, Kait trusted my judgment, but if she had to choose between someone with no medical degree versus someone who had studied melanoma for 25 years or more, I wouldn't expect her to go against the recommendation of a doctor, nor would I blame her.

But, I must admit that I had quickly developed a somewhat cynical opinion of oncologists overall. As much as I respected Dr. Robertson, I couldn't help but feel discouraged. First of all, I know their library of knowledge is vast when it comes to the disease. They know most of the mechanisms at work, how the beast functions (sort of, not really), what it likes best, what it feasts on, etc. However, they know very little about what it takes to actually kill the beast, i.e. cure the disease. Nobody knows. If they did, people would have more than a 3% chance of survival in Stage 4. Secondly, there is a set protocol for treating cancer. A committee convenes on the subject of treatment strategies, trying to decide how patients should be treated. During Kait's battle with melanoma, the general order of therapies for a typical melanoma sufferer was IL-2 first, then Ipilimumab, and finally Zelboraf, and when those didn't work, they start throwing other drugs at it. Again, it's a one-size-fits-all attack, absolving any responsibility from the individual oncologist so they don't have to stress about whether or not they are choosing the right treatment option. As much as I understand that need to lighten up the stress-load oncologists face, adhering to a blanket strategy was unacceptable to me. Every patient's cancer is different, and using the same exact playbook for each one is completely inefficient and uninspired. Some oncologists take the liberty of devising individualized treatment plans for their patients, but for the ones that don't want to bear the immense responsibility or risk their careers, they can always turn to the standard playbook.

Another huge obstacle was that if a combinational therapy had not been approved by the FDA, then the likelihood of getting insurance to pay for the treatment was slim. In some cases, if the combination of two drugs has shown results and the prescribing doctor fights for the patient, the insurance company will budge. Or, if there is a justified need to introduce a second method of therapy, for instance, if Kait was on Ipilimumab and needed radiation on a specific tumor that was causing discomfort, then insurance would likely cover it. There are various ways to skirt around the insurance machine, but it certainly isn't easy.

With that, I began calling around to various institutions to inquire about the clinical trials they were running. I quickly realized that most of the studies excluded patients with brain metastases since their prognosis is so poor, and clinical trials cost millions upon millions of dollars to conduct. If a melanoma survivor does have brain tumors, they typically have to go through a procedure to remove or stabilize the tumors, like radiation, and then two or three months later they must show that the tumors have remained stable.

One particular phone call almost triggered an emotional reaction out of me. As I was sitting outside of my work building on break, I called Memorial Sloan Kettering in New York, inquiring about a clinical trial combining Ipilimumab and Zelboraf. When a receptionist answered, I asked for the specific doctor in charge of the particular study. While she politely put me on hold, a slow, sad piano melody began playing through my phone. It sounded like funeral music to me. Suddenly, images of Kait in a church, looking up at me while lying in a casket started flashing through my head. My throat developed an immediate lump as I desperately tried to allay the visuals that brought forth tears to the back of my eyes. Luckily, as colleagues were walking by, I was able to wring those depressing thoughts from my mind, swallowing down the golf ball in my throat, evading a potential emotional breakdown.

It quickly became apparent that at any given moment, any little sound, any little comment, any little anything could trigger the most random of thoughts having the potential to snowball into an avalanche. Rarely could I control them.

After working for a few days in Madison, I returned to Kenosha to take care of my darling. During my time away, Kaitlyn made a decision to give herself a sort of, makeover. For as long as I had known her, Kait always had long, blonde, silky soft hair. But, with brain radiation looming, it was inevitably going to fall out. All of it. Kaitlyn had always teetered with the idea of cutting her hair to shoulder length, curious of what it might look like. And now that she was going to lose it anyway, she figured it was as good a time as any to give the new look a try.

Upon returning to her mother's house, I wasted little time before taking my bags up into Kait's room, anxious to see the new hairdo.

As I slowly turned the corner into her room, I saw her sitting on her bed watching TV with cousin Alexa. The sight of her new haircut left me speechless. She looked absolutely stunning! It stopped right above her shoulders, and somehow she was able to cover up the hairless left side, and I couldn't even tell.

"Oh my God, honey, look at you! You look amazing with your new haircut!"

Kait smiled as she sat on the bed wearing a tie-dyed shirt she and Lex made. "I'm glad you like it," she replied softly. Alexa left the room briefly to give us some alone time.

I walked up to Kait and gave her a big hug and a kiss. "Seriously, I had no idea what you would look like with short hair, and I'm blown away!" When she used to tell me she wanted to cut her hair shorter, I always had a hard time imagining what it would look like. And now that I could finally see it, I couldn't get over how cute and sassy she looked.

I took a seat next to her on the bed and began evaluating her progress whilst making conversation. Four days had passed since I had last seen her, and I was curious to know how far along she had come. Though she still seemed relatively distant, after talking with her for a few short minutes it was apparent to me she had made great strides in her recovery, which was a treat to witness. From the day of her seizure up to that point, watching her improve daily, one step at a time, it was more gratifying to me than anything

I had ever experienced or accomplished in my life. All of the self-congratulatory achievements, all of the self-appeasing glory bestowed upon me in my 27 years of existence, all of it combined paled in comparison to watching Kait persevere through her daily struggles. I couldn't have been more proud of her.

Of course, as much as she was improving, she still had a long way to full cognitive recovery. While we were sitting on her bed talking, I noticed her looking at me, puzzled. She had difficulty recognizing me the exact same way she did before. "I feel like I don't really know you," she said calmly, "I mean, I know who you are, but it just feels different."

For a split-second, my eyes fluttered open in surprise before quickly putting her comments into perspective. "That's okay, sweetheart! You haven't seen me for a week. You've been through a lot. I'm sure after a little bit, you'll recognize me the same way you always have."

Really though, the fresh painting that was Kait's life had just been smeared by the malevolent hand of cancer, and she was now gradually repairing the damages. She was slowly putting her life back together. And I had been gone for nearly a week. A week! After seeing each other every single day for many months. Obviously she knew who I was, but it was understandable if she didn't recognize me in the exact same way she was accustomed to in that moment. Her brain had a difficult time fully recalling my face as the one she shared such an intense connection with.

However, after enjoying a few quality hours in each other's company, which included good conversation and boneless chicken wings, that recognition problem rapidly faded. She remembered our love!

For the rest of my weekend with Kaitlyn, I became her watchdog once again, though she didn't need someone hovering over her quite as often as she did a week prior. We went for three walks a day, played games, and hung out with family as often as possible, trying to take advantage of every single minute.

At one point, it was apparent we all had overestimated how much Kait had recovered from her seizure and craniotomy. Though her reactions and ability to process thoughts were still lagging a bit, she seemed almost like her normal self at times. So, one night, with Mark and Vicky over, we began watching *Inglorious Basterds*, a movie containing subtitles when the characters are speaking German. After about 10 or 15 minutes of sentences flashing across the screen, the overstimulation in Kait's brain became too much as she couldn't handle having to read the words and comprehend their meaning before a new sentence would appear. She tried so hard to follow along and keep up with the movie, but the overexertion on her brain produced a sharp headache. Once the pounding in her head began, not even her pain medication could dissipate the pressure. Sleep was the only other option. With that, she was done for the night as she retired to her bedroom to lie down and relax her head. We all felt terrible for subjecting her to a movie we should have known would cause a sensory overload to her fragile mind.

In other instances, it was also apparent that we underestimated where Kait was in her recovery process and her ability to understand her situation.

On one particular evening, a group of us went for a nice, leisurely walk, enjoying the perfect Wisconsin weather whilst avoiding the onslaught of summer's mosquitos. After returning from our short trip, we all sat around the picnic table behind the house, taking advantage of the remaining sunlight. As became usual, with the walk increasing her blood flow and neural functioning coupled with the clean, fresh air, Kait was extra talkative during our evening powwow.

We began revisiting the whole ordeal with her seizure, talking about events that went on during the week.

"Gosh, I just remember being in Alexa's bathroom, and everything just felt so weird. And then I don't remember much after that. Just a few things here and there," she claimed.

"Yeah, that was scary, sweetheart. We were all so worried about you. Then you had your seizure and luckily Uncle Dale was there to catch you."

"Yeah, that was so weird." She continued, "Then I remember being outside at UW, and Dr. Robertson came out. Then everyone was crying around me for some reason."

"We were all just worried about you," Jessica replied.

"Yeah, the previous girl that went through the same surgery as you ended up passing away, so we were nervous," I explained. I didn't want Kait to know about the heartbreaking comment she made on the roof. It would only cause her to stress and worry more after realizing it was her statement that brought us to tears at that moment.

"Oh wow, really?"

"Yeah."

Suddenly, Kait grew silent. A new thought had obviously emerged, and it was weighing on her I could tell. She then turned and looked at me, concerned. "This means we probably won't be able to have kids, huh?"

Not expecting that topic to be broached, I began scrambling for the proper answer in an attempt to wipe the growing dejection from her face. "No, no! It doesn't mean that at all. We just gotta get you better first. It may be a couple years down the road, but it can definitely still happen. One step at a time."

"Yeah......"

My reassurance didn't seem to help much. In reality, her ultimate dream of having children of her own, a dream that would have made her life complete unlike any other dream she had, was seriously endangered. For a few moments, she sat in silence, pondering my words, her future, our future, before changing the subject. It was obvious Kait was much more aware than she let on. She worried about us. But, in an attempt to insulate us from emotional turmoil, she internalized most of her stress-inducing thoughts.

As the purple and orange clouds slowly darkened, we headed back inside where Kait's spirits seemed to be resurrected. In the kitchen with her mother and Jess, Kait was talking, laughing, and making jokes like her old self again, full of love and positive energy, as though her mental vise had been released. Sitting back, I tried soaking in the moment as much as I could, taking mental pictures of her beautiful smile and of everyone's happiness from being together. I loved observing it!

Again, those instances of complete clarity she seldom experienced left me utterly befuddled. What in our brain causes us to go from confused and sluggish one minute to sharp and quick the next? Why can a coma patient briefly awaken and have full conversations before returning to his unconscious state? The brain is truly one of life's great mysteries. As much as we are advancing toward our understanding of this powerful organ, it seems we have merely scratched the surface when it comes to how it works and its capabilities. Then again, I'm no neuroscientist, so I shouldn't make such assertions.

After spending a few more quality days with my love, I once again had to return to Madison for work, back to the reality outside of our own. Blah! Being around Kait in Kenosha, it felt like we were in a completely different world, isolated from all other walks of life. The serious nature of our situation left us with temporary tunnel vision. We were closed off from all other happenings around us, as though we were encased within a foggy glass ball, with the smog of our stress and worry clouding our view of the outside world. It became easy to forget about the lives beyond our walls. It became easy to forget that we were not the only ones on this earth suffering from physical and emotional torment. Within our own world, it really felt like what we were dealing with was completely unique and different from anything anyone else was experiencing. Like we were the only ones going through something so harsh. But we weren't the only ones. We had to remember that.

19 WORLD OF PHARMA

Back at work, I was making great progress in developing what I perceived to be effective strategies to combat our cancer infestation. Not only was I researching conventional methods, but I began researching heavily on alternative methods, too.

The first four alternative treatments I devoted my attention to were the Hydrogen Peroxide (H2O2) therapy, Hemp Oil, Intravenous (IV) Vitamin C, and the Gerson Therapy. As I was trying to find statistical data on any of these methods, I found it to be nonexistent. Why? None of these methods had gone through clinical trials, yet, but all of them carried anecdotal evidence from people around the country. Looking deeper into the matter, I began to discover the large role pharmaceutical companies, the FDA, and money play in the world of medicine.

Unfortunately, because H2O2, Hemp Oil, and Vitamin C are all natural substances, they cannot be patented by any pharmaceutical company. That means, if a company decides to spend millions upon millions of dollars to take, say, High Dose Vitamin C through clinical trials to test its efficacy, and they find out it is successful at fighting cancer, then any other company would be able to package and sell the product, competing for the lowest price. Consequently, the company that spent all of their money on testing the Vitamin C would lose big because they wouldn't be able to sell it for an amount that would recuperate their investment. So, for most treatments involving natural substances, very little to no scientific data exists. Companies can't risk profits and shareholder value. That's why most of the cancer fighting methods within the medical community consists of dangerous, highly toxic chemicals. The compounds used in chemotherapy can be patented and sold for thousands of dollars per treatment. Kaitlyn's three Ipilimumab doses alone totaled around $200,000.

In many cases, evidence exists of pharmaceutical companies actually trying to discredit and even ban natural methods or other treatments. Why? I don't know. Maybe because if a cheap method is discovered, it would cut into the billions of dollars the medical world commands.

As one example, Vitamin B17 is another alternative, natural substance that has been highly touted as an effective cancer combatant. Many people from around the globe have claimed it to have successfully defeated their cancer. However, the FDA decided to put a ban on Vitamin B17, also known as Laetrile, in the United States with the justification that the substance is poisonous and, therefore, dangerous if taken in excessive amounts. But, contradicting that assertion is the fact that various forms of chemotherapy administered in fighting cancer are extremely poisonous and dangerous, killing healthy cells in a person's body and many times even being the cause of death over the cancer itself. Yet, these treatments are allowed to flourish even though their success rates are extremely poor. Why? They bring in enormous amounts of cash.

Another example I found through my research involved the infamous doctor, Stanislaw Burzynski. In the 1970s he discovered what he called "antineoplaston therapy" to help destroy cancer. Even though his method has been proven to successfully fight the disease, especially in cases where other doctors have told the patients nothing more can be done, the FDA and pharmaceuticals have been trying to discredit and shut him down for 30 years and have failed every single time in their attempt. In one instance, in an apparent attempt to disprove his method, a pharmaceutical company decided to test his antineoplaston therapy without consulting him on the proper way to administer the treatment even though he was the brain behind the idea. Needless to say, they gave the treatment in an ineffective manner to various cancer patients, and as a result were able to "report" that Burzynski's methods do not work in order to sway public interest away from him. A very interesting documentary can be found online called "Burzynski: Cancer is Serious Business." It's eye-opening and I would recommend it.

The same thing happened with Dr. Nicholas Gonzalez and his Kelley Treatment which had garnered success stories from across the nation. A study was conducted by a Columbia University group to test the efficacy of this nutrition-based therapy. One of the requirements to be accepted into the clinical trial - since it was based on nutrition – was that the patients needed to be able to eat, of course. But as the study commenced, not only were patients being accepted into the trial who were unable to eat, but many patients were so sick they were dying before even starting the treatment. However, the study was set up so that as soon as a patient entered the trial, they were counted as having received the treatment protocol, even if they never actually began it. So, essentially, patients that died before ever beginning the Kelley Treatment were still counted. By the end of the study, Dr. Gonzalez stated that out of 39 patients accepted into the study, maybe five or six actually started the regimen, yet all 39 were counted as having received it. In the end, the Columbia team was allowed to publish the negative data and "prove" that the Kelley Treatment doesn't work. Did I mention that the head investigator with this Columbia group was previously in charge of developing the chemotherapy regimen that the Kelley Treatment was going up against? Conflict of interest?

Interestingly enough in the above case, a complaint was filed with the Office of Human Research Protection, and after a two-year investigation, it was found that the majority of the patients in this clinical trial were in fact admitted even though they did not meet the admission criteria. However, the Columbia team still published their negative findings based on fraudulent practices, and the results from the investigation never made it to mainstream. All of the funding raised for the clinical trial had essentially been wasted, and a potentially life-saving treatment was effectively discredited.

This "twisting" of data happens all too often, as has been documented, when healthier and potentially curative approaches make an attempt at scientific backing. Once these alternative methods fail in these rigged clinical trials, the doctors are labeled quacks and the methods are buried and forever ignored by mainstream medicine. Just over the last 100 years, the methods of such practitioners such as Dr. Burzynski, Dr. Gonzalez, Dr. Tullio Simoncini, Rene Caisse, Dr. Max Gerson, Linus Pauling, John Hoxsey, and so many more, have been suppressed even though they've proven to be safer and less toxic than traditional chemotherapy and have garnered positive results. Now I'm not saying the methods presented by these people would necessarily work better than anything else available, but they should at least be given a fair shake when it comes to the testing phase.

The more I read and the more I discovered, the more infuriated I became knowing people were dying of cancer all over the globe, and it seemed that greed and the mighty dollar inhibited those with novel and potentially curative approaches from entering this great fight. Money and power has a unique way of crushing its weaker competitors and directly and subliminally manipulating the masses to scoff at and alienate those simply trying to help humanity. It would seem the FDA, a government agency created to protect us, is plagued with corruption, which isn't surprising since it's run by humans, and many humans can be coerced when the smell of greenbacks is wafting in their faces. A bitterness began to grow over my body upon realizing how low those in power will stoop in order to maintain their status and wealth. (Now, that's not to say that I believe oncologists are corrupt. They want a cure just as bad as everyone else and work tirelessly to educate themselves on how to most effectively attack cancer, but the tools they've been given are very limited. If anything I feel bad for them.)

Trying to set my frustration and disgust aside, I continued researching to locate a potential cancer deterrent for Kait. Atop my list was Hemp Oil, the liquid extracted from the marijuana plant, the one my brother said he had a dream about. From extensive reading, it seemed the most promising as the oil had been shown to have medicinal and curative properties to combat not only cancer, but also numerous other ailments. Backed by thousands of people who have found success with the liquid, this method involves ingesting the oil as opposed to smoking it, which causes zero harm to a person's body, even if they take too much.

As much as I wanted to obtain this alternative medicine, I ran into a large obstacle - marijuana was banned in the United States. Though it's NOT harmful in itself, it's been banned under the pretense that it can lead to the use of other drugs, which sounds like propaganda to me. I mean, alcohol IS actually harmful and can also lead to the use of other serious drugs, so why is it not banned – because of the ability to tax it and because it doesn't threaten other industries, maybe? I had never been an advocate for the use of marijuana, but the more I researched, the more I discovered what an effective plant it is. It seems as though the main reason it has been banned is basically because it poses a threat to multiple industries as its purposes extend beyond simple consumption through ingestion and inhalation.

I soon learned finding alternative methods would pose a much more difficult task than I had originally thought with unforeseen obstacles standing in my way, which added to my frustration and stress.

20 NOT ANOTHER SEIZURE...

It was around lunchtime on the Thursday of my week back to work, and I had taken a break from research, turning my attention to my daily chores.

As I sat in my cubicle, I felt my phone vibrating in my pants pocket. Surprisingly, it was Kaitlyn. Always on high alert, I answered immediately fearing something could be wrong.

"Hey sweetie, what's up," I said softly so as to not bother my coworkers.

"Oh not much." She sounded happy. "I don't want you to be worried, but I wanted to let you know Vicky and I are driving up to Madison."

What? Blood instantly rushed to the forefront of my face as my heart began drilling through the walls of my chest.

"Driving to Madison? Why what happened, sweetheart?" The volume of my voice increased.

"Don't worry, Trav. We're just coming up as a precaution. Vicky and I were walking, and all of a sudden I was having a hard time talking. I kept trying to say your brother's name, and I couldn't. I kept saying Te...Te...Tyson. Then my head started hurting really bad. But, DON'T WORRY, my head doesn't hurt as much anymore and I'm able to talk better now."

I could feel my hands shaking. Flashbacks of her disorientation and inability to properly speak at Lex's right before her seizure began running through my mind, and I feared it was repeating itself. I feared one of her tumors was bleeding again.

"Oh boy! Okay. So you guys are leaving right now," I asked nervously.

"Yes."

"Okay, that's a good idea. Please tell Vicky to drive safe."

"I will. Vicky's been great. Just don't worry, sweetheart, I'm fine. I promise."

I chuckled at her impossible suggestion. "I'll do my best, honey. I love you so much and I'll see you when you get here!"

"I love you so much, too, Trav!"

With that, I hung up the phone, wrote a quick note to my boss, packed up my few belongings, and immediately left work.

As I waited for Kaitlyn at the hospital, I couldn't control my heartbeat. The images of her suffering a seizure while Vicky drove her to Madison kept reappearing in my head. I naturally feared the worst. *What if she has another seizure? Will her body be able to handle another traumatic episode? Will her body be able to handle another brain surgery? She's already been through way too much. This can't happen again.*

To my relief, when Kait and her family arrived, I could see she had already been improving. Her speech had returned for the most part, and her headache was almost gone.

I gave her a big hug. Sensing my tremendous worry, she did everything she could to reassure me she was okay. The only remedy for my uncontrollable nerves was her presence. Just seeing her in front of me, seemingly okay allowed me to relax once again. Now, just as a precautionary step to make sure Kait's tumors were not bleeding, the medical staff took her back for a CT scan.

Oddly enough, once Kait returned from imaging, Dr. Kuo, her neurosurgeon just happened to walk by and noticed us standing in the room. Curious, he walked in and inquired as to why we were in the Emergency wing. With minor help from us, Kait did her best to explain step by step what had happened just a couple hours earlier.

Dr. Kuo was perplexed. He began running the same tests he ran with her just a couple weeks earlier. Commanding her to raise her hands, press down on his hands, stick her tongue out, look side-to-side, etc. She passed every one of them, easily. Then, as the final part of his assessment, he pulled out his pen and held it up in front of Kait.

With a smile, he asked, "Can you tell me what this is?"

Kait smirked. "A pen!"

We all laughed. She finally answered correctly!

When the scans arrived, Dr. Kuo examined them quickly, trying to detect any problematic areas where bleeding may have occurred.

"Well, the good news is I don't see anything on your scans that would indicate anymore bleeding."

That was great news! "Then, what could have caused her episode of confusion," we asked.

"It could be a number of things. It could be extra stimulation, possibly from the walk. It could be nerves, but it's impossible to tell. The main thing is that there is no more bleeding."

What a relief! We could all relax.

With a potential emergency averted, Kaitlyn and company had to head back to Kenosha, much to my dismay. However, with brain radiation beginning in four days, Kait was set to return permanently to our apartment in Madison. I couldn't wait to have my baby back.

That night, a sudden epiphany struck me upside the head.

Kait received brain scans on May 12th right after her seizure. Now it was June 7th, almost a month later, and she had just received another set of scans on her brain. I wondered, was it possible that between her first scans and her second scans that those brain tumors could have shrunk? Or, were they stable? Did they grow?

Before the Ipilimumab began working on Kait's body, back in March and April, all of her visible tumors noticeably increased in size every week. But, with the Ipi and her immune system attacking her melanoma cells right around the time of her seizure, in May, not only did her tumors decrease significantly, but they had remained stable ever since.

With my reasoning, it seemed logical that if the Ipilimumab was not working in Kait's brain, those brain tumors would have grown noticeably within the 3 to 4 weeks between the May 12th scans and the June 7th scans. However, if her immune system, aided by the Ipilimumab, had been working in her brain, then it made sense that those tumors would be stable just like the tumors in her body.

Excited and curious about a possible discovery that could lead to an effective treatment strategy, I searched high and low for the man most knowledgeable about her brain and those tumors – Dr. Kuo. After scouring the Internet, searching through every nook and cranny for a way to contact him, I dug up his email address. My message to him simply asked whether or not Kait's tumors had grown, shrunk, or remained stable when comparing the two scans from the different dates.

In his response, he confirmed that the tumors were "essentially similar."

What did that mean? Did "essentially similar" mean they had not grown? It was absolutely conceivable to me that if they weren't stable, their growth within the timeframe of one month would have been noticeable. Like I said, with the tumors on Kait's body, they noticeably grew every single week. "Essentially similar" after almost 4 weeks to me indicated they had been stable, meaning the T-cells, proliferated by the Iplilimumab, had traveled up into her brain and had begun attacking. She was responding to the Ipi! I just needed to know what to do with that knowledge since Kait wouldn't be approved to receive any more of the drug.

I had more fuel to power my research, nevertheless.

21 TOMOTHERAPY: A FALLING OUT

A full month had passed since Kaitlyn stepped foot in our Madison apartment, and I was overcome with joy to have her back. Unfortunately, with her return, that meant she was beginning her brain radiation. She couldn't drive, so for the three-week duration, we developed a schedule so we knew who would be taking Kait to her appointments and on which days. Also, because Kait was still at risk of suffering another brain hemorrhage, and for other reasons, we deemed it necessary for someone to be around her at all times, at least during radiation.

I decided to work 10-hour days during the week to free up my Fridays so I could chauffeur Kait to her therapies on those days. Jessica set aside a full week of time to come stay with us and take her to the hospital, and as for the remaining days, my mother and aunt filled in as needed.

As for Kait's first day of radiation, the four parents and I were in attendance so we all felt like we had a grasp on what to expect from the 15 days of treatments.

Dr. Miles Stevens was the expert in charge of delivering a specialized, precise treatment termed, Tomotherapy. How it worked was Kait would enter an MRI machine with a mask fastened tightly to her face to keep her head from moving. As the machine rotated around her head, it would deliver a small dose of radiation to her whole brain, and when it arrived at the sight of the visible brain tumors, a much higher amount of radiation would be administered. For this reason, it was imperative Kaitlyn kept completely still during treatment to lessen risk of heavy radiation being delivered to the wrong areas of the brain.

In the waiting room, the five of us sat patiently as Kaitlyn received her first round of Tomotherapy in a back room. We were informed a typical treatment would take between 15 and 20 minutes, so I made sure to grab myself a cup of complimentary hot chocolate and cookies.

As we waited for Kait to walk out of the room so we could congratulate her on completing her first day, we watched the time slowly tick past the 15 minute mark. Nothing to worry about, we figured. It was the first day, and we figured they had to make adjustments and work out the kinks.

Soon, we were approaching the 25 minute mark, and we began to wonder when Kait would emerge from the entrance leading to the MRI room.

After about 35 minutes of waiting, Kaitlyn finally appeared.

"Hey, there she is," I exclaimed.

"You did it! How was it Kait," Kathy asked excitedly.

As Kait got closer to us, my happy gaze morphed into a concerned frown as we noticed she was distraught over something.

"Sweetie, what's the matter?"

"Here, come sit down, pumpkin," her dad suggested, using his hand to guide Kait to a chair in between us all.

As she sat down, my poor baby used her hands to wipe the tears from her face. Vicky handed her a tissue.

"What happened, honey," I asked concernedly as I rubbed her back.

Weeping, she explained, "The machine kept on stopping, and they would have to pull me out and adjust it and then put me back in. I'm worried it's not working right."

"Oh, I'm sure it doesn't mean it's not working. It's your first day and they probably had to make sure it was lined up properly," Kathy explained.

Curious, Mark walked away to ask the radiation therapist about the malfunctions Kait described.

Brushing away the tears with her tissue, Kait explained her woes further, "And then the mask was screwed on so tightly that my head was pressing down real hard against the bed the whole time. After about 10 minutes it began hurting really bad."

Now, we were all well aware that since her seizure and craniotomy coupled with the effects from the steroids she continued to receive, Kait was extra sensitive when it came to her emotions. However, after being subjected to 30 minutes of having her head pressed tightly against a hard slab, unable to move a millimeter while pain pulsed from the back of her head down through her neck, I would say her tears were more than justified. If it were me in that claustrophobic chamber, I know for a fact I would have been yelling for the nurses to release me at once.

We all felt so bad for her as we tried calming her down. Mark came back and explained why the machine kept on stopping.

"Kait, I asked the nurse, and she said the machine had to recalibrate to make sure it was hitting the right spots. All of the radiation that was supposed to be delivered to those tumors WAS delivered. So you don't have to worry about whether or not it was working properly."

"Ok," Kait replied, sniffling.

"And, I told her about the mask being too tight, and she said they would cut some holes so you would have a bit more freedom. Also, she said you can take one of those anti-anxiety pills before each treatment to help relax your muscles."

"Okay, but I don't know how much that'll help."

"Well, if it doesn't help, we can ask Dr. Stevens if maybe they can loosen the screws just a bit."

Soon, Kaitlyn began calming her emotions down as we left the hospital.

In better spirits once we took off, we all celebrated by going out to dinner. Kait completed the first day of her next step toward defeating her wretched disease, and we all wanted to shower her with love and praise. She deserved every bit of it.

The next three weeks of radiation therapy ran seemingly smooth for Kait and the rest of us. Mentally, Kait had improved to the point where she no longer struggled to hold conversation. She was back to talking fast and plentiful, which was beautiful to see. The one deficiency that remained was in her short-term memory. Still, words she just learned for the first time after her seizure were likely forgotten, no matter how hard she tried to remember them. Unsure if her short-term memory was capable of being strengthened, I tested her daily by having her answer a series of questions.

By linking new words and names to older words she was familiar with, I hoped eventually her mind could be conditioned to improve her memory. For instance, for Dr. Kuo, I would have Kaitlyn remember Koala Bear to help her arrive at his name. I would ask, "What's the name of your surgeon?"

She would slowly work toward the correct answer. "Ummm. K-. K-. Ko-. K-, koala. Ko. Kuo? Kuo. That's it, Kuo."

Watching the wheels in her mind churn until she dug up the proper word was rewarding, and I would rejoice and praise her every time. Even if the right term didn't emerge, I would still praise her.

At work, I continued my research in between my chores, taking notes and calling clinical trial institutions when I could.

As planned, Kait's sister, Jess, stayed with us for a week. At first, a part of me was apprehensive as I wasn't looking particularly forward to the uncomfortable silence and forced conversation for five whole days. However, my foolish anxieties were quickly silenced when I came home from work for the first day and saw how comfortable Kait was interacting with her sister as opposed to my family members. Normally, when she was around my family, as comfortable as she was Kait felt like she had to entertain the entire time, even if they assured her they didn't need to be. She constantly challenged herself by trying to fill the time with fun conversation, making sure her guests never faced a dull moment.

But, with Jessica around, Kaitlyn didn't care. She watched what she wanted to watch. She talked when she felt like talking. And, she could eat with her mouth open and not care about the potential judgments coming from the other person in the room. For me, knowing the pressure was off of Kait to entertain, knowing she could just relax and genuinely be herself around her sister, I was relieved.

At around the two-week mark of her radiation therapy, Kait's hair began falling out. When she would wake up in the morning, hair would be scattered all over her pillow, and in the shower, clumps of long strands would gather at the surface of the drain. It was coming out fast.

So, at the three-week mark, after Kait willed her way through the completion of her brain radiation, she decided she wanted to buzz off what little hair she had left atop her head. With that, we headed over to my parents' humble abode to allow my mother to give Kait her haircut.

I had to mentally brace myself. What I learned during our struggle that began on May 12th (the seizure), was that it was impossible to predict when my emotions would decide to come out of hiding and pay me a visit. Watching Kait say goodbye to her once long, bright, blonde, beautiful locks was nothing to take lightly. Her hair was the one physical feature she took great pride in, and that feature was going to be gone completely. I wasn't sure if my sadness for her would become overwhelming or not.

But Kait was genuinely looking forward to the new look as she took a seat in the high chair my mom used for cutting our hair. She smiled!

"I'm so excited to see what I'll look like with short hair!"

She amazed me!

The only nervous one in the room was me as my mother pulled the clippers from her bag and turned them on. I took a deep breath as Kait continued to smile.

"Okay, you ready," my mom asked.

"Yup!"

Kait's face was radiant. There was no fear. There was no sadness. Only a dazzling smile. Using her strength as a support beam, I no longer felt the sadness I initially burdened myself with coming into the evening.

Bit by bit, my mom slowly ran the clippers along Kait's round head, sending small groups of blonde hair plummeting to the floor. Before long, she was sporting a stylish mohawk, fit for a bad-ass biker chick, a personality trait she couldn't have been further from.

My mom continued to buzz away. Kait continued to smile with each stroke. Trying to peel back the layers to assess whether or not Kait was simply wearing a disguise to mask her sadness, I swiftly concluded that Kait's smile was genuine. She courageously embraced her unfortunate circumstances, and in her acceptance, she was genuinely happy and excited for her new look. I could only shake my head in amazement and disbelief. Her incredible strength and ability to carry such a burden, to face such a daunting challenge was undeniable, and the proudness I felt for my great love was enormous.

As my mother finished her final stroke, we watched the last strands of hair float gently to the floor, and Kait's hairless head was revealed to everyone in waiting. Looking at her in a "natural" state for the first time, my jaw loosened uncontrollably as the bottom portion of my mouth jutted open. Her beauty was majestic, breathtaking! It was causing me to melt all over and I just wanted to wrap my arms around her.

Without hair, Kait's smile was bigger, shimmering more than ever before. Her perfect eyes were accentuated, and looking into them was like being awarded a glimpse into heaven. All of the softest features of her face that were once hidden by her long locks of love were now exposed, and they glowed ever so brightly. Without her hair taking attention away, now all of her most striking features were magnified, and she looked amazing!

I knew she would still be gorgeous with a shaved head, but I never in a million years could have anticipated how gorgeous she would still be. Gazing upon my beautiful Kait, the air was literally extracted from my lungs.

As she looked at herself in the mirror, grinning ear to ear, I could tell she was satisfied. We all sounded like broken records as we kept telling her how great she looked. It was unanimous, she could rock the bald look if she ever decided to again in the future.

After a quick photo shoot, we all headed downstairs to enjoy a night of board games.

For Kait, donning a new look also represented new beginnings, in a sense, as she transitioned from Step 2 of her journey back to health and was now preparing for Step 3, which was yet to be determined. Though whole brain radiation was mentally and physically draining on Kait throughout the three-week period, she was unwavering in her determination toward completing it. To her, whether she was miserable or not, it was something that had to be done.

The proudness I felt toward her continued to grow at a rapid pace. Not only was she put through the gauntlet of surgery and then brain radiation, but then she was forced to part with one of her most prominent identifiers, and yet she took it all in stride. She never flinched. She never felt an ounce of sorrow for herself. As she stared unfazed into the face of this unimaginable challenge, not accepting defeat no matter the magnitude of the setback, Kaitlyn continued to quietly flaunt her tremendous strength. I was left in awe!

22 DESTABILIZATION

For just over one month, the tumors in Kaitlyn's body had remained stable, neither increasing nor decreasing in size. Around the middle of June, as I was feeling the tumors on her back and neck, it was apparent that they were no longer stable. They had begun to grow once more. The steroids and brain radiation in aggregate were destroying the legion of T-cells her immune system had worked on for months to build up.

Because she was in the middle of receiving radiation therapy at the time, we couldn't put her on any other form of conventional treatment. The earliest we could begin any new therapy was around mid-July. So, I intensified my research, actively seeking a safe alternative to possibly lessen the rate of growth within those cancer cells.

To start, my grandparents lent us an expensive water system that allegedly ionizes the water dispensed from it in order to detoxify one's body. In my mind, I knew this attempt at slowing the growth of her tumors would likely prove futile, but I had to try it. After consulting Dr. Robertson of its safety while she was receiving radiation, not wanting the ionized water to counteract against the toxins from the Tomotherapy, Kait began consuming about 10 cups on a daily basis. I drank it, too. Maybe it was all psychological, but I did feel like I felt better. It sure cleaned me out the first week I began drinking it (use your imagination).

In the meantime, I searched high and low for anyone that might have any information about producing Hemp Oil for us. It seemed promising, and though I knew it was illegal, the health and well-being of my girl superseded any man-made law, especially a law as outdated as that one.

Unfortunately, though I tried for months, even extending my reach overseas, I failed in my attempt at acquiring the Cannabis medicine, which disappointed me greatly.

I was at a crossroads now when it came to conventional medicine. My goal was to initially get Kait qualified for a promising clinical trial that combined two drugs – Dabrafenib and Trametinib. However, that trial, like most clinical trials, required Kait to wait until two months after her last day of radiation to be accepted. But with the tumors growing again, I concluded that waiting around two months would likely be detrimental. In my mind, it seemed wise to get Kait started on a treatment as soon as possible, which would be about three weeks after her last day of radiation.

I wanted her to go back on Ipilimumab, but if it took another two or three months to regrow her T-cells, I didn't know if we could afford that kind of time.

Reading through medical literature, analyzing novel approaches to fighting melanoma, I wanted to find anything besides Zelboraf, because in my mind once Zelboraf stopped working the cancer cells would become too powerful, rendering all subsequent treatments ineffective.

The one method I dug up which was experiencing success in clinical trials at the time was an approach combining Stereotactic Body Radiation (SBRT) and IL-2. SBRT is basically just a method of delivering a high dosage of radiation to specific tumors within the body. The theory behind the method is that by delivering radiation to a specific tumor, it weakens the melanoma cells and damages their cloak, exposing them from hiding. Next, IL-2 is introduced into the subject's body, boosting the immune system. With the T-cells revved up and the radiated cancer cells weakened, the idea is that the immune system would be able to locate and destroy the melanoma more efficiently. Then, after the T-cells have had a taste for "melanoma blood," they would essentially be programmed to seek out the remaining cancer cells in the person's body. As I touched upon earlier, this is known as an Abscopal Effect.

Even though Kait couldn't qualify for that clinical trial, both SBRT and IL-2 were approved separately, and it was a strategy any clinic could do with proper justification. To me, it was a much more novel, inspired approach compared to just Zelboraf alone, and the promising results only supported my desire for the combo. I just had to convince everyone else.

23 GRANDMA'S FUNERAL

In early July, just after Kaitlyn completed radiation on her brain, my dad's mother, my grandmother, sadly passed away. The passing of our sweet Edna was bitter sweet. Bitter in the sense that we would no longer have the opportunity to be graced with her wonderful presence here on earth. And, sweet because she was finally reuniting with her soul mate, Victor, whom she had lost to cancer almost 30 years prior.

Donning her brand new wig, one that resembled the short style she wore just before losing her hair, Kait accompanied me to Grandma's wake. Upon entering the funeral home, Kait and I walked straight up to my Grandma to pay our respects and say goodbye as she lay peacefully in her casket.

Always trying to put on a mask and act like a tough guy for some unknown reason, probably due to massive insecurities, I do everything I possibly can at wakes and funerals to keep my tears at bay. If ever I feel a cry about to break loose, I use all of my might to squeeze it in. However, at my Grandma's wake, things were much, much different.

After Kait and I paid our respects to my Grandma, we stepped back and looked on as the priest tried getting everyone's attention. With her 11 sons and daughters, some 30 grandkids, and many more standing in silence, the priest began to pray. I stood quietly next to Kaitlyn with my hands folded in front of me, listening intently to the words the priest was speaking.

As the priest was talking kindly of our lovely Edna, I found my gaze fixated on her lifeless body in the casket. Suddenly, a wave of morbid thoughts began pummeling my mind. My head began projecting visions of another wake, a wake possibly set just months in the future, a wake for my dear Kaitlyn.

With the room still calm and in silence as the priest continued his brief sermon, I was anything but calm on the inside. The harder I tried to quell my thoughts and bring peace to my nerves, the harder my heart thumped against my ribcage. And it only got worse. My imagination began replacing my Grandma's body in the casket with Kaitlyn's. For short moments I could shake those awful images from my head, but they aggressively pushed their way back in immediately after.

As the whole family and some friends stood by, listening to the prayer, the emotional torment was becoming unbearable, and I was losing the battle within my mind. I could feel I was about to disruptively burst into hysteria. On the brink of completely losing my composure, I walked briskly out of the room. And before I could even turn the corner, tears began flowing from my eyes. With everyone out of sight, I let it all out. I was a mess, crying uncontrollably. My dear, sweet, amazing, loveable Kaitlyn was standing in the room next to me, with all of my family, smiling, full of vigor, full of life, and I couldn't bear the idea that it could soon be coming to an end. The thoughts were wrenching my heart and the pain was excruciating.

After about 10 minutes, I finally reined in my emotions and silenced my cries. Taking a deep breath, I composed myself as I walked back into the room to rejoin my love and my family. For the remainder of our evening, my emotions remained under control. I just hoped Kaitlyn wouldn't question the source of my tears. I hoped that she thought they were for my Grandma.

The following morning I headed to the church for my Grandma's funeral. Kaitlyn stayed back at the apartment with my aunt Wendy because it was going to be a long day, and being fresh out of intense brain radiation, Kait became fatigued rather quickly, and we didn't want her straining her mind to fight through mental exhaustion. Her brain didn't need that kind of stress as it needed time to recover from her treatments.

At the church, all of the family members said our final goodbyes to Grandma Edna. The glue that somehow kept a huge family of 11 bound together was now an angel watching over us. For the most part, I felt like all of the tears in my body had been cried out during the wake. As we took our seats in the pews, I felt composed and in control.

With Grandma's casket resting at the front of the church, right near the altar, the priest began his sermon. The crowd listened peacefully to the priest's words. So did I. But suddenly, the very same thoughts that plagued me the day before crept up again. It had been a mere five minutes into the sermon, and I found myself using every last bit of strength to fight back tears.

Heartbreaking images began sweeping through my mind, and once again, I had no control over them. As much as I tried thinking of anything else, my thoughts continued to put my Kaitlyn in the closed casket resting just in front of me. My thoughts continued to replace "Edna" with "Kaitlyn" in the priest's speech.

Suddenly, my emotions hit me like truck, only this time I was trapped in the middle of the pew and couldn't get out. Using every last bit of energy in my body, I desperately tried suppressing and redirecting my thoughts. It didn't work.

My head was like a glass tank, and the pressure from the water became too much as tears shattered through my fragile walls. Hunching over in the pew, I began sobbing terribly. The whole church was silent except for the priest, so I used all my might to at least be respectful and cry quietly. But, I don't think I succeeded in that regard, either.

The people looking on around me assumed my cries were for the deep love of my wonderful grandma. As much as I loved her, if anything, I was happy for her. Toward the end of her life, she wanted nothing more than to be with her dear husband again, and that wish had finally been fulfilled. She lived a fruitful life filled with children, and grandchildren, and great grandchildren, and love, and laughter. I was elated for her.

Still, I feel foolish in admitting, but my tears were all for Kaitlyn and her potential fate. The thought of such a perfect woman being constantly confronted with death at only 23 years of age became torturous for me as I sat in that church. I felt terrible for what she had to face. She didn't deserve it.

For the remainder of the sermon, I stared at the statue of Jesus in the church and prayed, pleading with him over and over again to spare my Kaitlyn. I was growing desperate. And desperation has a way of corrupting one's mind. I found myself, at times, wishing hardship upon others in exchange for my loved one's health. I found myself asking, "Why can't it be the 77 year-old who has lived a full, happy life instead? Why can't it be the man who chose to rape or murder?" Sometimes I couldn't stop myself from allowing those negative thoughts from entering my head, but with Jesus staring back at me, I realized it was wrong to be so selfish. I was just so desperate for Kait's life to be spared.

24 COMFORT IN THE LORD

Almost every night before bed, I read to Kait from her book containing daily excerpts taken out of the Bible. Kait continued making significant improvements since the hemorrhage, but reading was still difficult for her as it put a heavy strain on her mind. Letters on the page looked like a jumbled mess, and trying to separate them and then comprehend the meaning of their words required her to expend a great deal of energy. Though I had her read to me on a limited basis to try and exercise her brain during the recovery process, I did most of the reading so that she could focus on listening and understanding the message being conveyed, since that was the point of reading the passages in the first place. The short excerpts gave Kaitlyn hope.

It was shortly after my Grandma's funeral, and I slowly read from Kait's new favorite book as she sat up in bed with her legs folded, listening as intently as she could. As I finished reading our fourth passage of the night, I looked up at Kait and asked, "Do you want me to read more?"

"No, that's good. Thank you, sweetheart."

I closed the book and placed it on the nightstand. Returning to bed, I took a seat in front of Kait as she sat quietly, in deep thought. For a moment, I stared at her, analyzing her body language, trying to read her mind only to find out my telepathic abilities needed further development.

Kait interrupted the silence, "I really think the Lord has a plan for all of us."

"Yeah, it is possible. I wonder. I wonder sometimes if these trials and tribulations we go through are his way of challenging us."

"It could be. It might be a way to see who still maintains their faith through their suffering."

"Hmmm, as a weeding out process," I said as I pondered.

Kait paused for a moment before adding, "You know, I just hope the Lord's plan for me is to beat this, that one of the treatments I go on will kill the cancer."

Pursing my mouth together, I replied, "Yes, I hope so badly that is the case. And, I think it will be."

"But, you know what, Trav, I trust the Lord, and if he says it's my time, then it's my time, and that's okay. I'm completely okay with that."

Wow! I was speechless! At first her words caught me off guard as I nodded my head in silence, trying to absorb what she said. I was astounded! Her statement, it was made with such enthusiasm and such conviction. It seemed as though she truly was comfortable with the notion that she may not be physically on earth for very much longer, and she trusted God would take care of her. She trusted in a greater purpose.

Though it scared me and made me a bit uneasy hearing her talk about her possible death, it also provided me with the comfort in knowing she was accepting should the day ever come where her time on earth was up.

Once again, Kait just continued to amaze me. There she was, in her early-20s, having a mature conversation with me about the notion of passing on. Kaitlyn had acquired a perspective normally reserved for those 50 years her senior, giving her the profound ability of coping with such an unfortunate circumstance. Her attitude left me beside myself, though it shouldn't have been surprising.

After reflecting on her comments, I began to question whether or not Kait was aware of her dire prognosis. But how? Nobody had told her. But, ever since her surgery, Kait seemed to carry with her a certain level of calmness, an otherworldly sense of peace, a sense of knowing. I was left wondering even more whether or not she did experience some sort of supernatural event following her seizure, or maybe some sort of spiritual revelation.

25 ZELBORAF

Almost three weeks had passed since Kaitlyn's final day of brain radiation, as we sat in Dr. Robertson's office ready to discuss treatment options. The tumor on her back had grown to about the size of a golf ball, at least the portion that was visible, and beneath her skin the bump may have been even bigger. With that tumor and other tumors increasing in size, it seemed imperative to begin a new treatment regimen as soon as possible.

Clutching my notebook with pages of questions as I sat next to Kait, we awaited our oncologist's arrival. I had a whole lineup of different strategies I wanted to discuss, both conventional and alternative.

However, as prepared as I was, I found myself at a crossroads. What if Kait ended up going with a method based off my encouragements, it didn't work, and she passed away shortly after? I would feel responsible and second-guess myself for the rest of my life. But, on the other hand, what if Kait were to go on Zelboraf, and after it only worked for a few months, her cancer developed a resistance to the drug and ended up taking her life that way? I would still feel responsible and second-guess myself for not trying a different strategy. I didn't know what to do. Deep down, though, I knew Zelboraf was not the right choice. Like I mentioned earlier, it worked for 6 to 7 months, on average, and then once it stopped working, the cancer would start growing at an accelerated pace. A couple people had remained on the drug for two years, but to pray for that miracle was analogous to pulling a slot machine. And, the side effects were extensive – ranging from nausea, skin rashes all over, accelerated heartbeat, hair loss, and sunlight sensitivity all the way to possibly acquiring another form of skin cancer. So even if her life was to be extended, it sounded to me like she would be miserable, and her healthy cells would be poisoned, too. Though I knew the odds were astronomical, I was focused on the word "cure," not on palliative care or simply extending her life a mere few months, and that's all Zelboraf offered.

With Dr. Robertson in the room, I began running through my multitude of ideas, beginning with the SBRT and IL-2 combo, divulging the positive results shown in clinical trials at the time. As I ran through my list, reintroducing Ipilimumab to the mix and talking about a number of clinical trials, explaining my justifications for each, nothing seemed to trip his trigger. Zelboraf was THE approved method with conclusive data attached to it. Though the other methods had some statistics and anecdotal evidence, they were still in the testing phase.

Needless to say, after much discussion, we agreed to the conventional route, the prototypical next step in the playbook – Zelboraf. Before even walking into our meeting with our oncologist, though, I accepted the fact we would likely elect that chemo pill. Having back-up plans, my hope was that if we did go on Zelboraf, it would shrink her tumors considerably, and then we'd be able to qualify Kait for a promising clinical trial. So, on July 19th, Kaitlyn began treatment with the chemotherapy, which required her to take four pills (they smelled like truck tires) in the morning and four pills at night.

And, much to our delight, after consuming Zelboraf for only a week, we began noticing shrinkage within the subcutaneous tumors on Kaitlyn's body. We were both elated! The quick results, no matter how temporary they were, helped rekindle the dimming confidence both of us were feeling. We were injected with a newfound hope for the future, and we were excited to watch those tumors continue to shrink.

Results aside, however, I would still not allow myself to lighten up on my research. If anything, I had to be more diligent and airtight in my studies, ready to adjust to a different treatment or strategy at the drop of a dime. Zelboraf was like a ticking time bomb. At any moment her tumors could discover an alternate pathway, rendering the drug useless, and at that moment, the cancer would become exponentially more aggressive. For that reason, I kept daily tabs on her tumors, which Kaitlyn had no problem with.

The only problem she had was how much pressure I was putting on myself to discover a way to cure her.

One evening, I was sitting on the couch, discussing with Kait some of the various treatments I had been finding. I didn't talk about it often because I never wanted to overwhelm her. But as she listened to my testimony about the different methods, she eventually came and sat next to me. "Honey, maybe you should give yourself a break from doing research."

Looking at her, I replied, "I can't sweetheart. We have to be prepared in case those pills stop working."

"But, Trav, it's working now. My tumors are shrinking. If it's going to last two years, that gives us plenty of time to find other treatments." With the look on her face, I could tell she was adamant about me giving my mind a rest.

"But, the average on Zelboraf is 6 months or so, and I…."

Just then, Kait's eyes began to well up with tears as she rested the side of her head against the backrest of the couch. *Oh no! What did I just say? I can't believe I just dashed her hopes by telling her the average was 6 months.* As Kait began to sob, my heart was crushed at the thought that I may have caused them with my unfiltered mouth. I gently put my hand on her shoulder. Feeling overwhelming guilt about possibly causing her tears, I found myself briefly tongue-tied, unable to find the words. For some idiotic reason, I sheepishly asked, "What's wrong, sweetie?"

I wanted to know if she was crying upon the realization her probation from cancer was likely going to be shorter than the two years she had assumed, or if the tears were for something else. Her answer surprised me, yet it didn't.

With her mouth quivering as tears streamed down her face, she said, "I'm just worried about you. I don't want you to be putting so much stress on yourself."

"Honey, you don't have to be worried about me," is all I could mutter. Inside I was closer to speechless. Her tears were for me! She already knew the average was six months. Deep down she knew her likely fate. Instead of me being the one trying to convince her to be hopeful whilst hiding my own worries, Kait was the one at that moment attempting to convince me. She knew the positive results from the Zelboraf would likely not last two years, but she wanted ME to believe that.

Upon realizing the source of her tears, I melted inside. With everything going on in her life, she was worried about me, not herself, even with the end possibly on the horizon. The thought left me numb and in awe. As I said before, looking back now, it seemed as though Kait knew much more about her situation than she would lead everyone else to believe.

26 TALE OF TWO LIVES

It was essentially a Tale of Two Lives in my world. One of rising tension, and one of infinite love.

When I was with Kaitlyn, it was all genuine happiness and laughter in her awakened presence, in spite of cancer. When I was with Kaitlyn, she helped me free my worries and harness my stress. And our love continued to grow and grow and grow. But away from Kait, even if she was napping on the couch next to me, my shield would weaken and my sadness for her would seep through the cracks, though I never ever revealed to her how much I worried on the inside about her future and well-being. I saved all of my outward stress for when we were apart. Away from Kait, tension was perpetually rising from within as I could sense the Grim Reaper hot on our trail in his unrelenting pursuit - I could feel him. His footsteps were loud and drawing near, and it terrified me. I felt a constant pressure, a constant burden to remain a step ahead of him, but I was foolish to think I had any control. I was powerless.

However, I had to continue to consciously ward off despair, because Kaitlyn was still alive and recovering, and she needed me just as much as I needed her. And throughout July, she had even improved to the point where she was almost restored to her original form. The main, and almost only element she still lacked was short-term memory, but even that was beginning to improve slightly. With cancer a heavy burden in our lives, we needed to do our best to distract ourselves and maintain a normal lifestyle, even if those distractions merely served as a thin veil to conceal our reality.

In our attempt at normalcy, in between the almost weekly trips to the hospital for checkups, Kathy, Tom, and other family members rented a cottage on Lake Wisconsin where we spent a weekend together, hanging out, laughing, enjoying the weather, jet skiing, and goofing off around the camp fire. Because of Kait's heightened skin sensitivity due to her chemo, she had to be extra cautious about how much time she was spending in the sun. Of course she didn't let that hinder her ability to have fun.

On another weekend we attended Lex's graduation party. As expected, the piano man was present, performing and entertaining for hours. To my surprise, he was actually quite a good musician and I thought it was an inspired choice by Uncle Dale.

With my family, we attended a Milwaukee Brewer game. Unable to work, having extra time on her hands, Kait created a special shirt for her favorite player on the team at the time, Norichika Aoki - a small Japanese player with the heart of a lion. The front said "Okee-Dokee Aoki" and the back displayed his name and number. It was great!

Either with one of her wigs or bandanas, we attended movies, hung out with friends, ate out at restaurants, or whatever we could do to maintain that façade of normalcy.

Kaitlyn even developed a new friendship.

During the days while I worked, Kaitlyn remained home alone. On some days, my aunt Wendy or other family or friends would stop in to keep her company, but for the most part, she entertained herself until I returned.

One day, while sitting on the couch at the apartment after going for a walk, Kaitlyn began noticing a baby bunny perching its furry little body right outside our porch door.

After many consecutive days of this miniature, long-eared critter loitering outside our apartment, a light bulb illuminated in Kait's head. She decided she wanted to feed him. With the lettuce we had in our refrigerator, Kait grabbed a handful and dumped it on the cement just outside our door. Frightfully darting away at first, the bunny apprehensively returned with Kait out of sight and devoured every last bit of that lettuce.

From that day forward, he was Kait's little buddy, as he would sit by our door on an almost daily basis, waiting for his yummy meal. With a third mouth to feed, our grocery list grew by one item (a bag of lettuce containing a mixture of other veggies).

After only two weeks of consuming Zelboraf, Kait began experiencing its hellish wrath. The main side effect was nausea, and with each passing day it worsened, getting to the point where it was difficult for her to keep down food. Frequent trips to the toilet became the norm. I felt awful for her. Just after being poked by needles, throwing up was her second biggest phobia. She HATED it! Then again, I don't know many people who are okay with vomiting.

One day I felt particularly bad for her. After a typical day at the office, I returned home, excited to see my baby. Normally when I entered through the door Kaitlyn would greet me with a "HI, SWEETIE!" and project herself into my extended arms. With her arms wrapped taut around my body, I would squeeze her as tight as I could without harming her, gently caressing and rubbing her fuzzy little head, and kissing her on the forehead, lips, cheeks, eyeballs, etc. It was always the perfect way to unwind and start my evening.

However, this one particular day was different.

As I walked through the doorway, I noticed the lights were off, setting off a gloomier ambience within the apartment. Only the TV was on, and the rest of the place was silent. I waited to hear a voice or see Kait jump out excitedly from around the corner. But nothing happened.

After a moment I heard a soft, "Hi honeyyy." Concerned, I set my things on the kitchen table, took my shoes off, and went searching for my girl.

Entering the living room, my head cocked to the side and my eyebrows sloped upon seeing my sweetheart quietly lying on the couch. The Zelboraf had ravaged her body, and she could no longer mask it. She felt really sick. She felt really weak.

"Sweetie, don't you feel good...?"

"Noooo....," she replied in her soft voice. After days of throwing up her food, she appeared nutritionally depleted.

I gently knelt down next to her, kissing her forehead and slowly rubbing her arms and back. "You poor thing, can I get you anything?"

"No....I'm okay. I'm sorry I didn't come to the door when you walked in."

My heart melted. She was so cute. "Sweetheart, noooo....I would feel terrible if you came to the door when you're feeling this shitty."

"I know," she continued softly, "But, I'm still sorry."

Though I felt absolutely awful about the intense nausea she was experiencing, her unparalleled sweetness made me smile as always. If only my hugs could alleviate the symptoms. Once again I was helpless. Water didn't help. Food didn't help. Nothing helped. At least the tumors were shrinking...for the time being.

27 DIVINE INTERVENTION?

Through mid-August, as I continued to monitor the visible tumors on Kait's body, the bumps were still shrinking. Unsatisfied, knowing the results were merely temporary, my research for alternate answers remained active. A novel approach crossed my path as I combed through the hundreds of clinical trials – cancer-fighting T-cells taken from the patient's body, genetically modified and cultured in a lab to attack the melanoma, and then reinserted into the body to seek out the cancer cells. The main criterion was four weeks of stable disease. I was thinking we could temporarily stop Zelboraf, put it back in our pocket for future use, and try to get Kait qualified for that trial. I knew it would be a long shot, but worth the effort.

In the meantime, along with researching for answers, I found myself praying a lot. I was asking for some sort of divine revelation to be sent down to me, one that I could use toward helping Kait overcome her disease. I prayed to God. I prayed to Jesus. I prayed to my deceased Grandparents, Kait's deceased Grandparents, my cousin Nicholas, and everyone I could think of to send me a sign, any sign. And after about two or three weeks of Kait being on Zelboraf, I believe an answer was delivered to me. The answer wasn't vague. It was very clear, and very specific.

I was driving home from work, mindlessly listening to my music as I tried to eliminate my stresses from the day. Suddenly, a clear idea hit me right upside my head.

Intermittent use of Zelboraf.

As the epiphany in my head explained it, Kait would take her chemo pills for three or four weeks straight. Then, she would stop taking it for two weeks. After the two-week vacation from Zelboraf, she would start up again, taking it for another three or four weeks. Then, she would stop taking it again for another two weeks. That cycle would continue for as long as the Zelboraf was working.

I became so excited with enlightenment I almost had to stop my car. The idea made more sense than anything I had thought of prior.

Zelboraf basically works by choking the B-Raf protein (a protein essential for the cancer's growth) within the melanoma cells, causing mass confusion and death within the cancer community. However, eventually, in their oppression, the cancer cells discover a different pathway where they no longer need the B-Raf protein to grow. At that point, Zelboraf becomes useless, and the cancer begins to prosper once more.

However, with the idea that popped in my mind, instead of taking Zelboraf continuously until the melanoma cells simply discovered an alternate pathway to grow, Kait would stop after four weeks. The chokehold on the B-Raf protein would then be released, and the cancer cells would essentially be "tricked" into thinking they could use that pathway again. Then, after a couple weeks of allowing the cancer cells to grow through the B-Raf protein like they were accustomed to, we would reintroduce Zelboraf just as the cancer was getting comfortable, putting the stranglehold back on the B-Raf protein, and essentially causing confusion and melanoma death once again. We would basically be tricking the cancer over and over again.

Flushed with invigoration, I rushed home to tell Kaitlyn all about the idea behind the magically illuminated light bulb in my head. I explained everything in a manner that was simple to understand, using hand gestures to suggest the choking and subsequent releasing of the protein. Kait's eyes lit up. She understood, and it made great, perfect sense to her, too. But we didn't feel comfortable simply changing our regimen without consulting Dr. Robertson. Even though I had been gaining more and more knowledge about melanoma and Zelboraf, I was still no expert. We wanted his opinion. Maybe it had already been tested. Maybe they found out that once someone stops taking Zelboraf it never works again. We needed to be cautious.

Upon divulging the idea of intermittent use of Zelboraf to her oncologist, he sat and pondered briefly. He lauded my novel approach, but because no research had been knowingly done to test the particular strategy I brought up, he advised against it. With that, my excitement began to deflate, and I started second-guessing myself. I don't know why. I knew it would have been professionally irresponsible for Dr. Robertson to offer his blessing on an unproven method. He could not risk Kait's well-being or his career by advocating an untested approach – a sentiment I respect. But, I feel like I shouldn't have let it alter my confidence in the idea.

Needless to say, I cowered away from my potentially divine thought, and we continued on the original course of constant use of Zelboraf.

Well, sure enough, six months later, in January of 2013, I just so happened to stumble across an article touching upon the very same strategy that had come to my mind. Scientists had been testing intermittent use of Zelboraf after all. In their data, it was concluded that using it "on" for four weeks and then "off" for two weeks greatly reduced the melanoma cells' abilities in finding an alternate pathway. Upon reading that article, my heart sank. The answer delivered to me in my car was correct, and though it may not have cured Kait's cancer, it could have extended her life much longer.

Disappointment consumed me. It seemed I had ignored an obvious, clear sign from an unexplainable source, potentially a source from above. Neither did I have the courage, nor enough belief in the Lord to trust the blatantly distinct pathway laid out right in front of me.

Sure, you can call it simple intuition. You could say it came to my head because of my adequate knowledge of melanoma and Zelboraf. But, I don't think so. It wasn't the only sign or answer I ignored throughout our fight. It seemed I had turned my back on the calls of fate on numerous occasions, purely through ignorance. Possibly stupidity.

As of that January 2013, I told myself I would do my best to never again ignore a message that I had been actively seeking.

28 UPON FURTHER REFLECTION

The more I reflect back on my life, the more I realize how true the old cliché really is of "It's the small things in life that matter." So many of my most vivid memories aren't of extravagant vacations or things I bought Kait or she bought me. It's the seemingly trivial, simple moments that replay in my mind and put a smile on my face more than anything.

Just reflecting back on that August alone, I remember the warm greetings I would receive coming home from work. The big smile. The lunging hug. The feel of wrapping my hands around her fuzzy head, holding it against my body. The feel of her forehead pressed against my lips, or the feel of her soft cheeks gracing mine.

I remember an evening when Kait had become so restless from sitting at home all day, unable to drive anywhere because of the risk of a seizure with the cancer still in her brain, that she couldn't stay there any longer. So, after I returned from my job, we jumped into my car and took off to one of our favorite parlors to get ice cream. The small diner was neat in that it had little knick-knacks everywhere, old antiques, train sets, and activities to occupy our time. Together, we consumed so much ice cream that we couldn't even eat dinner that night. It was delicious and well worth it, I must say.

I remember coming home to a shocked Kaitlyn as she sat on the couch anxious to tell me of her odd experience for the day. While she was eating lunch, out of the corner of her eye she saw movement. When she looked, nothing was there, so she refocused her attention back to her food. A minute later, she saw something move again. This time when she glanced over, she saw a chipmunk sitting under our kitchen table. Startled, she grabbed the broom and chased it out of the apartment. As she told the story, I couldn't stop laughing just thinking about her reaction to seeing the tiny little intruder. The chipmunk had apparently chewed a hole in our screen door and slipped right through. Duct tape was Kait's remedy to keeping the unwanted critter out.

I remember the look of pure jubilation on Kait's face and the uncontrollable laughter after prank calling her cousin. Just seeing her beaming with delight and that bubbly smile, after everything she had gone through, it made me so happy.

I remember her rubbing my back on many nights to help me fall asleep.

I remember Kait waking up at 6 AM with me some mornings, when she was feeling good, to fix my lunch as I got ready for work. Those mornings, I would be bouncing off the walls, teeming with energy, as I danced and sang and talked her sleepy little ears right off. I completed my routines like a zombie on the mornings without her.

I remember for about two weeks straight, it was so hot in our room at night, even with the air conditioner on, that it was causing Kait to feel even more nauseous. So, we slept out in the living room where the temperature was cool and comfortable. She took the couch, and I blew up an inflatable mattress and laid it across the floor, pressing it right up against the couch next to her. And I couldn't have been happier, because I was with her.

Those memories may seem so small, but it's the seemingly insignificant memories that leave such an indelible mark. It's those small memories that have created such a lasting impact in defining our relationship.

29 SEIZURE SCARE...AGAIN

It was a sunny Saturday morning in mid-August as Kait and I snuggled up on the couch watching one of her all-time favorite TV shows, *Spongebob Squarepants* – entertainment for children. "It's not a boulder, it's a rock," Kait would quote with a smile as I pretended like I didn't find the show to be hilariously amusing in order to maintain the illusion that I was an adult. Throughout our relationship, at the most random of times, Kait would often recite quotes from her favorite episodes. At first, I didn't know what she was referencing when she would yell "Techniqueee!!!" as we were shooting hoops or playing Mario Party 5. I thought maybe she was just special. But when I finally found out those lines were in reference to Spongebob, I couldn't help but fall just a little bit more in love with her and her childlike exuberance.

Plopped in front of the TV as we slowly allowed ourselves to come into the day, suddenly, I heard her say, "Uh oh!"

"What's up honey?" The mood instantly changed.

"Ro...Ro....Rob. I can't say his name." Kait was trying to say Dr. Robertson's name, a name she spoke of almost every day and never had troubles.

"Ok. What's our address," I asked, trying to test the severity of her aphasia.

"Um. Um....," she worked hard to retrieve the place in her mind storing that piece of information, but she couldn't. "I don't know."

"Can you remember your other doctor's names?"

Looking at me concerned, she shook her head, unable to verbally communicate effectively. She then grabbed a notebook and pen in order to deliver written messages to me. Feverishly scribbling on the paper, she presented what she wrote. It said, "We need to call need to call Dr. Robertson."

Shit! Here we go again. She's going to have another seizure. Visions of her dropping to the floor and her face turning blue began swarming my mind. Another bleed in her head could spell disaster as we were told that any time a brain experiences hemorrhaging, there is a risk it could shut down completely. My heart began pumping rapidly and my pupils constricted as I tried to focus on the proper course of action. I didn't want to worry her, so I tried remaining as calm as possible.

"Okay honey, I'm going to move the table out of the way, just in case," I gently explained as I moved the coffee table away from the couch. If she did begin seizing, I wanted to make sure hard objects were cleared from the area.

Next, I debated whether or not to call the ambulance or take her to the hospital. If I took her to the hospital and she began convulsing in the car, that seemed more dangerous to her health than if she had a seizure at the apartment and I just called the ambulance then. But, I couldn't call the ambulance just yet because I didn't think they would respond to someone who "might" have a seizure. I decided to give her a few minutes to see if her disorientation improved.

Kaitlyn continued writing sentences in the notebook that didn't make complete sense as I sat next to her, gauging her status as best I could.

After a couple minutes passed, I decided that driving 10 or 15 minutes to the hospital would be the best course of action. Though the risk of a seizure in the car was eminent, waiting in the apartment for chaos seemed unwise and possibly more detrimental to her health. So, we entered my vehicle and departed.

On the way to the hospital, Kait called her mom to get the number for the on-call oncologist at UW. Since it was a Saturday, all of the doctors we were familiar with were gone. As Kathy delivered the telephone number, Kait wrote down the seven digits.

"Here Kait, let me see."

Kait showed me the number so I could call the oncologist on duty at the time.

"Kait, can you put the phone on speaker quick?" Kait complied. "KATHY," I yelled so she could hear me properly, "Can you repeat that number to make sure we have the right one?"

"Sure, Travis." Kathy repeated the telephone number as I listened. As I compared what Kathy was saying to what Kait had written in the notebook, I could see the numbers were all wrong.

"Uh oh, Kait, the number is wrong."

"Really?"

"Yeah. That's okay, sweetie.......Hey, Kathy," I yelled again. "Can you repeat the number one more time?" I figured I could just memorize it since it was only seven digits.

After disclosing the number once more, we ended our conversation, and I called the doctor on-call.

Surprisingly, upon arriving at the hospital, Kait had already begun to improve. Her ability to verbally communicate was returning, but her head ached. For the moment, it seemed we avoided another potentially catastrophic episode, but just to err on the side of caution, Kait received a quick set of CT scans to make sure there wasn't any excessive bleeding going on.

As the time passed at the hospital, Kait returned to her normal self and the scans came back fine. No bleeding took place in her brain. It was just another one of those unexplainable episodes of confusion, possibly brought on by nerves. Either way, we were just relieved nothing serious happened.

Just over a month had passed since Kait began her journey with Zelboraf, and it had noticeably taken its toll on her. The negative side effects of the poison were increasing to the point where she could no longer keep anything down in her stomach. She was miserable.

Malnourished, dehydrated, and becoming so weak she could hardly do anything, we had no choice but to have her admitted to the hospital to receive IV fluids. Kait's body desperately needed water and nutrients.

Arriving at the hospital, we quietly awaited her name to be called back. Kait was tired, her skin was pale, and her face was slightly drawn. My stomach churned for her anguish.

Once we were called back, the medical personnel hooked Kait up to a bag of fluids. As the liquid was being delivered into her veins, it wasn't long before the positive effects became apparent.

For some odd reason, the nurses administered an allergy medication to

Kait while she was receiving the fluids. Suddenly, she began reacting adversely to the medicine as she began shaking and running a fever. Her temperature rose to 102 as the nurses cautiously monitored it in case it jumped even higher. Secretly, I welcomed the fever. In my research, I read that our body goes into hyperactive fighting and healing mode during fevers, trying to flush our system from all foreign invaders. I thought and hoped that her immune system would work extra hard to seek out those pesky tumors.

After receiving two bags of the IV fluids, we were allowed to leave. Kaitlyn's skin regained its color and her energy returned immediately. I was thankful for that.

Dr. Robertson advised Kait to go on a weeklong vacation from her chemotherapy, and she happily obliged.

30 WEDDING PLANNING RECOMMENCED

With September rolling around and signs of fall whispering through the leaves, we had good reason to be optimistic. It had been almost two months since beginning her chemotherapy, and we were seeing a substantial reduction in the size of her tumors. The tumor located in the middle of her back, the one I used as my main tracker, had shrunk to the point where I had a hard time finding it. It was wonderful!

Though we knew the shrinkage was likely temporary, it felt good to hide reality behind the mask of positive results, and I think we deserved a reason to celebrate and be cheerful.

Even though she still wasn't feeling the best due to the chemo side effects, we attended a family cookout in Kenosha on her dad's side. Just as she did when she was a wee child, Kait helped her Papa Don lather the meat with barbecue sauce on the grill, for old time's sake. A special moment for her Grandpa. Throughout the evening, Kait fought through bouts of nausea and did her best to enjoy the company of her family, lawn games, and drinks.

Swept under the rug in lieu of recent events with her seizure, radiation, and chemotherapy were our wedding plans. Though we, especially Kait, never forgot we still had a wedding to make arrangements for, it became less important given the circumstances. But, finally, with Kait's cancer becoming stabilized, we felt safe to begin planning and preparing for our wedding day once again.

The wedding was nine months away, just around the corner, really. So, as a first step toward getting back on the saddle, we scheduled engagement pictures with my sister-in-law's mother.

And, on a beautiful day in early-September, we completed our photo shoot to get the word out about our upcoming day of holy matrimony. I looked like a goon, as always, but Kait, she looked as gorgeous as ever wearing her short blonde wig as her bright blue eyes sparkled in the sun. It further supported the notion that she could pull off any look.

Overall, we had some wonderful pictures to choose from, which made us ever so happy.

Second, third, and fourth on our list, respectively, was finding and hiring a DJ, a photographer, and a cake designer for the day of the wedding. During her free time while I worked, Kaitlyn kept herself occupied by exploring and contacting many prospective clients. Obviously, Kaitlyn's cognitive functions had been almost completely repaired. Even her short-term memory was improving.

After pouring over all of our options, we finalized our decisions and made our hires. Items two, three, and four were checked off our preparation list.

Whether our wedding day would actually come to fruition remained unclear, however, making plans reignited our flame of excitement, as marriage seemed closer and closer. With the success of her treatment, we felt confident the positive results would extend beyond the 6-month average and carry us to May 25th of 2013.

I must add, as close as that day seemed, it couldn't have felt further away. Even with the tumors decreasing in size, just getting through Christmas was ahead of making it to spring.

31 CONFIRMED SUCCESS

"And I'll…find strength in pain and I….will change my ways, I'll know my name as it's called again…." Holding our Kindle tablet by her ear, Kaitlyn nervously bobbed her head back and forth to the feverish banjo strumming of *Mumford & Sons*, the only band we loved together, as we sat in the waiting room of the hospital. It was MRI day, the day we had all been anxiously preparing for. Our skittishness was fueled merely by anticipation, and frankly, it was a waste of energy. Both of us knew the scans would present positive results. The tumors on her body had been noticeably decreasing in size as I measured them every day with my fingers, some to the point where they had almost disappeared. And, sure, we couldn't see the lesions in her brain, but Kait's vast mental improvements since being on the drug suggested definite tumor-shrinkage within her skull.

For some reason, though, even with obvious signs of cancer reduction, we still worried about receiving negative results. I suppose it's only natural, expecting the worst.

I sat in my chair observing Kait as she escaped into her folk music, trying to hum away her worries, and I found myself mesmerized once again by her incredible cuteness. Over the previous couple of months, I had been shaving her head once a week since her hair had only been growing in select spots. Now, it was starting to grow evenly all over, producing extremely soft hair that mimicked the down coat of a duckling. I loved the feel of it against my fingers as I gently grazed through the field of light-blonde fuzz.

Coupled with her adorable hair and bright, jolly cheeks was the fact that she was adorned with a white medical gown three sizes too big, throwing her head grossly out of proportion with her body. As bad as I felt for her because of how uncomfortable she was mentally preparing for her scans, I just wanted to squeeze her tight. I loved her so much! Faced with such adversity, our bond became unbreakable. We had truly become one as our love continued to blossom.

As the minutes ticked by, Kaitlyn was called back for a brief session of MRI scans.

Two days passed before our scheduled appointment to hear the results of her brain scans from Dr. Stevens. Going into the meeting, I expected good news, but didn't want to be too overconfident.

Displaying the images of Kait's brain scans on the computer screen, Dr. Stevens began toggling through until he arrived at a point of interest - a tumor. Comparing the most recent scans to images taken months earlier, it was clear, the five masses in Kait's brain had decreased significantly. Some had almost completely vanished, and the others had shrunk by more than 50%. We were thrilled by the news! Was it from the focused radiation or from the Zelboraf? It was impossible to tell. But, what mattered was the fact that we were seeing results in the most difficult area to treat.

Additionally, the news delivered by Dr. Robertson was equally good as he explained the images from Kait's full body scan. As assumed, the tumors in her body had decreased all over, and still, none had appeared in any organs. Throughout Kait's entire journey with melanoma, not once did a body scan reveal tumor growth in any of her organs, which included her liver, lungs, bones, etc., remaining only in the fatty tissue in her body. Of course, it did make its way up to the brain, the worst possible spot it could have decided to take refuge.

Out of all the positive news being passed along, Dr. Robertson did make one statement that raised a red flag in my mind. As he was explaining the results, under his breath he mentioned it looked like there were a couple new tumors. Did that mean Kait's cancer cells were beginning to find a way around her chemo already? Or, did it mean those were new tumors that appeared just before Zelboraf started, but after her June scans? I didn't know. Nevertheless, through my research I had a number of different clinical trials I had been making phone calls about. With Kait's brain tumors stable, it seemed logical to put Zelboraf back on the shelf for future use while we were able to qualify her for one of these novel studies. If Kait's cancer developed a resistance and started growing again, it was likely she wouldn't qualify for any clinical trials, so now was our best shot.

However, with too many unknown variables, my ambitions fell short in the doctor's eyes. Staying the course with Zelboraf remained the plan. But I can't blame our oncologist. If I truly felt confident in my ideas, we could have ventured off on our own and attempted to enter a clinical study. Like I said, it would have been extremely irresponsible for Dr. Robertson to recommend a strategy that hadn't been proven. He couldn't. He sincerely cared about Kait and was doing what he thought was best in order to keep her alive. But, fighting melanoma is far from an exact science. A hundred doctors in a room might have a hundred different answers or opinions. I can only blame me for being a coward, not trusting myself, and not taking responsibility. I was too scared to be the one responsible should Kait pass away because my method of choice didn't work, which was silly because most of my ideas were backed by data.

32 TRANSITIONING PERIOD

In October, I began a new job. For a year, I had wanted to venture off to new challenges, and, well, get paid more money, but with Kait's health in limbo, our life became unstable and I didn't think it was fair for any new employer to acquire such a burden. What if our situation changed drastically, forcing me to leave or take extended time off?

However, with Kait's cancer in remission, I felt like the time was right.

As the days passed and as I continued to monitor the tumors on Kait's body, my optimism slowly started to drift toward pessimism. For two straight months starting at Zelboraf's inception, I could noticeably feel a difference in the tumors on her body. I was always 100% positive they had been shrinking. Now, it was becoming hard to tell.

Before Kait's scans, I had a difficult time locating the tumor in the middle of her back, near her spine. Now, combing her back with my index and middle finger, it seemed like I was having an easier time finding it. I didn't want to panic just yet, though. What if I had just gotten so used to locating the tumor that it became natural? What if my mind was playing tricks on me? Maybe Kait was standing at a different angle before. Maybe her posture was pushing the tumor out more? Maybe since she lost five pounds the tumor was more prominent? I didn't want to jump to any conclusions, and her other tumors seemed to be the same size. A part of me, though, was beginning to worry that the mass on her back had started to grow once more. Either way, it was no cause for alarm at the moment.

Progress on wedding planning continued to be made as we were charging full steam ahead. It was October 13th, and Kaitlyn was up and out of bed bright and early to prepare for a wonderful day – a day of modeling an assortment of wedding dresses, hopefully discovering the perfect one for our big day. With all the calamities that had occurred since springtime, with all of the bad news, with the chemo, and everything else, the likelihood of this day ever arriving was murky at best. Now that it had actually came to be, it was an event to cherish for Kait and some of the most special women in her life.

With Kathy, Vicky, Sherri (my mother), Jessica, and Lex, Kait and the bunch journeyed off to hunt for the perfect dress.

For months and months, Kait had explored all over in hopes of finding the right look for her special day, zeroing in on a short list of dresses. With the desired style and design set, her frugality was poised to be the biggest obstacle in finalizing her wedding ensemble. Family and friends knew Kait as the ultimate bargain shopper. On one football Sunday in October, she insisted she wanted to shop alone, walk the mall, peruse at her own pace, and spare me from hours of wasted energy. As much as I told her I didn't mind missing football, she was adamant about going by herself. After three hours of browsing a multitude of stores, she brought home six or seven articles of clothing and spent a mere $20. Her cheapskate ways were wholly amusing to me. Even if I told her I would buy anything for her on any clothes rack, she could never bring herself to pick out anything above $40 or $50, a blessing for any man.

Adhering to her thrifty ways, Kait set herself a limit – no dresses over $1,000.

The first store they went to was somewhat of a let down for the group. Not only were the dresses undesirable, but they were also given a time limit. Everyone knows it takes four days just to put on a dress, so it seemed completely inappropriate to rush the bride in her difficult decision. Needless to say, the first store wasn't appreciated as the women left and didn't look back.

Moving on to option number two, Kait and the flock of hens traveled with high aspirations to the second bridal shop, confident they would strike gold.

The second store was completely opposite from the first. With a long, elegant staircase and a much calmer, comfortable atmosphere, shop number two made its guests feel completely welcomed; not rushed.

Skimming through a multitude of dresses, Kait and family picked out a handful of different options, keeping Kait's budget in mind. She paraded down the catwalk modeling the various ensembles. And as beautiful as Kait looked in the dresses, they just weren't "it." Either the material wasn't right, the color was off, or there was some other glaring deficiency, but none of the dresses piqued the group's collective interest.

Slowly perusing through the floor of dresses, Kathy noticed a gorgeous outfit matching exactly the style and design Kait had in mind. Without consulting Kaitlyn first, Kathy swiped it off the rack even though the price tag revealed an amount well above Kait's range. But, it looked so wonderful Kathy at least wanted her to try it on first.

To make her mother happy, Kaitlyn agreed to give it a chance.

"Don't let her see the price," Kathy advised the store manager. Nodding her head, they reached a silent accord as the lady took Kait back to put on the dress.

The five women sat patiently as they awaited the beautiful bride-to-be.

After a few minutes, Kaitlyn stepped out from behind the curtain. With the dress shimmering as she walked and her face sparkling with delight, Kait looked enchanting.

The reaction of the audience was unexpected. Silence! Kaitlyn's stunning beauty left the crowd speechless. This was THE dress she was to marry me in and everyone could sense it. Everyone could feel it.

No more than a few seconds after presenting her outfit on the catwalk, tears began streaming down the faces of every woman in the room, even employees standing in watch. It was that magical moment every mother waits to have with her daughter, and that moment was fully realized, and it was beautiful!

Kait was set. She had found the dress she had been hoping to find. But then she saw the figure on the price tag, and it almost caused her eyes to pop out of her head.

"Mom, I can't buy this dress, it's way too much!"

"Kait, honey, don't worry about price. That dress is so perfect for you!"

Everyone agreed.

"But, mom, I can't afford this. It's way out of my budget."

"Don't worry about it, Kait. I'll take care of it."

As much as she didn't want to accept the charity, she couldn't resist the dress's beauty and the way it made her feel. The offer was one she couldn't refuse. They purchased the dress.

The group left the store feeling euphoric and triumphant. With the future uncertain, even if things were to take a turn for the worse, at least the family had this one special day to look back on and remember. And, what a special day it was.

From what I had been told, I couldn't wait to see her adorned in her beautiful dress as she walked down the aisle to make me the luckiest man in the world!

It was the middle of October, and I was starting fresh at my new job — learning new tasks, a new system, and meeting new people. I was excited.

My boss, who was also the Vice President of the company, happened to be a pretty cool guy. I didn't reveal my personal situation to him during the interview, which only lasted 15 minutes, but on the first day of work I brought it up because I felt it was important for him to know in case I needed to leave suddenly for any reasons. Shocked at first, he informed me that the owner of the company lost a sister to melanoma back in the 80s, a sad coincidence. Either way, I felt at home in my new gig and it seemed like the perfect fit.

During my breaks I continued my routine of searching up and down the Internet, hoping to come upon answers. By now, I had become quite knowledgeable about melanoma and how it functioned, about conventional treatments, and about alternative treatments. Now that it was questionable whether or not Kait's cancer was still stable, I felt like I had to have a plan ready to go along with five or six back-up plans.

Because my company was so close to home, I was able to go back to the apartment on my lunch break and see Kaitlyn. It was wonderful coming home, absorbing a big hug, talking, and eating lunch with my sweetheart!

Unfortunately, the upper half of the hourglass was already almost empty for my new job.

33 DARKNESS LOOMS

From the beginning of October, Kait began experiencing minor discomfort just beneath her lower right ribcage. Whenever she laid on her side, she felt a slight amount of pain. As much as I feared the worst, I tried to convince myself not to worry too much. Not yet.

Nausea also crept back into Kait's life, progressively becoming more volatile, making it harder to keep meals down. The sickness wasn't nearly as bad as what it was back in August, but it still wasn't comfortable.

On the Friday evening after successfully completing my first week of work, I did my usual check up on Kait to measure her tumors. Again, there was something peculiar about the one on her back. It did feel slightly bigger, but I still wasn't sure if maybe my mind was simply having a difficult time telling a difference. It was still too early to jump to any rash conclusions.

I continued checking her other tumors to see if they had increased in size. Kait joined in, performing a self-assessment on her body. Fixated on the tumors I was evaluating, Kait interrupted my focus with a concern of her own.

"Hmmm. Here, Trav, feel this one," she said, "It feels bigger."

Her left hand was just under her right armpit, a spot I frequently monitored. As my hand replaced hers, I felt the bump in question. It was definitely bigger.

"Hm. Yeah, I don't know. It does feel bigger."

That's weird. This tumor feels lower than usual. I could have sworn it was located higher up. I thought to myself. I continued feeling around the large mass when suddenly, I found the original tumor, and it was still small. That meant….the tumor we were questioning…..was a new one. My heart sank.

"Uh oh…… Honey….. This is a new one."

"Hmmm." She felt it again and then felt the old one to compare. "Yeah, you're right." She paused. "Here's another one."

Just under the new tumor, she spotted a second. *Shit!*

It had only been a couple weeks at most, and those tumors were already large in mass, evidencing the fact that they had grown at a rapid pace.

I continued searching around. Right above her chest, we found another tumor that wasn't there before. My heart sank even more…..

Fuck!

After a mere three months on Zelboraf, her cancer had built up a resistance and now seemed stronger than ever. We immediately called Dr. Robertson, but it was late on a Friday and he had already left for the weekend, so we agreed to do our best to just wipe it from our minds until Monday. A couple days couldn't hurt. At least that's what we thought.

The bottom line now – it was time to kick into overdrive. We had to move to our next treatment, and we had to move fast. I would not allow myself to rest until we found our next strategy.

On Monday morning, after struggling to maintain focus through a meeting with two investment bankers, I requested a quick meeting with my boss. For an hour and a half, I prepared myself on what I was going to say. And no matter what, I absolutely was not going to cry. My plan was to simply present him with the facts and tell him what I needed.

We entered his office. I sat down.

"So what's up," Bill asked.

I composed myself.

"When I took this job, Kaitlyn's cancer had been in remission for a while. It was under control. That's why I felt safe to take a new job. And, last week, when I told you about our situation, everything was stable. But, now, a week after starting…..," my mouth started to quiver as my body began to shake while trying to hold back my tears, "….it's growing again."

As I finished my last sentence, I could no longer hold back as I began to sob.

"Oh shit," my boss replied, sincerely concerned for Kait and me.

"I'm sorry. Just give me a minute. I didn't want to cry."

"Are you kidding? If it were me I'd be a bumbling baby."

I smiled.

Bill asked me if I needed anything, informing me I could come and go as needed. His understanding was greatly appreciated. I also had the support of the owner, which was reassuring.

Throughout the rest of the day, I tried going about it as normal as I could, working on assignments and learning new tasks.

Feeling the sharp pinch, I was restless and in a frenzy. During my breaks, I got on the horn, contacting multiple universities who were hosting clinical trials. I was calling Sloan Kettering in New York, Vanderbilt, University of Illinois, M.D. Anderson in Texas, UCLA, and others, and each institution needed Kait's records, so I jumped on the phone and began coordinating with UW to get them dispersed. I was printing and filling out forms, faxing them to UW and faxing them to the other universities. The switch to shut off my adrenaline was broken.

Even though Kait's tumors began growing again, there existed a small chance that her brain mets remained stable. But, if they were still stable, it would only be a matter of time before they did start back up, so we had to be extremely hasty in finding a formidable study. And it became frustrating, because as I was trying to coordinate the delivery of Kait's medical records, I had to call UW multiple times only to find out something had been forgotten about or misplaced on their end, and her records weren't being sent. Time was of the essence, so it was crucial that they be processed quickly. I knew everyone was busy, but I was told they would fax over her information immediately, so I trusted that. If they couldn't, I would have appreciated it if they would have at least been honest and tell me it could be a day or two.

The next day, I did some more research and found out that once the cancer cells find a way around Zelboraf, it essentially becomes nourishment for the cancer cells and can cause them to grow faster. So, I called Dr. Robertson and we discussed that concern. He then advised Kait to stop taking the Zelboraf for the time being.

As the week progressed, Kait began feeling more and more discomfort in certain areas. I had no doubt in my mind the cancer had moved to her organs or her bones. My stress level remained at a maximum, and I didn't expect it to cease in the foreseeable future. Not until we were safely on a new treatment.

On October 29th, Kaitlyn turned 24 years old. To celebrate, we went out to dinner at an elegant Italian joint in downtown Madison. It was a lovely dinner. We talked about everything except for cancer. The food was great, and we thoroughly enjoyed each other's company as usual. Unfortunately, when we got home, for some reason Kaitlyn threw it up. Was it too rich? She had stopped taking Zelboraf, so we didn't know what caused her to vomit.

To keep the ball rolling, I had set up an appointment for Kait with the University of Illinois, hoping to get her qualified for one of their clinical trials. After that, I set up another appointment with Vanderbilt for a week later. But first, Kait needed to go in for scans to assess her situation and see where the cancer had moved. Because Kait didn't seem to lose any of her mental capabilities, I remained slightly confident the tumors in her brain had remained stable. Then again, when the cancer was growing in her brain back in April and May, her intellect never wavered. So, it was impossible to tell for sure.

In the meantime, I had a dichotomy of strategies. Down one road, in the scenario where the cancer in her head was stable, we would enter one of many clinical trials. However, down the second road, if the tumors in her brain had started growing again, I wanted Kaitlyn to go on a combination of Ipilimumab and a drug called Temodar. Over the span of a couple weeks, I came into contact with a couple of people who had had success with that very combination of drugs. One in particular had 14 brain tumors and cancer all over her body. After receiving the Ipi/Temodar cocktail, all of the masses in her brain disappeared, and almost all of the spots in her body were gone. I called the doctor that administered the combination to that particular patient, and he said many people under his care were given that combo, receiving positive results in the majority.

So, I started researching the duo of drugs a bit more. I found out a Phase II clinical trial had been completed, and it had experienced an overall disease control rate of 67%, which was much higher than either agent alone.

Then, I called an institution that had currently been running a clinical trial, MD Anderson in Texas, and they informed me of the success they were having with the combination of Ipilimumab and Temodar.

I was convinced. After a few amazing anecdotal stories, the blessing from more than one professional, and positive evidence from an actual study, I felt the Ipi/Temodar combo was THE option to go with should we find out Kait's brain tumors had begun to grow again. If not, we would keep it as our "ace in the hole."

All of the frenetic research and scheduling was mentally draining, but giving into exhaustion was out of the question. Love and the fear of it being taken from me was my cocaine.

Scans were done in early November on Kaitlyn's brain and body.

Though I thought for certain the melanoma had spread into her bones or at least some organs, I was relieved to find out it had remained in her fatty tissue. If only the news from the brain scans was equally as good.

Sitting inside a small medical room, we waited for Dr. Robertson to come in with a smile, shake Kait's hand, then mine, before sitting down and delivering positive information like he always did. We played games on our tablet as the time passed.

A short while later, Dr. Robertson walked in. His face revealed no joy.

"Well, I'm afraid I don't have good news."

Foregoing any handshake or greeting, he didn't hesitate before taking a seat and popping up the reports on his computer.

I could feel the blood in my body accelerating in speed as my face became flushed with redness. This was not good. I held Kait's hand tight, gently rubbing her back with my other hand.

"It looks like the lesions in your brain have increased in size, and there appears to be a few news ones."

FUCK!

Any chance of qualifying Kait for any clinical trial was killed at that moment. Right then I began regretting in my head not temporarily delaying Kait's Zelboraf to get her entered into a study back in September.

Dr. Robertson continued explaining the results, informing us that Dr. Stevens would not do brain radiation again. With that, I knew what Dr. Robertson's next suggestion would be because I was well acquainted with the universal melanoma playbook. He was going to recommend Temodar as a single agent. No combination. Just Temodar.

And I was right.

I had done my due diligence on Temodar beforehand. When taken alone, the results were poor. Some articles listed its success at 10%, others at 20%. If it did work, it would only keep the tumors from growing. It wouldn't promote shrinkage.

Kaitlyn was on board with me. She heard the story about the woman and others who had received the Ipi/Temodar combo, and she really wanted to receive the two together. Kaitlyn agreed that if we were serious about fighting the disease, Temodar as a single agent would not be an option.

So, with that, I immediately brought up the Ipi and Temodar combination. Dr. Robertson wasn't so receptive to it, however, because the data and testing still wasn't complete. But I was convinced that there WAS enough evidence out there to support the combo. He liked the idea of going on Temodar by itself for a while and then eventually transitioning back to Ipilimumab, but to me that also wasn't an option. Ipilimumab needed a couple of months to kick in. If we waited until Temodar stopped working, her tumors would grow out of control before the Ipilimumab could ever begin to work.

Kait's oncologist still wasn't convinced. I could understand his reservations, but I wasn't satisfied.

As the doctor continued to gently refuse our treatment request, Kait began to sob. She was going against Dr. Robertson, a man she completely trusted and respected. It broke her heart just thinking of the idea that we may have to find another oncologist willing to honor our request. Kaitlyn agreed with me that Temodar alone was not the answer. So, Dr. Robertson advised us to still go down to the University of Illinois and at least get a second opinion since we no longer qualified for the clinical trial there.

We entered the hospital confident a plan of attack would have been devised and decided upon. However, we left discouraged and disappointed with nothing. We had the exact treatment strategy in mind that we wanted, and it wasn't like we were reaching. It was a well-known combination of drugs used by a number of doctors, and it had been garnering success. Why couldn't we get what we wanted? Why wasn't this our choice? Now what were we to do? Kait's cancer seemed to be galloping as new tumors began popping up almost every day. Should we just go with Temodar alone, even if we had almost no confidence in it? I didn't think we should.

But, we seemed backed into a corner with little choice. It normally takes weeks to even get set up with a new doctor and become acclimated with the new team. Additionally, if Kait were to begin Temodar, no other doctors would likely take her in if they saw she was currently on a treatment. Frustration set in.

Fortunately, all on her own, Kaitlyn had been making phone calls and setting up appointments at the Cancer Treatment Center of America (CTCA) in Goodyear, Arizona, right next to Phoenix. Kait received the recommendation from her aunt, Julie, who worked at a CTCA in Illinois, informing her of a quality melanoma doctor.

As proud as I was of Kait for taking the responsibility and initiative to contact the institution on her own, I wasn't overly thrilled about the idea of actually checking it out mainly because of my lack of knowledge about the hospitals. Those reservations were quickly squelched, however, after I read all of the positive reviews and found out they were willing to take innovative approaches toward attacking cancer. I felt more confident they'd be receptive to the Ipilimumab/Temodar combination we so desperately wanted. Also, I was interested in hearing what other ideas they would have in mind.

So, with that, we booked our trip to Arizona for November 14th. A part of me thought that if nothing else, traveling to Phoenix during the cold month of November could at least be a mini-vacation, and we needed to get away.

In the meantime, while we awaited our trip, I had Kait start consuming apricot seeds, hoping they could at least slow the growth of her cancer in the interim. When typing "apricot seeds" into the Google search bar on the Internet, the first option that appears is "apricot seeds and cancer." Additionally, she began ingesting Turmeric, Green Tea supplements, Resveratrol, and other regular vitamins. In my mind I didn't really believe those supplements would do much, if anything, but I believed there was a chance they could help decrease the rate at which her cancer was growing, and a mere chance was all I needed to justify their use.

With my mind busy and exerted beyond its limit, working and learning new tasks at my job became increasingly difficult. As I continued searching around desperately for clinical trials that took patients with brain tumors, because I wanted as many backup plans as possible, my mind was in a state of perpetual worry. The walls inside my world were slowly moving in. Tumors were blooming all over her body.

One of my greatest fears was that I would return home from work to see Kaitlyn lying on the floor after having suffered a seizure. I text messaged her often throughout the day to check in. Also, every single night after having gone to bed, I would wake up multiple times during the wee hours and stare at her until I saw her chest rise. Another one of my greatest worries was that she would suffer a hemorrhage and pass away in her sleep, so I had to make sure she was still breathing. In some instances, because she was such a light breather, I would wait 8 to 10 seconds before she inhaled. Those moments almost sent me into a panic until she finally took a breath.

Visions of a future without Kait littered my mind, and it hurt. I feared we wouldn't even make it to Christmas together.

On November 13th, we had an appointment set up to see Dr. Gresky at the University of Illinois. We no longer qualified for his particular clinical trial, but we at least wanted a second opinion.

The evening before our meeting with Dr. Gresky, while staying in Kenosha, my gut was screaming at me to forego our scheduled appointment and spare Kait the misery. Traveling to Chicago with the horrendous traffic would potentially cause an excessive amount of stress on Kait, and with tumors growing again in her brain, the risk of hemorrhaging increased. I wanted to evade that risk. Plus, I had no doubt in my mind that our next treatment would come from CTCA in Arizona, essentially rendering the rigorous trek to Chicago a waste of time.

After sleeping on my worries, I woke up the next morning with the same nagging intuition. My mind was scrambling to find a way to tell everyone we shouldn't go to Chicago, but I didn't want to come off as the irrational, impulsive type. In my cowardice, I remained silent.

We took off.

As expected, the morning Chicago traffic was awful. Kait's stomach had already been weakened by months of chemotherapy, and the constant rapid acceleration and deceleration on the road induced a carsickness not felt before.

After only a few miles of jerking and jutting, Kait's stomach had all it could take.

"Oh no, I'm gonna throw up," she cried.

Frantically feeling around the vehicle, we luckily pulled out a plastic bag. Quickly opening the bag, Kaitlyn immediately released all that had been stored in her belly. She was miserable. Unfortunately, Tom didn't realize he could remedy the situation by simply easing on the gas and easing on the breaks while ignoring the negative judgments of other drivers around him.

"Please stop," Kaitlyn implored.

"I'm sorry, Kait. There's nothing I can do," Tom said. He felt terrible.

By the time we arrived at the hospital in Chicago, Kaitlyn was extremely weak, and she felt like she was going to pass out. To compound our woes, we couldn't find a parking spot, of course. Up and down the parking ramp we went, unable to find a single opening. Finally, as my anxieties increased for Kait, I just told Tom to let us out so we could at least stop moving and get some fresh air. It seemed like I could feel every bit of Kait's agony, as though we were connected in some mysterious way.

After exiting the car, I grabbed Kait's bag of vomit and tossed it in the garbage, although she was reluctant and self-conscious at first because of the repulsiveness of it. Feeling physically shaky and frail, Kathy led Kaitlyn to a bench where she could regain her strength as I sought out a wheelchair. Kait badly needed food and water to replenish all that she had lost.

I found a wheelchair, some water, and some food for her to snack on, as she slowly improved.

Even though we made it to Chicago, I sincerely regretted not speaking out and stopping the trip from happening. To me, it really was more harmful and meaningless than it was positive as it caused unneeded stress on a body that desperately needed its immune system in full working order.

Inside the building, we met with Dr. Gresky. His goofiness was on full display, but he was a very nice guy, nevertheless. After the usual meet-and-greet and summarizing Kait's medical history, we began to deliberate. When I mentioned the Ipi/Temodar combination, I was surprised when my idea wasn't immediately rejected as he said, "We could certainly do that if that's what you want."

His first suggestion was Stereotactic Radiosurgery (SRS), which, as a basic explanation, is a method of pinpoint radiation to target specific brain tumors, similar to the Tomotherapy Kait received in June, however, SRS is more precise and delivers higher doses of radiation. Dr. Gresky's hope was to stabilize her brain tumors in order to quickly get her qualified for one of his clinical trials, a notion I was on board with. But, we found out a day later from Dr. Stevens that any more radiation to the brain could cause severe damage, possibly resulting in death. So, the option of SRS was thrown out the window.

We left Chicago with some ideas, but nothing decided upon. I appreciated Dr. Gresky's openness to listen and consider all options, keeping our desires in mind, but it seemed in the end our trip to Chicago merely resulted in wasted energy. My initial gut instinct was ultimately right.

34 ARIZONA BOUND

The next day, we were on a plane headed to Goodyear, Arizona, confident we'd return home with a new treatment.

During the flight, when it felt like a cloud literally slapped the top of our plane, inducing gasps from multiple passengers, it was Kait's turn to comfort me. With my heart pumping like rabbits mating, with my palms sweaty and eyes fixated on the landscape below, I assumed we were headed for a fiery crash – an assumption I always make at the slightest bump of turbulence, I'm ashamed to admit. To calm my frantic nerves Kait began rubbing my arm, encouraging me to "breeeeaatthe…..," as if I was going into labor (that's how I acted). And when I looked over at her, meeting my eyes with hers, I could just see the sincere care and love pouring out at me. She was so amazing! But then it dawned on me; here was this girl trudging along in life against terrible circumstances, actually facing death. And here I am, facing basically nothing, and I'm the one needing comfort and support? Geesh….how despicable of me. That's why I loved her so much, though!

Eventually, we made it to Phoenix and were immediately escorted to the hospital. Kait was anxious to get started.

On that Wednesday, one of Kait's physical features captured my attention and concern – her gorgeous smile. I noticed it had begun to change slightly. When she smiled, it remained straight for the most part, but her left side appeared to be just a bit weaker. Though we couldn't see her brain tumors, monitoring the functionality of the left side of her face was a good indicator of how fast they were growing.

Also, becoming more frequent was the fact that many of the tumors springing up just beneath Kait's skin had begun to bruise, and some were in delicate spots near her joints. When we were shopping for groceries in Arizona, Kaitlyn accidentally dropped a box of food. As an almost involuntary, natural reaction, she quickly reached out to try and catch it before it crashed to the ground. With a tumor growing around the joint of her elbow, inhibiting movement and pressing up against her muscles, extending her arm as rapidly as she did caused excruciating pain. She immediately keeled to the ground, wincing. When I looked at her arm, I could see inflammation instantly rising from an already black and blue area on the inside of her elbow. I felt bad for her.

As concerned and worried as I was though, I felt confident that whatever treatment we started at CTCA would destroy the tumors causing those painful obstructions.

Between Thursday and Friday, we had a slew of appointments set up to meet with doctors of various specializations, like a nutritionist, a naturopath, etc. The perpetual skeptic in me began to wonder whether or not all of those appointments were scheduled simply so the hospital could charge our insurance company and "earn" more revenue. I mean, we were given about 15 minutes with each specialist, and we weren't necessarily enlightened in that short, rushed time span. The nutritionist gave us a list of "cancer foods" to eat and the naturopath gave us a meditation CD to listen to, information easily found on the web.

Though both days were long and exhausting, we were still able to spend quality time together while at the hospital. The weather was wonderful, so we took advantage by going outside and playing shuffle board, putting golf balls on their miniature green, and just sitting back and talking. Kait bought gifts for family and friends, and we also picked out a cute new purplish bandana for her to wear.

When Friday evening rolled around, we were finally scheduled to meet our new melanoma oncologist. By that time, the bruising in Kait's arm from trying to catch the box of food had basically covered the whole inside of her forearm with a wide array of colors. And the droopiness in the left side of her face had become more noticeable than from two days earlier, indicating the tumor on the right side of her brain was growing at a fast rate, further reinforcing the need to move quickly.

As we sat waiting in a small room for our new doctor, watching television on the flat screens provided, a short Asian man with gray hair combed back to his shoulders walked in. His name was Dr. Lee. He had a very calm, compassionate demeanor, and Kaitlyn took a liking to him immediately, though he was no Dr. Robertson. After shaking our hands and introducing himself and his team, he asked questions to gain a better perspective on Kait's situation. I was anxious and curious to hear about his ideas. What concerned him most, of course, were the tumors in her brain.

"You've been dealt a tough hand with those brain tumors," he said. In a way, I interpreted his posture and tone of voice to mean he thought her situation was almost hopeless. Then again, maybe it was just my fatigue inducing my cynicism.

When it finally came time to talk about treatment options, I immediately brought up the Ipilimumab and Temodar combination. He briefly pondered the idea, but then dismissed it based on the fact we had just increased her steroid intake to reduce inflammation in the brain. I was regretful.

Dammit! I thought to myself. *Why couldn't we have started that combo two weeks ago when I suggested it, before she even began taking steroids again?*

With my desired combination off the table, Dr. Lee had a different treatment plan in mind, one involving a combination of three different chemotherapy drugs – Lomustine, Vincristine, and Bleomycin – along with a steroid called Prednisolone. And to be completely honest, at that point I didn't even really care what the drugs were, I was just relieved to hear of another approach besides Temodar alone. Then, come to find out, Lomustine and Temodar are quite similar, anyway.

As Dr. Lee explained the justification behind his approach, he informed us the combination had been used multiple times on patients with a good amount of success.

"Well, do you have any statistics, by any chance," I asked.

"Well sure. Around 40% receive an objective response."

That percentage was higher than anything else we had been offered. As he continued explaining the idea behind his recommendation, he threw out the "magic" word, the word most oncologists consider irresponsible and misleading – cure. Dr. Lee mentioned that some patients had achieved a complete response. They had been "cured." Of course, our ears perked right up. Either what he was saying was true, or he was a good car salesman working with a for-profit organization trying to persuade us into purchasing their product whether it was effective or not. I hoped it was the former.

Though we were intrigued, we wanted the weekend to mull over our options. It was likely we would elect to go with the three-drug cocktail, but we wanted to involve everyone else before finalizing.

Before leaving for Arizona, Dr. Robertson had requested us to ask our CTCA oncologist to contact him to confer about whatever potential treatment plan was suggested. When I asked Dr. Lee about calling Dr. Robertson, he was hesitant before explaining that most oncologists don't agree with his approaches because they haven't gone through every phase of clinical testing, yet. To avoid ridicule and confrontation, he preferred not to consult with other doctors.

Upon returning to our hotel room, we discussed the presented option with the family, and I researched other variations of Dr. Lee's treatment plan to examine its efficacy. Pressed for time as the walls around us continued to close in, we really didn't have much of a choice. We had to make a move and make it quick, and Dr. Lee's idea seemed better than any other concept readily available to us (though I still wanted the Ipi/Temodar combination). So we scheduled Kaitlyn to begin treatment starting that following Monday.

And with images and aspirations of an obliterated cancer dancing through our heads, we were honestly excited to begin treatment. As for myself, it felt like a huge weight was lifted off my shoulders and I could finally relax, a little bit. After a month of intense research, contacting institutions, and coordinating appointments, compounded with my immense worry for Kait, my brain needed the break. Though I know in the end all of my research proved to be futile, like I figured it would, I would have never forgiven myself if I didn't try.

After days of non-stop appointments and hours spent at the cancer facility, we welcomed the weekend with open arms.

We rented a car to escape the constraints of our hotel and explore the surrounding area in Phoenix. To get some exercise and enjoy the fresh, open air, we decided to take a hike on Camelback Mountain, our second choice from the beautiful Red Rocks in Sedona. We didn't pack warm clothes for the cold, wintry weather of Sedona so we had to settle for

Camelback.

As we ascended the mountain, following the trail, a couple small tumors buried within Kait's legs slightly obstructed her motion as they pressed against her hamstrings. The accompanying pain was not enough to hold her down, however, as her strength and enduring resilience allowed her to overcome the annoying impediments. Other than that, her ability to walk was perfectly normal.

After hiking through eight different checkpoints, we stopped at every subsequent one, and I would ask Kait if she wanted to proceed forward or head back down. She wasn't ready to stop, so we continued climbing. Passing by tall cacti on the barren, desert-looking side of the mountain and taking pictures at various stops, we finally decided to turn around at about the 18th checkpoint.

The descent actually ended up being more difficult, as we had to gently lower ourselves from tall rocks onto the loose gravel below. It was tiring and caused soreness to our ankles and leg muscles, but as avid exercisers we both welcomed the pain from a good workout. Eventually, we reached the bottom.

I do mean to be trite in saying how proud and amazed I was of Kaitlyn and her awesomeness, yet again, as she was able to traverse three miles without a hiccup or complaint. Aside from the lack of hair on her head, one would have never guessed she was battling a life-threatening disease. Her toughness astounded me.

Then, as another way to explore Phoenix, and because we sadly hadn't been to a zoo in all of our years together, we decided to pay a visit to the animal facility in Phoenix, which oddly turned out to be a depressing experience after having seen how miserable many of the animals were.

The visit started out on a positive note as we bore witness to a pair of turtles in a creek entertaining the masses at no charge as the male positioned itself atop the female to consummate their love. Laughing, Kaitlyn couldn't resist as she quickly pulled out her camera to capture the beautiful moment of procreation.

With her camera still out, Kait decided to snap a picture of the two of us, something she often did. Because she never smiled at herself in the mirror, this was really the first time she saw her evolving smile, and she didn't like it. She began deleting the photos. By that Sunday, the left side of her face had become almost completely paralyzed, and her smile was even more asymmetrical. I did my best to reassure her that her tilted grin was even cuter than before, but she didn't believe me. Unfortunately, she had little choice but to accept her physical "imperfection," so she did just that. It was only supposed to be temporary, anyway. We just had to wait for the growing tumor on the right side of her brain to be destroyed. Also piquing my concern was the fact that Kait's paralysis began creeping down into her arm as she started losing strength in her left hand. As much as I smiled for her on the outside, my soul wept on the inside.

We continued hiking through the zoo, checking out every single animal we could. To our disappointment, most of the animals were either out of sight in their cages, or in hiding. The ones that weren't hiding all seemed to be suicidal, as they hated the quarters they were being contained in. When we stopped at the orangutan enclosure, the two that were inside were hunched over on the ground, turned away from the crowd, and using their fingers to draw pictures in the dirt. One got the sense how much they hated their existence. Most of the animals at the zoo expressed the same sort of disdain for their habitat and conditions, and we felt bad for them.

Either way, we were at least glad to be out in the fresh air, enjoying the sub-80-degree temperatures while getting good exercise.

Monday rolled around rather quickly, and Kaitlyn was ever so anxious to begin treatment.

To start the morning off on a sour note, however, we found out that Dr. Robertson waited by his phone on Friday evening, hoping to receive a call from our CTCA oncologist, and that call never came. We felt terrible. But, we were also grateful that he cared enough about us to be willing to spend his afterhours at work to make sure his patient was properly taken care of.

Before beginning treatment, Kaitlyn was scheduled to have a port installed, which is a medical appliance inserted beneath the skin and is perpetually attached to a vein, in order to easily draw blood or administer chemotherapy. That way, Kait wouldn't need to be stabbed with a needle every time labs were required or drugs needed to be delivered. With her enormous aversion to needles, it was a perfect solution.

Unfortunately, in order to install the device, an IV needed to be connected to her veins before they could begin the procedure. With Kait's tiny veins, the nurses struggled to successfully connect the line to her nearly invisible vessels. They made multiple attempts and failed each time.

The pain started getting to Kait, but the psychological torture was cause for the majority of her discomfort. Also, with the tumors in her brain, she had less control over her emotions, and she began sobbing. She was miserable. The nurses kept poking, unable to find a vein. With Kait under increasing and considerable distress, the nurses decided to wheel Kait into another section that had more effective tools, a section where I was not allowed. I was forced to leave behind a scared, distraught Kaitlyn, and it pulled at my emotional strings.

As I walked out of the surgery wing, I felt a sea of tears flooding my head, trying to filter through my eyes, but I kept them subdued. For the first time, I felt like the disease had taken hold of Kaitlyn, and the physical defects and deterioration from the rapidly growing cancer were becoming more and more apparent, and I felt awful for her. She was becoming frail. She was becoming brittle. She was falling apart. It was all happening right in front of my eyes and I had absolutely zero control over her fate. It was breaking my heart. And, it tore me up inside knowing this small, sweet girl had to endure such a tragic circumstance. To add to my sadness, the visuals being manufactured in my mind were of her in the back surgery room, miserable from the physical and emotional pain of the needles, crying to be liberated from the torment. I wished so badly I could take her place.

Drowning in a pool of mental anguish, all I could do was sit down on a chair and wait, powerless as usual.

As the time passed, I was like a puppy in distress, waiting for the return of my loving owner who I depended so dearly on. Finally, after only 45 minutes and a successful surgery, I was allowed back to see Kait in the recovery room where she would remain for another hour.

Still groggy from the anesthetics, Kaitlyn looked quite tired with blankets piled on top of her to keep her shivering body warm. With her bandana off, exposing her fuzzy head, and the tint of light reflecting off her glasses, she looked so incredibly adorable. Her demeanor was so calm, so quiet, and so lackadaisical that I just wanted to squeeze her as hard as I could. Once again, it was moments like this I wish I could freeze just so I could appreciate her sweetness just a bit longer.

As a result from the surgery, a small protrusion appeared above her right chest, near her shoulder. That was the port. Now, we just had to wait until Wednesday before Kait could receive her chemotherapy through that port. Her treatment regimen was split up into two parts. The Monday portion of her treatment consisted of orally administered drugs, which she completed before surgery, and Wednesday was the intravenous part. After 28 days, she would return to Arizona to receive a second round.

With Kait's chemotherapy scheduled, we were able to finally book our flight home, enlisting the help of a man named PJ to get our trip coordinated for us. We were looking forward to going home.

On Tuesday morning, Kait and I feasted on a delicious breakfast in the CTCA cafeteria.

When it came to meat, the nutritionist we had met with gave us one guideline to try to adhere to – if it <u>flies or swims</u>, it's good for you. In other words, chicken and fish were the healthiest forms of animal to consume.

So that morning, with Kait's breakfast plate filled with pancakes, eggs, and some bacon, she grabbed a crispy strip and held it up before taking a bite. Just as she was about to sever the bacon with her teeth, donning her cute, crooked smirk, she said, "Pigs fly, right?" And then she chomped down on the sliced pork.

After taking a moment for my miniscule brain to process her joke, I finally got it, causing me to laugh uncontrollably. I couldn't stop; it was so unexpected and perfectly timed. She started laughing, too. And then, amazingly, I noticed that when she laughed, her smile became full and symmetrical once again. Apparently, a different part of our brain controls our mouth when we laugh than when we just smile normally.

A few moments after her gem of a quip, after the laughter settled, we changed topic. PJ, our travel coordinator told us to come back and grab our flight information at some point on that Tuesday. Remembering his words, Kait wanted to remind me so we didn't forget. However, her short-term memory was still not as good as it once was, and she continued to struggle with remembering names of people.

So, reminding me of our one objective for the day, she instructed, "Oh yeah, don't forget, we have to go talk to….," she realized she couldn't recall his name, "…….AJ?....BJ?......shit…," she said as she dropped her shoulders and smiled.

The mere sheepish look on her face knowing she screwed up PJ's name, followed by the conceding "shit" had me just cracking up inside. She was so adorable as she bashfully laughed about it.

I loved that girl so!

Wednesday had arrived, and we were excited for Kait to receive the second part of her regimen.

After being lead back to a small cubicle-type of area, Kaitlyn was hooked up to IVs through her port, which meant no stabbing of needles into her tender arms. She was quite relieved.

Once the IVs were connected properly and the bags of chemo attached, the liquid began entering into Kait's veins. And, a mere two hours later we were all done and sent on our way.

Thankfully, with our new treatment regimen side effects were much less potent than other forms of chemotherapy, so we likely wouldn't have to worry about nausea or other discomforts.

And with everything accomplished, drugs fully administered and appointments completed, we boarded our plane destined for Wisconsin, feeling hopeful and confident in positive results. We absolutely needed this treatment to work. If it didn't, in my mind, I feared we wouldn't get a chance at another. We placed all of our eggs into the three-drug cocktail basket, and I had to trust that Dr. Lee's knowledge of melanoma qualified and justified his approach.

35 A COLD RETURN

Before our hope-filled departure to Arizona, the only visible sign of cancer on Kait's body was the missing locks of gold atop her head; the lumps on her body were normally hidden from public view. However, after being away for a mere eight days, her body had experienced significant and unsettling changes. The left side of her face was almost completely paralyzed, she was losing ability in her left arm, and bruises were scattered across multiple areas of her body.

We returned to Wisconsin just in time for Thanksgiving, and everyone was absolutely elated to see our angelic Kait. We had the privilege of eating wonderful feasts on both sides of the family, telling stories about our trip to Arizona, all that we experienced, and the plan going forward. At one point I had to choke back tears as we all went around the table and professed one thing that we were thankful for. When it was my turn, I took a deep breath, swallowed a lump in my throat, and simply said, "I'm thankful for Kait."

On the Friday after Thanksgiving, we spent most of the day resting and relaxing. Her body and mind craved it after a week of constant appointments, procedures, and travel! Unfortunately, cancer could never just let us live our lives in peace...

With the sun bowing out that night, Kait and I nestled into the couch at her mom's house to partake in further relaxation, conversing and watching TV with many of her immediate and extended family members.

Laughing as we awaited the arrival of greasy, yet delicious pizza, Kait tapped me on the arm.

"Trav, I kind of feel funny. My left arm is going numb."

Numbness was one of the potential side effects of her new treatment.

"Really?"

"It could just be one of the side effects," she responded.

"Yeah. Well, let me know if it gets worse."

We diverted our attention back to the familial congregation as we both tried hiding our concern.

Five minutes later, I felt another tap on my arm.

"Trav, can we go upstairs and call CTCA?"

"Sure, sweetie," I replied with worry in my eyes as we stood up and removed ourselves from the living room.

When we got to Kait's room, she sat on the bed as I pulled out my phone to call CTCA and ask for their professional advice. Right when I began dialing, her little brother Benjamin entered the room with a group of his friends, excited to recite the events of his youthful day, unaware of Kait's current predicament. Not wanting to scare him by rushing him out, I gave him my partial attention and had a hasty conversation with the wee lad.

Just as he left, I heard Kait say, "Travvvv?"

When I turned around, my worried eyes instantly transformed to fear. The left side of Kait's face was twitching along with her left hand as she sat on the bed. Terrified for her, but under control, I prepared for a grand mal seizure.

"Get mom and Lex," she said. I yelled down the stairwell, calling for the two women, and they scurried up the stairs to attend to Kait.

As soon as they entered the room, I called CTCA, and the doctor advised me to err on the side of caution and call an ambulance, just in case she experienced a major seizure. Her mother pulled out her phone and immediately dialed.

With Kathy on the phone with a 911 dispatcher, I tested Kait's mental clarity by asking her simple questions, expecting her to lose consciousness and start convulsing at any moment. However, unlike her previous seizure, she was able to correctly answer my questions and maintain conversation through her spasms. She knew our address, the names of her doctors, everything.

After a few minutes of waiting and monitoring Kait, the medics arrived, and her twitching had already subsided. Thankfully! Though what she had experienced was likely a minor seizure, we were completely relieved it didn't lead to a major episode, yet.

With many family members wrestling tears away, the EMTs secured Kait onto a stretcher and loaded her inside the ambulance to be taken to the nearby hospital. Even though the spasms had ceased, we agreed it was safest to transport her with medical professionals, just in case.

I jumped into the front seat and we took off.

"You doing alright back there, honey," I asked, looking back at Kait.

Facing away from me, unable to turn, she held her thumb up. "I'm good, Trav."

Immediately after arriving at the hospital, Kait was wheeled to the imaging department for scans. Using the newly installed port, Kait was relieved her veins and skin could be spared from the onslaught of needle pokes.

As I assumed, the scans revealed minor hemorrhaging in the right side of her brain, likely from the very tumor causing her left-side paralysis. Unfamiliar with Kait's situation and not wanting to take any chances, the doctor recommended an ambulance deliver us to UW-Madison for further evaluation by their oncology experts. So, at 10 PM on that Friday night, Kait and I filed into the ambulance and headed for Madison, arriving just after midnight.

Anxiety began setting in as we were introduced to our room for the night at UW because I knew the medical personnel there would likely want to run tests on Kait, and it was already way past her bedtime. With everything going on, with her grueling last week and a half, and with her damaged body poised for likely one last stand, rest was vitally important.

By the time we settled in, Kait's immediate family was already there waiting for us. We huddled around her bed, trying to make room for the large group. Kait kept everyone entertained and laughing by performing one of her many unrehearsed comedy routines, all while lying in her medical bed. She was adorable, as always.

Into the wee hours of the morning already, people quickly dispersed, heading off to their hotels for a restless night's rest. And just after everyone departed, around 1 AM, a nurse came in to take Kait for a set of MRI scans.

"You get some rest, honey. Don't wait up for me," she said as she disappeared from my view.

Figuring she'd only be gone about an hour, a typical time frame for an MRI, I tried getting some rest on the cot while I waited. I also figured she would doze off while inside the imaging chamber, a silly thought, really, considering how loud those machines are.

Dazed and confused, I abruptly woke up to nurses wheeling Kait back into the room. To my surprise, when I checked my phone it read 4:30 AM! Perturbed, I whispered to Kait, "What the heck happened, sweetie?"

"Ughh, it was hell…."

The way Kait explained it, the nurses were unclear about whether or not they could deliver the MRI liquid through the entry in Kait's port made by the hospital in Kenosha. So, playing it safe, they removed the needle left in her port and replaced it with what they considered to be a proper needle, which I could understand. However, the previous needle was tightly lodged into her port, so the nurses were yanking and pulling to remove it. Having not even been a week removed from the initial surgery to install the device, it was extremely painful for Kait. I was quite agitated of all she had been put through, but there was nothing we could do about it.

With Kait's body desperately needing sleep to recover from everything, we didn't stew over the painful event for long. It was almost 5 AM after all, so we both expressed our love for one another and closed our eyes.

And, of course, adding to my frustration and stress for Kait, she was woken up a mere two and a half hours later for evaluation. I couldn't believe it. It seems to me that depriving patients of sleep is quite contradictory to a hospital's mission of health and wellness. I think any expert, or layman for that matter, would agree that sleep is essential for good health and healing, yet every time Kait and I were at a hospital, she could never get sleep. How can any person be expected to recover when their body is under so much stress?

At around 9:30 AM, with Kait's family present, a neurosurgeon entered the room to discuss Kait's MRI results. She began by confirming the fact that the tumor on the right side of her brain had bled and what she experienced in Kenosha was a minor seizure. Secondly, the doctor began talking about options, or lack thereof. Surgery was a possibility, but it carried great risk. The problematic metastasis was in an extremely delicate section of the brain, increasing the chance for brain damage if we were to elect to go with another craniotomy. Because multiple tumors were growing inside her head and just removing one wouldn't make much difference, she advised against surgical resection.

Shaking our heads, as obvious as our answer was, we were briefly stumped, telling the surgeon we'd need time to think about it and that we would like to confer with Dr. Kuo first.

We carefully ran through our options. Should we take the one tumor out, the one causing the paralysis on her left side, the largest one in her brain? Should we subject Kait to further torture only to realize the benefits would be very little in the long run? Or should we simply wait and see if the new treatment regimen does its job and zaps away the metastases? Realistically, even if the one tumor were removed, it wouldn't be long before other tumors grew large enough to create life-threatening problems. With that, our decision became less difficult. We decided to forego surgery and its tremendous risks.

With the pressure rapidly rising as the walls continued closing in, my head frantically skimmed through ideas, hoping to reveal an overlooked solution. After all my research, after hours of scouring the web, after hours of reading medical literature, I had nothing. We were diminished to mere spectators, at the mercy of her cancer and the chemotherapy.

One aspect we could control, however, was whether or not we wanted to stay at the hospital. I wanted to leave. Undergoing rampant exhaustion and in desperate need of proper rest, Kaitlyn wholeheartedly agreed. Fearing another potentially dangerous episode, her family opposed the idea at first, and they wanted Kait to stay at the hospital just in case something happened – valid thoughts, indeed. My argument, however, remained the same. Kait's mind and body had been put through the gauntlet over the last week and a half and was never given a chance to recoup since returning home. She only slept for two and half hours the previous night, and sleep deprivation subjects the body to varying degrees of stress. Stress and cancer have a direct relationship with each other as stress suppresses one's immune system, allowing cancer to grow more uninhibited. In my mind, it was imperative and obvious we needed to get Kait out of that friendly dungeon and into the comfortable bed inside our cozy home. Many more sleepless nights in the hospital might just be the catalyst in shutting her body down.

Eventually they agreed, but only after receiving the doctor's go-ahead, which we obtained just a few hours later.

Happily discharged from the hospital that evening, we headed back to our apartment for the first time in two weeks as her family departed for Kenosha. With appointments set up for just a few days later to further discuss Kait's MRI results and possible next steps, they would be returning.

That night, finally sinking into our soft, sponge-like bed in the quiet of our apartment, Kaitlyn was able to peacefully doze off after accepting my goodnight kiss. After falling asleep, she slept, and slept, and slept. She ended up sleeping uninterrupted for 13 straight hours, not even waking up for a bathroom break. It further reinforced the no-brainer that I surmised – Kait desperately needed rest. Relief and happiness pulsated throughout my body at the simple fact that my baby was finally able to enjoy a peaceful environment in order to recuperate.

Over the next couple of days, Kait and I took every advantage of our alone time together, holding deep conversations and each other as we prepared for possible change. However, I was unprepared for how drastic our change would be.

36 A CRUSHING BLOW

Kathy, Tom, Mark, Vicky, Kaitlyn, and I sat inside of a small conference room at the UW hospital as Dr. Stevens, usually the facetious one out of Kait's team of trusted doctors, somberly addressed us about our options and possible next steps. Our first and foremost question was whether or not Kait could receive SRS, the highly concentrated, pinpoint radiation to eradicate the lesions inside her head. One of our main concerns was that her rapidly growing brain tumors would overwhelm Kait before the new treatment regimen would even get a chance to work. We were hoping we could at least destroy the problematic tumor inhibiting the movement on her left side, which had now gotten to the point where she could barely squeeze her hand.

"Can Kait receive more brain radiation," we asked.

Taking his time, it was apparent Dr. Stevens was consciously bracing us for a crushing blow.

"Normally, you only get one shot with brain radiation, and most doctors will refuse to do anymore because it can cause necrosis, or brain cell death. I'm actually one of the few doctors in the nation who is willing to do brain radiation a second time, but normally, it's only after a patient's brain has been given enough time to recover."

We all listened intently as he continued to explain, sensing his likely denial of our request for SRS.

"Now, you received Tomotherapy with Whole Brain Radiation back in June. Only.....five months ago, and I gave you a high dosage. Kaitlyn, I'm afraid if we did another round of radiation this early, it could cause brain damage, or…….it could even shut your brain down completely."

Trying her best to smile, Kait nodded her head politely as she followed along.

"Oh, we wouldn't want that. So, maybe radiation is not such a good idea," she replied.

"No. I don't think so." Dr. Stevens got even more serious with us. "Now, Kaitlyn, I want to be completely honest with you. I've seen the images sent to me from your scans, and the one tumor right now in the right side of your brain has grown to about the size of a walnut."

We all gasped. *Holy shit!*

"The way it's growing, you've already been losing movement on your left side, and in a few weeks you may not even be able to walk. Kaitlyn….I'm afraid…in the next couple of weeks…..this may end up taking your life."

Complete silence instantly, but briefly inhabited the air before sounds of sniffling and whimpering brought life back into the room and tears could be heard splashing against the table. I foolishly strained and squirmed from within to remain tearless, as if crying were a sign of weakness. We were all shocked. We were paralyzed with sadness. We couldn't believe it. Weeks? Even though we knew how dire Kait's situation was going into our meeting, it never occurred to us that we may only have "weeks" left with our beloved sweetheart. It was agony for everyone.

His words hit us like 5,000 anvils falling from the sky. As much as the radiation expert kept his composure, it was obvious it pained him to have to be the one to deliver the soul-crushing news.

And the hardest part of all was that for the very first time, Kait was being told by a doctor of her likely mortality. It broke my heart that she had to hear the demoralizing and devastating prognosis. I never wanted her to have to face those words.

Trying to keep her sobbing controlled, a teary-eyed Kait responded to Dr. Stevens with quivering lips. "Okay. Uh. That's okay," she said as her voice crackled. In typical Kait fashion, amidst the awful revelation, she wore her beautiful smile for Dr. Stevens as she addressed him.

As Dr. Stevens continued, he recommended hospice care for Kaitlyn, assuming we would need a trained professional's assistance within the next few weeks.

After ten more minutes of informing us, making suggestions, applauding Kait for her courageous battle, and injecting us with small traces of hope, Dr. Stevens stood up to let us be.

With her emotions somehow subdued, Kaitlyn delivered a grateful farewell to the doctor, knowing she may not get another chance. Smiling, she said, "Thank you so much Dr. Stevens, for all you've done. You and Dr. Robertson have been so great."

"Thank you, Kaitlyn," he replied. "As you know, I'm the guy who gives hugs."

Dr. Stevens walked up to Kait and gave her a hug. One last time. And then he left the room.

With the oncologist gone, we all did our best to console each other. It was all too surreal. We couldn't believe, after everything, that we had arrived at this point. In the early stages of her bout with cancer, there was always this inner feeling that instilled a sense of optimism within us, the feeling that Kait was going to be okay, that something would eventually happen to ultimately save her. Even after her seizure, we had this sense, maybe from denial, that the cancer would miraculously disappear at some point and never come back. I mean, it just had to, because something so awful and tragic as Kaitlyn succumbing to her disease just couldn't happen. No matter how dull that inner voice became, that belief was always there. However, with Dr. Stevens's words, that voice was all but silenced. It seemed our window of opportunity for a miracle had just about closed.

All I wanted to do was comfort Kait and assure her a glimmer of hope still existed with the treatment she was on, but I couldn't. With the news so prevalent in my mind, all I could think about were the few weeks we likely had left with our beautiful Kait. It hurt.

After giving ourselves ample time to emote and gather ourselves, we had to go to our scheduled meeting with Dr. Robertson. At that point, I was like 'why?' What more could be said that would be of any benefit to us? But, Kaitlyn had a strong admiration for her primary oncologist, so it was important for her to see him. It didn't really hit me that it would essentially be our farewell.

Distraught and defeated, we entered the room to speak with Dr. Robertson. As we somberly asked for his opinion, unfortunately, he couldn't offer us much. At that point, not much could be done. His confidence in Kaitlyn's chemotherapy combination was low. He suggested that once the potency of the drugs waned in about four weeks, we could possibly shift to Temodar. But four weeks was a LONG way off.

Normally during our meetings with Dr. Robertson, I came prepared with a plethora of questions. But, that evening, I remained tight-lipped. Any movement risked provoking an emotional breakdown, and I didn't want that, not yet. After Dr. Robertson finished explaining his position and opinion on Kait's situation, he asked the group, "Does anyone have any questions?" Then, he assumingly looked straight at me, waiting for me to ask something. Hunched over with my arms leaning on the table, all I could do was gently shake my head and weakly mutter, "No."

Just saying the word 'no' nearly triggered an emotional reaction out of me.

Demonstrating her indomitable strength, Kait expressed her thankfulness to her oncologist with a smile. "Thank you for everything you've done, Dr. Robertson. You've been so wonderful."

He shook her hand. Then he shook ours before leaving. We wouldn't see him again.

We slowly filed out of the room, one-by-one, and as we did, Nurse Sue just happened to be walking by. Kait talked to her as if nothing was out of the ordinary, bubbly and with a sparkling smile, but Nurse Sue knew everything that had been going on.

The two talked briefly, but before departing, the nurse gave Kaitlyn a big hug and said, "Ohhhh, you are just the nicest person I have ever met." Words that made me feel good for Kait, knowing she made an indelible impression on the people who she came into contact with.

Without saying a word to me, giving me a look as if to say 'I'm so sorry, but stay strong,' Nurse Sue rubbed my arm as we walked away. The only response I was capable of returning without having a tear-filled tantrum was a quick glance back at her with my lips pursed. She knew what it meant. It meant 'thank you.'

We left the hospital, for the last time.

Afterward, we decided it would be most wise to stay in Kenosha with Kait's family for the time being. So we headed back to the apartment for one last night to relax before having to pack our bags the next morning.

Kathy and Tom dropped us off at our home and headed to their hotel. Finally. It was just Kait and I. Away from everyone else. In the quiet of our apartment.

And, there we were, looking each other straight in the eyes. After a full year of peaks and valleys. After a full year of triumphant victories and heartbreaking defeats. After a full year filled with laughter and tears. It had all culminated to this one moment as we stood facing each other, eyes glazed, with the sad realization our time together would likely be cut much too short. All of the hopes and dreams we had for our future was likely lost.

In front of Kait, as we gazed into each other's souls, I broke down. Tears began pouring out of me uncontrollably. I immediately thrust myself into Kait's body, and we shared a tight embrace.

"I'm sooo sorry, sweetheart....... I'm so, so sorry," I said as a waterfall of tears streamed down my face.

She cried with me. "It's okay, sweetie....."

"No it's not......... I just... can't believe this is happening. It's not fair...." My now high-pitched voice crackled as I struggled to speak every word.

"I know, honey....... It's weird, isn't it?" Water droplets were rolling past her lips. "...To think I might not be here in a couple weeks."

"Kait, I don't want you to go.............please don't leave meee. You're my best friend.....I don't know what I'll do without you...........I'll be lost."

Tears continued gushing from my eyes as we consoled each other.

"I don't want to leave you, either, honey....," she replied. "You have to promise me you won't shut down. You have to find someone else someday."

The mere thought of moving on at that juncture twisted my heart even more.

"I can'tttt.....," I whimpered, ".....I want you."

"I'll be with you, Trav."

"Do you promise....?"

"Yes.... Always."

We stood embracing each other in silence for a few moments longer before separating. Again, I was staring at this beautiful, beautiful woman standing in front of me, soaking in her perfection while I could. I started shaking my head.

"I can't believe this....... This is YOU," I said as I extended my arms halfway toward her, pointing at her with my palms facing the ceiling, "This is Kaitlyn Julia we are talking about. This is so stupid."

"I know. I just hope….," she had to pause to collect herself as her lip began quivering again. "I just hope people remember me as being a good person who always tried making people smile, and someone who always tried doing the right thing."

"Oh sweetheart, that's not even a question….. You're the kindest, most good-hearted person I have ever met. People love you so much."

"I hope so…."

The moment was just too surreal. I felt like I was floating, weightless.

"You know, Kait, sometimes I've thought that maybe you were a gift from God sent down here to brighten up the world, but that we weren't ready for you and took you for granted, so God decided to take you back until the time was right."

Those words brought a slight smile out of her as she tried to restrain her sobs. "You think? That'd be kind of neat."

I went in for another warm, tight embrace. "I just love you so much, Kait."

"I love you, too, Trav."

"But, then again, it's not like all hope is gone…. With the treatment you are on, there's still a chance. We can't forget that."

"Yeah, that's true. If we can just get to the second round then who knows."

Gradually, we calmed down. After our tears settled, Kait expressed to me how she had a craving for pizza and just wanted to pig out. I smiled. I then ordered for delivery right away, saying 'Screw you!' to health-consciousness for a day.

When that Italian pie arrived, we devoured it, packing as much saucy dough into our twisted bellies as we could, washing it down with Pepsi from a 2-liter bottle, something that took her back to her childhood days.

"You know, Kait. I suppose I can tell you now."

"Yeah?"

"Back in May, Dr. Kuo told us that you only had a couple months to live. And, now it's gonna be, like, eight months. You've far surpassed his estimation."

"Really? That's pretty cool," she replied with a smile.

"Yeah. I'm just so proud of you honey. The way you've handled yourself through all of this, I couldn't imagine anyone doing it better. You've maintained your sweetness throughout, never letting this stupid cancer hold you back or get you down. I just, I'm amazed by you."

"Thank you, Trav. You're a good man, you know that? You've handled yourself pretty well, too. Thank you for staying with me."

With my arm around her as we sat on the floor, I kissed her and leaned my head against hers.

That night in bed, we held on tightly to one another, not wanting to let go. Of course, I never wanted to let her go.

37 PLEASE, DON'T GO!

The next day, November 27th, we packed our bags to head to Kenosha. Before we left, Kait turned around to look at the apartment one last time, trying to soak in the image of our first dwelling as a couple.

"It's crazy to think this could be the last time I ever see this place."

"Nahhh. We'll be back."

"Yeah...," Kait said as she smiled at me, allowing me to remain in denial. But she knew. We both knew. Her return was highly unlikely.

With that, we closed the door, locked it, and took off.

Upon returning to Kenosha, the family, Kait, and I did our best to make every single day count. We tried dividing up Kait's time so she could be at her dad's and mom's equally, giving them ample attention since everyone wanted to be around her at all times.

Unfortunately, because I would be out of town indefinitely, I decided to leave my job. They were willing to hold the position for me, but I felt like I couldn't let them do that. It wasn't fair to the company. I was the only accountant they had, and I had no idea how long I would be gone for. Since I had been with them for merely a month, I would have to relearn everything all over again if I did return. And, if Kait did end up passing away, I had no way of predicting how much time I would need before feeling comfortable enough to go back to work and give at least some of my focus. So, it made sense to me for the company to move on and find someone else.

"Do you still want to get married, Trav," Kait apprehensively asked while we sat in the living room at her father's abode.

She wasn't sure anymore if I still wanted to get married given the fact that she would likely be passing on soon, which would leave me a widower. I felt so bad for her in that moment. It pained me to know she was even questioning whether or not I still wanted to take her hand in marriage. If anything, I was sorry we didn't get it done much sooner.

"Honey! Absolutely I do!"

"Okay. Are you sure? Because I can understand if you don't want to anymore?"

"Sweetheart, I want to get married to you more than anything. Do you still?"

Kaitlyn smiled and nodded. "Of course. I was just asking because, if you still wanted to, I was thinking maybe we could move up the date and get married in the coming weeks."

"Absolutely! That's a great idea. Do we have a calendar?"

Vicky quickly found us a calendar and set it on the coffee table in front of us. We began looking at the upcoming weekends, tossing out various ideas and talking about certain obstacles with each one. Because it took a couple of weeks to apply for and receive the marriage license, and because Kait would be headed to Arizona in about a month, we ultimately decided to go with January 5th, 2013. So, with that, it was settled. In just four short weeks, we were to officially become man and wife. A thought that made us both smile radiantly.

With a new date agreed upon, Kait's excitement grew. "Oh my gosh! I can't believe we're actually gonna be married soon!"

"I know," I replied gleefully as I sunk my head into my shoulders with a smile. "I can't wait!"

At that moment, being that January 5th was only a month away, and because Kait still seemed healthy aside from her off-centered smile and weakened left hand, I thought we'd easily make it to that date. I mean, she was just hiking up a mountain nine days earlier, it would have been silly to think otherwise.

But I didn't truly realize how rapidly her cancer was growing.

Our original wedding date of May 25th was officially called off, sadly forcing us to cancel all prior reservations and plans. After calling or emailing the various companies and informing them of our extenuating circumstances, they all agreed to return our down payment without a fuss, except for one – the DJ. Legally, we were bound to the contract we signed, and the DJ wouldn't waiver from the agreed upon terms even though we were cancelling merely a month after signing on with them, giving them a good six months to refill that slot. And our situation went far beyond a simple piece of paper and ink, so I found their decision to be unacceptable. After a string of stern emails from myself and some extended family members, all avoiding cussing, the company eventually decided to budge and give us our refund. And really, though, I couldn't care less about the money. It was the principle of the matter that drew my ire. If you ask me, it was pretty despicable for them to oppose in the first place.

While one company sunk to distasteful lows, another rose to the occasion (not that we ever expected any sort of charity). As we sat on the couch watching TV one Saturday at Kathy's house, suddenly the phone started ringing. The TV displayed a phone number that included a '212' area code along with the name 'Waddell.' Assuming it was just another annoying telemarketer, we ignored the call.

Well, about 15 minutes later, the phone rang again, and again it was that same number. For the second time, we ignored it. But then I started pondering – where have I seen that area code before? The wheels in my head began spinning. I knew I had seen it recently, but where? Ahh ha! A light bulb turned on in my brain – I remembered when calling Memorial Sloan Kettering they had the same area code. They were located in New York. Okay, if anything, we at least knew where the telemarketer was calling from. But then Kathy began putting the second piece of the puzzle together – Waddell. She knew she had seen that name somewhere before, but where? Waddell. Waddell. She thought hard for a few moments. Hmmm. Ahh ha! Kait's wedding dress. Judd Waddell was the man who designed the dress Kait was originally going to wear on May 25th.

By the fourth time that same number called, Kathy picked it up. Sure enough, it was Judd Waddell. After introducing himself, he immediately expressed his sincere sorrow to Kathy after hearing of Kait's terrible status which forced her to have to cancel her dress order. Revealing his deep desire to do something nice, he then mentioned he had designed an elegant, beautiful, simple dress specifically for Kaitlyn to wear during our wedding ceremony on January 5th, at no charge. And he was shipping it immediately! Shocked and amazed, we couldn't believe it. Mr. Waddell's unbelievably kind gesture brought tears to Kathy's eyes as she spoke with him on the phone. We were extremely grateful. But, I'm sure he would agree that it was the least he could do (not that he was obligated to do anything in the first place).

Cancer was quickly progressing, and it effected Kait more and more with each passing day. Every morning after waking up, her vision would remain blurry for three or four hours, and it was difficult for her to focus or think during that span. Like a venomous snakebite, the paralysis slowly worked its way down the left side of her body, inhibiting movement more and more every day. By early-December, she could no longer squeeze her left hand.

Some of the tumors began causing extensive amounts of pain as they pushed against her stomach, her bones, and her muscles. At times, the pain would become so excruciating that nothing could remedy the intense discomfort. The fast-acting medication we gave her for the "breakthrough" pain didn't seem to act very fast, and sometimes it didn't even act at all. Lying down wouldn't help. Sitting didn't work. Standing did nothing. Sometimes we simply had to wait for the episode to pass as we didn't know what to do.

And then with the tumors growing in her brain, Kait's ability to focus on anything was greatly hindered. We tried going to church – an activity she was looking quite forward to. And when we arrived with her mom and stepdad, we four took a seat in the pews, positioning ourselves near the aisle just in case we needed to scurry out for any number of reasons. Shortly after settling in, mass began. Kait sat, listening intently to the priest's words, doing her best to absorb and comprehend everything. She followed along with everyone, standing when we needed to stand, singing when we needed to sing. But with all of the vibrant colors shining from the stained-glass windows, and with the priest's loud, resonating voice echoing back and forth off the walls, making it sound like he was speaking five words at once, it became too much for Kait. Trying to focus on everything, all the mental stimulation, it hurt her head, so we decided to leave after only 15 minutes.

Hopefully God forgave us.

It was Kaitlyn's favorite time of the year, and even with her health in decline, she wasn't going to forget it. As a memento to help carry on her memory, Kait began working on a special Christmas gift to be given to each member of her immediate family. She wanted to create an individualized photo album for each person. Each one would consist of pictures of her with the specific family member the album was for, along with a meaningful saying or quote on every page. I thought it was such a wonderfully sweet idea.

Because she was reduced to typing with only her right hand, I tried helping her as often as I could. But, the project was meant to be a surprise, so she made sure my assistance was used minimally. Her dedication was adorable to me, and it was a great way to occupy her time and keep her mind off of cancer. We ordered the albums and they were set to arrive just a few days before Christmas, giving her just enough time to paste the pictures to each page and finish the project.

Meanwhile, after counting the weeks out on my fingers, I realized it would be safe to administer Kait's second round of treatment as early as December 17th, almost three weeks earlier than scheduled. Upon this elementary epiphany, I began calling CTCA in Arizona to try and reschedule her January appointment.

Because we feared the long distance travel might be too strenuous on Kait's mind and body, we also made an attempt at moving her treatment locale to Zion, Illinois, which was only 20 minutes away from Kenosha. It made much more sense to have her treatment done locally rather than travel all the way to Arizona. However, we didn't realize how difficult the approval process would be to move her treatment to the nearby hospital. Apparently, there had to be a doctor there willing to administer the specific regimen that Dr. Lee laid out. Dr. Lee couldn't simply make a phone call and direct the Zion doctors on how to administer the drugs using simple instructions, which seemed silly to me. Unfortunately, because his regimen was not FDA-approved, no doctor was willing to take on the novel approach since their asses would essentially be on the line should anything go wrong. Just another example of how things are much more difficult than they need to be.

In preparation for our wedding, we realized we needed to pick out a ring for me. Together, Kait and I researched local jewelers online and settled on a couple different options. However, none of the local stores seemed to have what we were looking for, until we arrived at Kay Jewelers.

Wearing her adorable purple bandana, I held Kait's hand as we entered the store. We began by browsing around, checking out all of the different ring designs through the glass cases.

"Since I had to pick out your ring, I think you should have to pick out mine," I said to Kait.

With a smile, she accepted the challenge as she increased her focus on the rings in front of her. "Hmmm, what about this one right here?"

She pointed to a silver ring lying in front of us. "I don't know. You tell me? Do you think it fits me?" I wasn't going to let her off that easy.

"I don't know. I think so…yes."

I smiled. "Okay. Should I try it on?"

Kait pondered for a moment. "Well, wait. Let me look at a few others." She navigated through the glass case just a bit longer. "Honey, this is too hard."

I started laughing. "Okay, how about this. You pick out three rings you think would fit me, and then together we'll choose one." That was a compromise she could work with.

After scanning over the variety of designs, Kaitlyn narrowed down the choices to a select few. She understood my tastes and personality enough that she knew I wouldn't want anything overly gaudy. But at the same time, she knew I wouldn't want anything overly plain. With the three choices she singled out, each one seemed to fit my tastes perfectly. It didn't take long before we selected a ring and had the jeweler remove it from behind the enclosure and take it up to the register.

Kait turned to me and quietly requested, "Do you think you could just step outside for a moment, Trav?"

"Sure!"

I exited the store and stood outside. Looking through the glass windows like a puppy dog, watching my master converse with the store clerk, I made the assumption Kait was asking about adding a special inscription to the wedding band, but I didn't want to be nosy so I didn't ask.

After a few minutes, Kait walked out of the store with a luminous smile, emanating with happiness and joy.

"So do you have the ring?"

"Nope. They said it should come within a couple weeks."

"Cool!!! How exciting!"

"Come here," Kait said as she pulled me closer for a kiss. I could feel her positive energy. Her delight. And that made me happy! We were both beaming with excitement as we held hands on our way to the car.

The walls continued closing in and were now pushing against us as Kait's cancer continued to progress. Two weeks had passed since receiving her new treatment and her tumors showed no signs of slowing down. I kept my hopes up, though. I remained confident the drugs would kick in shortly and begin evaporating the cancer cells. That sliver of hope kept me from dwelling on our almost-inevitable and bleak future.

What was intriguing to me, however, was the fact that it seemed as though Kait's short-term memory had improved, as she was able to easily remember names of people she just met. It made me wonder if the treatment was partially working.

Planning ahead and preparing for the worst, we hired a hospice care company to assist in the home in case Kait's health declined. Though we would be able to take care of her ourselves, it was reassuring and comforting to have an educated professional help with the aspects of healthcare we were unfamiliar with.

The name of our primary nurse assigned to our case was Amy.

The days slowly and quickly passed, and we continued doing our best to simply live life to the fullest and enjoy every waking hour. Hoping to aid her chemotherapy along, Kait ingested her morning handful of vitamins and other supplements, washing them down with a fresh cup of green tea. She usually tried drinking two or three cups every day, because we were told it was great for one's body. And then for every meal, we did our best to include foods listed on the sheet of paper given to us by the Arizona nutritionist. Our lunches and dinners normally consisted of either chicken or fish along with several helpings of various green vegetables. Would the foods help the treatment or her body fight the cancer? We didn't know. But an educated nutritionist was suggesting the healthy diet, and we figured it couldn't hurt.

Also, Kait kept her body active for the most part to keep the blood flowing and the oxygen cycling through her system. Like during the summer, we went for our daily walks. Then at night Kait would either walk for 15 to 30 minutes on the treadmill or bike on the stationary bike in Kathy's basement.

As much as we wanted to ignore the seriousness of our situation and pretend like everything would turn out okay, the reality was things were rapidly getting worse, and the chemo didn't seem to be doing much. And Kait knew it.

One evening, Kait, Jess, and I sat on the couch watching TV. Somehow, I don't remember what triggered it, whether it was a conversation from the show we were watching or what, but we arrived at the topic of death and the afterlife.

"I wonder what happens when we die," Kait pondered.

Her inquiry caught Jess and I completely off guard. Not knowing what exactly to say, I simply replied, "Yeah, I don't know. It's hard to say."

"I don't know, when I think of heaven, I like to think of it as that wonderful place with clouds and bright lights. I want to believe that is where we go when we die, and that we don't just stay in the ground in the dark…and I don't think there's anything wrong with thinking that."

I didn't know what to say as Jess snuck away to the kitchen for a glass of water to keep from losing her composure. "That's good honey. There's definitely nothing wrong with believing that. I think that's a good thing."

I was partially shocked. Kait was bravely speaking of such a scary, sad, and heavy topic, yet she didn't seem to be bothered by the thought of passing on. Not at all. Was she saying this because she knew her fate was likely sealed? Was she hinting to Jess and I that she was comfortable and accepting of her bleak future? I didn't know. A part of me wanted to cry for her. A part of me wanted to hug her. But her strength! It amazed me. She always made me so proud.

I sat next to Kait on her bed on a Saturday afternoon. For the first time, she was experiencing an episode of extreme pain – in her abdomen, caused by a tumor - as she laid on her back squirming in discomfort. I could do nothing as I looked on helplessly. I had already given her multiple doses of her "fast acting" medication. And after that didn't work and after calling her hospice provider, I was advised to switch medications and administer the alternative drug right away. So I did just that. At that moment, we just had to wait. I began wondering what could have caused this sudden breakthrough of pain.

Though Kait was quickly losing mobility in her left arm, her legs still worked properly, allowing her to partake in one of her favorite activities – shopping. Christmas shopping, no less. Just a few hours before the sharp pain began shooting through her abdominal region, Kait went shopping with her mother and sister to search for the perfect holiday gifts for everyone. The trio gleefully scavenged through various Kenosha retail stores, and Kait had a blast hanging out with her family and perusing through the discount racks in pursuit of hot deals. However, because she was physically weak and had a difficult time focusing amidst all of the holiday commotion, shopping took its toll on her.

As she laid on the bed wincing in pain as sensations pulsated through her stomach, I surmised that the chaos and walking from store to store likely caused this episode. But, to be honest, because Kait had such a great time, in a way I was happy. She was able to spend quality time with her family, and for all we knew, it was probably the last time she would be able to go shopping.

"Just breathe slowly, sweetheart," I helplessly suggested. We hadn't experienced anything like this before, so I had no idea what to say or do.

"I'm trying," she responded. She really couldn't take deep breaths since the air filling her lungs was pressing up against her stomach, causing even more discomfort.

I could hear the agony in her soft whimpers as she altered the angle at which she laid in an attempt to allay the pain. When that angle didn't seem to help, she switched to a different angle. But every bit of movement only caused more excruciating pain. The best option was to simply lie still and wait for the medication to kick in. I wanted so badly just to take her away from all of her anguish. Seeing her cringe. Seeing the tension in her face. Seeing the beads of sweat develop on her forehead. It was psychologically torturous. I felt so bad for her. All I could do was hold her hand and gently massage her, but I didn't even want to do that for fear it would send ripples of pain throughout her body.

For an hour, Kait laid as still as she could, taking long, deep inhales and slowly exhaling through her mouth. Eventually, with the medicine kicking in, she was able to lull herself to sleep. The unbearable discomfort was gradually subsiding. Finally. In total, the episode lasted two hours. I could only pray that would be the last of them, but we knew there'd be more to come.

December 8th, 2012. It was a day marked on our calendar for months, a day in which Kaitlyn was looking particularly forward to – the yearly tradition of decorating Christmas cookies with her dad and stepmom.

This year, for everyone involved, it was poised to be especially challenging knowing it could be Kait's last year to participate. Nevertheless, it was going to be a special day, and we were going to take full advantage of our opportunity to spend it with her. It was these types of family get-togethers Kaitlyn enjoyed and loved most, so we were going to make sure we made the best of it, at least for her sake.

Ever the organized woman, Vicky had all of the ingredients and tools laid out on the table along with a large batch of cookies cut out in various holiday shapes.

Sadly, at that point, Kaitlyn lost all mobility in her left arm as it hung lifelessly by her side, leaving her with one hand to decorate cookies. However, her resilience would never let something so "trivial" keep her down. Utilizing the squeeze bottles of frosting and sometimes my hand to hold the cookies down as she spread the icing with a knife, she ended up designing some unbelievably beautiful cookies. I know if it were me in her situation, I would have exploded in frustration and expletives just trying to spread the icing with one hand as the cookie slid all over the table. But, Kaitlyn never let her hindrance consume or frustrate her, staying upbeat and smiling the whole time, just enjoying the special moment with her family. She left me in awe.

I guess to make it fair, we all should have been required to use one hand to match Kait and even out the playing field. Then again, she wouldn't have wanted that.

After we finished decorating cookies, Kait let me put what little hair she had atop her head into a mohawk. I loved it. We concluded the evening by playing cards, watching a movie, and just hanging out and enjoying everyone's company.

All and all, it was a great day and a wonderful experience we were all able to cherish together. Kait was full of positive energy and didn't have a single episode of pain or confusion, which was remarkable considering how things had been as of late.

I consider our day of cookie painting to be the last great experience

Kait had. She was able to enjoy everything most precious to her in life — her family, laughing, loving, smiling, talking, and more. I'm thankful for that.

On the day after cookie decorating, a Sunday, with her cousins Lex and Samantha and her aunt Judy paying a visit, Kait's paralysis slowly began seeping down into her left leg. She was able to walk, but with each step she took, her left foot dragged behind slightly. Although the progression was expected, still, this new development was rather disconcerting, but nothing could be done.

After conversing with her family members for a bit, Kait's head began to hurt, so we cut the socializing short. It was almost as though Kaitlyn bottled up all of her remaining energy and expended it on the day prior with decorating cookies.

When we woke up the next morning, Kaitlyn had difficulties simply walking. Her left leg had become much more weak as she was quickly losing mobility, a rapid change from a mere two days earlier when she was walking perfectly fine, or at least it seemed that way. Unable to put much pressure on her leg without losing her balance or falling over, we had to help her down the stairs and guide her into her chair.

Watching the effects of the cancer mercilessly steal her abilities day by day was extremely painful. The person in this life I was most responsible for was crumbling right before my eyes, and I could do absolutely nothing to stop it. My soul wept for her as she took her misfortunes in stride.

To make matters worse, I had to leave her to go home for a day in order to grab certain supplies and items from the apartment and briefly spend time with my family since they were worried sick. I did not want to abandon my love, but we figured it'd be best for me to go now before her situation worsened even more.

With that, I kissed her, almost breaking down in tears as I said goodbye, and I left. As I drove off, I released the floodgates of my tears, crying on and off throughout the two-hour trip home. I would be away from Kait for the first time in I don't know how long, and I didn't like it.

And of course, just moments after I took off, Kait began experiencing another episode of awful pain. Hoping to stop it before it could worsen, she quickly took her "fast-acting" medications. But the drugs didn't kick in fast enough. The pain became unbearable. Wanting to lie down, Jess helped get Kait upstairs and into her bed.

Kait's breathing labored as she struggled to deal with the shooting pain. Jess did her best to talk her through the severe discomfort. "Just keep breathing, Kait….deep breaths."

With her face tensed up, Kait followed along as her sister coached her through. "Jess…..do you think I'll still be here when Travis gets back?"

Taken aback, Jess didn't know how to initially respond. The truth was, she had no idea. There was a chance that something could happen in my absence that would ultimately take her life, like if one of the tumors in her brain began bleeding or any number of other things that could occur. She didn't know. "He's only gonna be gone for a day or two, Kait. If anything does happen, he is only two hours away."

"Yeah. I guess I'm just worried…..but he needs to see his family. I want him to."

Kait was concerned she would pass away while I was back in Madison, a revelation that broke my heart when Jess informed me of their conversation. But it also confirmed, once again, one of the many reasons why I loved her so much. I'm just glad nothing detrimental did happen in my absence.

For the two nights I was gone, Jess took my place in bed with Kait. It was important for someone to be nearby just in case something were to happen. And, because she was on a schedule to take her pain medications every eight hours, it also didn't hurt having someone to help with that, too, when she would wake up at 2 or 3 in the morning.

Upon my return on Wednesday, I had no idea what to expect when I walked into Kathy's house, dreading what I might discover. Before entering the abode, I braced myself and pushed my emotions to the depths of my stomach just in case they unpredictably wanted to barge through. I didn't want to cry. I knew the cancer likely progressed, and I could only imagine how bad things had gotten while I was away.

As I walked into the house, I was tested immediately. Through the opening into the kitchen, I saw Kaitlyn with her arm around Jess as her sister guided her to the bathroom. Her left leg was extremely weak and she could barely use it. Taking a big gulp to ensure I remained strong for her, I made my presence known.

When Kait returned to her spot on the couch, I greeted her and did my best to catch up without overwhelming her with questions and conversation. Not so surprising, she did not let her most recent physical declination crush her spirits, as she was positive as usual. I don't know how she did it.

What did surprise me, however, was when I was ambitiously feeling her tumors, hoping the chemo had begun doing its job, I discovered that a few of the metastasis had actually decreased in size, some significantly. Unfortunately, the most problematic ones, especially the one on the right side of her brain causing the left-side paralysis, had continued to grow. It seemed as though the rate of growth in her cancer was much too high, and the drugs struggled to keep up. My hope was that a second round of treatment would be the turning point in our battle.

Friday, December 14th. Kait could no longer walk. Her left leg wasn't completely paralyzed, but it had become so weak she couldn't use it at all. We used a wheelchair to guide her throughout different areas of the house, and we had to pick her up and carry her to places like the couch or her bed. The most difficult part, physically, was having to transfer her up or down the stairs. To do so, I would lift the front end of Kait's wheelchair while Tom, Jess, or whoever was available would stabilize the back end. Then, as a team we would slowly move from one step to another, doing our best to keep Kait balanced so she wasn't bouncing around in her chair. We typically did a good job in that regard.

The disease was completely taking over, and it was difficult to suppress our sadness as it was consuming us all. But in front of Kait, we remained strong. Unfortunately, because of Kait's rapid decline in health, it was deemed too risky to fly her to Arizona for her second treatment. Dr. Lee agreed to send the oral portion of the regimen by mail, but we somehow had to find another doctor willing to administer the intravenous part, which seemed impossible.

Due to one of the drugs included in the chemo-cocktail (Lomustine), Kait's blood count became alarmingly low, and it was noticeable. Her energy was down. Her skin was pale. And her face was slightly drawn. We were advised to take Kait to the nearest hospital for a blood transfusion. So, on that Friday, after I lifted Kait out of her wheelchair and gently set her into the car, we drove her to the local medical facility to receive a couple bags of blood.

When we arrived, we lifted Kait out of her wheelchair and situated her comfortably in her bed, placing ice packs behind her back to alleviate the persistent pain she had been experiencing for days. The pain literally never ceased at that point. It was always nagging at a minimum, in her back, stomach, legs, just about everywhere in her body. Even the smallest tumors caused severe discomfort as they would push against her muscles, bones, and quite possibly even her organs. And the heavy regimen of medications just didn't seem to do the trick to quell the constant pain.

A nurse walked in while we were waiting for the correct blood type to arrive. As we were talking to her, we mentioned our current dilemma and how we were struggling to find a doctor willing to take on Kaitlyn's case. We mentioned how we called around and no doctor was comfortable administering Dr. Lee's treatment regimen because it wasn't FDA approved. However, we were in luck. The nurse just so happened to know a particular doctor within their facility who was known for administering basically whatever treatment the patient requested. I was intrigued! The nurse gave me his number.

I called the doctor right away. When he answered, I wasted little time before divulging Kait's situation and every bit of pertinent information I could.

"Hmmm, well it sounds like something I could do, but can you tell me more about this treatment regimen," he asked. He was initially reluctant. "What is the justification behind it?"

I didn't know what to say exactly. I felt like I had to choose my words carefully. If I said the wrong thing, I feared he would change his mind. "Well, our doctor in Arizona has given his regimen to multiple patients and he says he's seen about a 40% success rate."

"I get that, but I want to know what the justification is on your end."

I was confused. It seemed obvious. We wanted to keep Kait alive.

"Well, we were told that sometimes patients don't respond until after their second dose. Because we've seen some shrinkage after the first dose, we're thinking a second round will work even more."

Using my unoccupied hand, I wiped the beads of sweat above my lip. My heart was pumping because I knew how important it was for Kait to receive her second round, and I was nervous I would say something that would cause him to recant.

"Okay. I think you've told me enough. Like I said, it sounds like something I could certainly do, but I'd have to see her first. I'll set aside time on Monday to see her then."

My eyes shuddered in excitement.

"Great! Thank you so much! We will see you then."

When I hung up the phone, I immediately pumped my fist. With a doctor willing to administer her chemo regimen, we once again had a glimmer of hope to cling to. A miracle was still possible.

After several hours and a couple bags of blood later, we were discharged from the hospital. The color in Kait's face had returned, but she didn't feel any different. "Kait, you look so much better," Mark said.

"That's good! But I don't feel any better. Maybe it takes a couple of days to feel the effects."

When we returned to Kathy's, we wheeled Kait inside and situated her on her designated corner spot of the couch. I wish we would have left her there. She was comfortable as she ate a few bites of French toast. She hadn't really eaten anything all day.

Since it was already late, we decided to go to bed shortly after returning home. So, I picked Kait up off of the couch, gently set her down in her wheelchair, and guided her toward the bathroom where Jess was waiting to help. As I began lifting Kait back up and out of her chair, a sudden sharp sensation began shooting through her back and traveled throughout her body. "Oww….pain…," she softly cried out. It was excruciating for her.

Thinking as fast as I could, I immediately tried placing her back in the wheelchair, but as I was setting her in, the chair started rolling away from us. *Dammit!*

And because I was bent over in an awkward position as I tried situating her on the seat, my back was quickly giving out, and I was losing strength fast. I couldn't hold her up any longer. Plus, holding her up by her armpits as her legs dangled beneath her, it was causing her even more pain, so I had to set her down. Slowly and gently, I lowered her to the floor and placed her on the soft mat below. But I messed up. As I was setting her down, I didn't pay enough attention to the positioning of her legs. After releasing my grip on her, I noticed they were all contorted and bent as she sat on the ground, and it caused her to cringe in even more excruciating pain. "Owww…..ow….hmmp," she repeated. I felt terrible. How could I be so careless? She was trying hard to be quiet in her agony, but through her gentle cries and whimpers, we could tell the pain was extreme. We could feel her torment. Frantically, yet gently, Jess and I tried repositioning her legs so she was no longer sitting on them. But that didn't help. Nothing did.

After a few moments and zero improvement, we decided we needed to get her upstairs and into her room where the recently delivered adjustable bed from hospice awaited – a bed that came with a mattress much thinner than her old one and a metal frame that looked extremely uncomfortable. Anyway, Jess and I picked Kait up from the bathroom floor, placed her into her wheelchair, and brought her to the bottom of the staircase. I then bent down using my knees, grabbed the front end of the chair, and lifted. With Jess stabilizing the back end, we guided her up the stairs. As soon as we entered her room, I picked her up from under her armpits and set her on the bed as Jess situated her legs properly on the mattress. "Hmmp....hmmm...," Kait continued to whimper with every stuttered breath.

At that moment, my back felt like it was about to snap in half. With Mark and Vicky entering the scene, I immediately keeled over on the floor. I had to lie down. All of the lifting throughout the previous few days, and especially on that evening had taken its toll, and I had no choice but to briefly tap out. I wanted to remain tough, but I couldn't any longer. I sprawled out on the ground on the side of her bed.

Kait's extreme pain persisted as Mark, Vicky, and Jess did everything they could to help remedy the throbbing discomfort. They placed ice packs on certain areas of her body. They massaged her legs. They tried talking with her, coaching her through the pain. Nothing helped. When I tapped back in just moments later, Kait's left arm and the left side of her face began to twitch from the severe distress she was experiencing.

"Just breathe Kait," we suggested. "Just take slow deep inhales, and slowly exhale."

"Okay....," she said as she helplessly looked up at us.

Kait followed our instructions. Focusing on her accelerated breathing, she tried slowing it down with those deep inhales and slow exhales. Gradually, she was able to calm herself, and the minor spasms halted.

With all four of us gently massaging her legs and arms, moving the ice packs to different areas of her body every 15 minutes, the pain eventually dissipated to a tolerable level, and Kait's misery had temporarily subsided. We were left exhausted, but so relieved.

With another lengthy episode of pain behind us, the others exited the room so Kait and I could get some sleep. We needed it. Because Kait's new bed was only big enough for one person, I set up a blow-up mattress and placed it next to her bed. "I love you so much, sweetheart," I said before nestling into my bed.

"I love you, too, Trav." I turned off the lights and we both did our best to get some rest.

Unfortunately, rest was not an option for either of us. Kait was in constant, varying levels of pain throughout the night, and I did my best to help her through each episode. "Trav...?," is all she would say.

As soon as I would hear her voice, I would jump out of bed and take a seat next to her. "What's up, honey?"

"Pain again...."

The only things I could think of to do besides giving her pain medication was massage her arms and legs, switch out cold packs for heating packs, and talk to her until the discomfort receded. Usually after at least a half hour, the pain would go away, and I would tuck myself back into bed after kissing her on the forehead. But each time, after only 10 or 15 minutes of silence, pain would flare up again. I would immediately jump out of bed and repeat the same cycle as before. I felt so bad for her. Kathy even had to come in once or twice to help soothe Kait back to a comfortable state.

Finally, at about 4:00 in the morning, the pain decreased to a tolerable level for good and Kait was allowed to go to sleep. "Travy," she said in such a soft and sweet voice before dozing off, "Do you wanna come lay with me?"

Her request melted my heart. She was so adorable. "I'm sorry, honey. I want to lie next to you so badly, but that bed is too small for both of us."

"Are you sure? I'll scooch over for you."

I smiled. My heart melted even more. I wanted nothing more than to lie next to her and hold her - forever.

Eventually, we got through the night and Kait was able to get some rest. After her family woke up, I went into another room and crashed for a few hours, knowing I would need my energy as the days passed.

Through the weekend, with the left side of her body completely immobile, and because she was in constant pain, Kait became completely confined to her bed. Her appetite had all but vanished, and she was eating less and less. Aside from a miracle, the end seemed to be upon us, and it terrified me. It was killing me inside.

The appointment with her new oncologist was on that Monday, and we had to somehow figure out a way to transport her to the hospital without causing too much pain and discomfort. We were baffled. How the hell were we to do that when any slight movement felt like her tumors were stabbing her? Either way, we had to figure it out.

When Monday arrived, we found ourselves pinched between a rock and a hard place. Damned if we do, damned if we don't. CTCA sent in the mail the oral portion of her treatment, which meant we only needed our new oncologist to administer the intravenous portion. Kaitlyn's appointment was later in the morning and we just had to find a way to get her safely to the hospital. With tumors spread across her body, every single movement sent burning sensations pulsating through her system. None of us felt comfortable with the idea of moving her, but we all felt like we had to. This second round of chemotherapy seemed like our last chance to save her life. As much as my gut was screaming at me to cancel the appointment and keep Kait stationary, I felt like we had no choice.

We loaded her up on pain medications beforehand in hopes of offsetting the pain, at least a little bit. We even contemplated adding Lorazepam to the mix, but we didn't want her to be completely out of it while the doctor made his assessments.

A transport van arrived to the house, pulling into the driveway to pick us up. As we stood in her room, we talked and talked and talked about how to move Kait from her bed to the wheelchair whilst inflicting the least amount of pain. No one could think of an effective method, and it seemed like we were running in circles trying to catch our tails. We were accomplishing nothing. Finally, I just decided to act. Whether it was the right or wrong thing to do, I approached Kait, wrapped my arms around her while gently supporting her legs and back, and moved her to the wheelchair. We then swiftly secured her in and carried her down the flight of stairs. She was in extreme discomfort.

The driver of the van opened up the side door, and I noticed the back was completely empty. The wheelchair was then automatically lifted into the van and we strapped Kait safely inside. Due to her weakened and paralyzed neck muscles, Kaitlyn could no longer hold her head up properly, so I knelt down behind her in the vehicle and tried as hard as I could to gently hold her head in place through the bumps of the road.

The 15-minute trip to the hospital was miserable. Kait was in pain the whole ride. My anxiety for her seemed to increase every second.

When we got to the hospital, we wheeled her up to the waiting room and signed in. Nothing made Kait comfortable. We tried ice. We tried giving her water. We tried massages. Nothing helped. All she could do was endure the pain, because not even her pain medications were effective. Eventually, to spare Kait anymore suffering, we decided to give her the Lorazepam even though it would likely cause drowsiness during her appointment.

Finally, after 30 agonizing minutes, we were called back, and the doctor entered the room just moments later. Immediately, he could see how miserable Kaitlyn was as she sat there in front of him trying her best to block out and ignore the pain. However, he didn't seem to acknowledge it or care. At first, he tried impressing us by displaying his memorization skills as he slowly rambled off Kait's history without using his notes. With no urgency whatsoever, he stood there and pondered for long moments, trying to recall bits of important information as she sat in torture.

After he finished his evaluation of Kait, he allowed us to leave. However, he wanted to speak with Mark, Kathy, and I separately. So, Jess and Vicky accompanied Kait during the trip home. I dreaded their ride back to the house and what she would have to endure.

The three of us entered the doctor's office and took a seat. He sat at his desk.

"Now, I know I said I would administer treatment, but I didn't realize how advanced Kaitlyn's disease was. Just from the looks of her, I would say she is only days away. I don't think I'd be willing to treat someone who is that sick. I think it would only make things worse in her last days. At this point, I think we should be talking about quality of life and keeping her comfortable," he admonished.

We all sat there listening intently, understanding where he was coming from as he continued explaining his position. Desperate to keep my baby alive, I didn't want to hear the word "no." I still believed in my head she

268

could be saved.

"You know, I realize how bad her situation is. I realize the chances of the treatment actually working are slim, but even if there is, say, only a 10% chance, then it's worth doing in my eyes," I stated.

"At this point, 10% would be great odds. I would say the probability is much less."

"Either way, I'm not ready to give up, yet."

"What I always try to help people understand is even if you decide against treatment, you are never giving up. By giving her a quality life in her final days, you are never giving up."

"I understand that. What I mean is, I'm not ready to give up on fighting the cancer. I know she's expressed to me on multiple occasions how much she wanted this second treatment."

As the doctor continued, he made it clear he wasn't willing to administer the chemotherapy and potentially make her last days on this earth even more miserable. Mark agreed. Kathy was on the fence. I was opposed, but there was nothing I could do. In hindsight, however, I realize it was a good thing we didn't administer the three-drug combo. She probably would have suffered even more. With the love of my life rapidly floating away from me, my desperation to keep her alive clouded my judgment. As much as I was against traditional chemotherapy, it seemed like it was the only option given Kait's severe circumstances.

We left his office. My head hung low.

Once we returned to Kathy's, I braced myself for the worst. I could only imagine how miserable the van ride home must have been for Kait and the others. I was prepared to walk into her room and see her cringing in extreme pain from everything we put her through. But, to my amazement, when I walked upstairs, Kaitlyn was sitting up, calm and comfortable, and my worries instantly vanished.

While we were gone, a new bed arrived at the house. It was electric and had a thick, soft mattress. By pressing a button, the firmness could be adjusted or the bed could be moved up or down. It was much, much better than that other piece of shit bed with the paper thin mattress and metal frame.

Most importantly, wrapped in warm blankets in her new bed, she was comfortable. She was talkative and happy, and I was so relieved as I walked over and kissed her. I thanked Vicky and Jess for making sure she was safe during the ride. I thanked the van driver and Tom for their wonderful help. Apparently, when they arrived, they wrapped Kait in a cocoon of blankets and carried her upstairs. It was effective and not as jarring as our wheelchair method.

Nevertheless, I felt awful for putting Kait through such a stressful ordeal. It was obvious how much it took out of her, and it ended up being completely unnecessary and a waste of time.

Now, with the oral portion of her treatment from Arizona still in our possession, we had to decide whether or not it would still be worth giving it to Kait. I wanted to. But, I agreed to wait and think it over for a couple days.

Tuesday, December 18ᵗʰ. My parents traveled to Kenosha on Tuesday for a few hours to visit Kaitlyn, and, essentially, say goodbye. The last time they had seen Kaitlyn, her smile was symmetrical and full, and she could walk and talk perfectly well. But after only a month, she could no longer walk, and she talked less and less. With the growing tumors in her brain coupled with her now heavy drug regimen to ward off pain, her ability to communicate and comprehend her surroundings was becoming greatly stunted.

Together, my mother and father entered Kait's room, approaching her as she lay awake in her bed with her eyes mostly closed. It was difficult and heart-wrenching for them to see her struggle like she was, and it was hard for me to see them so saddened. Never in their lifetime could they or any of us have imagined witnessing such a young and vivacious woman we loved so much slowly wither away at the hands of such an unforgiving disease. It was surreal.

As they stood next to her bed, they told her they loved her and said their teary goodbyes. It was the last time they would see Kaitlyn alive. And after spending about another half hour or so in Kenosha, they made their way back to Madison.

Just moments later, Amy came downstairs and informed us that Kaitlyn was running a high fever, indicating she likely had an infection somewhere in her body. Our hospice nurse somberly explained that because Kait's body was in such a battered state, if she did have an infection, her system would likely be too weak to fight. Her last breaths were likely only hours away.

The feeling of vertigo overtook my mind and body as blood rushed to my head. I couldn't believe what I was hearing. My Kaitlyn, was about to......die. I quickly scampered upstairs and entered her room. Standing over her, staring with glazed eyes, it was that very moment I had been dreading for months, one that I prayed over and over in hopes of avoiding, but also one I knew was almost inevitable. It was time for me to say farewell to my great love.

Bending over, I leaned the right side of my head against hers and held her hand. With streaming tears and a quivering lower-lip, I whispered, "Kaitlyn. I love you so, so much. I never ever thought......I would be so lucky......to meet someone as perfect as you. I'm going to miss you so much....."

I could barely get my sentences out, I was so devastated. But, at that very moment, as much as I didn't want her to leave me, I was ready to let her go. More than anything, I wanted her to be freed from any further physical or emotional suffering. I wanted her pain to end.

Kait's family gathered around her bed, waiting for her final breaths as our hospice nurse stood behind us. For minutes on end, all was silent except for Kait complaining of pain in her head. Soon, five minutes became 10, and 10 minutes became 20. With time passing by and all of us quietly anticipating her last moments on earth, it became apparent to me that she wasn't ready to pass on. Not yet. My nagging intuition projected outward, "She's not going anywhere right now."

And she didn't. Her high fever eventually cooled down that evening, though it remained between 99 and 101 degrees for days.

Considering Kait's condition and accepting the fact that she was beyond the point of medical help, we decided against administering the oral portion of her chemotherapy, surmising it would do more harm than good.

Thursday, December 20th. We had begun taking turns sitting upstairs with Kaitlyn to keep her company and to monitor her. I spent as much time as I could next to her, rubbing her arms, her hair, massaging her legs, itching spots on her body she couldn't reach. Along with her left side being completely paralyzed, her right side was losing strength and mobility, too. Unfortunately, even though she couldn't move her extremities, she still had feeling in them.

Four days had passed since she had any semblance of a meal. Because installing a feeding tube was considered "life-sustaining," hospice was restricted from doing so, which was quite upsetting to me. The only thing stopping her from being able to eat were the tumors in her brain inhibiting her movement. Though she had superficial tumors, by looking at various signs and indicators it seemed like her organs were functioning properly. I didn't want her to starve, and it pissed me off.

As I sat quietly in my chair next to Kait, suddenly another epiphany just smacked me upside the head. Over the course of the previous many months, I had read multiple articles of studies being done to test the effects of fasting while patients received chemotherapy. The thought behind that approach is that when a person goes multiple days without eating, the healthy cells inside the body go into a defense mode and close down. In this defense mode, they significantly decrease their consumption of the body's resources as they no longer require as much energy. However, the cancer cells remain completely open, starving for anything ingested and absorbed into the body. And, cancer cells eat at a much higher rate than healthy cells, so whatever resources become bioavailable within the system are "hogged" by the slobbering cancer cells. Now, with Kait not having eaten anything in four days, my thinking was that her healthy cells were likely closed down in defense mode and her cancer cells were likely famished for anything that entered her body.

Expanding on my discoveries, I also read about a study involving mice and chemotherapy. In the study, one group of mice was deprived of food for two days, and the other group of mice was allowed to eat as normal. Each mouse was then delivered an equal amount of chemotherapy. For the mice that went on a two-day fast, the potent drugs left their body generally unharmed, proving that their healthy cells went into this defense mode from hunger and put up a sort of shield. That shield protected them from the poisonous drugs. As for the mice on a normal diet, most of them died from the toxic effects of the chemo.

Going even further into my studies, not only were institutions doing clinical trials involving fasting, but I also read personal accounts of people fasting on their own, stating the heightened effectiveness of the treatment they were on and the decreased side effects.

So, I was convinced that if we were to administer the oral portion of her treatment regimen, her healthy cells would remain generally unharmed and her cancer cells would gobble the poison right up. The idea got me excited as I now thought a miracle was possible.

I ran my thought by Mark and Kathy. They both heavily contemplated the idea, but wanted professional advice first. After conferring with our hospice nurse, she asserted it would likely do more damage than anything, so the two parents opposed the idea. And the notion of giving Kait the Lomustine was put to rest once and for all. As disappointed as I was, in the end I believe it was for the better. Things seemed about as bad as they could get, but I would have hated for Kaitlyn to be throwing up in her final days. I'm glad we didn't give her the chemo.

From the moment she became bedridden (of course, even before that), every day was torture for us watching her as the cancer shackled her to her bed, causing her constant pain and suffering, both mentally and physically. It seemed as though we were increasing the dosage of pain pills almost every day, and eventually we reached a level that seemed to subdue her uncomfortable sensations. For Kait's sake, we all just wanted it to be over. Then again my bipolar emotions teetered every few hours.

Everyone expressed to Kait that she no longer had to continue fighting. They kept telling her it was okay to 'let go.' However, deep down, as much as I didn't want her to suffer any more, I still hoped for a miracle. I still thought a recovery was possible, no matter how miniscule the chances were. So, aloud, I would tell Kait she could let go at any time, to make her family happy. But then, when no one was around, I would bend over and whisper into her ear, "Please, sweetheart. You can still beat this. Please keep fighting. Tell that cancer in your body to go away. Ask Jesus. Ask your grandparents. You can beat this. I neeeeed you."

Selfishly, I couldn't let her go just yet.

Through hospice care, we ordered an oxygen tank at the suggestion of a doctor who the family knew. Kait's oxygen level was hovering around 99%, so it wasn't completely necessary just yet, but wise to have on hand.

Needless to say, when the appliance arrived, we hooked it up immediately and placed the tubes into Kait's nose. She HATED it! But because she couldn't move, she was unable to remove the annoying tubes herself, and she began pleading with us to take them out.

"Travvy. Travvy honey can you get this off of me," she implored.

With her family around, I didn't know what to do. I didn't want to press any buttons, so I said, "Well, let's just wait a minute, sweetie, and see if you get used to it." It pained me to deny her request.

Her little brother Benjamin then came into the room. Somehow she sensed his presence, though her eyes were closed. "Bennie. Benjamin, sweetie. Can you take this thing off of me?" Ben didn't have the confidence or authority to do so. "Please, someone get this shit off of me," she continued.

Finally, unable to bear the shrill cries, I removed the tubes from her nose to potentially be used at a later date. She didn't need the oxygen, anyway. Her levels were normal.

38 THE RING

Saturday, December 22ⁿᵈ. The weekend was upon us, and though only days had passed since Kait became confined to her room, it felt like months. Discerning one day from the next seemed nearly impossible at times, as it felt like all the days were cobbled into one.

Kait's newly designed wedding dress arrived in the mail, but I was not prepared to look at it, not wanting to break tradition. Lying in her bed, Kait reminded us we still had to go shopping for wedding shoes, expressing her excitement on many occasions for our big day on January 5ᵗʰ. It was heartbreaking talking with her about our wedding that would never be.

Continuing the wedding themed weekend, my ring also arrived in the mail. Tom drove to Kay Jewelers, usurped the item, and returned it to me. Like the wedding dress, I didn't want to look at it just yet. Keeping it stored away in its miniature box, I placed it atop the dresser in Kait's room, right next to her bed. Because her ability to communicate and comprehend seemed spontaneous and unpredictable at that point, I wasn't sure she would ever realize the memento she had purchased for me to symbolize our love had arrived.

As the evening wore on, I sat in a chair next to her bed as she slept peacefully. Kathy was in the room with me. Suddenly, as I was reading, I heard a soft, angelic voice. It was Kaitlyn's. "Did you read the inscription on your ring," she asked.

Taken aback by her question, I instantly sat up alertly in my chair and responded, "No. I haven't looked at it, yet. I wanted your permission. Do you want me to read it?"

"Mmhmm," she acknowledged with her eyes partially closed.

I grabbed the box off of the dresser and removed the top portion, revealing the shiny cylinder of white gold inside. Removing it from the box, I used the little light in the room to read what she had secretly inscribed. It read in beautiful italics 'I will love you always & forever.' How sweet! I was so moved. A group of tears instantly escaped my eyes, passing down my face as they fell to the floor. "Oh, you are just the sweetest damn thing in the world," I said as I leaned over and kissed her cheeks.

Satisfied by her sweetness, not expecting her to expend any more energy by responding, she surprised me and replied, "Travis Dean, I will love you always, always, always."

Kathy left the room to give us a moment as more tears streamed down my face. Her wonderful words made me smile, and cry. "I will love you always, too, sweetheart," I said, slightly struggling.

She continued. "Does that scare you?"

I chuckled a bit and shook my head. "Nooo… not at all. It makes me so happy….."

"Hmmm….," she sighed with a soft smile. She then closed her eyes. I bent over and gently pressed my forehead against hers, moistening her skin with my tears. I then hugged her cautiously tight, and rubbed my cheek against hers before giving her a kiss. In that moment, my profound sadness was met with an equally profound happiness for having the rare privilege of being blessed with a living, breathing angel. All I wanted to do was lift her up and squeeze her as hard as I could. But I couldn't.

With our time together seemingly coming to a premature end, I was extremely grateful Kaitlyn gave me this memory to carry on and cherish forever. I love her for that!

Even through her suffering she still found a way to make us smile, whether it was by rubbing Vicky's arm as Vicky massaged Kait's legs, or by expressing her love for me. It was a further reflection of her perfect, loving character.

Christmas was just days away, and we thought it would be nice to decorate Kait's room with some Christmas lights, so we did. When we turned on the lights, she opened her eyes and acknowledged the colorful display. "It's beautiful. It's just so, so beautiful," she said.

With her infinite adoration for Christmas, it made us happy to hear her utter those words.

As the cancer was rapidly overwhelming Kait's body, her concern for our wellbeing remained strong. Realizing her likely fate, she made a request to her father. "Dad, you have to look out for Travis for me."

Mark proudly obliged.

"And Asian food is shit," she continued, taking a jab at my substandard diet devoid of fruits or vegetables, and packed with processed foods. When Vicky told me this, I laughed. Kait knew I loved my Asian food, but it certainly is bad for me.

To maintain order and give everyone ample opportunity at much needed sleep, Kathy created a nightly schedule for people to rotate in and out of monitoring Kait and administering drugs throughout the wee hours of the mornings. Fortunately, unlike some families where only one or two family members are charged with the heavy burden of being primary caregivers, we were never short of volunteers with all four parents, siblings, aunts and uncles, family friends and me wanting to assist as often as we could. And, it was an honor being able to spend time with and take care of her.

On one particular night, with only the white Christmas lights illuminating her room, I sat alone with her as the monotonous hum from the bed lulled her to sleep. It was 3:30 AM. With my shift ending soon, Kait's uncle - uncle Mark - entered the room to substitute in for me. He took a seat and we talked for a moment.

"Pound for pound, Kait's THE strongest person I know," uncle Mark said to me.

Over the previous many months, he had come across a rather rough patch in his life (I won't delve into the details, but really it had been an ongoing ordeal for a few years). Obviously, with everything going on in Kait's life, he would never verbalize his situation because it didn't seem appropriate to him, but it was emotionally draining, nevertheless. Anyway, during the summer when Kait was visiting in Kenosha and he was over at the house, she could sense the gloominess and defeat in his face.

"How's everything going, uncle Mark," she asked. Typically, he always felt comfortable divulging the details of his situation to her, but with everything that had happened with the seizure and surgery, he wanted to spare her from his seemingly "trivial" matters (when compared to hers). However, her tone made it apparent she wasn't asking just to make small talk. Not only was her look of insistence giving uncle Mark permission to speak about his life, it was urging him to do so.

"Well….," he caved. He began telling Kait all about the most recent developments in his story. About all of the unnecessary stress that came with it. She listened intently, interjecting with words of encouragement when she could. And when the conversation had ended, Kait approached her uncle and gave him a big hug.

"I love you, uncle Mark." He embraced her as she continued, "You have to know, you're a great man!"

Those few words and warm hug had a lasting impact on her uncle, and it meant a lot that she would set aside her battle with cancer in order to comfort him. And now helping her during such a crucial time of need was the least he could do to pay back the *strongest* person he knew.

After briefly conversing in the dark blue of the room as Kait remained asleep, I rose up out of my chair to leave and get some rest. Uncle Dale had just arrived, as well, so I knew she was going to be in good hands while I slept. I exited the room.

"You're leaving?.....I was hoping you could stay and chit chat for a while."

I stopped right in my tracks. The request came not from the uncles, but from the soft, angelic voice of my sweetheart lying in bed. Kait had woken up! Not wanting to miss a special moment with my girl, I immediately turned around and reentered her room.

"Hey sweetheart! You're awake! Of course I'll stay a while."

She smiled. To my wondrous surprise, with her eyes partially opened, only looking up when necessary, Kait began holding a legible conversation with the three of us. We began by talking about both Dale's and Mark's dating life. Addressing her uncles, she said, "I wish I could have taken you guys Christmas shopping. I would have helped you pick out such nice gifts for your girlfriends.

We all smiled. "Yeah, Kait, we could have used your help," Dale replied.

"You're always able to find the perfect gifts," I added.

We continued talking as Kait displayed her beautiful smile at many points for us during our conversation. It warmed my heart to see it.

"Hey Kait," Mark said as he changed the subject, looking to quiz her, "what's the name of that restaurant in Sauk I like to go to?" Sauk is my hometown. His girlfriend's family owns a cabin on a lake nearby, so he spent a lot of time there over the summer.

She answered, "Ummm. Green Acres?"

She was right. My eyes opened wide as I shook my head and smiled! I couldn't believe it. At some points she was barely able to speak, and now she was holding a clear conversation, recalling minute details that I thought she had no chance of recalling, at least not with the way her memory had been. It boggled my mind. But I loved it!

However, after every smile I shared with my girl, I wept on the inside. Moments like this were running out, and it twisted my heart...

Lying in my bed, trying to sleep, I was still not ready to surrender as I prayed to God and everyone I could think of to send a miracle or an answer.

Suddenly, shortly after my request, lightning struck. Flipping through the pages of my mind of everything I had read over the course of six months, I stopped on an article I remembered about the use of turmeric to combat cancer in clinical trials. In one of the studies, otherwise healthy patients with pancreatic cancer received turmeric alone as a treatment. Out of the study group, 10% saw a benefit. Sadly, in the medical world that's considered successful. But, that got my wheels spinning once again. If Kait's healthy cells were currently closed down and her cancer cells remained open, starving from having not eaten for a whole week, then they would essentially devour the first thing that entered her system. Maybe turmeric would be strong enough to poison those cancer cells.

So, the next morning on Christmas Eve, I went to the store and purchased a bottle of turmeric supplements. Right when I got back to Kathy's, I mixed the yellow powder with a liquid into a syringe. Kait could no longer swallow pills, so we delivered everything in liquid form. To test the flavor, her brother and I ingested the mixture. It was not good. I began to ponder whether or not I should even give it to Kait. To lessen the taste, I diluted it even more.

As I sat next to Kait with the syringe filled with one turmeric pill and liquid, I contemplated back and forth about having her consume it. Convinced there was a chance the concoction could save her, I decided to give it to her, at least once to see how she handled it.

Not so surprisingly, she did not like it. Not at all, telling me it tasted like 'shit.'

After that single dose, I gave her no more in fear it would eventually make her vomit. I reasoned with myself that it was a silly idea anyway.

Looking back, I now kick myself. Back at our apartment I had a bottle of tasteless and odorless turmeric supplements that I had forgotten all about. I don't know what I was thinking. Sure the probability was slim, but there was still a chance. I wish so badly I would have driven back to Madison to grab those pills.

Later that night, Kait was more talkative than she had been in the previous few days, and we actually fed her a couple of small banana pieces. Mark then acknowledged that the tumor on her belly seemed a bit smaller. Did that one turmeric supplement have a positive effect? It didn't seem like it could work that fast, but maybe it could have. Nevertheless, I figured it was all psychological.

To this day I regret not trying more.

Tuesday, December 25th. Christmas had arrived - her favorite day in the whole wide world. To Kait, it meant celebrating the birth of Christ with family and love. However, on this Christmas day, a deep, dark emptiness filled the atmosphere as she lay motionless in her bed. Extended family members did come over to "celebrate" on the eve, but no one was in the mood. Everyone wanted to be there just to make it feel somewhat like Christmas, but it couldn't.

To our great sadness, Kait never was able to finish her photo album project she invested so much love and passion into. Though, as the months passed, with pictures and quotes saved on different computers, her family was able to piece together a couple of the albums.

With the negative effects compiled from the cancer, the onslaught of medications, and lack of nutrition, Kait began incoherently chattering nonstop for two consecutive days. The difficulty was in discerning whether or not she needed something or if her mumbling was more or less involuntary. Either way, it was tough to ignore, especially when she would say, "Travyyy…," or for Mark when she would say, "Daddy poo….." For two straight days, she barely slept. And when she finally did fall asleep, we would do everything in our power not to awaken her.

Thursday, December 27th. Following two days of nearly constant chatter, Kaitlyn fell into a deep sleep. A coma, really. For two whole days we couldn't even wake her to administer the liquid medications. To get it into her system, we would have to slip it slowly under her tongue and wait for it to absorb. For two whole days, the only water entering her system was the miniscule amount from the IV connected to her port. I hated it. My great fear was that she wasn't going to be taken from her cancer, but from malnutrition and dehydration (I know, it was because of the cancer that she couldn't eat or drink, so essentially the cancer would still be the cause of her passing on). I just prayed she couldn't feel it.

As she laid lifelessly in front of me, I began to wonder if it was possible that her spirit was outside of her body looking down on us. I entertained the idea.

Friday, December 28th. Unless a miracle happened in the coming hours, our wedding would never be. Our dream of marriage was gone. With that in mind, and with immediate and extended family members present, we decided to hold a small, makeshift ceremony to "unofficially unite" Kaitlyn and me. But we were already fully united in my eyes. We had already been married for quite some time. A piece of paper with meaningless signatures meant nothing to me. It would have added nothing to our love.

Deacon Jim Francois from the family's local Catholic Church, the man who's duty it would have been to marry us originally, and a woman from the hospice company joined in reading passages from the Bible and sharing stories. With all of my remaining energy and might, I made absolutely sure I would not break down in front of everyone as we gathered around Kait's bed. Even though I could feel my tears punching my eye sockets, I was determined to keep them confined within. I just didn't feel like crying. I didn't feel like receiving sympathy from anyone. I didn't want it. At one point, when the hospice woman said, "…..and I know your heart may be cracked….," my tears almost burst through with sadness and nervous laughter as I wanted to replace "cracked" with "shattered." Tensing my jaw, pressing my tongue tightly against the roof of my mouth, and blocking out all thoughts, I temporarily quelled my emotions.

At the conclusion of our small ceremony, I placed the ring on Kait's left ring finger, kissed her on the forehead, and told her I loved her as eyes watered in the crowd. For the duration of the event, Kait remained in a deep trance, not moving once. And though I'm not sure what the ceremony really meant to me, if anything, it was still a nice moment. I wanted to believe Kaitlyn was watching over. I wanted to believe she could still hear everything that was going on.

With everyone gone, I sat quietly next to Kait amid the soothing lull of the electric bed humming and gazed upon her now emaciated figure. Two weeks had passed since her last meal, and nearly all of the muscles and fat on her body had atrophied and withered away. She was probably two-thirds her original size. Watching her gradually melt to nothing was just agonizing. But she was still so cute. She had such soft, rounded, and small facial features. I just couldn't believe she had to endure such a horrible disease.

As I sat and blankly stared at my love, I also noticed her once colorful, glowing aura had nearly faded away, too. The dullness of her fleeting energy indicated her time was sadly near. I no longer believed a miracle would swoop down and save us. I officially threw in the towel. Nothing more could be done, at least not by any mortal being. And though I could never accept Kait leaving me, I knew at that point it was for the best. As gaunt as she was, I wanted it to be over as soon as possible, for her sake, to end the suffering. I didn't care about my suffering. I would have been happy spoon feeding her for a lifetime.

Almost floating in my chair, mentally numb, billions of thoughts, reflections, and questions projected through my head. *What will life be like now, after she passes? What will I do? What will the apartment be like? How long will it take to "heal"? Will I ever? What will the wake and funeral be like? Will I be expected to speak? I don't think I'll be capable. How will I react when the casket closes? I need to buy a new suit? Where will she go? Will she be floating around, or does life literally end after our bodies permanently shut down? I hope she stays with me. Then again, I'd rather her be up in heaven. But, if she can move back and forth from heaven to earth, I'd like it if she came and visited often. Does she see me now? Does she feel pain? Is she jumping back and forth from her body? Is that possible? Am I being punished? Did I do something wrong in my life? I don't know. Is there meaning in suffering? Is suffering meaningless? If suffering does carry meaning or purpose, then Kait would certainly be worthy to bear it.*

I didn't know the answer to any of my questions, but they were abundant.

During Kait's hibernation, I made a peculiar discovery. As I was feeling her back through her many bedsores, I could no longer feel any of the tumors. It seemed as though they had vanished. But, how? For two weeks she had been lying on her back with a body temperature above normal levels, creating an oven-effect capturing the heat. Maybe the heat became too much for the tumors on her back, causing apoptosis. I knew at certain temperatures cancer cells died off. It made me curious, but it seemed sadly too late.

Saturday, December 29th. Kaitlyn was not conscious for most of the day. We were merely in waiting. I sat next to her bed for most of the afternoon and into the evening, and though she was still breathing, technically still alive, she was already gone. I could feel my numbness intensifying within me. My blank stares were lasting longer. With Kaitlyn essentially no longer in my life, physically, I was shutting down. As a defense mechanism, apathy was the strongest medicine, the strongest shield against the oncoming pain.

As the sun slowly waved goodbye to the day and with my stomach grumbling, I made my way downstairs for a quick bite and a quick break. Others were gathered in the living room watching *The Dark Knight Rises*, so I decided to join for a brief period.

Moments into the film, Vicky suddenly rushed down stairs. "Kait's blood pressure has dropped, and her breathing has become labored. You may wanna go upstairs."

This is it... I immediately darted upstairs and met Mark who was standing at Kait's bedside. It was just two of us for a short moment as I prepared my final goodbye.

All of a sudden, to my shock and amazement, Kait opened her eyes. For the first time in days, she actually opened her eyes, even making straight eye contact with us, something she really couldn't do throughout the week and a half prior.

Then, she tried speaking. But she was so weak, and her mouth was so dry from not drinking any water for two straight days that she struggled. "Mark, let's give her some water."

Mark quickly filled a syringe with water and we slowly delivered it to her in small amounts so she wouldn't choke. The moisture helped. Mustering every last bit of her strength, she began talking. Her voice was raspy. And it was soft. Making it difficult to discern her words, but Mark and I could clearly hear key phrases.

"I love you," she said as we bent over for a closer listen. That sentence was certainly discernible.

"They are here….but I don't want to go, yet," was another phrase we could clearly understand.

With her vitals in rapid decline, both Mark and I were communicating with Kait the best we could.

"I love you, sweetheart…… You can go whenever you want to. You don't have to fight anymore. You can let go…," I muttered with misty eyes. This time, I meant it.

The rest of the family filed into the room shortly after, all awaiting Kait's final breaths. It was time. We were as ready as we could be (whatever that means).

The room fell silent as we awaited Kait's last moment. I held her hand and rubbed her arm. With the hospice nurse standing by, we were calmly on edge. We were scared, but at peace. But suddenly, as the minutes ticked by, Kait began showing signs of improvement. Her blood pressure increased and her breathing normalized once again. I couldn't believe it.

"I don't think she's going anywhere tonight, guys," I claimed. And she didn't. Somehow she held on.

Feeding off of pure adrenaline and stress through multiple, consecutive sleepless nights, my body was beginning to cave. My legs grew feeble, and I felt like I was going to pass out. Instead of fighting the obvious cries from my body to rest, I gave in as I went and laid down. Somehow, I fell asleep. I didn't wake up until around 8:30 the next morning.

39 FAREWELL MY LOVE

Sunday, December 30th, 2012. My dad's birthday. After awakening at roughly 8:30 A.M., I jumped out of bed and rushed upstairs, slowing down my pace as I approached Kait's room.

I entered. As she laid motionless in her bed, the golden rays of morning sunlight shone through her window, blanketing her with its comforting warmth. Mark and Vicky were sitting with her. I walked up to Kait and kissed her forehead first thing. "Good morning, sweetheart." I turned my attention to her family. "How did she do last night?"

"Uhh. Good. She basically just slept for the most part," Mark answered.

"Good. That's good."

All of a sudden, just a minute or two after greeting her for the morning, Kaitlyn began to labor. She was struggling to breathe. This time, I could feel it. Instantly. And it was obvious. The end was upon us. Kathy walked into the room and approached Kait, worriedly looking down at her laboring daughter. I looked up at her, prim-lipped, tight-jawed, porcelain-eyed, and with absolute conviction and said, "This is it."

Her brothers, Brian and Benjamin rushed into the room along with Tom. Shortly after, Alexa entered. The last family member to arrive on the scene was Jess as her boyfriend, Carlos, stood just outside Kait's room. And as soon as Jess entered the room, with all of the family present, Kait began to let go. It was almost as though it were a conscious decision on her part, as though she decided to wait until every family member was present before allowing herself to pass on.

The intervals between each of Kait's breaths became more extended. 11 seconds would tick by. And she would take a breath. Then 14 seconds would tick by. Another breath. 18 seconds......another breath. The silence between each heart-pounding inhalation had us on edge. 22 seconds passed from her previous breath, and then she surprised us with yet another. 26 seconds.....she inhaled. With the seconds ticking by again, I held her hand and rubbed her shoulder as we waited anxiously for one more breath. But that breath never came.

And just like that.....it was over. At 8:48 AM, Central Standard Time, Kaitlyn Julia had been cast into the eternal light. Now among the angels - her true kin.

As we huddled around her bed in silence, I wrapped my arms around her and wept. In a slow motion freefall since December, my crumbling heart shattered beneath me. The being that meant more to me than anything in the world, the one who I loved more than anything, more than myself, was gone.

I was stricken with the deepest sadness I had ever felt. I was crushed. But also, I was relieved. Relieved she no longer had to endure the emotional torment and physical suffering from her ailment. She was finally freed from the limitations of her surrogate form. She was finally, at peace.

For many minutes, we all stood in silence. It was difficult to grasp. 24 years of life. Gone. Just like that. A person once so full of life and vigor, laughter and love, was now lying in front of us, lifeless. The full gravity of our loss hadn't completely sunk in, yet. Our month of December was a gauntlet of stress and despair, and coming up for the occasional breaths of air was rarely an option. In a way we were delirious from mental exhaustion.

Eventually, I went downstairs and started making phone calls to family and friends. During each conversation, my emotions spilled over. I pulled the phone away from my mouth during each one to hide my cries. My stomach convulsed as I tried to keep my weeping as silent as possible.

After notifying everyone, I sat by myself, collecting my thoughts as I apathetically gazed forward. I just couldn't fathom it all. All the years we spent together. Gone. Vanished. In the blink of an eye. I kept pinching myself, hoping to wake up from this nightmare we were living, have things return to normal. But it didn't work. This nightmare was our reality. And there was no escaping it. No matter how hard I tried.

And in our nightmare, I had failed. I needed to try harder. Reflecting back on our harrowing journey that lasted for more than a year, it seemed answers of possible solutions had been sent down to me multiple times. They were clear answers, too. I heard them. I was listening. But I was too much of a coward to follow through. I was too afraid to veer away from conventional wisdom. And now my girl was gone.

Shortly after sulking in my own sorrow, I made my way back up to Kaitlyn. She was still lying there. In the same position as when I left her. The coroner and funeral director arrived to take her away. We all were given the chance to kiss her and say goodbye one last time. I didn't want to leave her. But I had to. As the men entered the room, I slowly walked out, looking back more than once before exiting and heading downstairs. It was the last time I would see her body as it was.

Minutes passed. Eventually, the men in long coats carried Kait's lifeless body down the stairs in a body bag. It was a difficult image for me to accept, so I shielded myself from the depressing sight. But then I recanted. I had a strong feeling inside telling me that I needed to be a part of every single moment of Kait's life, even the most horrible parts. Just because something was difficult to witness, didn't mean I should ignore it. I didn't want to ignore my love. So, I saw her off as she was loaded into the vehicle and chauffeured away. In my numbing sadness, I felt hypnotized as I watched her physically disappear from my life.

Suddenly, the house was quiet. Over the last month, people were over all of the time, bringing meals, providing emotional support, helping in any way possible. Now. Everyone was gone. It was eerily quiet. And I didn't like it. I had grown accustomed to the daily commotion and outpouring of love. I found great comfort in it. The screeching silence was deafening.

Then, Mark and Vicky, who had been staying at Kathy and Tom's during the previous many weeks, began packing their bags, too. Preparing to go back home. I didn't like that, either. Life was carrying on. I suppose it had to, no matter how badly I just wanted it to pause for a moment.

Lying in bed at Kathy's that night, I finally felt my adrenaline secretions just beginning to subside, after having been essentially on overdrive for a year straight. In my unfamiliar calmness, I started contemplating whether or not I would give a speech at Kait's funeral. Like I had dreaded for months in my daily imaginings. I contemplated whether or not I'd even have the strength to. But just in case I felt the urge to speak, I began writing. Even if I ended up not speaking at her service, I at least wanted to express my feelings for her in words. I at least wanted a meaningful tribute to her, though any combination of words would fall sadly short of adequately describing her. Nevertheless, I ended up creating a potential speech, and below is what I came up with:

Kaitlyn Julia was the sweetest person I have ever met in my life. I'm not even going to talk about her outer beauty, because that is obvious. She was so much more than a beautiful face.

She was such a bright, radiant person, bleeding with joy and happiness. Every room she entered instantly seemed brighter. When we were living in the dorms, I would be sitting in my room, alone, things were quiet. Then, she would come in. And as soon as you knew it, the room was filled with people and conversation and laughter. People gravitated to where she was. Even with my family. I'm not much of a talker around them. Normally during football Sunday, we'd just sit on the couch, not saying much. All of a sudden, Kait enters the room, sits down on the couch, pretty soon people are talking, I'm telling stories, and I'm actually smiling and laughing in front of my family. That's not me at all, but she brought that out of me, she brought that out of everybody.

And, she was so funny. You would not guess that when looking at her. But, she was always equipped with these witty one-liners that you would never see coming, and soon you would find yourself laughing uncontrollably. Whether it was laughing with her or at her, she made people laugh. She didn't mind looking silly in order to get a loud chuckle out of me. There were times when she would pull her pants up way high and do a dorky dance that would just have me in stitches. I don't laugh often from other people, but Kaitlyn had me laughing all of the time.

She was a modern gal, but classical in the same sense. Her most memorable, most enjoyable moments were sitting around with her family, with her cousins, or sitting around with her aunts and uncles, or friends, or whomever just telling stories and laughing away. Those were the moments that she truly cherished, something money could not buy.

For the period I knew her, Kaitlyn lived her life doing everything the right way. She worked hard to achieve her goals and she earned her success. She was humble, never seeking attention. While other people strive to constantly be noticed, Kaitlyn accomplished her goals quietly. Kaitlyn was absolutely selfless, in a world where it seems selfishness and inward focus are rewarded. Very few people know she achieved straight A's in six consecutive semesters. The only reason few people know is because I or someone else told them. One semester, Kaitlyn had to get up at 5:30 AM to go to one of her jobs, get off at 9 AM and go straight to her classes, be done at 2 PM, go to her second job, get home at 5 or 6 PM, workout, do homework, eat dinner, etc., and repeat the next day. She did this a whole semester. She never complained, rather, she saw this as something that simply had to be done. You would think she would then take a break that summer after such a tough semester, but no, she proceeded to take classes full time and work full time. I couldn't believe how dedicated she was.

Kaitlyn had a vision of the teacher she wanted to become. She never strayed from that path. Her unwavering discipline allowed her to obtain the tools necessary to make sure she was providing children with the best education and opportunities possible. When she was a student-teacher, the day came where she had to be evaluated and be given constructive criticism on where she could improve. During her evaluation, her instructor basically told Kaitlyn she was doing pretty much everything great. Then, this woman picked out one flaw in Kait's techniques. One! Kait was so upset at herself for this, for she worried she was going to be short-changing children of their education because she wasn't perfect with her teaching skills. That's how Kaitlyn was. She cared so much about the children she would be mentoring that she accepted nothing less than perfection from herself, even if I told her that was impossible. She then pushed herself even harder. She would never admit it, but she succeeded time and again with children.

After graduating from Whitewater, Kaitlyn began substitute teaching in the Madison school district. One of the main schools she taught for was Kennedy Elementary, where she was called on for many months. It didn't take long for other teachers and even the principal to take notice of Kaitlyn's natural ability to connect with children. The principal of Kennedy eventually told me that she called Kaitlyn the "child whisperer", because she could somehow connect with children that no one else could. I thought this was so neat. Even though I already knew Kait had this ability, it's always nice to hear it from someone else. Of course, Kaitlyn never told me about this because she was never boastful if she received praise. She would accept the praise and then move on, continuing to improve. One day I even told Kaitlyn, and this was after the umpteenth story she told me of a kid that seemed to open up to only her. But I said, "Kaitlyn, you have to realize that you have a gift when it comes to connecting with children." She said, "No, no." I said, "But Kait, do you know how many stories you tell me of all of these kids that absolutely love you? It's crazy." By the way, I brought up things like this to her before. But finally, she replied, "Travis, I do sometimes realize that the kids do like me, but I don't ever want to think that way because I don't ever want it to go to my head. I feel like if it goes to my head, then I won't be as good of a teacher." Of course I'm paraphrasing here, because I don't remember exactly what she said. But, after she said that, I just sat back in the passenger seat of the car, and in my head I said, "Wow! This girl is amazing." And she really was, in a number of ways.

Her principal called her the "child whisperer". But, then I got to thinking. She wasn't just a "child whisperer." Kaitlyn was able to break down the barriers of any person she came into contact with. It wasn't just children she was able to connect with, she had the gift of being able to connect with anybody. She didn't care who you were, she didn't care where you came from. She didn't care if you were a nerd or a jock, white or black, rich or poor, she was going to treat you like you were the king of the world. She was going to put a smile on your face whether you wanted to or not. And it's not even that she would TRY to put a smile on people's faces, she just naturally did.

She could get any "tough" man to let down his guard with that sweet smile and bubbly personality. I mean, she broke down my walls, and no one, and I mean no one was able to get inside me prior to her. I truly believe I speak for everyone when I say this, but she just made you feel comfortable. She made you feel like you mattered. And, she made you feel like she wasn't judging you, no matter how crazy your thoughts were. She was always there to listen. She was always there to give you words of encouragement. She was always there to help you pick up the pieces. And, that's one of the many areas where I will miss her greatly. Whenever anything on me broke down, Kaitlyn was always there to pick up the pieces and put me back together. She is gone now, and with a heart now shattered into millions of pieces, the task of putting it back together seems impossible without her.

But, she wouldn't want me sulking or feeling sorry for myself. I don't, though. I feel sorry for her. I feel so sorry for her. She absolutely didn't deserve this. No one deserves to have to endure what she had to go through, but she deserved it the least out of anyone I know. However, Kaitlyn would never wish this upon anyone else. If there was anyone tough enough to endure this hardship, it was Kait. Pound for pound she is by far the strongest person I have ever known. Throughout this whole struggle, one would have never guessed she was stricken with cancer if it weren't for the hair loss to give it away. She maintained her wonderful, happy, positive persona at all times. Even after having surgery and radiation to her brain, somehow she maintained her sweetness.

This sweetness she possessed, it made her so huggable. People couldn't help but want to hug Kaitlyn when they saw her. She just had this warmth that people would be drawn to. It was okay to be vulnerable around her. My dad, my uncles, her uncles, everyone wanted to hug her. She was just that much of a sweetheart. Everything about her was so darn cute and adorable. The first time she played the board game, Pictionary, with my family and I, the other team guessed a drawing correctly. Kaitlyn proceeded to cheer and praise them. Coming from a competitive family, we all looked at her, me especially because I was on her team, and I said, "What are you doing?" Sheepishly, cutely, she looked around and said, "Well they did a good job." Half-joking, I said, "Don't do that. Don't cheer for them." But on the inside my heart melted. That was early on in our relationship, and that instance showed me so much about her character.

And, that brings me to our relationship. Kaitlyn and I, we were much more than simply fiancés, more than husband or wife. No labels adequately describe the bond between us. We shared a lifetime of love in just 4.5 years. We loved each other, we loved each other more than anyone could ever see. We were quite guarded around others. But, not a single day went by where we didn't tell each other 100 times over how much we loved and appreciated the other. It never grew tiring, it never seemed like overkill to express this feeling with her. It seemed right. I couldn't believe I was with someone that made me feel this way. It felt wrong not to let her know how special she was to me.

Because of the strength of our bond, Kaitlyn and I truly became one. I gave much of myself to her, and she gave much of herself to me. We looked out for one another constantly. We developed a sort of psychic connection where it seemed like we always knew what the other was thinking. If I was thinking about ordering pizza for the night, ten minutes later she would say something like, "Should we maybe order pizza tonight?" This happened all of the time.

From the very beginning, I knew I had someone special in Kaitlyn. It was the second time I had met her. We were both standing, waiting for the 9th floor elevator on the first day of classes at Whitewater. After we said our greetings and stuff like that, we were both silent. Out of the corner of my eye, all I could see was this girl smiling. I thought to myself, "Why is she smiling so much?" Of course it certainly wasn't a bad thing. It was quite endearing. But, she wore that smile the whole time. I was fascinated.

Then, a few days later, I was sitting in my dorm room, playing *Super Mario Bros. 2* on the old Nintendo. She walked by and happened to notice. She stopped and told me she used to watch her dad play this game. Then, we began a long conversation about Nintendo, and Super Mario, and Tetris. Little did she know, she struck a chord with me. I was obsessed with old Nintendo games, and I couldn't believe this little girl was having a conversation with me about it. That's when I started taking interest. See, I was her RA. I wasn't supposed to be taking interest on any girls on my floor, so I tried really hard to stay uninterested. But, I kept on running into her, and every time I would see her, her cheeks would always be bubbling with joy. Her smile rarely went away. How could any sane man not gravitate toward this? Well, needless to say, she had won me over.

From that point on, we shared something that will never be matched. Sure we had a couple of low points, a couple of arguments, but those were very few and very far between. Whenever we had a concern, we simply communicated that concern and worked together to find a solution.

In a dark world, I truly believe Kaitlyn was a gift from God sent here to try and brighten things up. She was sent here to offer her love. And boy did she ever. I've said this before, but I'm saying it again. Kaitlyn loved to love and be loved in return. She spread that wonderful feeling to everyone she came into contact with. Sadly, for reasons I will never figure out, this mission of spreading joy and happiness was ended much, much too soon. There will never be a plausible explanation for why this horrible disease entered her life. I can come up with any number of possibilities, but nothing seems to make sense.

Out of chapters and chapters, if each of us took a page out of Kaitlyn's book, this world would definitely be a better place. If there was anything Kaitlyn would want us to continue to do, it would be that we love and love and love and love. Cherish one another and love. Focus on the positives in people instead of dwelling on the negatives which I know I'm guilty of often. She was always willing to forgive and look past a person's flaws. She was always willing to give people multiple chances. She didn't hold grudges. Kaitlyn was the perfect person. Perfectly flawed. She was perfect.

This world will never be the same without her. My only hope is that one day we are reunited.

Kaitlyn Julia, you are the love of my life and a true inspiration. I'm so proud of you and everything you've done. I'm so proud of how strong you were and how hard you fought during the darkest times. The deck was stacked against you but you didn't let that affect you. You are truly one of a kind. You truly were an angel on this earth and now an angel in Heaven. I love you more than anything in this world.

40 FINAL GOODBYES

Friday, January 4th, 2013. Kaitlyn's wake. A day I had been dreading for many reasons and for a long time. In Kathy's kitchen, I paced back and forth as perspiration lurked beneath my suit and tie. I was nervous. I was anxious. I had no idea what to expect. I had no idea what it was going to be like walking into the funeral home and seeing Kait lying in her casket. I wasn't sure how I was going to react. I had no idea what she would look like. I had no idea how I was going to hold up for all of the people as they walked through the line, bidding farewell to Kait and offering their condolences. The anticipation uncaged a flurry of butterflies within my abdominal region, nurturing my growing timorousness. I needed help. I needed the one person I could always turn to for inner strength and courage.

"Kait, sweetie?" I put my ring on my left ring finger. "Please give me the strength….please help me make it through this day. I love you, and I miss you."

I closed my eyes and imagined Kait's spirit standing over me. I imagined her loving arms embracing my body as she rested her head on the nape of my neck. It comforted me. The thought of her presence helped calm me down.

As the afternoon progressed, I took multiple deep breaths, and we took off for the funeral home.

Inside the funeral home, we all stood in a group as the doors to the room Kait was in were closed off for the moment. As the director instructed us on the evening, Mark made one quick request. "If it's okay with everyone, I'd like a moment alone with Kait."

I certainly respected his request and had every intention of adhering to it. However, as soon as the funeral director opened the door and I saw Kait's casket through the opening, my body involuntarily thrust forward. My mind and ability to control myself seemed to completely shut off at that moment. As I began my walk toward Kait, I immediately burst into tears. I just couldn't believe it. It just wasn't right. The 24-year old woman with whom I invested so many years, happily discovering every aspect we could about one another, the only person in the world I could truly be vulnerable around, the love of my life, was lying lifelessly in the wooden box just in front of me. It was so surreal.

As I stood over her with tears flooding my eyes, I suddenly felt an unfamiliarity toward the figure lying in front of me. It was so weird, but I quickly realized why. It was because this figure, it was not Kaitlyn. It was an empty capsule. A shell. And what gave that shell life, the real Kaitlyn, her spirit, her consciousness, was no longer inside. It was in that moment I discovered what should have been obvious my whole life, and that is our physical body is simply a tool, a vehicle for our spirit to express itself. Oddly, however, I could still feel Kait's energy, her presence, but no longer was it emanating from the empty body in the casket, from the source I was used to feeling it from. Rather, the source of this all-enveloping energy was an invisible one, and it was all around me. The real Kait was present, I just couldn't see her.

Looking around the room, I found myself visually captivated by the overall setup, with the grand display of beautiful flowers adorning her casket and the surrounding area and the picture boards people constructed, including my own, to help us remember our sweet Kait.

Just before visitation commenced, we gathered around as Deacon Jim led us in prayer. He started by telling a story. In this dreary, but relevant tale, a woman was flying a kite. And the kite, hovering above her head, slowly drifted toward the sun. Suddenly, a forceful wind came and violently pushed the kite farther into the distance. Nature caught her off guard, and the woman began frantically reeling to bring it back in. But the wind was too strong. Eventually, with the kite pulling on the string, extending farther and farther out, it reached the end of its spool. And no matter how fast and how hard the woman tried turning her wrists, she couldn't retrieve her kite as it floated toward the clouds. In one final attempt, the woman summoned every last ounce of strength to rescue her beloved toy, but she still couldn't bring it back. The kite's fate was out of her control. Unable to do anything to retrieve it, she had to learn to let go. She cut the string. Sadly standing by, she watched as her kite faded into the heavens and out of her life.

My eyes glistened as I related Deacon Jim's story to our own situation. No matter how hard I tried to reel Kait back in, I couldn't. Eventually, realizing her fate was out of my control, I had to let her go. A tough notion for me to accept.

After reciting the 'Our Father' prayer, we prepared to begin the visitation service, and I took my place right next to Kait. My soul mate. A short moment later, the doors were opened and a procession of supporters rolled in. With an overwhelming number of people waiting in line, it was apparent to me Kait had answered my prayer. I felt at ease. I felt a sense of peace. I was no longer nervous or anxious. She gave me the strength to hold myself together and keep my composure for the duration of the service. Only when certain people walked through did I allow myself to break down. Not that it mattered if I cried, but I didn't want to be a sniveling baby throughout the entire evening.

Hundreds and hundreds of people paid their respect to Kait and the family, which made me feel good knowing she was truly loved. As the immature young adult I was, I never realized how much it meant having so many people show their support. In the past, during my short life, there were many times I decided to not attend a service or send a card because I didn't think my presence or support mattered. Now, being on the opposite end, it became clear how much EVERY SINGLE person's support means. To this day, I remember every single one of my family and friends who put in the effort to make an appearance, give me a phone call, shoot me a text message, or send a card. And I'm profoundly grateful. Conversely, you also remember all of the people who didn't outwardly show their support. As an imperfect human being, it's difficult not to feel a slight bitterness towards ones you felt should have. Then again, they are imperfect human beings, too, so the ability to forgive is essential.

As the hours passed and my throat became weak and hoarse, the last groups of supporters filed through, bidding farewell to Kait and lending their condolences to the family. After that, only family remained. With visitors gone, we finally took a seat on the chairs neatly scattered in front of Kait's casket and turned our attention to the flat screen monitors in the room, silently watching as pictures of our beloved angel filtered through. We officially made it through the first day of services, but one more remained, and my dread remained prevalent.

Saturday, January 5ᵗʰ, 2013. The day we were supposed to be wed. But instead of taking Kait's hand in holy matrimony, I was laying her to rest.

We arrived at the funeral home bright and early in the morning to prepare for the funeral service. Before taking a seat with the family and other attendees, I greeted Kait and stood over her casket for a brief moment. With a lack of sleep and a lack of energy, my ability to focus and restrain my emotions felt greatly impaired. I contemplated whether or not I should deliver my speech, but eventually I decided against it. My strength came into question. I feared I wouldn't be able to maintain my composure as I addressed the teary-eyed crowd. I was afraid I would break down after every other word. But I didn't feel like I needed to give a speech in order to prove to anyone how much Kait meant to me. It should have been obvious to those who knew us.

At the commencement of service, a couple of people stood up at the podium and spoke about our beautiful Kaitlyn, including Vicky. As a sweet and touching tribute, Vicky read a letter in which Mark had written to Kait when she was just a 5ᵗʰ grade girl. In the letter, Mark wrote of wonderful qualities and attributes she possessed even as a 10-year old. He talked about her compassion for other people, about her incredible work ethic, about her propensity to always want to help those in need, and more. I was amazed! Those traits she possessed as a child were the very same traits she held onto as a 24-year old young adult. For a moment, I thought maybe Mark tweaked the letter, but when I asked him if he made updates, he said, "Nope, that's how Kait's always been." I shook my head. I was astounded. Kait never wavered from her core values. She never let society or any other outside influences corrupt her belief system. That letter struck a chord with me, and holding my emotions back as Vicky spoke proved to be difficult.

Then, it was time to close the casket. Anticipation leading up to the moment caused me great anxiety. I didn't know how I would react. I feared that the magnitude of my pain as the lid was closed for an eternity on Kait's body would be too much. It would be the last time I would ever get to see her. But then I reasoned with myself. *The figure lying in the casket in front of me is not Kait. I'm only saying goodbye to her physical form, a superficial representation. I said goodbye to the real Kait a week ago.* My reasoning didn't help.

After the congregation of supporters paid their final respects as they passed by, I walked up to Kait. As I stood over the casket, gazing at what was once the person I invested my whole life into, the person my whole future was based around, the person with whom I had spoken to every single day for the last few years, and the person I planned on growing old and saggy and wrinkly and decrepit with, I lost it. The ground beneath me began to shake, and my legs buckled. Hunched over my love, I wept. I wept hard. I wept uncontrollably. No words could describe the grief I felt at that moment. Her body represented all that was left of her in the physical world, and I didn't want to let go. But I had to. I had to cut the string, again.

Eventually, I pulled myself away, allowing others a final moment with their girl. And after every family member said his or her sobbing, heartfelt goodbye to the youthful beauty, it was time. The lid was shut and permanently sealed. We all exited the funeral home and waited for the casket to be wheeled out the doors. Feeling as though it was an obligation and a duty of mine to take my love home, I requested to be a pallbearer. It wouldn't have felt right otherwise.

Shortly after arriving at the church, the hearse pulled up as we pallbearers took our place at the back of the elongated vehicle. I took my ring off, briefly, and put it in my pocket, fearing it could be damaged while carrying the casket.

One by one we grabbed hold of the sidebars of the wooden coffin and carried Kait into the church. The building was packed. We proceeded down the aisle, past all of the wonderful supporters, and positioned Kait at the front of the church before finding our seats.

Through the stained-glass windows, the sun was shining brightly onto my face as I stood with my family. I liked it. I wanted to believe Kait was shining on me and on the rest of us.

Deacon Jim spoke again at the church. In his speech he addressed the special bond Kait and I shared, elaborating on various stories he had heard. I was touched by his kind words. Not knowing Jim all too well before Kait's passing, my admiration and adoration for the Deacon soared that weekend. He was a sweet man.

As I involuntarily began tuning the speakers out, I found myself reflecting on the past. Sitting quietly in the pews, I recalled my sadness during my Grandma's funeral back in July as I imagined Kaitlyn in my Grandma's place. In my recollection, I realized the nightmarish scenario I envisioned had come true. Feeling my emotions quickly invading my mind, I swiftly erased all thoughts and returned my focus to the violinists readying to perform.

Surprisingly, Kait's former high school violin teacher volunteered his talents along with three others to close the ceremony. Together, they performed "Silent Night." The wonderful melody of strings gracefully entered my body and touched my heart and soul, making it difficult to hold on. It was the most beautiful, magical rendition of "Silent Night" I had ever heard and a most fitting way to conclude the funeral mass.

Following the church portion of the service, we followed the hearse to Kait's gravesite. Though Kait was to be laid to rest outside, we held one last ceremony with her casket inside the mausoleum where we gathered round. Once again the sun shone perfectly through the opening of the building and shimmered off of her casket. As in the church, I wanted to believe it was Kait making her presence known.

Finally, for the very last time, we had to walk away from Kait, forever. As people grabbed flowers off of her coffin, I stood by. Though I knew the real Kait was not in the casket, I still didn't want to leave. But I had to let go. And eventually, I did as I dragged myself out of the mausoleum, looking back a couple times before she disappeared behind the structural walls.

And to complete our grueling weekend, which concluded a grueling month, which completed a grueling year, we had to attend a group lunch. I certainly was in no mood to throw on a smile and mingle with everybody, but I had to. We all had to. Aside from a few moments of having to tense up my jaw in order to quell my tears, it turned out to be a nice get together of our family and friends.

Then, just like that, it was all over. All of the dread. All of the fear. All of the anxiety that had billowed within leading up to her funeral services. It was completely over. Finally. We all seemingly made it through, but not unscathed.

As exhausted as we could be, we stumbled into Kathy's house and totally unwound. I took a seat on the couch and didn't plan on moving.

Then, all of a sudden, almost as a wink and a nod from Kait, white crystal flakes began descending from the sky. It was snowing! No snow was in the forecast, and it had been sunny all day long, but it was actually snowing. In my mind and in the mind of others, we like to think it was Kaitlyn sending us a sign. She loved snow as it exemplified Christmas. It was a most fitting way to conclude everything and bring closure to our treacherous journey. It brought me a brief feeling of comfort.

Unable to keep my eyes open as the evening wore on, I made an early exit and crashed after nestling into bed. The beginning of a long journey through the rest of my life laid ahead, and it made me queasy. How was I going to survive the next 60 years, alone?

41 A DESOLATE APARTMENT

....
....
....
.... (tick) ......
.... (tock)
....
.... (tick) ....
.... (tock) ....
.... (tick) .... (tock) .... (tick) ....
.... (tock) .... Our apartment ...... (tick)
.... Once full of laughter and life ... (tock) ...... Once full of love
.... Once full of positivity .... Completely silent ......
(tick).......... Aside from the nearly inaudible ticking of the clock .....
(tock) ....Complete silence.

....
....
....I sit on the couch......By myself........Empty....... (tick) ....
...... (tock) ....Staring blankly forward ....
...............My social cushion.......... Gone .... My
breathing has slowed.... Significantly .... I'm suffocating ......
...................................My phone sits on the coffee table in front of
me......Waiting for it to vibrate......Waiting for a text from Kaitlyn......
(tick) ....(tock) .... I ate two chocolate chip
cookies today...... Want to pick up the phone and tell her........I

can't...................

....Silence.........

....

....birds chirp

outside..............................Hindu babies scream and cry in the
hallway.

My head's a balloon......... weightless ....My body
tingles.................................I look around the apartment ......
.......Everything remains................but it's desolate. Barren.
Lonesome......................

I'm drowning .... Deep, dark ocean of despair .... I keep
sinking .... deeper .... and deeper
.... The light of the sun .... vanished .... no
strength to swim.

Who can I talk to? .... I need Kait ....
.... I only want to talk to Kait .... Kait
where are you?.........................You were the one and only person I trusted
to pick me up .... You were the one and only person I trusted to admit
when I needed help.....or when I was sad.....mad.....glad.

...........................I can feel my heart trying to repair itself
.... This hurts................hurts badly ......
....................Is this what the rest of my life will feel like? ....
..................It's only been an hour.............How will I make it through this
week? .... How will I make it through this month? ....
.... How will I make it through this lifetime? ....
.... Kait...... can you come back?

Everything I do, I can still sense Kait. Taking a shower. Walking
around the apartment. Lying in my bed. I still feel her presence. It feels
like someone is constantly looking over my shoulder. I can feel a certain
foreign energy wrapped around my neck, my back. Is it her? Is my mind
fooling me? It's impossible to differentiate whether I feel this presence
because my memories are still so fresh, or because she actually is present.
My mind can't tell. It could be either. For self-appeasing purposes, I want
to believe it's her. So, it is her. It's definitely her.

"Hi, Kait," I say with a smile. "I miss you. I love you so much. I'm
sorry I couldn't do more."

Reminders of the life Kait and I had together are everywhere in the apartment. Our rings lying next to each other. The mound of shoes taking up a whole portion of the closet. Jewelry sprinkled across our dresser. Her clothes hanging in the closet. Family pictures throughout the apartment. Her cute snowman hot chocolate cup resting in the cupboard. Candy and chips and green tea and cooking supplies and her favorite chili from her dad and her nutritional drinks to combat the ill effects of cancer and more, littered throughout the kitchen. Her wedding magazines. Her wedding planner. Her career information – letters of recommendation, resumes, references. The letter and a picture from the little boy at Kennedy Elementary sent to Kait to update her on his progress and let him know he missed her, nearly bringing her to tears. Halloween decorations still up from October. The prayer she wrote down on a sticky note and taped to the inside of our bathroom cabinet. Her makeup. Her shampoo. Her hair straightener. Her wigs. Her bandanas. Her coats hanging from the coat rack. Every decoration in the apartment, all her touch. The coffee table she bought for $5 at a garage sale that she sanded down and beautifully refinished the summer before we moved in together. The plant stand my grandpa made for us that she sanded and spray painted to match the color scheme of our living room.

Reminders of Kait are scattered throughout. I like it. I don't like it. They make me happy because they bring back certain memories. They make me sad because they remind me that Kait's gone, for good.

Hours and days pass. I sit on the couch. Pondering. Reflecting. In pain. My head is boiling. My heart. I feel like I've coded. No pulse. I'm a zombie. Darkness envelops me. I'm frightened. Am I in hell? I think so. I can't be sure. Purgatory?

I can't believe people experience similar pain every day. Some worse. Some face the challenge of cancer for years. Some at a younger age. But it's not a competition. A tragedy is a tragedy, and pain is pain. Comparing situations would seem immature. Not everything in life needs to be reduced to a competition.

What do I do? I have to start clawing my way out. But the shroud of blackness is too thick, too overwhelming. I need help.

I can't live the rest of my years as a lifeless, wooden replica of a man. I have to live, somehow. But, everything that gave my life meaning. A purpose. She's gone. The one thing I was responsible for I let slip away. The one thing I completely devoted myself to can no longer be my devotion.

Now what? What's the point? I had goals. I had aspirations. Then disease entered. Those goals and aspirations became completely and utterly meaningless. I set my sights on a new goal. It was my only goal. Kaitlyn. Doing everything I could possibly do to help return Kait to health. I worked harder to achieve that goal than anything I'd ever aspired to achieve. My only purpose in life then was keeping her alive, and it was more important and meaningful than anything I'd ever done. Even if I couldn't do much, even if I had almost no control over her outcome, I wanted to work tirelessly to acquire all of the necessary tools to make my new dream a possibility. And then a reality. I was all in. Pledged all of my being. And, not only was I to keep her alive, but I was also to make damn sure she was happy. All of my stress. All of my worries for her, the person I loved more than anything in the world, had to be swept under the rug. It had to remain hidden from her view.

I would never outwardly admit it, but I knew there was a good chance she wouldn't come out of this in the end. That also had to remain a secret, even if she knew it, too. And, if she was to succumb to her ailment, then I had to make sure in her final months that she was not stressed, and that she was able to love, laugh, and live her life happily until the end.

Above all, no matter how much stress and worry I was under, I always kept myself grounded in the reality that what she was experiencing was so much worse than what I was experiencing. She was actually dealing with her own mortality and physical pain. So, whatever stress I was under paled 100 times over in comparison to what she was dealing with. I always had to remember that fact then, and I still have to remember that fact now.

I still went to work, but I coasted because that was a trivial part of my life. My job mattered little in the grand scheme of things. More of an annoyance than anything. It kept me from my real task. If I was fired, I would hardly flinch because I knew what awaited me at home was infinitely more important than a simple job. Time with her was potentially running out. Every activity not involving Kait was time wasted.

For a year, that was my life. That was my goal. Kaitlyn was my true job. Now what? No job could ever compare to the job I undertook 12 months ago. What's even the purpose? What's the purpose of doing anything now? Whatever task I undertake from here on out will never compare in importance and meaning to the one I had. Money no longer carries the weight it carried before. Everything severely lacks meaning. From here on out, everything I achieve will seem pointless and miniscule in the end. So, what's the point? What can I do that would even come close to the importance of the previous goal I had?

I just don't know.

My purpose is gone. I am obsolete. I've passed my expiration date. What to do...

I wake up in the middle of the night. Still sleepy. Still groggy. Kait's leg is nestled up to mine. She likes to feel my presence when we sleep, so she always keeps her leg against me. Every night. I love it.

I continue waking up. I lift my head and turn my body, wanting to give Kait a kiss on the forehead. Letting her know she's safe and she's loved. Maybe I'll squeeze her, too. It depends how she responds. I don't want to wake her.

My grogginess becomes complete consciousness as I turn over.

Kait's not there.

That's right.

She's gone.

The feeling against my leg was just the fold of the blankets.

Oddly, I found myself only partially disappointed. On one hand, the sense of dejection upon realizing Kait was not there as I had anticipated was profound. But, on the other hand, for those 5, 10 seconds as I was waking up, I genuinely felt a familiarity of something I had just months earlier, something I had gotten used to for years. For those 5 to 10 seconds, she was alive again in my head. She was actually alive. And I liked that feeling, however short that feeling was.

Once again, I sit on my couch, staring blankly forward. I feel like I should be doing something productive, but I can't. The mere thought of moving, even lifting a finger seems like a daunting task. It's as if the blood in my veins has hardened to concrete. I'm cemented to the couch.

What's the point? Will I always feel like this?

My heart hurts. I literally feel an intense pain in my heart. After every lub-dub, I feel it mourn for Kait and the suffering she had to endure.

In my head a pair of vise grips clamp around the backs of my eyeballs, squeezing tightly. Beyond my control and beyond my prediction, they add and release pressure at their own will. At times, like they are squeezing lemons. My eyes well up and fluids drain.

My body and my spirit are constantly at war. Somehow I feel like I'm floating and falling at the same time. My physical body continues plummeting down this dark abyss, but my head feels like it wants to detach itself from my body and float away. This must be my spirit trying to leap out of my shell. My face feels like pins and needles. Tingly. I'm completely numb.

Am I half dead? I mean, I know I had this nice theory saying that I gave myself to Kait, and when she died, a part of me went with her. Could that be true, after all? It seemed like just a cute, crackpot theory, but now it seems viable. Essentially, I feel like a part of me is dead.

If the rest of my life is going to feel like this, pure agony, should I just end it now? I mean, maybe that whole suicide and hell thing is just a myth.

But, what if it's not?

What would it feel like to put a bullet in my head? What would it actually feel like?

Would it hurt? Would it be peaceful? Would it relieve all of the built up pressure in my head? Hmm…

But I can't put our families through more heartache. That wouldn't be fair.

This isn't how life is supposed to be lived, and I don't have the strength to change it, so what's the purpose of living if it's always going to be like this?

But it won't always be like this. Right? I mean, everyone says time heals. Is that true? Or, do we simply learn how to cope with the pain as time moves forward? Do we simply learn more effective methods of managing our wounds?

Weeks passed. Some days I would feel a spark, thinking I must be getting over some sort of hump. But then, hours later, that spark would vanish, the plank would drop beneath me and I would plunge deeper into my limitless sorrow, dispassionately treading to keep afloat. I never felt sorry for myself, though. Just Kait.

Every day I replayed every aspect of our battle against our cancer insurgency. From the day we first met, to the day we first learned she had the disease, all the way up to her final moments, the same images cycled through my mind, hitting rewind and starting over every 15 minutes.

Every day I pondered my future. Will I ever work again? Will I ever find love again? I don't think so. How could I? People say I have to, eventually. But, I don't know if I'll ever be ready. It feels like it won't be fair to the girl I pursue. Will she have difficulty understanding my eternal love for Kaitlyn? Will she have difficulty understanding when I have a moment of sad memories and tears for another woman? Will she feel like she is my consolation prize?

I question whether I'd ever be able to fully commit myself like I did with Kaitlyn. I feel I will always be inhibited in love. If I'm showing affection to another girl, I might pause and think to myself – *this is what I used to do with Kaitlyn. Am I betraying Kaitlyn?* Every woman deserves full commitment from the man she is with. Not 80%. Not 98%. But an immense 100%.

Have I exhausted my ability to love? Is there a finite amount of love within each human being, or is it infinite?

I constantly long to feel that companionship. But, it's Kait's companionship I long for. My happiness soared to unimaginable heights with Kait's love and friendship, and I miss how that bond made me feel. One day I'm sure I'll open myself up to that companionship again, but I don't know when. I suppose it may be never.

Even after a year, there are times I see a girl who I am physically attracted to, and a part of me wants to pursue her. My damaged heart temporarily ignores any inhibitions and races toward that attraction. Soon after, my thoughts interfere. Why even try if I'll be essentially leading her on? I don't want to hurt anyone. So, shortly into my pursuit, my brain constructs a great wall that I come barreling into, stopping me dead in my tracks.

I don't know if it's okay to love someone else again. People tell me I have to move on and "let Kait go." In my irritable state, I want to tell them to screw off. Maybe I'm simply destined to go the way of the nun, living a life of celibacy.

I don't even know if it's okay to truly be happy. How can I be if my primary source of happiness is gone?

I ponder whether grief will always be a prominent part of my life. I feel like if I'm not grieving, I'm doing Kait a disservice. How dare I smile!? Kait suffered and died, I should not be smiling.

Then the hypochondriac in me starts wondering whether or not the long-term stress I experienced could have caused damage, effecting my ability to think in the future. For over a year I pushed my neurons as far as I think they could be pushed. Can neurons burn out and die? Of course. I feel like I'm having a hard time with short-term memory now. Things in the past, which would never escape my mind, are beginning to escape. Remembering simple names of people, or simple processes I've done over and over suddenly become more difficult as I question myself every time. I can't focus. I can't concentrate. Will that last? Is it just because I'm still stricken with grief and guilt? Or, maybe old age is simply setting in.

Sitting in my apartment, I think and I think and I think. All the thoughts become overwhelming. So, I take advantage of the skill I acquired from suffering through cancer – I blank my mind. A complete whiteout. I never thought it was possible to halt all thoughts, but I learned how.

After briefly clearing the brush of sadness from my mind, I soon come upon anger and disgust aimed heavily at pharmaceutical companies and a system which perpetuates such evil, self-serving behavior. Through all of my research, I received a rude awakening in that we are nowhere near a cure because money trumps compassion and human values. While our most beloved suffer and die, we are fed stories through the media of "breakthrough" discoveries to instill hope in us, making us believe they are doing everything possible to destroy cancer. That may be true, but only if it helps the bottom line.

I was so angry, because instead of taking advantage and testing the natural, God-given resources expressing similar DNA to our own, like plants, we continue using toxic, carcinogenic chemicals, which poisons and destroys our bodies. After 30 years and trillions of dollars spent, the methods employed today have hardly changed. So many novel, natural approaches have been ignored because they wouldn't be profitable, or are banned because they threaten the monetary gains of the pharma industry. When cheap, healthier, and potentially more effective alternatives are brought to light, the heads of these corporations with the help of the FDA will do whatever they can, going to great lengths to discredit the method, steer people away, and even ban it.

Ineffective, damaging poison will continue to be the preferred approach because it brings in the most money (approaches like effective, yet costly Stem Cell Therapy, Gene Modification, etc. are years away). If you were the head of a company and your job depended on increasing shareholder value, which study would you lean toward? The one where you can charge a patient $200,000 over a few months (Kaitlyn on Ipilimumab)? Or, the one that can't be patented because it's natural, where competition will drive the price down to unprofitable levels (like with High-Dose Vitamin C, say)? The answer is simple. I understand it. But, I don't like it. In fact I loathe it. This kind of behavior is promoted by a gaming system with its rules that need changing so that human life is put ahead of monetary gains. However, that won't happen.

I become angry because I see so many people defend the aberrant behavior exhibited by those in charge of these companies, when just a smidgen of research exposes their intrinsic mission. And, that mission is not geared toward you or me.

Don't believe me? Good. I encourage people to be skeptical, question everything, and to do their own research to discover unsettling truths.

In the meantime, with stress rampant, with carcinogens in our air, our food, and our water, and with pharmaceuticals merely seeking profit, cancer and other major diseases will continue to rapidly increase, causing the deaths of millions of people. People who you and I love dearly. People way too young, who deserve a chance at a full, fruitful life.

It angers me because I feel like Kaitlyn would still be alive today if greed didn't play a role in the medical world. That anger, that rage fuels my utter disdain for pharmaceutical companies and the money-driven "men" at the top who play a role in stunting true medical progress. As much advancement has been made in remedying other ailments, cancer remains big, big business.

Shortly after my rage would dissipate, sadness would return and the life cycle of our relationship would begin again in my head. Overall, I was in bad shape.

I needed reminders that life goes on, that I can't sit and sulk in sadness and depression. And, oftentimes those reminders would make themselves known in subtle ways.

It had been a month, and I was sitting on the couch during the evening with the blinds agape in our apartment. Through the mound of snow surrounding our porch, a full-grown rabbit appeared. Standing right outside the window of the sliding door, he looked in. *Could this be the same rabbit from before? It must be. Do rabbits grow that fast? I suppose they do.* Remembering how Kait used to feed him during the summer, I quickly scanned the fridge, but I didn't eat vegetables, so we were empty. Feeling a duty to Kait and to the furry critter, I grabbed my keys and hurried to the store to buy lettuce.

When I came back, the bunny was gone, but I still dumped a large handful of food on the ground. As the minutes passed, our rabbit friend returned, munching away at his tasty meal. From that night on, I fed the adorable rodent almost every day. For Kait. And because I didn't want him to starve. Hopefully it made Kait happy.

It was a gentle reminder I may still have purpose. That others may need me, yet, in this world. That I can't be sitting on my butt feeling depressed forever.

42 FAITH RENEWED

Weeks kept passing by, and my struggle continued as I attempted to rediscover a purpose worth living for. So many questions remained. Where is Kait now? Is she still with me? Is she following me around? Is she with her family? Does she jump back and forth? Or, is death the final frontier? Is life on earth the only life we experience, and once it's over, do we resolve to nothing while the planet gobbles us up? I wanted answers so badly. I desperately wanted to believe a life existed beyond that of our own two eyes. I desperately wanted to believe Kait was in a place much better than the place we inhabit.

In my quest for answers, like with my cancer studies, I began a foray into heavy research. As I saddled up and prepared to delve into the world of death and God, I made sure I would not fool myself. I was aware of how desperately I wanted Kait to still exist on a different plane. So, I wanted to make sure I wouldn't trick myself into believing in an afterlife just as a coping mechanism and to appease my own desires. Whatever conclusions I arrived upon had to be from overwhelming evidence, and I had to keep confirmation bias subdued. I realized little to no scientific research existed when it came to what happens after death, but I wanted to find out as much as I could.

Before Kaitlyn passed away, I was one of those half-and-half believers in God and heaven. I believed, but I didn't really "believe." I would pray only when I needed help, but I didn't truly believe my prayers were capable of being heard. Quickly, my belief system started to evolve. It began with my anecdotal findings.

RESEARCH – NDES, OBES. In my endeavor into learning whether or not an afterlife existed, I began by scouring the web, looking up everything I could imagine that dealt with death and the great beyond. I Googled topics such as "heaven", "afterlife", "what happens when we die", and even obscure, yet related topics like "Ouija board stories". I wanted answers, and I wanted to hear what people had to say.

Through my research, I read hundreds of stories of individuals who experienced Near-Death Experiences (NDEs) and Out-of-Body Experiences (OBEs). I watched documentaries and read books touching on topics such as the afterlife, NDEs, OBEs, psychology, and the history of spirituality across many different civilizations. I navigated through many, many, many interviews of people and their stories about having brushes with death and meeting an entity they claimed was Jesus. From all of the anecdotal stories and all of the studies, it became difficult not to believe something more existed after we die. Of course, I know that the more one is exposed to a certain subject or belief, the more apt he is to begin to align with that belief. With that in mind, I continuously reminded myself to do my best to remain objective.

I listened to scientists' attempts at explaining what really happens during a near-death experience in an attempt to "scientifically" explain the heavenly visions people receive. The common and accepted claim is that when people see the proverbial light as they ascend into what they perceive as heaven, it's merely our brain's response as it begins shutting down. As the brain ceases to function, one of the last parts to work is the area that captures light.

That same concept is also used for the scientific explanation as to why people have their lives flash before their eyes before death. Like with the light, it is explained that as our brain is shutting down, one of the last functioning areas is the part where memories are stored. The problem I have with this idea, however, is that we don't know exactly where memories are stored. We know that declarative memories seem to begin their path in the hippocampus via the perforant path, and then like a librarian the hippocampus finds a spot within the brain to log those memories. But, where exactly those memories end up is still a mystery. I mean, generally speaking, the frontal, parietal, and temporal lobes seem to be a main storage unit for our various memories, but it still isn't quite clear.

So, maybe NDEs are purely biological. Even though the current scientific explanations are not convincing to me, maybe they are on the right path to eventually proving that these experiences are merely an illusion.

But then, there are the out-of-body experiences. What's the explanation for when people exit their bodies during surgery, and then, even though their faces are completely covered, they can see exactly what is going on not only in the room of their procedure, but in other rooms, too? How does one explain the incidences where a person is born blind, has an OBE during a procedure or medical emergency, and can suddenly see what's going on around him as he's hovering above his body? Many of these experiences are later verified by shocked doctors and nurses as the patients recite everything that was going on during their surgeries. And, so far, no explanation exists for these occurrences.

Above near-death experiences, I believe out-of-body experiences are the proof that we actually do have a soul or a spirit that can be detached from our physical bodies. This reaffirms my assertion that our physical bodies are merely shells for our souls, or our conscious beings, to experience life here on earth. In my opinion, I don't think there can be a scientific explanation to simplify or reduce out-of-body experiences.

And as for NDEs, I truly believe that many (not all) of the people who say they traveled to an alternate reality during their brush with death actually did travel to an alternate reality. For the most part, the stories told by thousands of people across the globe are essentially similar. The unifying principles of most of these experiences are heightened sensory, unconditional love, no pain, unexplainable beauty of the landscape, interactions with deceased loved ones, and an overwhelming comfort that makes it difficult to want to go back to earth. The experiencers feel love like they've never felt love before. They feel warm. They feel safe. They feel absolutely wonderful.

Many people claim to have seen relatives who they had no idea existed – siblings who died in the womb, uncles they've never met, etc. Once these experiencers reenter their human form, they later verify that the people they met in "heaven" actually were their relative. Many people claim to have seen Jesus. They all say his presence is completely loving and wonderful. Many people have had experiences where they've been given insight into future events, which, later on, do actually happen. Just about every single person that has had an NDE comes back to earth completely changed and enlightened. Their perspectives altered forever.

After compiling all of this anecdotal evidence of people entering alternate, spiritual worlds, I was almost completely convinced an afterlife existed. But, no matter how many claims I come across, I'm always skeptical. Unless something happens to me, or people I know, I have a difficult time completely committing to a belief system. I needed personal evidence.

Which brings me to certain occurrences that happened to us. Most of these could be considered mere coincidences, but when compiled together, it becomes difficult to dismiss each happening.

A CHILLING REVELATION. "……I was supposed to die for you." To this day, that one statement she made in the wake of her major seizure still gives me chills. It's a comment I ponder almost every day, leaving me to wonder, what did she mean?

"I was supposed to die for you."

"I was SUPPOSED to DIE for YOU."

What could that have possibly meant? As I explained earlier, even in her disoriented state of mind, there was a chance she was able to partially comprehend her situation. Knowing Kait, if she did realize her life would be forever changed, there is a chance she may have wanted to die for me so she wouldn't be "dragging me along" during her intense struggle going forward. But, in her state of mind at the time, I don't think her level of thinking was that advanced.

When she made that statement, I simply tried to shrug it off, believing it likely meant nothing. Unfortunately, Kaitlyn's recollection of her stay at the three hospitals after her seizure was very poor, remembering only bits and pieces. Also, I never asked her about it because I feared it would be a topic too stressful for her to talk about – death.

However, after all of the stories I read, and after other things that happened which I'm about to discuss, I believe Kaitlyn might have had an out-of-body experience during her seizure. At one point, she did begin to turn blue while she was convulsing. I believe it is possible her soul could have detached temporarily from her body. I believe it is possible she could have entered a alternate dimension. I believe it is possible she could have met and conversed with another entity. And, I believe it is possible this entity might have gently explained to her that she was supposed to die for me, and maybe others, while explaining the purpose of it.

I have absolutely no way of knowing for sure, nor will I ever, but I think she did briefly go to a heavenly realm.

ESCORTING SPIRITS. "They are here for me, but I don't want to go, yet." For two straight days before she passed away, Kaitlyn was completely unresponsive, not even waking for water or her medications. Then, hours before her final breaths, she woke up and made that statement in her attempts to speak. And, she looked directly at us, whereas during the previous week and a half, she was unable to look straight. That in and of itself was extraordinary to me, but her statement was what set that moment apart.

"They are here for me, but I don't want to go, yet."

What did she mean? Who was there for her?

Could she have been hallucinating? Yes. Do I think she was? No.

I think it is possible deceased relatives could have been in her room waiting to take her home, to a better world. I believe she saw something real.

PERFECT TIMING. Another instance I refer to as potential proof of a spiritual world is the perfect timing of Kait's passing. On December 29th, by all signs, with her laboring and her blood pressure dropping, she was supposed pass on that night. But, she didn't.

I went to bed.

The next morning, I entered the room at about 8:30. Just minutes after I greeted her, as though she had been waiting for me to wake up, she began laboring again. Swiftly, we called every one of her family members in to be by her side. Jessica was the last one to enter her room. Maybe two minutes after she came in, Kait let go, as though she was making sure to hold on until all of her family were present.

What a coincidence that would be, huh? First of all, she could have died at any point during the night. Essentially, she should have. But, seemingly conscious of her surroundings, she held on. As soon as I got in the room, she began the process of dying. And, as soon as the last family member arrived, she passed away. I don't think it was a coincidence at all. I think she was aware and possibly outside of her body looking over herself. I think she knew exactly what she was doing. The timing of her passing was too perfect.

A FATHER'S DREAM. Months had gone by since Kait's passing. Every single night, Mark dreamt of Kait. All of the dreams were essentially similar. Either Kait was no longer with us, or Kait had passed away and came back to life, or Kait was alive again but she still had cancer and we were trying to figure out how to beat it. Although dreams always feel real when you are in them, we wake up knowing they were merely dreams, nothing more. Except for one night for Mark.....

It was early-June, and for several weeks, Mark had been having a rough time coming to grips with his daughter's death. As expected, emotional pain was prevalent every single day, but more pronounced during those weeks leading up to June.

Well, on one particular night, Mark had gone to sleep early as usual to recharge for work the next day. Hours into his nightly slumber, Mark awoke. Only, he wasn't in his room. He found himself in an unknown place, completely surrounded by a soft white light. The light was not blinding or overpowering. It was a warm and comforting light. Nothing else existed in this large, luminous space, except a strong presence.

Something in Mark's head immediately alerted him.

"Kait's here!"

He began looking around. Not long into his search, he found her. Kait was standing before him! Curiously, when Kait revealed herself to him, her image was sort of flickering, rapidly changing back and forth from a sick Kait to a healthy Kait. Eventually, the flickering stopped. Kait was healthy.

Excited, ecstatic, speechless, Mark approached her and they tightly embraced. With his head rested on Kait's shoulder, he wept uncontrollably. This was real. He could feel it. He could sense it. This was no ordinary dream. Holding each other as Mark continued shedding tears of joy, he could feel Kait with her unconditional love supporting him as she seemed to hover slightly above whatever ground was beneath them. After releasing his cries, the stress and anxiety he had been feeling for weeks and months seemed to completely vanish.

Then, Kait took Mark by the hand as they walked a couple of steps before taking a seat on seemingly nothing. Mark turned his attention to the white nothingness in front of him. With their hands still intertwined, images of Kaitlyn began to appear before his eyes. The images were of Kait through all phases of her life – as a baby, as a toddler, as a child, as an adolescent, and as a young adult. They all had one thing in common – Kaitlyn was smiling and she was happy.

No conversing was done, but Mark could feel a strong sense of pure joy, pure bliss, pure love and happiness emanating from Kait as she sat with her father. Without words, Mark felt like she was trying to convey the message, "See Dad, I lived a great, happy life. You don't have to worry about me. I'm okay!"

Astounded by what he was experiencing, he wanted to go tell everyone before it was too late, but then he got the feeling that this experience was for him. No one else would be able to see or understand what was happening.

Then, the experience was over.

The next morning, Mark woke up feeling rested for the first time in a long time. He felt like the weight of the world had been lifted off his shoulders. All day he felt calm and serene, walking around with a tingling feeling of chills pulsating like gentle waves of electricity throughout his entire body. He felt comforted. He knew his daughter was all right.

Mark and I both strongly agree. He wasn't simply dreaming. Kait crossed over to send him a message that night.

Five months later, Mark woke up in the exact same setting of soft white light, feeling Kait's presence once again. Only this time, before anything significant happened, Mark woke from his actual sleep. He wonders if a connection was trying to be made. So do I.

A GRANDDAUGHTER'S REASSURANCE. It was around the same time in June, possibly even the same night as Mark's dream. Kaitlyn's grandpa, Don, had an extraordinary experience himself.

Since Kait passed away, Don talked with her often, praying to her every single day and night. And every single night, he would sleep with a special wooden cross in his hands, holding it near his chest.

Well, on one particular night, Don woke up in the wee morning hours. And when he awoke, he glanced to his side and saw a faint image. It looked like Kait. But, tired, groggy and assuming he was hallucinating, Don turned around and fell back to sleep.

Time passed throughout the night before Don awoke once more. Glancing to the side of his bed again, the soft, white image of Kait was still there. And, again, he shrugged it off as just his imagination before trying to fall back to sleep. With his eyes closed, feeling a warm presence, he decided to look one last time to make sure he wasn't seeing things. When he opened his eyes, the image was still there.

More awake and seeing clearly now, Don affirmed with himself what he had questioned. The foggy spirit standing next to him was the granddaughter he loved so effusively. It was Kait! When she smiled at him, his initial shock turned to complete comfort and joy.

Then, she approached him. Putting her hand on his arm, she said, "It's okay, Papa."

So profoundly touched by his amazing experience, talking about it induced chills and emotions.

For weeks, Don kept his story hidden from Mark, fearing it could potentially cause pain and sadness. When he finally decided to give testimony to Mark on what he had witnessed, he became emotional. Mark could tell the old man was sincere. Don was not making it up.

Could it have been a hallucination? Of course. But, I don't think so. Especially since both Mark's and Don's experiences occurred around the same time period. Possibly the same exact night. We wonder if Kait was more active at that point. It's possible, but impossible to know for sure.

A COMFORTING TOUCH. Only weeks had passed since Kait crossed over into the afterlife. Late one night, struggling mightily to cope with everything her lovely daughter was forced to endure, Kathy laid in bed restless, distraught, full of grief, and unable to fall asleep. Unable to suppress her sadness just long enough to doze, she reached out to Kait for help. To herself, Kathy asked her daughter to give her a sign, to let her know she was okay.

Just then, as she waited silently under her covers, Kathy suddenly felt a light pressure on her leg, as though someone or something was pressing down, patting it. Relieved and comforted from receiving this unexpected, warming response, Kathy was able to fall asleep for the night.

Could this have been all in Kathy's mind? Absolutely. But, I'm not about to dismiss it as such.

NIGHTLY APPARITIONS. It was February. I was sleeping in my childhood room at my parents' house. At around 2 AM, I woke up. In my fogginess, I turned over to face the empty side of my bed. Immediately, my eyes alerted me to an abnormal presence, accelerating my heartbeat. Lying next to me was an image of a person. Trying to assure myself I wasn't hallucinating, I began blinking my eyes and shaking my head to see if it would disappear. But it didn't. Looking on wide-eyed, the person suddenly smiled at me with white teeth. Because my room was so dark, and because I was so tired, I couldn't ascertain who the image was portraying.

After maybe 30 seconds had passed, I exited my room to go to the bathroom. When I came back, my room was empty again. With my adrenaline easing back to normal, I was able to fall back to sleep eventually.

Then, as more weeks passed, four more times I woke up and saw an image of someone lying next to me. It happened once at my apartment and three more times at my parents' domicile. In my grogginess, I never could tell exactly who it was. But, I know for sure I was awake. And, I know for sure I saw something. Could it have been Kait? Possibly. Could it have been projections manufactured by my own mind? Possibly.

As a side note, when I was 19 or 20, I began waking up in the middle of the night to ghostly images of people standing in my room. One time it was a little girl standing in the corner of my room. Another time it was a black woman sitting in a chair at the corner of my bed. On certain nights my alarm clock would go off at around 2:30 AM even though I never set it. Of course, many people experience alarm clock mishaps. But the images of people, I experienced those on many nights.

Are my experiences examples of hallucinations? Do I have early signs of schizophrenia? It's possible. But, between the age of 20 and 28 I stopped seeing things. All of a sudden at the age of 28, I began waking up and seeing images again. And, it was the exact same image each time, of a person lying next to me in bed.

Then, months later, after I moved into a new apartment, I had the same experience. It was the third different location I had seen this image of a person lying beside me. But it only happened once at my new home and hasn't since. Is it possible that Kait was appearing before me? I don't know. Is it possible when I wake up at night, my mind is in a relaxed state that allows me to see "things" or entities? Maybe. Is it possible I'm going crazy? Absolutely. I just don't know.

JESUS ANSWERING?. I had been having a particularly rough two weeks. My mind was in the gutter, and I couldn't seem to find energy or reason to do anything. My muscles, my bones, my thoughts, everything felt like molasses. Everything felt like slow motion.

Finally, one night, I decided to reach out. After speaking with Kaitlyn like I did every night, I made a call to Jesus. I proceeded to plead my case with him, divulging my most recent struggles. I then made a request. "Jesus…," I said, "…do you think, maybe you could show yourself to me? Could you somehow appear to me? In front of me right now or in my dreams or any way you see fit? I would appreciate it. And I think it would help."

I finished my prayer and went to bed that night. I wasn't expecting anything.

Well, hours into my sleep, my eyes opened. Was I awake or dreaming? I honestly do not know, because I was extremely groggy. Even the next morning, I couldn't discern which it was. But, when my eyes opened that night, I was in my room, lying in my bed on my side. I looked down at the edge of my bed, by my feet, and sure enough, standing tall, looking right at me, was Jesus. He was completely surrounded by a luminous, white light. The light was extremely bright, but not blinding by any means. Through the radiance I could see His beard, and I knew without a doubt that it was Him.

Like I said, I don't know if I was still asleep or awake, but shortly after I saw Him, I closed my eyes and fell back to sleep. And that was it.

Was it really Him? Did He reach out to me in my dream? Was I awake? I don't know. Nevertheless, I definitely saw Him in some form, and the fact that it happened the very night I asked for Him makes me believe that He really was reaching out to me.

A PHONE CALL FROM BEYOND? – After Kait had passed, Kathy could not bring herself to cancel Kait's cell phone plan with their wireless company. Every so often in the ensuing years, Kathy and others would call her phone simply to hear her sweet and friendly voice once more.

Well, one day, a couple years after Kait's passing, her sister Jess was going through a rough patch at work. A patient temporarily residing at their institution committed suicide. For any warm-blooded human with a properly functioning heart, this can be quite an emotional experience. It was for Jess and a number of her colleagues.

Struggling to cope with this tragic event, she and her coworkers decided to talk about the situation as a group. Moments later, as the group session concluded, Jess headed back to her office with a heavy heart. Upon entering her office, she noticed her phone was blinking, indicating she had a missed call. So, she grabbed her phone and looked to see who it was.

Shock!

Dizziness!

Chills immediately rushed down her spine as she processed the name of the missed caller!

It was Kaitlyn!

Impossible! How could that be?

After collecting herself and calming her nerves, Jessica quickly called Kathy to see if maybe she was messing around with Kait's phone. But she was not. Kait's phone had been dead and tucked away in a storage bin for many months.

With everyone's attention and curiosity piqued, they began investigating all of the possible ways this could have happened. They called the cell phone company, they searched the internet, but nothing seemed to make logical sense. How could Kait's phone have called Jess while being dead and stored away? It was a mystery. One that current information and logic could not solve.

Is it possible that Kait sent the call from beyond the grave? Was Kait trying to help her dear sister cope with an emotional event in her life? Of course, you know my response. Yes!

MY DREAM. I had a dream. Not too dissimilar from Mark's where the dream felt more real than most dreams I have.

For months after Kait passed away, I dreamt of her often. In my dreams, Kait was alive, her hair was long and flowing again, but she still had cancer and we were trying to figure out how to cure her.

However, on one particular night, my dream was much different. It felt more "real." Kait had returned to visit me, but unlike my other dreams, I knew she had passed away. I knew she couldn't stay long. Together, we were hanging out in our apartment again living normally, but we didn't speak. All I wanted to do was stare at her and soak in her loving presence because I knew it was only temporary.

Then, we went to the mall. As we were walking past the mass of shoppers, my family arrived. Immediately, I exclaimed, "Hey guys, look who it is," as I pointed to Kait.

Seeing Kait standing in front of them they all wept as they embraced her, expressing how much she was missed.

Soon after, we found ourselves back at our apartment, just hanging out together. In my heart I knew it was time. She had to go back to her world. Standing before me, Kait smiled and held my hand, letting me know we would do this some other time. With that, we hugged. I held onto her tightly and told her how much I loved her.

All of a sudden, I jolted awake. My heart was tingling along with the rest of my body. I took a deep breath, and the first thing I said was, "Thank you."

For those moments, Kait was real, and she was back to say hello. It wasn't like most dreams where deep down you sense you are merely dreaming. It wasn't one of those dreams where you wake up and have to slowly piece it back together through your fogginess. Normally, I have a vague recollection of my dreams, but this one was vivid and still is. When I woke up, I instantly felt it was real.

But, was it? It's impossible for me to know for sure. The whole part about going to the mall is what makes me consider it may have just been a normal dream.

AN ANIMAL'S SENSE. At Mark's house, a room was set up in the basement for the nights when Kaitlyn would sleep over. Normally, Kaitlyn lived at her mom's abode, but some nights she would stay at her dad's.

Vicky and Mark had a cat named Little Bit. This cat almost never went downstairs into Kait's room.

Well, one day, just a couple weeks after Kaitlyn passed away, Vicky was looking all over the house for Little Bit. To her surprise, she found the feline hanging out in Kaitlyn's room, and she was acting rather strange. As the cat sat on Kait's bed, it stared intently at a corner of the ceiling. It was completely fixated on something.

Like a ball on a swivel, the cat's head began turning slowly, as if she was following the movement of this "thing" she had her vision focused on.

Then, the movement of Little Bit's head stopped. For another few moments, her head remained stationary as her eyes continued to be transfixed on this invisible "thing". All of a sudden, the cat's eyes followed along a path leading to the closet. For the moment, with the "thing" seemingly escaped from Little Bit's view, she immediately jumped off the bed and ran to the closet to find it again.

Vicky followed her pet. Inside the closet, Vicky curiously watched her cat as it was fixated on one specific area in the closet for many, many seconds. Suddenly, Little Bit darted out of the closet following something, and then she stopped as she stared intently at another point in the room.

Confused by her cat's odd behavior, Vicky had a peculiar thought. Kait was present and her cat could see her.

"Hey Kait," she said with a sheepish smile, unsure if she was talking to herself or, well, Kaitlyn.

Taken aback by the cat's behavior, unsure of how to interpret her actions, Vicky told Mark about her experience later on in the evening. Intrigued, Mark decided to venture off into the basement. And, even though Little Bit never hung out in Kait's room, she was there again, resting on the bed.

Mark sat at the edge of Kait's bed, observing the room in wonderment. Then, breaking her calm demeanor, Little Bit suddenly sat up and seemed distracted again by something and began behaving exactly how she was with Vicky. The cat lifted her head and focused on a certain point on the ceiling. Again, Little Bit slowly followed this "thing" as it would seemingly move from one area of the room to another. This happened for several minutes. Eventually, as the cat's line of vision followed along the wall, her gaze stopped right in front of Mark, as though this imaginary "thing" was standing before him, just three feet away. For a few moments, Little Bit's eyes remained transfixed on this phantom object or being as it seemed to remain stationary while facing Mark.

Was it possible Kait was standing right in front of him? He didn't know. He wasn't sure what to think. Like Vicky, Mark simply said, "Hey Kait."

Was their cat just crazy? Or, did the cat see something? I tend to believe the latter. I do think Little Bit did see something. Call me delusional, but I believe it was Kait. Animals can sense things we cannot.

MORE DREAMS. Going back to the dream theme, I present exhibit C of the extra-real sleeping fantasies. This one involved my aunt, Michelle.

One night in March as she lay asleep in bed, Michelle suddenly found herself surrounded by a heavenly landscape, which she interpreted to be heaven. Waiting for her in this wonderful place was her mother, Edna - my grandmother who had passed away six months before Kait. Then, as Michelle approached her mother, she noticed Kaitlyn was standing right next to her (two other deceased relatives were also in the picture). They were smiling and very happy.

Like Mark's and my dream, Michelle explained that her dream felt more real than any dream she had experienced before. She recalled feeling unconditional love, warmth, and comfort. She didn't want to leave.

SUSPENDED ARM. One night, I was grieving as usual as I struggled to fall asleep. Missing Kaitlyn, I began talking to her, at least in my head I was. Wanting to feel her again, I lifted my arm up toward the ceiling and asked, "Kait, can you please hold my hand?"

Now, if you can picture this, my triceps were still lying on the bed. Only my forearm was extended toward the ceiling, so my arm was bent at a 90-degree angle.

While holding my hand in the air, hoping my request would be heard, I waited. After about 10 seconds, I suddenly felt a pressure on my hand that extended down my forearm. Surprised, I didn't know what to think. To test the validity of the potential bond, I decided to allow my arm to go limp and let it fall to the bed. When I released my arm, it didn't budge. It felt like it was suspended upright.

Testing it even further, I physically lowered my arm to a 45-degree angle and then allowed my muscles to relax. Again, my arm remained suspended in the air even though I was consciously trying to let it drop. Surrounding my hand, I genuinely thought I could feel an energy.

I'm fully aware this could all have been psychological, created solely in my mind. But, I don't know. It is also possible it could have been Kait. I can't be certain. I tried it on many other nights, and nothing happened. My arm fell when I relaxed my muscles, and I couldn't feel the pressure I felt before.

For that one particular instance, I like to believe the energy was due to Kait's presence.

EXTRAS. Searching for further proof of a possible afterlife and Kait's presence, I look to a few "smaller" examples of odd occurrences.

The day of Kaitlyn's funeral, when it started snowing for 20 minutes as soon as we returned home even though no snow was in the forecast and it had been relatively sunny. I'm aware this was likely just a coincidence, but I feel like it is possible Kait was sending us a sign as we were in great mourning.

As another example, one day when Mark was at his house, he saw the basement light turn on by itself.

In another instance, as Vicky sat alone in the quiet of her home, she heard someone whistle behind her ear.

Also, I look to the month of August in 2012 when Kaitlyn was on Zelboraf. I had openly asked for help to whoever was listening. Like a bolt of lightning, an answer was zapped into my head about how Kait should be taking her chemo in order to make it more effective. I didn't adhere to the instructions sent down to me, fearing it wouldn't work since it hadn't been tested, yet, or so I thought. Six months later, as I said earlier, a report was printed about a study where scientists were testing the very technique that had been conjured up in my head, and that technique proved to be more effective. I violently kick myself for not listening.

Mark and Kait had a special song together. A song they danced to the day Mark and Vicky were married – "Somewhere Over the Rainbow" by Israel "Iz" Kamakawiwo'ole, the big Hawaiian guy. To our great sadness, Papa Don passed away a year after Kait, near the same day. On the morning of Don's funeral, Mark woke up at about 4 AM with Iz's rendition of the Wizard of Oz song stuck in his head. And, when he fell back to sleep, he had a dream of Kait, one of three since his experience in June. Then, at the funeral, as soon as he and Vicky walked into the funeral home, "Somewhere Over the Rainbow" began playing over the speakers, and the song just started. Oddly, that song was not included on the CD used during the memorial service. Sometimes the coordinators turn on a radio station that only plays soothing instrumental music, but I don't think Iz's song would be on there. Seeing how the song began playing as soon as Mark and Vicky walked into the funeral home, I think Kait was trying to let them know she was going to be by their side to help them get through the day.

Months later, after Jessica finished her FINAL paper to complete her Masters program, she was anxious to share and celebrate her achievement with somebody; anybody. But it was 12:30 AM and everyone was asleep, including Carlos who had been sick. Suddenly, on her computer, on the internet station she had been listening to, "Somewhere Over the Rainbow" began playing. The song began playing almost immediately after Jess finished her project. To her it was obvious Kaitlyn was sending her a sign. Jess was able to share her success with somebody that night. Kaitlyn was there to give her sister a congratulatory pat on the back.

Again, these occurrences may be nothing. They may simply be coincidences, but I just don't know. I don't think they are.

So, as I sat in my apartment, pondering the possibility of an existence beyond our own two eyes, I began by compiling all of the evidence, or at least how I perceived it to be. From the hundreds of stories I read and heard to some of the seemingly supernatural occurrences we experienced, I found my belief system completely turned on its head.

God and heaven used to be almost unfathomable to me. As a "logical" person, it was difficult to accept an imaginary world, one that existed on a different plane, filtered from our mind and hidden from our sight. How could something like that exist? I sometimes felt like I had to be a lunatic to believe in such a world, as though by believing, I was exhibiting a primitive mindset. At times I believed my own two eyes told the whole story, and the only story.

No longer.

After countless hours of sifting through consistent anecdotal evidence, I not only believe a God exists, but in my heart I know a God exists. Without a semblance of doubt in my mind, I know now life continues after life on earth. And, I know it is absolutely wonderful.

However, what I cannot be sure of, and what no one can truly know is what exactly God is. Is He the universe? Is He the all-encompassing light? Is He you and me? Does He take the form of a human with a long grey beard? Is He neither male nor female? I know the Bible mentions something about God making Adam in his image. But, I don't consider the Bible to be a credible source because it's a human creation, therefore, corruptible. Is He Jesus? Who is Jesus and what does He really look like? I know Christians have an idea of what he looks like, but what if Jesus is an entity who takes on forms solely for our recognition, so we have an image we can relate to? It seems throughout the history of mankind, in different civilizations and different religions, they almost all believe in that one seemingly all-powerful, all-loving leader, like Jesus. What if throughout time, this was the same entity, but just appearing in different forms to blend in with the culture? Is it possible Jesus is Mithra and Mithra is Jesus? I suppose we can't possibly know until we die.

Additionally, it's impossible to know what exactly the afterlife is. Is it more or less an accentuated earth where everything is more beautiful and pronounced? Is it a bunch of clouds and bright light with transparent beings floating around? Is it merely a world existing outside of our human perceptions? Consider that our brains are only able to visually perceive wavelengths within the visible light spectrum – ROY G BIV. And, visible light is a tiny fraction within the vast electromagnetic spectrum, meaning it is certainly feasible that worlds could exist beyond are limited human senses. Are there different levels of afterlife? Or, different tiers in which we have to earn our way up the ladder by doing good deeds? What does it take to get into heaven? What causes some to wind up in a hellish place? What about reincarnation? Do our souls get to choose to reenter earth if they get sick of the omnipotence of heaven and want a challenge again? What are our capabilities in the afterlife? How far can we travel? Will I be able to haunt someone for fun? Energy cannot be created nor destroyed. Does that mean the cells or molecules containing our memories and other genetic attributes are passed along?

Even after concluding without a doubt that an afterlife existed, so many questions remained. Though people with near-death experiences have potentially given us a glimpse into what the afterlife may contain, we still can't know for sure. The bottom line is, I know there is one, and I know Kaitlyn is there. I know what she is experiencing far surpasses what we are experiencing here on earth. And I just can't wait to see her again.

43 EVOLUTION OF MIND

(*NOTE* - These next two chapters veer a bit from the main topic of this book. Feel free to skip ahead to the final, closing chapter. However, I feel compelled to keep what I have written, because it explains how Kaitlyn's death affected me and in what ways it helped me to grow. I talk about many of the things I have learned and have grown to understand since Kait's death. Her passing sent me on a path to discovery. I wrote these two chapters at the end of 2013 and the beginning of 2014, when I was just a baby. Since then, my knowledge and understanding of everything from life to our economic systems to the universe to our brain and beyond has grown exponentially. Feel free to ask any questions on topics you are curious about or simply disagree with. I do plan on writing another, all-encompassing book that talks about everything I have come to understand, because these next two chapters merely scratch the surface.)

Knowing in my heart Kaitlyn was all right, in a world full of love and warmth, I felt myself comforted. I felt more at ease. And when I lifted my head and looked up, I could now see a light shimmering up above piercing through the darkness. With my palms up, I raised my hands to my waist and peered down at my numb fingers. Slowly, I could feel a semblance of strength emanating softly from within me. The numbness all over my body was beginning to dissipate. I could sense there was still hope for a meaningful life! Somewhere a purpose still existed! Clenching my fists, I returned my attention to the light above. *Travis, Kaitlyn is fine! She loves you and will always be with you! You have to continue to live! It's time to start rediscovering your purpose!* As my eyes glistened with moisture, I pursed my lips and nodded my head. With a new sense of determination, I reached forward with my hands and began clawing my way out from the psychological hell

I'd fallen deep into. But the light was far off in the distance. I had a long way to go.

As I slowly traversed through the long, black tunnel, I gazed through the nothingness and completely tuned out the world. For the rest of my journey back to life, it was just my thoughts and I...and of course, Kaitlyn's guidance. In the tranquility of my dark space, devoid of any outside influences, I began to think and reflect upon everything I had ever been led to believe. And through my reflections, as I started dissecting and questioning all of my previous truths one by one, I found that my perspectives on life had completely changed. All of my previous belief systems had completely evolved.

For starters, I found myself more ready and willing to take on challenges I may have been too afraid to attempt before. Struggle. Pain. Tribulation. I no longer feared any of it. The love of my life, a woman half my size, was forced to endure a hardship I couldn't even imagine. And she faced it head on with indomitable strength. She faced the pain and the suffering with such dignity, never wavering from her loving self, and never complaining of her unfortunate circumstances. Kait could have given in to the struggle at any moment, but she didn't. By following her brave lead and drawing inspiration from her strength, I've come out a much stronger man myself. And if we could handle cancer together the way we did, I know now that I can handle anything; a revelation that has released me from my cement shoes of fear as I move forward in life. Now, when it comes to struggle, I say bring it on! I can take it.

Moving on, I found myself less fearful of scrutiny and ridicule. Less fearful of the judgment of others. When people say, "Travis you're going bald." I no longer care. I say, "Yup, that's true." If people say, "Travis you're weird." I say, "Yeah I am pretty weird, aren't I?" If someone tells me, "Travis, your face is crooked." I laugh and say, "Really? Hmm, ain't that somethin'." Life is short, who cares what people say or think. Big deal. I've learned to embrace the things that distinguish me from the rest and laugh at my "flaws." Who wants to be the same as everyone else, anyway?

Next, as I continued my slow crawl toward the light, I faced the concept of death – a notion that once terrified me. But as I revisited this frightening topic, I found that the idea of passing on no longer sent chills traveling down my spine like it used to. After experiencing death through

Kaitlyn, the concept of dying is one that no longer terrifies me. Why should it? Kait experienced it, so I should be able to, as well. And now that I know life continues after our earthly life, there really is nothing to fear. Death comes to us all. Whether it happens tomorrow or 50 years from now, the difference in that stretch of time is nothing compared to eternity. And as much as we like to sometimes believe we are impervious, death is inevitable. We all pass on at some point. Earth is merely a temporary playground. Unless a person's actions are causing pain to others, it shouldn't matter what endeavors they decide to take on, as long as they find some sort of satisfaction in doing it. To each, their own. Let bygones be bygones. In the grand scheme of life, it doesn't matter.

We struggle daily to make the "right" decisions, hoping our choices don't threaten our survival and overall wellbeing. But I realize now there is really no such thing as a right or wrong decision. If we choose to go down a certain path and the outcome turns out to be less favorable than expected, causing a certain level of pain and hardship, then we learn from it. If we are still alive after a "wrong" decision, we persevere and grow. Facing challenge is what adds to the intrigue of life. It's all a part of our short journey here on earth. And many times challenge and struggle make achievement and triumph so much more gratifying. The ups and downs are all a part of living, and if anything they at least give us entertaining stories to pass down to our loved ones.

On my arduous journey through the seemingly infinite space of my dark world, every stage of my life began to flash before my eyes. Like Mark's dream, the images whooshing by my face were attempting to instill in me an important message. Each and every image drawn from my memory was helping me to recall special times when I was smiling, when I was laughing, and when I was HAPPY. I recalled once again going for ice cream with Kait that one evening after work when she was sick, and how such a simple moment was the source of so much laughter. Reaching back even further into my memory bank, I recalled the hot summer nights when I was seven years old, sleeping in the living room in our sleeping bags, playing Nintendo into the wee hours of the morning with my dad, brothers, uncles, and friends. What fun we had. I recalled a time when we were sitting in our hot tub, and our pug, wanting to join us so badly, took the unknowing plunge into the steamy water. As he quickly sank to the bottom, I remembered connecting eyes with him before we swiftly swept him out. Though he was shaken, he was quite all right. I smile with a glint in my eye from that adorable reminiscence. Memories continued flooding my mind. I remembered as a 10 year-old, my cousin and I throwing apples at my younger brothers and younger cousin as they built a fort in the woods. I recalled playing cards and board games with my family on multiple occasions. I remembered my brother sticking his thumb up our dog's ass (an English Mastiff) when he was four and then innocently saying, "Dad smell," as he held his hand up to my oblivious dad's nose. The pungent odor almost knocked him out. I remembered so many times dancing in the kitchen while I "assisted" Kait as we cooked our meals together. I couldn't help myself, I was just so excited to be with her, and she was so much fun to have around. I remembered those sad nights when we would hold each other. And even though our physical bond was seriously being threatened, nothing else mattered in the world except for the fact that we were together, exchanging our limitless love.

As hundreds of images of treasured memories continued zipping past my line of sight, I began to realize it was those moments of seemingly less that I cherished most in my life. Those simple moments made me laugh. They made me cry. Most importantly, they made me feel. Somewhere, in the hustle bustle of everyday life in our society, that notion of what truly matters had escaped my conscious being. The idea of what life is really all about had been lost on me. I feel it's been lost on many in our nation and in our world.

Then, I began to realize that in all of my recollections there was one more uniting principle. In all of my happiest memories filled with life and laughter, money was never involved (unless it was playing cards with my family, and then it was simply spending time with them as we joked about everything that was the source of the happiness. I couldn't care less if I came out a winner, financially).

Suddenly, it hit me. I didn't care about money anymore. I no longer cared about the material possessions or the false sense of wealth it garnered. As I sifted through the memories of my life, it seems it has caused more stress and grief than anything else. All of those inanimate objects we scratch and claw and work so hard to obtain have become absolutely valueless in my life. That feeling is reinforced by the fact that I would give up everything, every single item I own if it meant I could have Kait back for just one hour. Simply being with her, holding her hand, hugging her, touching her head, and drinking in her magical beauty, nothing on Earth could match that feeling of profound wealth. That's a feeling of true richness money could never buy. That's a feeling of genuine happiness that even all of the world's material items combined could not equal. So, I will repeat it one more time since it has had such a profound effect on my outlook. I would trade everything, all of my material possessions without even a second thought for just one hour with Kait. And that let's me know just how unimportant all of this inanimate crap is.

Reflecting back on my time on our planet, I realize all of my happiest, most fulfilling moments have come while spending time with those closest to me. Even though we have been convinced to believe that consumption will provide us with happiness, it rarely does. We are left instead with a feeling of emptiness, thinking we need to make an additional purchase or go on yet another shopping spree just to fill that void. But it doesn't work that way, and the cycle just repeats itself over and over again until your garage is filled with junk. Going forward, my goals will never revolve around the acquisition of any material object or anything as artificial as money like they used to be. With my evolved perspectives, I will no longer be fooled into thinking true happiness will come from consumption or competing against my peers to have more.

As I continued confronting every single belief I once held, I began to feel a subtle sense of enjoyment. In some ways I felt like a blind man being given sight for the first time in his life. I was uncovering secrets hidden from my view that had been right in front of me the whole time.

In my pursuit of the growing light ahead, images of a 24-year old lying motionless on a bed began pummeling my mind. Kait's life was taken away so quickly, reminding me how short we are here on Earth. 24 years. Gone. In a flash. The years we spent together feel like just a couple of weeks. It feels like just months ago I was a small child imagining my dream world of having a beautiful wife with a perfect family. Now, it feels like just yesterday I was burying that dream.

Life is so short. So, so short! I feel like so much of the precious time I've been given on this Earth has been wasted on meaningless activities that don't make me happy or provide anything of value to society. Why? Well, I know the answer is to earn income since we sadly need paper to access the necessities of life. I've been so worried about how I'm going to survive into next week or next year or when I'm 70 years old that I've let so much of the best parts of my life pass me by. I've been so fearful of struggle and hardship in the past. Most people are. But going forward, I think it's high time I shut off the amygdala, the primitive "lizard" part of my brain, throw away fear, and start living. What does it mean to live? That I still have to figure out.

For years I've allowed myself to be confined within this bubble we've created in our society, where we devote our lives and expend a large portion of our energy working our way up this imaginary ladder (patting ourselves on the back along the way) in order to "make it." With Kait's passing, however, I've been able to pull myself out of this bubble and reassess it essentially from an outsider's point of view. As I stand alone, on the outside looking in, I've been given an opportunity to quietly observe and then question the validity of everything that I have been raised to believe about the world we've built. And only now, through my observations, have I realized how much more there is to life than this complex bubble we've created. Life is so much bigger than our suits and ties and our bear and bull markets. Only now have I awakened to realize there is no such thing as "making it." Because even after one "makes it," even after one "wins," the game does not end. He must continue playing. If he stops playing, if he lets down his guard even for a moment, there are hoards of players eager to take his spot. The game never ends, at least the way we have it set up.

Kaitlyn's passing has forced me to widen my vision. As I remained hovering outside of our perceived world, I began to make observations about how much time we are spending working in the name of progress compared to how much time we are spending actually enjoying life, the one life we have, with our loved ones. From that point of view, I ask myself, what are we actually working so hard to advance toward? Is our purpose on earth merely to produce, produce, produce? What's the end goal? Is there an end goal? Or, are we just working to pass the time and distract ourselves? I confess that I'm often guilty of the all work and no play attitude. I rarely stop and smell the roses. Why? Don't get me wrong, I don't want an easy life. I sincerely enjoy being challenged, but I prefer my challenges to have the potential for productive outcomes.

But what is so important that we feel we have to sacrifice our wellbeing and happiness to obtain it? Essentially, life as we know it goes on forever. It goes on and on and on and on and on. So, if life goes on forever, what are we in such a hurry to achieve? We have all the time in the world to make advancements. If life goes on forever, is it even possible to have an end goal to work toward? Is it even possible to get to a point where we feel like we've progressed enough and can take a break? No. Because with every hypothesis relative to a question arises several more hypotheses, meaning we will always discover ways of performing activities differently and more efficiently.

So what is it we are working so hard and so fast to obtain? The truth is, we don't truly know. We know we want to create a better, more efficient world for our families and humans to live in. And, in many, many regards, at least when it comes to efficiency, we certainly have. Healthcare, transportation, shelter, food production – we've made so many processes so much simpler and more efficient. However, even though our world is more efficient, does that mean it's better? At first glance, the answer seems like a simple one. Yes. But upon further inspection, as I navigate through society, the answer becomes much more complex. The key determinant in concluding whether or not our advancements have created a "better" world is by assessing our overall happiness. With all of our advancements, are we happier? That should be the most important factor. Certain indicators point to the fact that we aren't happier, as we've had a rise in suicides, crime, depression, drug use, incarcerations, divorce, murder, cancer and heart disease (stress plays an important role), and much more. And as I look around, almost everyone I know is stressed out, weathered, tired, and irritable, just praying they can win the lottery, not so they can be lazy and lounge around all day, but so they can have more time to live and not worry about whether or not their children will be able to eat day in and day out. Nobody seems to have time for life anymore as we yawn our way through our monotonous schedules, through the everyday chaos. Most of my friends and colleagues seem to just want to take a nap! They are worn out. And in our fatigue, we've lost that childlike wonderment. That desire to continuously ask questions of the unknown and explore to discover the answers.

Is progress truly progress if people are constantly in a state of stress and unhappiness? And would the consequences be so dire if we slowed down and placed more emphasis on balance and on the enjoyment of the one life we've been given?

My situation with Kaitlyn has propelled me to start asking questions again. About everything. Kait's passing has forced me to ask, what is the point of life? In my exploration to discover the answer to that impossible question, I begin by peeling back the layers and breaking it down to its most basic form. What seems to be the one universal thing people want most in life? As I sit and ponder that question, the answer seems simple – happiness. I think it's safe to say everyone on earth wants to live a life of happiness. Pretty basic. Right? They want a peaceful life, free of stress, free from worry, free from struggle, free from war and hate.

As I reflect and ask questions, leaning on Kait for advice, clear answers begin pouring in. "Kaitlyn, in order to 'live', if the overall goal in life is to be happy, then how do I, and we, find happiness?"

I hear a shout from afar as a response instantly manifests and echoes within my mind, and it's so obvious.

LOVE!!!

The path to overall, genuine happiness is through love. It's so simple. The more I think about it, as cheesy as it sounds, the more it makes sense. It's the absolute truth. The immense love Kait and I expressed with each other made me happier than I have ever been before. The love I feel from my pets makes me smile radiantly. We are creatures meant to love. We do things we love to do. We eat things we love to eat. We hang out with people we love to hang out with. Love makes us feel good. Love adds warm, positive energy to our hearts. It makes us tingle. It makes our nerves stand up. It makes us glow. Think about all of the times you were mad. Anger, hate, sadness, frustration, they hurt. Those feelings feel terrible. Love is what we were meant to seek and feel. Love fulfills us all. And, it shouldn't be hard to find. It flows abundantly within everyone. We just have to learn it's okay to free it. We don't have to keep it suppressed.

It is such a simple notion. So obvious. But, it's so easy to forget. And, it seems we have forgotten that. I know I have. Being a man, I've grown up with the mindset that to show love and affection is to be weak and unmanly. A wuss. As I think about it, though, to be afraid to express a feeling due to fear of ridicule from peers, that is actually much more unmanly. To be so insecure that you can't create your own path, and instead you have to follow another's path or go by the "books" of what it means to be a man, that's not manly at all.

Kaitlyn broke down the barriers of my icy heart and taught my soul what it meant to love. She demonstrated that love truly conquers all. Whenever I was grumpy and gloomy, her love always brightened my day.

Whenever negative energy was permeating within, clouding my mind, her love always cleared it away and replaced it with positive, warm light. And it felt good. Her love felt so good! That was living!

Vicariously through Kait, I essentially had my "death bed" moment as I watched her/my/our life slowly slip away. Through my intense grief and mourning, through my anger and sadness, through my guilt, I was forced to reflect on all aspects of my life. As I clashed within to find purpose and meaning again, I was forced to question and rethink everything I was taught throughout my years. What's really important in life? What really matters? What would I change? But unlike most people on their death bed, I've been given a rare opportunity to continue living, to make corrections and grow through tragedy. Kaitlyn's struggle and suffering instilled valuable lessons in me. She taught me what really matters in life. Conversely, she taught me about the things that truly don't matter in life.

I can't thank her enough for that!

44 REDISCOVERING PURPOSE

Weeks and months passed, and I still struggled to come to grips with the death of the love of my life. Some nights as I tried to sleep it felt like a train was roaring through my head. On some days anxiety would feel as though a hand was squeezing my heart, sending shockwaves through my whole body as it sputtered to maintain rhythm. Even with a completely evolved perspective, I still struggled to find purpose and meaning. I still struggled to put Kait's passing into perspective. Every time I recalled staring into her knowing eyes, I remembered how much she wanted to continue on living her life with me and those who loved her, but sensing she wouldn't get that opportunity. Every day I relived her final weeks of emotional and physical torment. It was painful.

As much as I wanted to dig a large hole and burrow into it for the rest of my life, I knew I couldn't. I knew Kait would not want me to sit and sulk and feel sorry for her as my years ticked by. And, self-loathing and self-pity are destructive, unproductive, and selfish. I couldn't do that. It was imperative I found meaning again. But, where would I begin? Everything seemed so unimportant. Was anything worthy of my attention anymore? I had already established the fact that the accumulation of money and material wealth had become a boring, empty, and endless challenge. That would just be a waste of precious life. I had to find something more meaningful. But, what?

Inner dialogue began chattering away as usual, replaying one line over and over in my head – "I was supposed to die for you."

"I was supposed to die for you."

What does that mean?

"I was supposed to die for you."

But, why? That single statement began to inspire me.

In my newfound spiritual enlightenment, I started to truly believe there might have been a meaning to those words. Somehow it must have been communicated to her that her life would be sacrificed for me and others. But, why? Is it so that I would open my eyes and become a better person? Was I living a life way too centered on myself? I know that before Kait passed, while she was living her life to help children and others, I was living solely to provide for her and I. The struggles of everyone else in the world were of little concern to me. If I didn't know them, or if I didn't see them suffering, it didn't affect me. That was my mindset. So maybe that's why she was supposed to die for me. To encourage me to live less selfishly. Or, was it because I didn't fully believe in Jesus? Was it because I didn't have him in my heart, and by Kait passing on, she knew I would seek him out?

"I was supposed to die for you."

"Kait, why did you die for me?"

Why did she sacrifice herself for me? If she did, what could I do to fulfill her sacrifice? I couldn't simply live for myself from here on out. Somehow I had to figure out a way to continue her legacy and find a way to provide a helping hand to those in need. I had to find a way to live for others as she did.

I realize there is a chance her statement might have meant something completely different. But, there is that old saying 'I'd rather live with faith only to die and find out God doesn't exist than live without faith only to die and find out he does exist.' In the same sense, what if Kait truly did sacrifice herself for me and I shrugged it off as not having any deeper meaning only to find out in the afterlife how much it actually meant? Her giving up her life would have been for naught. So, I'd rather live my life believing she gave herself up, trying to live up to and fulfill her sacrifice only to find out it meant very little in the end, rather than the opposite. And that's what I'm going to do. I have to live my life believing there was a deeper meaning to 'I was supposed to die for you.' I have to believe there was a greater purpose for her passing on so early in her life.

So, Kait was supposed to die for me. That's the motto I will use if I need something to motivate me or pick me up when I am down. But even with that, I still needed to figure out what it was I could do that would fulfill her sacrifice. What could I possibly do to reintroduce meaning to my existence? Struggling to discover the answers as I continued crawling through the dark shroud of ash and soot, I once again turned to Kait for guidance. "Kait what can I do?"

As expected, I suddenly heard gentle whispers nearby. She had answered my call with words of encouragement and direction. "Open your eyes," she said. "Open them even wider, and purpose will find you again."

I listened. Following Kait's instructions, I looked out, extending my vision even farther than before as I surveyed the landscape beyond my own backyard. And when I did, for the first time I truly began to see. I began to see things that were always in my line of sight, but I previously ignored. I finally began to notice the struggle and suffering endured by millions throughout the world. I started becoming truly aware of all the devastation and destruction plaguing every region of our planet. And the wider I opened my eyes and the more I could see, the more I felt appalled. The situation outside my previous world of sunshine and butterflies was bad. It still is. And it's rapidly getting worse.

What do I see that begs for help, that begs for change? I see what many have come to see.

I see a world in which my peers are afraid to bring children into.

I see a world where 20,000 to 30,000 emaciated children around the globe die of starvation every single day. Kids who want a happy life just like you and I. And the sad thing is, we live in a world of abundance. The earth has more than enough carrying capacity to be able to provide food for all of the humans in existence many times over. Yet, with the way things are currently set up, we essentially forced people into this slimy pit, into this gladiator ring where they have to compete against one another for survival. They must game each other in order to access the necessities of life. Though God has created a world where there is enough to go around, we have undermined him and created systems in which scarcity is the driving force.

I see a world whose beloved animals, crucial to the flow of our ecosystems, are likely to become extinct within our lifetime and possibly sooner than we assume. Wonderful creatures like rhinos, elephants, gorillas, and pandas. Lions, and tigers, and polar bears. Oh my! Cheetahs, chimps, gazelle, brown bear, black bear, orangutan, whale sharks, leopards, yak, sperm whale, humpback whale, any kind of whale whale. Thousands of other precious, but doomed life forms likely to be wiped off the map in months and years to come.

I see precious resources, life forces being ravaged, misused, and wasted. Resources that have taken thousands and even millions of years to develop being exhausted in just a couple hundred years. Air is becoming polluted. Water undrinkable. Food poisoned. Carcinogens are everywhere. We are killing ourselves. How can we be so careless, immature, and obtuse?

I see just about every ecosystem in severe danger.

I see a world with alleged men fighting over land and resources. Killing over power and wealth. Murdering over religious ideals.

I see half the world impoverished, equating to almost 3,000,000,000 people, a number that continues to steadily increase as our false idols hoard more and more, increasing the gap between those well off and the destitute.

I see 1% of the world's population hoarding 40% of the world's resources and wealth under the false pretenses of, "We've earned it." And we buy the justification of these so-called men. A "man" is not someone who selfishly hoards resources for himself and doesn't care as those around him suffer and perish. That is a coward.

I see beautiful, fruitful, life-providing rainforests being reduced to nothing. Rainforests, the "Lungs of our Planet" that once covered 14% of the earth cut, chopped, and bulldozed away to a mere 6% in only 40 years' time. Rainforests which provide precious plants used as ingredients in a large portion of our medicines and many other products. Rainforests, essential for recycling carbon dioxide and turning it into 20% of the world's oxygen. They are severely threatened.

I see our trash, garbage, obsolete electronics, etc. being strewn about various African regions, turning once beautiful landscapes lush with plants and rivers into desolate, barren wastelands.

I see us scrambling to patch a system destined for failure. A system driven by scarcity and bolstered by societal problems. A system that's needed war and destruction to break out of recession. A system of mass overproduction and mass overconsumption. A system that allows deceitfully indebting underdeveloped countries (Ecuador, for instance) whose people have little education on what they've entered into, only to be coerced into giving up their finite resources when they can't pay off these made up debts. A system that does not take into account the laws of nature, a nature which we are inherently at the mercy of, a nature which is the secret ruler of us all, a nature which is the true driving force of life. If we don't work for it, if we aggravate it enough, it has the power to chew us up and spit us out. Simple solutions lie right in front of us if we are willing.

I see us doing our part to indirectly enslave children and adults in countries all over the world. We empower it. These slaves in countries like Indonesia and Bangladesh work grueling hours for very little pay only so we can have our Macs or iPhones cheaper, or so we can get a pair of jeans at a lower cost, or so we can get our yearly Air Jordan's. We just turn our cheek and keep buying our cheaper goods as these kids and adults slave away for us and for the corporations who stand on their shoulders for a higher bottom line. Our higher standard of life comes at the depravation of others. But because we don't see or know these people, we don't feel their suffering. We don't care. They feel love and pain, too.

Instead of embracing and accepting our flaws and differences, I see us condemning them. We seemingly have an inherent need to compartmentalize everything and place people and things into categories. We like to try to find any difference we can and group people together based on similar attributes – skin color, gender, sexual orientation, religion, political affiliation, country, state, city, age. Anything. Then we like to create a perimeter and keep those distant whom we deem too different. But, our differences are what make us special and unique and fun. Same is boring. Kait's mantra, which I've tried to adopt, was as long as you were nice to her, you were "in" (actually, even if you weren't nice to her, she would forgive often and give you multiple chances at redemption).

I see a world with artificial borders separating our lands, creating artificial borders in our minds, keeping us divided. If we fly above earth, we cannot see these borders because they do not exist. They merely exist in our heads. As crazy as it may sound at first, there is no such thing as the United States. There is no such thing as Canada. Again, the borders we created to divide these areas of land are artificial and exist only in our minds. We all belong to one big body – Earth. So, when one country is attacking another, we are merely attacking ourselves in the big picture. Russia attacking the USA or vice versa is like the lungs attacking the heart. It's insane.

I see artificial, theoretical means of exchange limiting and inhibiting us from solving real life issues, inhibiting us from real progress.

I see an arbitrary numerical value hovering above our heads, denoting our worth in society. An hour of one person's life may be inadequately valued at $15 per hour, less than a shirt. Others may be arbitrarily worth $100 per hour. A person's intrinsic value cannot and should not be measured by monetary worth.

I see a permeating vanity syndrome in our society, shaping and misguiding our values. We are stuck on superficialities, on image. What I found with Kaitlyn is that I fell in love with who she was, not what she was.

I see elected politicians playing a despicable game of manipulation and deceit in order to elevate themselves among the ranks and obtain power and material wealth. The saddest part is, they use civilians as their game pieces, as their pawns, and the civilians actually think their best interests are being pursued.

I see attempts at true technological progress being thwarted by those who fear to lose power. From the suppression of Nikola Tesla's viable plan to provide free energy to the world with his Wardenclyffe project to the mysterious deaths of Stanley Meyer (allegedly poisoned) and Eugene Mallove (beaten to death at his home), wonderful minds behind the water fuel cell (water-powered engine) and cold fusion (clean, abundant energy), respectively, it's been happening for decades and even centuries. This behavior of suppressing inventions even goes back to the times of the Roman Empire. It's been said an inventor during Tiberius Caesar's rule had presented a plastic type of material, said to be flexible glass, which didn't break when it hit the ground. Fearing this invention would threaten the value of gold and silver, the emperor sentenced the man to death. Progress thwarted.

I see African children, and also adult workers, being exploited to mine the diamonds we seem so enthralled with. Kids as young as 5 years old working long days, six or seven days a week, under extreme conditions simply so we can put a shiny stone around our neck or finger.

I see a world in a perpetual state of warfare, where our most brilliant minds and most brilliant technological advancements are designed for destruction rather than for the benefit of man. And what's even sadder is that I observe a large portion of our population cheering it on.

And, overall, if these trends continue, I see a world on the verge of collapse.

Scanning the earth, noticing how abysmal things were, I felt a churning in my stomach. I felt guilty. I had lived a life of privilege while many had to endure similar, if not worse circumstances than I ended up coming upon with Kait. But through my guilt, I could hear Kait's comforting whispers of reassurance. "Travis, you shouldn't feel guilty. You can still change and improve. Everyone can change and improve. Things don't have to be the way they are. Things aren't supposed to be what they've become."

"But, Kait, there's so much. What possibly can I do?" Waiting for an answer, I felt a warm, soothing touch on my shoulder. And suddenly, everything became clearer. I needed to continue digging. I needed to go deeper and look beyond the surface issues if I truly wanted to grow and find meaning again. So I did. I began analyzing and questioning all that I saw, trying to figure out the source of so much pain. I began by assessing all of our issues in aggregate. And when I did, the answer I derived seemed so obvious. Greed! It seems as though most of the world's problems can be attributed to greed. Which is perpetuated by money and the pervasive idea that to have more means you are better and happier than others. Looking back on my life I realize that during my short time on earth greed and individualistic thinking have been encouraged in the sense that it drives our system forward and keeps it afloat. Even though Oliver Stone was trying to vilify his lead character in *Wall Street*, I see the infamous line "Greed is good" ringing true in countless social circles with many thinking it's acceptable to emulate and adhere to that sort of mindset and attitude. I know I'm certainly not the first to say this, but GREED IS NOT GOOD! It's destructive both for individuals and for the world. Greed and selfish thinking will only lead to more destruction, more suffering, and possibly complete decimation of our home.

Recalling various times in my life when I felt like I should do something about it, I remember being told by a number of individuals that all of our issues are out of my control and that I should just worry about myself. It seems as though a great number of us, at least in our society, adhere to that sentiment and live for ourselves. We live for power, money, material goods, and self-gain. We lust for attention and glory because we are not secure enough in our own bodies, and that glory, that attention validates our existence. It makes us feel like we belong, makes us feel like we have an importance in life. And, most of us want so desperately to feel that sense of belonging, that sense of acceptance that we will do things simply to fit in even if it means compromising our moral values. I used to want to fit in with the older men in nice suits, talking the financial lingo, using complex words only the financially astute understood, feeling like I was smarter than the lay person. But, then I realized how phony and artificial it all was. Especially when I learned a monkey has just as good a chance at picking profitable stocks than humans, well, aside from those with inside information.

With my eyes open, it's become obvious that we've been given everything we need to not only survive, but live abundantly, yet we aren't willing to share. And, in the process we have raped, pillaged, and destroyed so much in such a small time frame. We are so capable, and when allowed to flourish, have done so much good in the last couple hundred years. We've made remarkable progress in so many ways. Unfortunately, all of the great things we've accomplished are overshadowed by the bad since the bad literally threatens all forms of life.

But with Kait's hand caressing my shoulder, I could feel a genuine sense of hope permeating through my veins. Along with helping me become aware of all the current calamities of the world, she also showed me how things CAN be. She showed me how we as humans possess an innate desire to help each other out. How we have a propensity to want to lend a helping hand to our neighbor without expecting reward. And just that alone helped me to feel hopeful again. Hopeful that we can one day start thinking as a whole, as a species, and right the ship so we can feel confident in the world we leave for our children and generations beyond. Because the way things are right now, it truly, honestly does not have to be like this! We can do better! We can do so much better! I am hopeful.

Traveling through the space within my dark, suffocating tunnel of emotional depression, I finally felt the strength to lift myself up off the ground. With Kait's help, my slow crawl turned into a brisk walk as the glimmering light in front of me became bigger and brighter. I was rediscovering my purpose. I was redefining my reason to exist, and it was breathing life back into an otherwise lifeless existence. With Kait's guidance, she was showing me ways in which I could fulfill her sacrifice. It started with looking selflessly outward rather than selfishly inward. It started by living not only for myself, but for everyone else. The ultimate goal would be to find a way so that no one on earth lived in poverty. So that no one on earth suffered or starved. So that we wouldn't end up destroying everything most precious to us.

Initially, I felt overwhelmed by the proposal that would essentially pull me out of my hell and instill in me a new purpose. "But, Kait, that end goal seems utterly impossible. Wouldn't I be wasting my time," I said as I faithlessly shook my head. Once again as I sat waiting, an answer manifested in my mind. An answer reminding me that throughout our history, throughout humanity, we've constantly defined and redefined ourselves by achieving what was originally perceived as unachievable, by making the impossible possible. Why should we stop now? What makes this challenge any different than other daunting challenges?

Some people may say those ideals for a world where everyone gets along and sings songs and holds hands and skips around are Utopian, and therefore impossible. I agree that Utopia is impossible. Utopia essentially means a perfect world. But, can we ever arrive at a point where we can no longer improve? I don't think so. It's human nature to create and solve problems and continue to learn and improve. That will never stop, meaning Utopia is impossible.

Even if, say, those ideals happen to be Utopian, is it wrong to set the bar high, especially when we are capable of achieving so much more? Shouldn't we always be striving to make improvements? Does anyone in the world believe our structures or systems are perfect, or that they are as good as we can come up with? No! They are flawed. Every system ever put into practice is flawed. Since they are flawed, shouldn't we continue trying to improve instead of remaining stagnant and saying, "Oh well, this is just the way things are, so we have to live with it"? In all systems around the world, people are suffering and impoverished. That means we should continue with innovation until no one has to worry whether or not they will be able to eat in a given day. IT IS POSSIBLE! We simply have to aspire for more out of ourselves. We simply have to challenge ourselves to be better people, more caring, more selfless. More love!

Unfortunately, I'm also reminded that change throughout history has come at the hands of a few while the majority of detractors adamantly and, many times, violently opposed. We can be a part of the 99% who refused to believe the world was round. We can be part of the 99% who rejected the idea of the sun being the center of our solar system. We can be part of the large majority who thought aviation was impossible, or that exploring space was a galactic dream, or even that white and black people couldn't coexist. Or, we can be a part of the tiny minority who dare to redefine outdated belief systems, who dare to challenge the status quo and think beyond our invisible limits.

It seems, in order for improvements to take place, instead of immediately condemning or ostracizing a man who challenges what we "know" or think to be truth, a man who introduces fresh ideas to the world, we should ask questions first. When a man comes out and claims cancer is a part of the immune system, or that cancer is actually a result of fungus, or that he has ideas to improve society, or that he believes in a God, or that he doesn't believe in a God we should do our best to refrain from the impulse response of, "Pfff, that's crazy. What a lunatic...," as many say when a person introduces differing ideas or opinions into our world, and try to understand where that person is coming from first. I encourage to always, always, always ask questions and try to fully understand someone before criticizing his or her ideas or actions. Aim before firing. It's a principle so simple. So obvious. But so often broken, especially when conflicting interests are present. No ideas should ever be initially dismissed without objective, or even subjective, thought. At one point, in the 19th century, Ignaz Semmelweis correctly made the assertion that a doctor simply washing his hands before delivering a baby significantly reduced maternal mortality rates in hospitals, and instead of setting aside ego and investigating his proposal, the scientific and medical community heavily criticized him at the outset since it conflicted with the established opinions at the time. It wasn't until after his death that his theory was recognized as truth. Ego seems to be one of the biggest barriers against progressive thought. Sometimes we just have to swallow our pride and accept when we just don't *know* something and ask questions.

Change starts with peace and acceptance within ourselves, within the nucleus of our being, and expands outward from there. It starts with redirecting the "me first" attitude running rampant throughout our society. The childish attitude of "mine, mine, mine!" That's mine! That attitude only causes harm and strife. And really, it can be argued that nothing is truly ours, not even our bodies. Only 10% of the human body is actually made up of human cells and the remaining 90% consists of foreign bacteria, or microbial species, that filter in and out of our system. Even our thoughts can't truly be claimed as our own, because just about everything we know, all the information we've ever acquired has come from someone else, from some other outside source – parents, schools, television, etc. - and those outside sources have attained their knowledge from other sources, and so on and so forth. Knowledge is serial. It has been passed down and built upon for thousands of years.

With Kait's passing encouraging me to open my mind, I've now come to believe we are all somehow connected on this planet, like one big interwoven and interconnected series of molecules and energy. One big conscious organism (actually, studies are currently being done to try and quantify and validate the theory behind a collective consciousness). And if one person is suffering through hardship, then we all are. If we ever truly want to prosper and grow, it seems we have to start living not only for ourselves, but for everyone else. I am confident we can do that.

A part of me wonders if God's great test is to see if we can one day completely come together. Sounds ridiculous, but who knows. It'd be a fun challenge. It seems like just about every other natural system in the world (plants, animals, molecules) operates in harmony with its surrounding environment, except for the human system. We consume more than we need. We have little concern for the surrounding environment. We destroy other organisms in our way. We grow out of control. You know, the human system, as it currently operates, has many resemblances to something else I've come to know quite well – cancer. Is it too harsh to say we are a cancer to Earth's body at this very moment?

Many say, "Well, that's just how we are as humans. We are just animals who can't control our instinctual urges. We can't change that."

I don't believe that at all.

A part of that assertion may be true. The most primitive parts of our brain are instinctual and animalistic, where survival is the only purpose. But, what separates us from the animal kingdom is our advanced cerebral cortex and the development of the frontal lobes in our brain, giving us the innate ability to reason, solve highly complex problems, and feel empathy toward others. The cerebral cortex gives us the ability to tell the territorial part of our mind to shut up. Our advanced brains give us the ability to break free from our instinctual trance, to consciously control our urges. Our purpose becomes more than just survival and fulfilling those urges. With our advanced neurological functioning, we can find a solution for anything. Creative problem solving is what we are best at. The desire for challenge and the desire to create are two of the many driving forces among

345

humans.

With Kait's continued guidance, encouraging me to further evolve my belief systems, I've come to believe that life is a birthright. The first day we are born, we have a right to life, and the resources provided are a common heritage for everyone. No one man or one group can lay claim to something that has been around for millions of years just because they say they found it first, which they didn't. Simply look at the situation between Native Americans and the European explorers. By our standards of "finders keepers", every resource in America should essentially be the Natives'. But we murdered and stole everything and now claim we found it first, therefore it's ours to decide who gets what. Not right. Shouldn't be that way. There is enough to go around for everyone. We simply have to use what we've been so graciously given wisely.

Finally, I've come to believe everyone has a purpose on this earth. If you are here, that means you belong. If you are here, that means you are a gift to this world. Everyone is important. Every form of life plays a vital role on this planet. As long as you are breathing air on this earth, you have a purpose. Some people simply need a generous hand to help them discover what that purpose may be.

I think that's it! With her generous, loving hand guiding me through, Kait helped me reemerge from the thick, smoky fog of grief that had been choking me without end. She's helped me rediscover a purpose that seems worth living for, one that would fulfill her sacrifice and return the favor, at least in my eyes. And that purpose consists of devoting my life to trying to make a difference in the lives of those in need of a helping hand – both children and adults. That is the one activity, the one goal that can still provide for me a meaningful existence. It feels important. Going forward, I will do my best to no longer put myself before others. No more will I worry about petty material things. No more will I yearn for material reward for accomplishing tasks. The reward will be knowing that I helped someone in need.

Going forward, I won't allow myself to enjoy spoils while much of the world suffers. What kind of man would that make me to live in excess while children are famished and emaciated around the globe? And for those who think they need to keep acquiring tangible goods in order to find happiness, I would like to encourage them to sincerely reflect and recall the moments in life that truly made them laugh and truly made them smile. What was the source of that laughter? I would also challenge them not to be fooled by subliminally charged messages convincing us we need things we truly don't need, making us feel like we need to keep up with or surpass the Joneses to find true happiness. I would love it if we someday reach a point when, rather than striving to have more than the Joneses, we strive to make sure the Joneses have enough. A lifetime geared toward the constant pursuit of artificial wealth has left many to reminisce and wish they had spent more of their precious days with those most dear to their hearts.

No matter what, as I move forward, Kaitlyn's death cannot be for nothing. I have to do my best to make sure of that. Though her shoes are impossible to fill, I have to do everything I can to make them full. In that vein, I will either die succeeding in my quest, or I will die without having fully realized my goals. Either way, I will at least know that I lived my life trying. But hopefully, as time passes by and I become old and wrinkled, the problems I see plaguing our world today will eventually fade into the problems of a distant yesterday; and instead of saying 'I see,' hopefully one day I will be able to say 'I saw.' And at that point we will shake our heads and laugh at how stupid we once were.

45 UNTIL WE MEET AGAIN!

Sometimes, an angel descends from the heavens and forges for us a new path through the darkness. And though that path may not be entirely devoid of challenges or hardship, it ultimately leads to the sun.

Sometimes, an angel falls from the skies and challenges us to be transcendent. She inspires us to be more than who we thought we could be. To reach beyond our perceived limits and redefine ourselves and what it means to breathe life on this earth. To break free from complacency and artificial constraints. To gain the courage to detach from everything we've been led to believe as truth, assess its validity through a microscope, and be willing to stand up and face adversity and ridicule for the sake of morality.

For the most part, those angels remain hidden from our view, silently watching over and guiding us through our day-to-day encounters. But every now and then, one removes her heavenly cloak and reveals herself to the world. Every now and then one blesses us with her visible presence and spreads her unconditional love to everyone she meets.

I was one of the blessed. Kaitlyn so graciously revealed herself to the world and instilled in me wonderful new values. She taught me what life is truly all about. She taught me what it means to love. What it means to be selfless and make sacrifices. And when I had fallen deep into that shadowy abyss, my angel illuminated a bright new path for me and helped me emerge from the darkness. My angel helped me regain my vision – both in life and death.

As recompense, I see only one way I can properly express my infinite gratitude toward her, and that's through striving to be the best person I can be at all times. To practice altruism as best I can from now and for as long as I live. It seems the least I can do for all the gifts she bestowed upon me. Unfortunately, I am no angel. I am human with my infinite flaws. I am corruptible. I may be a hypocrite at times. I may contradict myself. I may even encounter spates of exhaustion and lethargy. I may grow irritable and lash out every now and then. That's all a part of the human experience. And a part of being human is making mistakes, but then learning and growing from those mistakes. There will be times where I will temporarily lose my sight and stumble off the trail, but with Kaitlyn's guiding spirit always by my side and her love forever in my heart, she will direct me back to the righteous path.

I miss Kait so much. Not a day will go by where the cavernous void in my life won't be strongly felt. Not a day will go by where I'm not haunted by her undeserved suffering. Though it's difficult to brush those images of heartbreak and trauma from my mind, I have to try. I can't allow the few painful moments steal the thunder from the overwhelming number of positive ones. We made every single day count. In our short time together, we created enough beautiful memories to extend through multiple lifetimes. It's important I don't forget to focus on those moments of immense, unconditional love and laughter, because they were abundant. They can and will always put a smile on my face.

My life with Kait truly was a blessing. And in time, it may also be revealed to me that her passing was somehow a blessing, too. In disguise.

From here and for as long as I live, everything I do, I do with you in heart and mind!

Kaitlyn Julia, I will love you always, always, always!

ABOUT THE AUTHOR

Shortly after Kaitlyn passed, Travis packed up and moved west to California as he tried making sense of such a senseless disease. It was while he was away that he found inspiration to write about the grim, yet love-filled journey he and Kait shared together. Now, with his book completed, it is Travis' new "lofty goal" (as he stated in the final chapters of the book) to spread Kait's positivity and grand personality throughout the world. It is his hope that people will be able to look to Kaitlyn for inspiration, because she was THE full embodiment of love and happiness.

Travis currently has a number of projects planned, which includes a book that explores our current economic system at its core, a documentary about the pervasive problem of child poverty and homelessness in America, and a few passion screenplays. For questions or concerns, Travis is always open for healthy discussion regarding any topic.

Made in the USA
Lexington, KY
13 May 2017